D1156854

OXFORD MEDIEVAL TEXTS

General Editors

V. H. GALBRAITH   R. A. B. MYNORS

C. N. L. BROOKE

DE GESTIS CONCILII BASILIENSIS COMMENTARIORVM

LIBRI II

AENEAS SYLVIVS PICCOLOMINVS
(PIVS II)

DE GESTIS CONCILII BASILIENSIS COMMENTARIORVM

LIBRI II

EDITED
AND TRANSLATED BY

DENYS HAY
AND
W. K. SMITH

OXFORD
AT THE CLARENDON PRESS
1967

Oxford University Press, Ely House, London W. 1
GLASGOW NEW YORK TORONTO MELBOURNE WELLINGTON
CAPE TOWN SALISBURY IBADAN NAIROBI LUSAKA ADDIS ABABA
BOMBAY CALCUTTA MADRAS KARACHI LAHORE DACCA
KUALA LUMPUR HONG KONG TOKYO

PRINTED IN GREAT BRITAIN
AT THE UNIVERSITY PRESS, OXFORD
BY VIVIAN RIDLER
PRINTER TO THE UNIVERSITY

GENERAL EDITORS' NOTE

THE series hitherto known as Nelson's Medieval Texts has now been transferred to the Clarendon Press. All new volumes, of which this is the first, will be published by the Press, and will be known as Oxford Medieval Texts; those which appeared before 1966 will continue to be published by Messrs. Nelson.

The original series arose during the last war out of discussions with Dr. H. P. Morrison, managing director of Thomas Nelson and Sons, and the first volume appeared in 1949. To Dr. Morrison's inspiration and constant support all those interested in medieval studies owe a lasting debt for the publication both of this series and of other valuable medieval texts.

C.N.L.B.
V.H.G.
R.A.B.M.

PREFACE

THE editors wish to express their thanks to a number of scholars who have assisted them. Dr. Max Burckhardt not only greatly facilitated the consultation of manuscripts in his charge at the University Library at Basle, but kindly drew attention to the sale of a manuscript which was acquired with characteristic promptness and generosity by the University Library at Edinburgh. In addition Dr. Burckhardt has been endlessly kind in answering specific inquiries. Help has also been forthcoming from Dr. Hans Baron, Mr. C. P. Finlayson, Professor H. S. Offler, Dr. M. A. Pegg, Professor Brian Tierney, and Professor Walter Ullmann. Professor Brooke, Professor Mynors, Mrs. Gweneth Whitteridge and the readers of the Clarendon Press have done much to improve the book.

Edinburgh, September 1966

CONTENTS

INTRODUCTION

PRINTED versions of the work here edited are to be found in the bigger libraries. While we believe that the reader is now presented with a text more reliable, pleasing, and manageable than that shrouded in the dense typography of the old folios, our principal reason for editing the treatise is that it has been neglected. This is due in the main to the remarkable circumstance that its author was later to disown it and to the failure of the entire cause in defence of which the book was composed. It is necessary briefly to sketch both developments in order to place the *De gestis concilii Basiliensis* of Aeneas Sylvius Piccolomini in its context.

I. THE CONCILIAR MOVEMENT AND THE COUNCIL OF BASLE

Councils were from an early date a regular part of the machinery of the Church. From the first generally accepted council (Nicaea, 325) they occur frequently down the centuries, though it would be a mistake to assume that they were held as a matter of course. They were from the start, and continued to be, associated with occasions of major dispute or doubt. Diocesan and metropolitan synods or assemblies gradually established themselves as part of the government of the Church, and these in theory had to be held at frequent intervals. But no attempt to make general councils of the whole Church a prescribed and recurrent element in ecclesiastical government occurs until the early fifteenth century.

Traditionally general councils, assembled to deal with weighty issues, were attended by senior clergy which—by the thirteenth century—meant that they were largely composed of prelates: cardinals, patriarchs, archbishops, bishops, abbots, and heads of religious orders; princes or their ambassadors also often attended. At this stage the part played by the most senior clergyman of all, the pope, was crucial. In effect by the eleventh century the pope alone summoned a council, appointed a president, and promulgated the resulting decisions or canons. A good example of such action is the fourth Lateran Council of 1215, in which a large

concourse of prelates approved canons drafted by Innocent III which defined the faith, dealt with heresy, laid down a mass of procedural rules, and legislated over the whole range of church law. Innocent IV called a general council at Lyons in 1245 which had as its main task to support the pope against the Emperor Frederick II. A second council met at Lyons in 1274, summoned by Gregory X to consolidate the abortive reunion negotiated with the Greek Church. At Vienne in 1312 Pope Clement V, under pressure from King Philip IV of France who was present in person, dissolved the Order of the Knights Templars.

Clement V was the first of the French popes of the fourteenth century. Political circumstances in Italy, which had made it hard for thirteenth-century popes to spend much time in Rome itself, led after 1305 to the gradual establishment of the Roman curia in the city of Avignon, then just outside the confines of the kingdom of France, being on the east side of the Rhone. Clement's successors for two generations were also Frenchmen and the cardinals too became predominantly French. The prolonged residence of the popes at Avignon did not prevent them from being heavily engaged in Italian politics. They were well aware that the English and the Germans suspected them of being the tools of French diplomacy and that many devout Christians attributed to the 'Babylonian Captivity' evils and corruptions in church life and administration. By 1377 a permanent return to Italy seemed feasible and the curia removed to Rome in that year. The pope was Gregory XI. Next year he died.

The ensuing conclave was held in a Rome whose citizens were determined that the new pope should not return to Avignon. A predominantly French college of cardinals found it hard to agree on a candidate and a compromise nominee was found in the Neapolitan archbishop of Bari—not a cardinal, but known to be both able and *persona grata* in France. Urban VI, as the new pope styled himself, proved a disastrous choice. He was pathologically suspicious and critical of the cardinals who had elected him, threatening reforms which would have seriously reduced the significance of these princes of the Church. For long the cardinals, collectively omnipotent during the brief period of the conclave, had sought ways of ensuring for themselves a position in church organisation which would reflect their outward panoply; in particular they wished to have constitutional protection against the

papal plenitude of power and to be regarded as the repository of ultimate authority. Faced now with a pope too tactless or too unbalanced to manage them, they revolted. Abandoning Urban VI, the French cardinals declared their earlier election invalid and in place of Urban they chose a French cardinal who took the name Clement VII; the rest of the college accepted and approved what had been done; the rejected pope had equipped himself a little before this with a new college of cardinals. Urban VI had been elected on 8 April 1378, Clement VII on 20 September 1378; a schism had begun which was to last until 1417.

The Great Schism deserves its name. Apart from the long-standing division between the Greek and Roman Churches, which had finally established itself by the eleventh century and had survived all attempts at reunion, the Great Schism was the only dispute over medieval church government based on something profounder than the political vicissitudes which in earlier times had occasionally prompted an emperor to support a rival pope. The Schism of 1378 would perhaps not have lasted as long if the princes of Europe had not associated themselves with the rivals—France, Scotland, the kingdoms of Spain supporting the 'Avignon' pope, England with much of Italy and Germany supporting the 'Roman' pope. But it could not have started without the action of the cardinals themselves.

In the event it was the cardinals also who took steps to end the Schism, though not before the issues involved had become a central preoccupation of governments and intellectuals. Three ways of dealing with the situation were canvassed. The two popes could each resign, thus opening the way to a new and unchallenged election; they could agree on arbitration; or a council could meet and exercise exceptional powers to meet this unprecedented crisis. Though the king of France, together with other kings, did his best to put pressure on the popes it proved impossible even to prevent the original popes of 1378 being followed by successors. Clement VII was followed in his obedience by the Spaniard Benedict XIII (1394); Urban VI by three Italians, Boniface IX (1389), Innocent VII (1404), and Gregory XII (1406). Direct negotiation between the rivals proved equally fruitless; each was confident of his rights and fearful of the consequences of conciliation or compromise. The nearest they came to it was a projected meeting in North Italy in 1408. This was probably not meant seriously by the two

popes, but it put the cardinals of each side in touch and a majority of cardinals in each of the two colleges took the momentous step of combining to summon a council at Pisa. For this they have been severely criticized by latter-day Roman Catholic writers;[1] in the circumstances of 1408 it is hard to see what else could have been done. The resulting Council of Pisa failed to secure its immediate objective. The deposition of the 'French' and 'Roman' popes deprived neither pontiff of all his followers: Benedict XIII was obeyed still by the Spaniards, Gregory XII had some scattered support in Italy. But Alexander V, elected at Pisa, was accepted by the vast majority of Christians as sole pope, as was the more controversial John XXIII who succeeded him in 1410.

In summoning the Council of Pisa the cardinals appealed from the existing popes to a future pope, and to Jesus Christ the infallible head of the Church. In proceeding thus they were reflecting notions which had been hammered out by theologians and lawyers during the dark days after 1378. Earlier exponents of what is called 'conciliar supremacy' had existed.[2] The English scholar, William of Ockham, was only one of a substantial number of doctors who argued that there were occasions when a council must be the final authority in the Church, more particularly when the pope lapsed into heresy. Heretics in the normal sense the schismatic popes were certainly not, but the deadlock following on the elections of 1378 forced an extension of the doctrine to cover pigheadedness as well as doctrinal error; to quote the civilian tag—*salus populi suprema lex*. Debates on the problem were particularly lively at the University of Paris, where a number of scholars evolved the theory that in a moment of crisis, the Church should have recourse to Christ and should express Christ's universality, so to speak, in a universal council. What remained

[1] See the relatively mild comment of Dom H. Leclercq: '... on doit s'étonner de voir des cardinaux s'arroger le droit de convoquer un concile du vivant du pape légitime, quel qu'il fût', Hefele–Leclercq, *Histoire des conciles*, VII. I n. Cf. Pastor, *History of the Popes* (trans. Antrobus), I. 178: 'The synod of Pisa, according to Catholic principles, was, from the outset, an act of open revolt against the Pope.' Note the changed emphasis but implied reproof in the recent volume of the 'Histoire de l'église'—D.L.O. p. 137: 'Ainsi aboutissait-on mais dans la révolte, à la maturation de cette idée conciliaire qui depuis trente ans cherchait son expression.' For full references to books referred to by short titles in the introduction, see the Bibliography below, pp. xxxvii–xxxviii.

[2] See Tierney, *Foundations of Conciliar Theory*.

doubtful was how to summon such a council after centuries when this had been done only by the pope. The cardinals at Pisa had tried to solve this problem in 1409; a few years later John XXIII, embarrassed in Italy and generally disliked, bought the support of the Emperor Sigismund by agreeing to call another council, to meet in the South German city of Constance and to deal with the final ending of the Schism as well as with a general reformation of the Church.

John XXIII hoped to dominate proceedings at Constance, where the Council opened in November 1414, by his own presence as well as by the large number of Italian bishops and prelates who attended. The other delegations were equally determined to prevent this. The Council deliberated by 'nations' (German, English, French, Italian, and—after 1416—Spanish) and doctors of theology and law were incorporated as well as more senior clergy. Only when there was a majority of 'nations' in favour of a proposal did it reach the 'congregation'. If approved in congregation the motion was then passed by a 'plenary session' (*plena sessio*) of the Council sitting in full solemnity. Such arrangements deprived John XXIII and his Italian supporters of any chance of managing the Council and the pope thereupon determined to wreck the proceedings by flight. Again he miscalculated. His officials and the cardinals stayed firm. He himself was declared deposed, and, with the resignation of Gregory XII (after himself convoking the Council, a move which in the view of modern Roman Catholics was to give it authority), and the process of deposition of Benedict XIII, the Council was itself in practice the supreme authority in the Church.[1]

This was also declared to be the theoretical position. In a celebrated canon, sometimes called *Sacrosancta*, the Council had declared (fifth session, 6 April 1415):

This holy synod of Constance . . . declares that, being lawfully assembled in the Holy Spirit, constituting a general council and representing the catholic church, it derives its power directly from Christ, and to it everyone, of whatever rank or dignity including the pope, is subject in those things which pertain to the faith, the ending

[1] On *The Council of Constance* see the collection of translated narratives under that title, prepared by Louise R. Loomis, ed. and introd. by J. H. Mundy and K. M. Woody; D.L.O., pp. 167–200 and the pioneering work of Valois, *France*, IV.

of the schism and the reformation of the church in head and members. It further declares that anyone, of whatever condition, rank or dignity, including the pope, who contumaciously neglects to obey the orders, canons, regulations or directions made or to be made by this holy council or by any other lawfully assembled council on or related to the aforesaid matters, shall (unless he comes to his senses) be subjected to condign penitence and duly punished, even by recourse to other legal sanctions if need arise.[1]

This canon would hardly have commanded general agreement save for John's impolitic action; the cardinals in particular resisted till the last, for there was a chance that they, rather than the Council, might become the final arbiters in all questions.

In the ensuing years the Council dealt with many other matters—for the future perhaps its most noteworthy act was the condemnation of the Czech heretic John Huss, which was followed by his execution by the civil authorities—but it made little headway with reform as such. National differences, reflected in the 'nations', impeded agreed decisions; even more important was a failure to solve the problem of the scope of papal prerogative. In the thirteenth and fourteenth centuries popes had secured the power to provide to a large number of benefices reserved to them by general or particular decisions. Over 'reservations' and 'provisions' and the fiscal rights involved in these papal acts debate ranged angrily. In general bishops were anxious to see them ended; but among university men, for whom the pope had for a century acted as a kind of employment agent, provisions were popular. In the end only a small number of 'agreed reforms' were passed in the thirty-ninth session, 9 October 1417, and the Council left other details to be worked out in national concordats between the future pope and the 'nations'. For a weary Christendom as well as for delegates who had in many cases been away from home for three years or more the election of a pope took on an overriding importance. In an extraordinary conclave, in which the twenty-three remaining cardinals were joined by six delegates from each of the five nations, Martin V (Oddo Colonna) was elected pope on 11 November 1417.

The only really significant item in the 'agreed reform' of October 1417 was an elaborate arrangement intended to secure that councils should meet regularly. This, the decree *Frequens*,

[1] Mansi, XXVII, col. 590; Mirbt, p. 169.

round which so much was to turn in subsequent years, may be summarized thus:[1]

General councils shall meet frequently in the future. The next will be held in five years' time, the second seven years after that, and thereafter they will be celebrated every ten years. These intervals may be shortened by the pope, in case of necessity and with the assent of the cardinals, but under no circumstances may they be lengthened. A month before the end of a council the pope, with the agreement of the council, shall determine the meeting place of the next council; if this is not done by the pope the council shall itself determine the place. The place named shall not be altered save for urgent reasons (such as a siege, war, or plague) and then only by the pope after he has obtained the consent in writing of at least a two-thirds majority of the cardinals. The new location must be near the originally-chosen place and in the territory of the same nation (*sub eadem tandem natione*); and if this is not possible it must be in an adjacent and suitable place in another nation. Any change of date or place must be published by the pope a year before the council is due to assemble.

Martin V, who reigned till 1431, disliked the conciliar atmosphere in which he had become pope and began the process of disengaging the papacy from the unequivocal statement of conciliar supremacy in *Sacrosancta* as well as the implied conciliar supremacy of *Frequens*. A council was indeed summoned to meet at Pavia in the spring of 1423, in conformity with *Frequens* and by resolution of the Council of Constance in its penultimate session. It was poorly attended and the pope moved it to Siena because of plague at Pavia. At Siena, where proceedings began in July 1423, little was accomplished. Delegations were rent by divisions, and they were suspicious both of the papal legates and of the pope's failure to appear. The council was dissolved by the legates in doubtful circumstances which indicated their disapproval of conciliar supremacy (March 1424), but not before the town of Basle had been chosen (February 1424) as the place of assembly of the next council, seven years later.

Martin V did much to strengthen the papacy in the next few years in the field of finance, administration, and foreign policy. What this additional strength might have meant if it had remained at the disposal of Martin we can never know, for he died in February 1431, a short while before the council was due to open,

[1] H–L. VII. 459; Mansi, XXVII, col. 1159; Mirbt, p. 169.

and he was succeeded by an upright but intransigent Venetian, Eugenius IV. To Eugenius, familiar as he was with the empty panoply of a doge, the conciliarism of the Fathers of Constance was even more repugnant than it had been to Martin V. Taken together, *Sacrosancta* and *Frequens*, with related documents, turned the pope into a limited monarch instead of the absolute sovereign who had reigned over the Church in earlier centuries; the Church was to be governed under a written constitution; there was forever to be an impending council to which all who opposed papal policies could appeal. The curious mixture of spiritual and temporal sanctions by which popes ruled not only the Church at large, but their own Papal State, was thus threatened with dissolution, and the pope as prince was stripped of his most valuable diplomatic weapons. All of this Eugenius and his supporters saw clearly enough, and there can be no doubt that had he been able to stop a council assembling at Basle the pope would have done so. He at once tried to dissolve it.

Cardinal Giuliano Cesarini had been appointed legate to the Council by Martin V before he died, but he was involved in the Crusade against the Hussites in Bohemia and did not arrive at Basle from the disastrous expedition until early in September 1431. Within a few months he was faced with a number of papal acts designed to end proceedings at Basle and notably with the bull *Quoniam alto* (18 December 1431) in which the pope dissolved the Council of Basle and summoned another to Bologna eighteen months later; ten years after that a council should assemble at Avignon. For this action, in open contradiction of the decree *Frequens*, the pope alleged many reasons, including the poor attendance at Basle, the proximity of war, and the willingness of the Greeks to attend a council at Bologna. (The Greeks were now under heavy pressure from the Ottoman Turks and prepared for union in the hope that it would be followed by military support.) The delegates assembled at Basle refused to accept this, and for two years there was open conflict between the Fathers and the pope. In this first period of tension the Council had, however, the advantage. Cesarini, whose character and attainments commanded universal respect and admiration, consistently urged Eugenius to recognize the Council if only as the unavoidable bridge to an understanding with the schismatic Czechs. In this he was insistently supported by the Emperor Sigismund, whose

Bohemian crown remained a shadow while the Hussite problem was unsolved. Eugenius himself became vulnerable to pressure. His ill-judged attack on the Colonna family provoked powerful enemies in and around Rome; the Visconti lord of Milan, Duke Filippo Maria, was intriguing against the pope in the Papal States. Although as late as September 1433 (*Deus novit*) Eugenius reiterated his conviction that the Council had behaved irresponsibly, he had in fact been gradually forced to accept the situation; the bull *Dudum Sacrum* (August 1433), though it was so framed as to be unacceptable to the Fathers, had accepted the Council. In December 1433 Eugenius finally capitulated in a revised version of *Dudum Sacrum*. The Council was recognized as ecumenical from its inception, all papal bulls issued against it were revoked, and its task was defined in approved terms: the rooting out of heresy, reunion, and reform. In June 1434 Eugenius fled from a rebellious Rome and for the next seven years the curia was established for long periods at Florence.

The Council which thus far had been victorious against Eugenius was in many ways organized differently from earlier assemblies, including that at Constance.[1] The 'nations', so important at the earlier Council, played a minor role as far as official recognition was concerned, though for certain purposes offices were shared between the 'nations' of France, Italy, Spain, and Germany (there was no English 'nation'). The basic deliberative unit was the 'deputation' or committee. There were four deputations devoted respectively to the problem of faith (i.e. of heresy), of peace, of reform, and for general business (*deputationes fidei*, *pacis*, *reformationis*, *de communibus*). Each deputation was composed of the same number of clergy from each of the four nations, and included clergy of different ranks. A president, who held office for a month, and a promoter for each deputation were elected. The deputations met three times a week and communicated their decisions to the other deputations. Each month a committee of twelve was elected, composed of three from each delegation, to steer business coming before the Council to the appropriate committee. No motion put before a deputation was to be carried the same day, save in case of necessity. Only business put before the deputation by its president was competent. Only when two deputations were agreed

[1] The most recent survey of the Council of Basle, with very good bibliographical references, is in D.L.O. pp. 227–92.

on a resolution could it be put to the general session, and such agreement was to be known in advance by the device of the presidents of the separate deputations reporting jointly to the president of the Council. If all or at least three deputations were in agreement the matter could be put formally to the Council in its plenary session,[1] an occasion of liturgical solemnity and panoply. Such consultative devices were ingenious, but not revolutionary. In addition the Fathers took *Sacrosancta*, which they repeatedly re-enacted, to its logical conclusion by constructing an entire curial organisation—camera (finance), chancery, penitentiary, and courts of law. But it was the wide vote accorded by the Fathers at Basle which was a real innovation. Incorporation was accorded, subject to checks which were not always very seriously applied, to practically all clergy. The prelates who had been the essential element of earlier general councils were greatly outnumbered by the lower clergy. By the summer of 1433 some five hundred clergy had been incorporated, eight cardinals were present as well as ambassadors (who were mainly prelates) from many princes; but prelates never numbered much more than a quarter of the total and that for a brief period only, in 1433 and 1434.

Meanwhile the Council was engaged in the solution of the Bohemian question and the pope was negotiating with the Greeks. The details of these transactions lie beyond the scope of this introduction.[2] It is sufficient to note that once the Council had helped to secure agreement of a sort in Bohemia it gradually lost its main *raison d'être*, at any rate so far as contemporary governments were concerned, and that once Eugenius IV arranged for the Greek Church to send its powerful delegation to an Italian town he had the whip hand. In July 1436 the 'Compacts of Prague' were signed, thus accomplishing on paper the reconciliation of the Bohemians with the Church. In November 1437 the Greek emperor, with the patriarchs and bishops who were to negotiate reunion, sailed from Constantinople in ships provided by the pope.

It was indeed the futile negotiations between the Council and

[1] Mansi, XXIX, cols. 377–80 and the fuller version given by Segovia, *Mon. Con.* II. 260–3; H–L. VII. 757–8; Valois, I. 311 ff.

[2] For the Czech negotiation see H–L. VII and E. F. Jacob, 'The Bohemians at the Council of Basel, 1433', in *Prague Essays*, ed. R. W. Seton Watson (Oxford, 1949); for the antecedents of the ending of the Greek Schism, see Gill, *Council of Florence*.

the Greeks which finally detached from the Fathers a substantial section of the moderates, including Cesarini. But tension between pope and Council had been increasing rapidly throughout 1436. The Council had earlier legislated general and acceptable reforms: the scheme of regularly held general councils laid down by the decree *Frequens* was to be supplemented by regular provincial and diocesan synods (session xv); concubinage was prohibited, interdict limited, and frivolous appeals in legal cases were condemned (session xx). More dramatic was the abolition of chancery fees, common services, and annates in session xxi (9 June 1435); at a stroke the main income of the pope was swept away and not replaced. In session xxiii (25 March 1436) the entire curia was reformed; rules for the conclave were laid down together with the numbers, rights, and quality of the cardinals; and a papal oath on election was to involve adherence to the canons of ecumenical councils, including Constance and Basle. In May of 1439 at session xxxiii conciliar supremacy (*Sacrosancta*) was declared to be an article of faith.

These steps, which would have made the pope not merely a figurehead, but a penniless figurehead at that, were met by Eugenius with a resistance strong in proportion to his own mounting resources. On 18 September 1437 he issued the bull *Doctoris gentium* which condemned the truculence and inactivity of the Fathers and transferred the Council to Ferrara. It was the moment when negotiations with the Greeks were coming to a head. A minority of the Fathers co-operated with Eugenius over this issue and in December 1437 Cesarini left Basle for the papally constituted assembly which opened at Ferrara on 8 January 1438, and which, after its translation to Florence, was to promulgate on 5 July 1439 the short-lived reunion of the Greek and Roman Churches.

The ultimate victory of the pope, who had been suspended by the Council on 24 January 1438 (session xxxi), appears predictable enough in retrospect. It was far from being so evident in 1438 and 1439. In France in 1438 the Gallican Church adopted the main reforming legislation of Basle and this was solemnly issued by Charles VII as a royal ordinance, the Pragmatic Sanction of Bourges. The French king sincerely urged reconciliation on both pope and Council but in truth the situation suited him well, as it suited other princes. In Germany the Emperor Sigismund had

died on 9 December 1437. Before choosing his successor the electors declared what amounted to neutrality between Eugenius and the Fathers at Basle; Albert of Austria was elected at Mainz in March 1438, and a year later the Diet followed the example of France by adopting the Basle decrees (the *Acceptatio* of Mainz),[1] while continuing to urge an accommodation between pope and Council. As for Italy, the two most powerful princes were Duke Filippo Maria Visconti of Milan and Alfonso V, king of Aragon and on the point of making good his conquest of Naples. The existence of the Council of Basle was for each a valuable weapon against Eugenius, and the Milanese and Neapolitan envoys at Basle played a tortuous and procrastinating game. This is particularly seen in the conduct of Panormitanus,[2] Alfonso's principal spokesman at the Council, who did his best to prevent the deposition of Eugenius. All in all, in 1439 it seemed possible that the Council might win its battle against the pope, at any rate until on 5 November 1439 it finally elected as pope the duke of Savoy, Amadeo, who took the title Felix V.[3] It is with the events of 1439 that the work here printed is concerned.

The remaining history of the Council can be dealt with in a few lines. Eugenius was triumphant in the acclaim of a Europe overjoyed at the ending of the Greek Schism—a Europe horrified that the upshot of the Council was a fresh schism. The pope came to terms with Milan and Naples, and by 1442 only in Germany was there much public support for the Council and the anti-pope. There the issue was delayed until 1447. But long before then Felix had abandoned Basle where the last formal session was held in 1443. At the end, a face-saving formula was evolved. The few remaining Fathers transferred themselves to Lausanne and there Felix V resigned in 1449 (he became a cardinal, legate, and papal vicar) and the 'council' elected as pope Nicholas V, who had succeeded Eugenius in March 1447.

The last paragraph may have suggested that the Council of Basle is solely to be measured in terms of the political significance

[1] Cf. below, p. 14, and *Reichstagsakten*, XIV.

[2] Below, p. xxii.

[3] The most recent account of Amadeo is the popular but on the whole reliable work of Queen Marie José: *La Maison de Savoie; Amédée VIII*, 2 vols. (Paris, 1962). It contains a useful bibliography of the older literature of which the most important work is the study by F. Cognasso, *Amadeo VIII*, 2 vols. (Turin, 1930).

it had initially possessed in the calculations of princes and popes. This is not the case. At Basle, as earlier at Constance, the Fathers were wrestling with the weightiest issues both in church reform and in church government. The two were intimately linked and for the protagonists of the Council it was only by securing the obedience of the pope to an assembly representative of the whole Church militant on earth and reflecting the will of God that good order could be secured in matters ecclesiastical. The issue was, indeed, more general even than that. Since the Church was to be presumed the least corrupt organization on earth, what was being determined in the councils was 'the depositary, the functions, and the limits, of sovereign power in a perfect society'. These words were written by J. N. Figgis,[1] and it is not easy to dispute his contention that at Constance and Basle the debate turned on constitutionalism as against absolutism, nor deny his conclusion that the failure of the Fathers and the victory of the papacy paved the way for the autocratic prince.

The arguments invoked by conciliarists and papalists are nearly all rehearsed in the work which follows and need not be set out here. Two points should, however, be made.

In the first place it is important to remember that the conciliar position had to a large degree been established before the Council of Basle opened. There is no doubt that as the clergy of Christendom drifted away from Constance in the autumn of 1417 and spring of 1418, the bulk of these senior and sober men felt that two constitutional points had been established: all men, including the pope, must necessarily obey a general council; and general councils must occur in future at regular intervals. In fact the supporters of traditional papal supremacy, of the vast *plenitudo potestatis* of the pope as *rex*, began slowly to gather strength, while it became the first objective of popes after Constance to disown conciliar doctrines. In the end it was the papalist position which won the day and the factious behaviour of many of the Fathers at Basle contributed to the discrediting of the conciliarist case. Nevertheless, many of the most heated exchanges, and indeed the final deposition of Eugenius IV, were occasioned by the passionate conviction that the pope and his supporters were trying to overthrow the decisions taken at Constance.

In the second place the violence of the action at Basle, the

[1] *From Gerson to Grotius*, p. 49.

undoubted presence there of lower clergy who were unworthy of representing the will of Christendom, of senior clergy who attended to further their own careers,[1] prosecute ancient vendettas, or intrigue for the political ends of their princely masters, all suggest that by the 1430's the calibre of the disputants had markedly declined from the more disinterested theologians, canonists, and prelates of the Schism and of Constance. This has a certain truth in it. By the time our narrative opens the nobler spirits had nearly all left: Cesarini, Nicholas of Cues,[2] Albergati. But those who remained had as their authorities an impressive literature—the works of Gerson, of d'Ailly, of Nicholas of Cues—written in the previous decades or in the early days of Basle itself; and there were still commanding personalities. Among the theologians the most impressive is Panormitanus—Niccolò de' Tudeschi, archbishop of Palermo.[3] He had arrived at Basle to support the political aims of his master, Alfonso V of Aragon, who was also king of Naples and the pope's enemy in Italy. Panormitanus, fortified by the procrastinating policies of Alfonso, undertook with vigour the resistance at Basle to the final deposition of Eugenius. Of the prelates the most significant is undoubtedly the saintly Louis d'Aleman, 'cardinal of Arles', who plays a dominant part in the proceedings recounted by Aeneas Sylvius.[4] He had become president of the Council on 14 February 1438 and sub-

[1] It has been plausibly argued that Felix V accepted the papacy to secure for the dukes of Savoy control over the episcopal town of Geneva. For Aeneas's later very unfavourable portrait of Amadeo's ambitions, see *Commentaries*, pp. 489–92.

[2] For Aeneas's view of him at this stage see below, p. 14; he was made a cardinal in 1448 and died 1464.

[3] Born 1386, died 1445. He was a Benedictine monk from Sicily and studied canon law at Padua. Made an abbot in 1425 he is sometimes referred to as *abbas Siculus* or *abbas modernus*. He was made archbishop of Palermo in 1434 and in 1440 Felix V made him a cardinal, the title being recognized at Rome after Alfonso V had made his peace with the pope in 1444. On Panormitanus at Basle see Z. Ranieri, *N. Tudisco ed un nuovo contributo alla storia del concilio di Basilea* (Catania, 1908), who prints, with many errors, a 'tractatus brevis' giving Panormitanus's 'sentenciam finalem' on the deposition of Eugenius, and the recent book by K. W. Nörr, *Kirche und Konzil bei N. de Tudeschis* (Cologne, 1964).

[4] See Pérouse. Aleman, who was born about 1390, was a doctor of canon law. He was made archbishop of Arles in 1423 and three years later Martin V made him cardinal. From this rank he was removed by Eugenius IV in 1440, but Nicholas V restored the title in 1449. He died in 1450 and was beatified in 1527 by Clement VII; see the somewhat embarrassed account of him in *Acta Sanctorum*, 16 Sept. (*Sept.* v. 436 ff.).

sequent events revealed him as a fervid antagonist of the pope, an able controversialist, and an adroit master of procedural technique. Against him the ambassadors (led by Panormitanus), whose princely masters preferred the existing equivocal situation to the deposition of the pope, proved in the end to be unavailing. The dispute over whether to pass the resolutions which would imply the 'heresy' of Eugenius or to postpone the issue, fills the bulk of Book i. It is dominated by the personalities of cardinal and archbishop. As Aeneas himself says (below, p. 172), the book is, in a sense, an account of the struggle between Aleman and Panormitanus.

Among those present at Basle was also the author of the work. Not quite twenty years later, on 18 January 1459, the man who in the present book evinced an ebullient support for conciliarism issued, as Pope Pius II, the bull *Execrabilis*. This (which we may regard as ending the conciliar effort of earlier generations) declared it anathema to appeal to a future council.[1] His own *mot* commenting on his change of heart was the advice: 'abandon Aeneas, follow Pius.'

2. AENEAS SYLVIUS PICCOLOMINI, POPE PIUS II

The Aeneas who was later to be condemned by Pius was born in the Tuscan hill town of Corsignano on 18 October 1405. His father, Silvio Piccolomini, and his mother, Vittoria Forteguerri, were both of noble descent and were both poor. The Piccolomini had once been rich and prominent in the life of Siena. Excluded from Sienese politics along with the other nobles in 1385, the Piccolomini were reduced to their meagre lands at Corsignano, some 30 miles to the south-east. Silvio and Vittoria had eighteen children and, though only three were in the end to survive, there was no question of a life of ease for Aeneas. His aptitudes, the experience of his father, and the help of the parish priest all turned him to a professional future. At eighteen he left his home for Siena, education, and a career.

Siena as Aeneas described it in later writings was a gay town, and the amatory adventures he and his friends were involved in were the occasion of self-reproach later in life, not least because he had committed them to paper in stories and verses. But for

[1] Mirbt, p. 181.

a penniless and unpatronized youth with a flair for letters the only way to promote his fortunes was by hard work, and there is no doubt that Aeneas was as diligent a student as he claims to have been a lover. The university of Siena was not among the most notable in Italy; and the town did not boast anything comparable to the groups of authors, scholars, and dilettanti who were evolving at Florence new attitudes to the past, new moral values, and a new educational programme. Nevertheless the excitement of Latin, the joy of literature, and the release of an active life rather than a clerical seclusion reached Siena, and Aeneas found particular inspiration and encouragement in the teaching of Mariano de' Sozzini, a lively and liberal jurist with wide-ranging enthusiasms which embraced antiquity. Sozzini's influence was clearly important but, like his illustrious predecessors from Petrarch and Boccaccio onwards, as a writer in the new manner (later to be baptized 'humanist') Aeneas was essentially self-taught. A new educational ideal was slowly taking root in the Italy of his time, but it had not reached expression as yet in schools. Though Aeneas seems to have spent some time in Florence and to have known Filelfo, there is no reason to suppose that his culture owes much to this visit, and it is certain that he learned no Greek from Filelfo. His scholarship, like his entire intellectual formation, was Latin and the result of hard work before he left Siena.

The scholar without support was usually able to fall back on a career of some sort in the Church or become one of the innumerable lawyers of the Italian towns. For the first alternative Aeneas had as yet no serious vocation; we know this from his own account of his experience of listening to Saint Bernardino.[1] Bernardino, one of the remarkable Observant Franciscans of early fifteenth-century Italy, preached magnetic, racy, vernacular sermons which stirred the towns of Italy and not least his native Siena. Aeneas in later life claimed that the preaching of the saint had nearly led him to join the Franciscan Order. As for the law, which Aeneas was professedly studying, he held its practitioners in contempt.

Chance, however, enabled him to avoid being committed as yet to a particular career; or, one should perhaps say, committed him to a period of self-advancement in the career of secretary. In the autumn of 1431 Cardinal Domenico Capranica passed through

[1] Cf. Ady, pp. 20–21.

Siena en route for the Council of Basle and took the young man into his entourage. Capranica had been a favourite of Martin V; Eugenius had stripped him of his dignity; the cardinal defied the pope by adhering to the recently opened Council. In his train Aeneas slowly moved from Siena to the coast, by ship to Genoa, from Genoa to Milan, and thence by the St. Gotthard to Basle, which the party entered in April 1432.

Capranica was reconciled with Eugenius two years later and in any case while at Basle was too poor to retain Aeneas's services. Accordingly he sought and found other employers: Nicodemo della Scala, bishop of Freisingen; Bartolomeo Visconti, bishop of Novara; and Cardinal Niccolò Albergati. Each of these employments proved precarious, but each enlarged his knowledge of the world. With the bishop of Freisingen he went to the diet of Frankfurt in 1434. His service with the bishop of Novara, an agent of the duke of Milan, involved him in intrigues in Italy and led to his being stranded in Florence. Taken under the charitable wing of Albergati at Florence, he accompanied him to the Congress of Arras, where England, France, and Burgundy were negotiating peace in 1435. Thence Albergati sent his secretary to Scotland on an errand which has remained mysterious despite Aeneas's subsequent account of his adventures by land and sea.[1] On his return from this mission, Aeneas in effect left the service of Albergati and struck out for himself. He went to Basle, where the Council offered a field for his now tried talents as negotiator, diplomat, orator, and pamphleteer. He was by now aged thirty.

The first public intervention he made in conciliar affairs was to champion Siena as a place for the meeting with the Greeks. It was unsuccessful, but the speech in which he advocated it brought him great publicity, and before long he was retained by the duke of Milan, who rewarded him with a benefice. He began to be nominated to the various committees in which, as we have seen, the Council conducted its business. When Cesarini, whom Aeneas greatly admired, left the Council, Aeneas remained at Basle, convinced (we must suppose) of the rightness of the conciliar position, contented also with the chances of personal advancement which might come his way. At first the decision seemed disastrous. Aeneas was desperately ill during the plague which raged in the

[1] *Commentaries*, pp. 16–21; cf. P. Hume Brown, *Early Travellers in Scotland* (Edinburgh, 1891), pp. 26–29.

city during the summer of 1439,[1] and the false news of his death enabled the duke of Milan to withdraw his support and appoint another clerk to his benefice; the Council provided him to a canonry in the cathedral at Trent.[2] He became one of the secretaries of the new Pope Felix V. It is at this stage that he wrote the work here reprinted.

This is not the occasion to deal with our author's subsequent career, but its main lines may briefly be indicated. He entered the service of the Emperor Frederick III in 1442 and proved a useful if unhappy member of the imperial chancery. In 1445 he was sent on a mission from the emperor to Rome—part of the negotiations which were finally to lead the emperor to adhere to the pope—and made his submission to Eugenius. Back in Vienna in 1446 Aeneas finally entered clerical orders as deacon, becoming priest soon afterwards.[3] His part in securing the obedience of Germany to the Roman see was rewarded by Nicholas V with the bishopric of Trieste, and from this point onwards Aeneas's promotion in the church was extraordinarily rapid: in 1450 he became bishop of Siena, and in 1456 he became cardinal priest of S. Sabina. Yet no one could have foreseen that at the conclave of 1458 the former enemy of the papacy would be elected pope. His activity as pope, with his efforts to call Christendom to Crusade and to bring order to the Papal States, his continued literary work (including the *Commentaries*, his history of himself and his own day), and his transformation of his birthplace Corsignano into the small but brilliant episcopal city of Pienza have long puzzled his biographers. Yet of the sincerity of his love both of letters and of Christendom there can be no doubt, even if they may be felt to be contradictory. No one knew Europe as well as Pius II. It was in the elusive hope of leading Christian Europe against the infidel that he summoned the Congress of Mantua in 1459. It was as a crusader that the pope died, at Ancona on 14 August 1464.

3. COMMENTARIES ON THE COUNCIL OF BASLE

(*a*) *The Work*

In view of the author's later change of heart, the reader of the *Commentaries on the Council of Basle* inevitably asks himself if it was a piece of propaganda, undertaken merely in the hope of

[1] Below, p. 196. [2] Below, p. 220 and n. 6.

[3] The exact date is doubtful.

securing promotion for Aeneas[1] and devoid of conviction. It is thus a further test of the consistency of Aeneas's whole career, with its sharp contrasts and illogicalities. Perhaps the fairest way of viewing the man is to see him as one of those personalities who readily assume the colour and the convictions of a given time and place. Just as circumstances during his student days in Tuscany when he was in his early manhood put him in touch with a world of new cultural and literary values to which he entirely responded, so among the zealots of conciliarism he became a conciliarist, and so when he entered a papal career under Nicholas V he was gradually persuaded of the essential correctness of the papal point of view. An indication of this emotional response to environment is the devotion roused in Aeneas by some of the strong personalities he encountered from time to time: he was the admirer and disciple of Sozzini, but felt the compelling attraction of Bernardino; he had unbounded regard for Cesarini, and then fell victim to the rigid uprightness of Louis d'Aleman. He is, moreover, a classic example of the changes induced by advancing years. As a youth he is poet and pedant; his thirties see him as radical politician and man of affairs; a decade later, a priest and a reformed character, he pursues sedately the career of prudence, 'full of wise saws and modern instances'. What he never lost was a love of writing. His pen never left his hand. As time passed his style became racier until he achieved complete self-expression and complete mastery, whether he was writing a prayer, composing a bull, or setting down the unedifying events in the conclave which made him pope.

By the time he came to compose the book here reprinted he had behind him a considerable variety of literary works—the *Cinthia* (1426–8), a collection of early verses, and a love poem, now lost, called *Nymphilexis* (before 1435), which later earned him laureation by the emperor. More solid than these, more indicative of his future field as an author, are his letters, of which over thirty survive earlier than the *Commentaries on the Council of Basle.* Many more of these lively epistles were to come later, but already we can see how the informality of the *genre* appealed to Aeneas. We must also suppose that he made notes on his travels, for it was on his experiences during his conciliar and Austrian period that some of the great works of his maturity partly depended: *Historia Friderici III imperatoris* (1452–8), the *Germania* (1457), the

[1] Cf. below, pp. 2–4.

Europa (1458), the *Historia Bohemica* (1458). Other works are evidence of the seriousness of his classical scholarship, like the *Rhetoric* (1456) and the *De Asia* (1461). In certain of these writings, as in many of his occasional pieces not mentioned here,[1] Aeneas is conventional enough, but his combination of history and geography was as original as it was to be influential. Above all he displayed all his talents in the long *Commentaries on the notable events of his own day*, a survey of his career and of public and papal policy in Europe and Italy, written when he was pope.

In 1440 Aeneas wrote two polemical works, a set of *Dialogues* and the *Commentaries on the Council*. His *Libellus dialogorum de generalis concilii authoritate et gestis Basiliensium*[2] is a curious mixture of straight argument in support of the conciliar position, Nicholas of Cues (who had abandoned Basle and entered Eugenius IV's service in 1437) debating with Stefano da Caccia, a conciliar secretary; and of scholarly and literary asides on a number of unrelated topics, the speakers being Martin Lefranc, provost of Lausanne, and Aeneas. It is indeed in these last exchanges, rather than in the formal discussion on the conciliar position, that the work comes to life.

The *Commentaries*, written at the same time as the *Libellus*, that is, between the election of Felix V in November 1439[3] and his coronation in July 1440, deal only with the final debates leading up to the deposition of Eugenius IV (Book i) and the election of the anti-pope (Book ii). They are followed in many manuscripts and in the printed editions by a letter from Aeneas to John of Segovia, describing the coronation of Felix, which is edited by Wolkan as one of the letters;[4] John of Segovia, a learned Spanish canonist, was a moderate supporter of the conciliar position whose own incomplete history of the Council is our fullest narrative account of it.[5] Voigt accepted that the *Commentaries* were originally

[1] A chronology of his writings will be found in Ady, pp. 349–51, and in Paparelli, pp. 361–6.

[2] A. F. Kollarius, *Analecta monumentorum omnis aevi Vindobonensia* (Vienna, 1762), II, cols. 691–790.

[3] Cf. below, p. 252.

[4] No. 34: Wolkan, I. i. 105–10. It appears as 'Book iii' in certain printed editions: below, p. xxxv.

[5] It was written after the event when the author was in disgrace, and it is printed in part in *Mon. Con.* vols. II, III. John of Segovia occurs several times in Aeneas's narrative (see Index). He was one of Felix V's cardinals (1440) and died after 1458 as titular archbishop of Caesarea.

composed in three books, of which one is missing, which dealt with the events between the decision to depose Eugenius (16 May 1439) and the election of Felix (October–November);[1] and there is certainly a chronological gap at this point.[2] Yet, though more manuscripts are now known than were available to Voigt, none of them has this alleged 'second' book, and its existence must be questioned; in particular the character of Vienna MS. 5104 suggests strongly that we have here the whole work.[3] It seems far more probable that Aeneas composed only the two books which we possess, intending at a later date to revise and expand. 'The *Commentaries on the Council of Basle* . . . has the form of an historical work, but in substance it belongs to the preliminary collection of documents.'[4]

A partial revision of the work was indeed undertaken by the author in 1450. This, the so-called *De rebus Basiliae gestis Commentarius*, is a long letter from Aeneas, now a bishop, to Cardinal Carvajal.[5] It is better written than the earlier work and, of course, represents a diametrically opposed point of view. It is the Council which is now presented as factious and condemned as schismatic, not Eugenius as in the history written in 1440. The actual events and debates of 1439, which fill the earlier work, are dismissed in a few pages in 1450.[6] The letter of 1450 might have been written to justify the bull *Execrabilis* which Aeneas was to issue as pope in 1459.

In his style Aeneas clearly aimed at Ciceronian diction and grammar. When one remembers that the book here edited was in essence a rapidly written tract for the times,[7] one is impressed by his success in capturing the true ring of classical Latin. The most noteworthy departures from Ciceronian practice which will be found in the following pages are:

[1] Voigt, I. 230, n. 1.

[2] Below, p. 186. As Voigt (loc. cit.) noted, there is a passage at the start of Book ii (below, p. 200) which mentions Guillaume Hugues and his part in the pope's process—i.e. the actual deposition of Eugenius IV—as though that event had earlier been described in detail. It is more likely that the author is here referring back loosely to his earlier note on Hugues (below, p. 12). There are a number of other glancing allusions to events between May and September, e.g., pp. 184 n. 2, 194 n. 3.

[3] Below, p. xxxii.

[4] Ady, p. 290.

[5] Wolkan, II. 164–228; C. Fea, *Pius II . . . vindicatus* (Rome, 1823), pp. 31–115.

[6] Wolkan, II. 198–202.

[7] The speed of composition doubtless explains several awkward sentences and some confusions in syntax.

(*a*) Indirect speech may either be couched in the accusative and infinitive construction, or in clauses introduced by *quia, quod, quoniam* (less frequently) or *ut* (occasionally) with a subjunctive;
(*b*) The ablative absolute construction may be used instead of a participle in apposition to the subject of a sentence;
(*c*) *Fore* = *esse*;
(*d*) The pronouns *se* and *suus* are not always used reflexively;
(*e*) Comparative of adjectives may be used for superlative.

These are all well-known habits of composition during the Middle Ages.

(*b*) *Manuscripts and editions*

In the circumstances Aeneas presumably took good care to destroy his autograph copy of the *Commentaries on the Council of Basle* and it is also significant that no manuscript is apparently to be found in the Vatican collections.[1]

The following manuscripts contain all or part of the *De gestis concilii Basiliensis*. They are all on paper and in hands typical of professional scriveners or clerks of the south of Germany and the second half of the fifteenth century.

Basle University Library

(1) MS. A. III. 38, ff. 157^{r}–201^{v}: [C] Book i only. The rest of the volume contains the sermons of John de Pistorio, 1446 (ff. 1–62); Opus anonymum in 6 tractatus distinctum historiam duodecim filiorum Israel narrans (ff. 63^{r}–72^{v}, breaking off with tract. 5, art. 2); Sermons on the Lord's Prayer by John Gartner of the Augustinian Hermits, 1454 (ff. 73^{r}–138^{r}); a sermon of Aeneas 'in festo Sancti Ambrosii'[2] (ff. 145^{r}–50^{v}); Oration delivered in the presence of Pope Felix V by Dr. John de Elgoth, canon of Cracow (ff. 150^{v}–2^{v}). Ff. 138^{v}–44^{v}, 153^{r}–6^{v}, 202^{r}–3^{v} are blank. According to inscriptions on the insides of the covers, the volume, formerly in the Augustinian library at Basle, was given by Prior Ludovicus de Kilchen to Master Johannes Fininger, and by him

[1] Voigt is mistaken in saying that Cod. Vat. Lat. 5603 is this text. It is a copy of Aeneas's later work on the Council.

[2] On this sermon, see Voigt, 1. 149–50; printed in Mansi, xxx, cols. 1207–16.

promised to the convent on his death. Ludovicus was certainly prior between 1500 and 1509, but may well have succeeded as early as 1468. Fininger was prior from 1513 to 1523.[1]

(2) MS. A. IV. 16, ff. 337^{r}–77^{v}: [D] Book i only. The rest of the volume contains a miscellany of papers relating to the Council of Basle, including Aeneas Sylvius's *Dialogi* (cf. above, p. xxviii) at ff. 8^{r}–31^{r}. There is no indication of provenance, but Dr. Max Burckhardt considers that it should be associated with a group of manuscripts presented to the chapter library at Basle by Johann von Vennigen, bishop of Basle from 1458 to 1478.

(3) MS. E. II. 14, ff. 117^{r}–47^{v}: [B] Book i only. The rest of the volume contains the *Historia Troiana* (ff. 1^{r}–115^{r}), De Lademonta filio Hectoris redeunte Troiam post finalem destructionem ipsius (ff. 115^{r}–16^{v}), the sermon by Aeneas as in MS. A. II. 38 (ff. 147^{r}–51^{r}) and Quaestiones ex opere Augustini de Ancona de potestate ecclesiastica excerptae (ff. 153^{r}–82^{v}). Ff. 151^{v}–2^{v} are blank. A volume in its original boards, formerly in the library of the Dominicans at Basle, it is inscribed 'ex libris bibliothecae Academie Basiliensis, 1559' in the hand of the first university librarian, H. Pantaleon.

National Library, Vienna

(4) MS. 5080, ff. 462^{r}–73^{v}: [W] Book ii only. The volume as a whole contains a mass of sermons, *acta*, treatises stemming from or related to the Council of Basle.[2] It has the appearance of a collection of papers nearly contemporary with the Council. There is no indication of provenance, but from the press mark it is evident that it was in the imperial collection in the time of the first librarian, Hugo Blotius, 1595–1608.[3]

(5) MS. 5104, ff. 28^{r}–56^{r}: [V] Books i and ii. The volume is also a miscellany[4] and includes at ff. 121^{r}–4^{v} the sermon by Aeneas as in Nos. 1 and 3 above. There is no indication of provenance but the volume was in the library in the time of Blotius.

[1] E. F. von Mülinen, *Helvetia sacra* (Bern, 1858–61), II. 6; *Matrikel der Universität Basel*, I (Basel, 1951), 257.

[2] The 132 items are not separately listed in *Tabulae codicum manuscriptorum in Bibliotheca Palatina Vindobonensi asservatorum*, IV (Vienna, 1870), 14.

[3] Cf. *Die oesterreichische National Bibliothek. Festschrift zum . . . Dienstjubiläum* (Vienna, 1948), pp. 14–16.

[4] See list of contents in *Bibl. Pal.* IV. 24–25.

Edinburgh University Library

(6) MS. 326. Book i only. Purchased in 1956 from a bookseller in Florence who ascribed it to the years 1462–70. Inquiries have failed to elicit the source of this fragment, evidently torn from some larger volume.

An inspection of these six manuscripts suggested at once that most confidence might be placed in the Vienna MS. 5104. Not only is it the only manuscript (save that which lay behind the *editio princeps*) which contains both books, but in addition it contains a colophon at f. 49 reading: 'Scriptum anno domini 1444° die xxv mensis Aprilis.'[1] There is no suggestion that this is the date of composition; by the spring of 1444 Aeneas was no longer a conciliarist and in April he was, in fact, in Austria[2] trying to dispose of his secretaryship to Felix V and rapidly accepting as desirable a future in papal service. But the copyist of MS. 5104 may well have been at work then; this seems more likely than that he transferred the colophon from an earlier exemplar. (As noted above,[3] the nature of this manuscript strongly supports the presumption that Aeneas did not compose a 'missing book': MS. 5104 is all of a piece; it is hard to imagine that as early as 1444 a substantial section, a whole book, dropped out of a text originally written only a year or two before.) These considerations were borne out in detailed collation, for MS. 5104 frequently offers better readings. We have therefore given particular attention to the text as we find it in this recension.

The other manuscripts have less to commend them and there are no clear external indications of their relative priority. Collation has, however, led us to regard Basle MS. E. II. 14 as the best of the manuscripts containing only Book i, and the Edinburgh manuscript as the least valuable; Vienna MS. 5080, containing Book ii, has also yielded some valuable readings.

In these circumstances the authority of the *editio princeps* is naturally considerable. The work was, after all, printed in Basle where the anonymous editor of the collection of texts which appeared about 1524 might have been expected to have had access to an authoritative text. In fact, the editor explains in his preface

[1] As Voigt noted, I. 230 n., though he wrongly gives the year as 1440 and this leads him, pp. 230–1 and notes, into unnecessary difficulties.

[2] Wolkan, I. i. 302–14.

[3] p. xxix.

that his volume consists precisely of one of those miscellanies connected with the Council: 'a kind of hotchpotch of treatises of different kinds.'[1] This is reflected in the book's title: *Commentariorum / Aeneae Sylvii Piccolominei Senensis, de / Concilio Basileae celebrato libri duo, olim quidem scripti, / nunc uero primum impressi. In quibus sic illam syno-/dum depingit, sic quicquid illic actum est, bona / fide refert, ut qui legerit, interesse et infula-/tos illos heroas disputantes, collo-/quentes, concionantesque co-/ram uidere se putet. / Nec solum iucunda est historia, uerumetiam utilis. / Vixque aliud Concilium extat pari fide & / diligentia descriptum. / Lege felix. / Cum multis aliis nunquam antehac impressis: quorum cognoscendo-/rum gratia ne te pigeat sequentem indicem aut epistolam percurrere.* The preface, antipapal in tone, not only comments on the other texts presented, it also discusses briefly but explicitly the present work. After explaining that Aeneas disowned as pope what he had written as a conciliar supporter and pointing out the value of the work as the account of an eye-witness, the editor goes on:

The rarity of this work can be inferred particularly from the fact that they say it is not extant at Basle. For only the first book is kept there, but it is badly written and full of mistakes, despite there being in the town a large number of books in which the proceedings of that synod are contained.[2]

[1] '. . . ueluti farrago quaedam erat uariorum tractatuum', 'Ad Lectorem', sig. A 1v. Apart from the *De gestis Concilii Basiliensis*, the contents of the volume are as follows: Aeneas Sylvius Senensis domino suo Iohanni de Segovia (see above p. xxviii); Exemplum literarum quas Iulianus cardinalis sancti Angeli legatus in Germania . . . scripsit ad Eugenium; Vita et gesta Hildebrandi; Vita Henrici quarti Caesaris; Epistolae aliquot Henrici quarti; Oratio excusatoria [fratrum Valdensium] ad Vladislaum; Excusatio fratrum Valdensium; Articuli Ioannis Wiclephi, Angli, impugnati a Wilhelmo Wideforde; Articuli Ioannis Wiclephi damnati per Concilium Constantiense; Rationes . . . articulorum Wiclephi et . . . Ioannis Huss in Concilio Constantiensi damnatorum; Quonam pacto doctrina Ioannis Wiclephi in Bohemiam venerit . . . ex historia Bohemorum, cuius author fuit Aeneas Sylvius (see above, p. xxviii); Poggius Leonardo Arretino (*sic*); Leonardi Aretini . . . Aduersum hypocritas libellus; Synodus Aribonis archiepiscopi Moguntini . . . anno domini M. XXIII; Quomodo Bohemi uocati, productique sint ad Basiliensem synodum Oecumenicam; Petitiones Bohemorum . . . in sacrosancta synodo Basiliensi; Paradoxa D. Ioannis de Wesalia; Examen . . . Ioannis de Wesalia; Sententia damnationis doctrinae Ioannis Wiclephi; Sententia definitiua lata contra Ioannem Huss; Tenor sententiae definitiuae latae contra Hieronymum de Praga.

[2] Ibid.: 'Cuius operis raritatem uel ex hoc collige, quod aiunt illud apud Basileam non extare. Nam primus liber tantum illic habetur, misere tamen et mendosissime scriptus, cum tantus numerus librorum illic sit quibus acta eius synodi continentur.'

Thus the first edition, we must presume, was based on a text which was *not* kept at Basle; it is, however, probable that the editor did consult a manuscript of Book i which was kept in the town, though he found it of little use.[1] None of the surviving collections containing the *Commentaries* corresponds with the contents of the first edition and it thus has independent value. While we must allow for printer and editor correcting mistakes in their exemplar, and while the first edition contains a large number of patent errors, it does, in fact, give very good readings, and is frequently to be preferred even to the best of the manuscripts, Vienna 5104.

To summarize, the only two texts which contain the whole work, Vienna MS. 5104 and the *editio princeps*, are also the best. Of the remainder Basle MS. E. II. 14 has most independent significance. We have therefore collated MSS. 5104 and E. II. 14 throughout with the first edition. The other manuscripts have only been consulted in cases of difficulty.

Apart from the *editio princeps*, the printed editions are of small interest.

The folio which appeared at Basle, in which our text occupies the first sixty-eight pages, can only be dated inferentially. At the end of the preface the editor justifies the interest in publishing the heretical doctrines of Wyclif condemned at Constance,

> also the reasons why they deserved condemnation, in case anyone imagines that there happened here what was criticized by many in the theologians of Paris, who recently published the condemnation of Luther without any reasons.[2]

This occurred in 1521 and the book must therefore be dated shortly after that. The copy in the University Library at Basle is provisionally dated 'about 1524' and plausibly attributed to the scholar-printer Andreas Hartmann ('Cratander'), who was active as a publisher in Basle from 1518 to 1536.[3]

[1] Probably E. II 14. In this MS. from f. 140^{v} brief underlinings with a cross in the margin (both in an ink different from that of the original copyist) are found at the points where the corresponding printed pages begin. Someone, most probably the printer, collated it with the printed sheets.

[2] 'Item rationes propter quas damnari meruerunt, ne quis hic putet esse factum, quod in Parisiensibus Theologis multi reprehenderunt, Lutheranam nuper damnationem absque rationibus nudam proferentibus', 'Ad Lectorem', sig. A 1^{v}. Cf. Voigt, loc. cit.

[3] He died about 1540. The ascription to Cratander and the approximate date 1524 by the library at Basle are based on the initials and their arrangement. This

This text was subsequently reprinted as follows: *Fasciculus rerum expetendarum*, ed. Ortwinus Gratius, Cologne, 1535; in Aeneas's *Opera quae extant omnia*, Basle, 1551; and in the reprint of O. Gratius's *Fasciculus*, ed. E. Brown, London, 1690.[1] The text as it figures in Ortwin Gratius's edition was reprinted at 'Cattapolis' (i.e. Giessen) in 1667 with the misleading title *Commentariorum libri iii*. Here the third book is simply the letter of Aeneas to John of Segovia (see above, p. xxviii), and this edition was reprinted at Helmstadt in 1700. Finally it should be observed that very full extracts are included by François Pinsson in his voluminous *Caroli Septimi Francorum Regis Pragmatica Sanctio*, Paris, 1666, pp. 761–821.[2]

In editing the text we have normally retained the orthography of the *editio princeps* which does not differ significantly from that of the manuscripts, while modernizing the punctuation. Errors of an obvious kind have been silently corrected and alternative readings from the manuscripts are given only where they are necessary. Marginalia in the manuscripts consist partly of corrections to the text by the copyist, partly (in Book i only) of words and phrases indicating or summarizing the adjacent passage. Such marginal indications and summaries are also plentifully supplied by the first edition in both Book i and Book ii. While we have, of course, incorporated marginal and all other corrections in the manuscripts, we have not judged it helpful to reproduce, either from the manuscripts or the *editio princeps*, the other material, since it figures only as a rough guide to the contents in the absence of an index.

The translation has aimed at reproducing the text as faithfully as possible. The few words that have had to be supplied are printed in square brackets. Quotations from the Bible are given from the Authorized Version where Aeneas Sylvius reproduces the Vulgate text and where the Authorized Version corresponds with this. Though unusual spellings of proper names have normally been retained in the Latin text, a correct form (where known) is given in the translation.

For a note on the author's Latin, see above, p. xxix–xxx.

ascription is also given in the *Short Title Catalogue of Books Printed in the German-Speaking Countries . . . in the British Museum* (London, 1962), p. 700.

[1] On this see *Annalen des historischen Vereins für den Niederrhein*, XXIII (Cologne, 1871), 192–224.

[2] On this cf. V. Martin, *Les origines du Gallicanisme* (Paris, 1939), II. 303 n.

SELECT BIBLIOGRAPHY AND ABBREVIATIONS USED IN THE NOTES

The Councils and Conciliarism

The Council of Constance: the Unification of the Church, trans. Louise R. Loomis, ed. and annotated by J. H. Mundy and K. M. Woody. Columbia Records of Civilization, Sources and Studies, no. lxiii (New York and London, 1961).

D.L.O. — E. Delaruelle, E.-R. Labande, and P. Ourliac, *L'église au temps du Grand Schisme et de la crise conciliaire*, 'Histoire de L'Église', ed. Fliche and Martin, vol. xiv (Paris, 1962–4).

Figgis — J. N. Figgis, *From Gerson to Grotius*, 2nd ed. (Cambridge, 1931).

Gill — J. Gill, *The Council of Florence* (Cambridge, 1959).

H–L. — C. J. von Hefele, rev. and trans. H. Leclercq, *Histoire des conciles*, vols. i–vii (Paris, 1907–16).

Jedin — H. Jedin, trans. E. Graf, *A History of the Council of Trent*, vol. i (Edinburgh and London, 1957).

Tierney — Brian Tierney, *Foundations of Conciliar Theory* (Cambridge, 1955).

Valois, *France* — Noel Valois, *La France et le grand schisme d'occident*, 4 vols. (Paris, 1896–1902).

The Council of Basle: Sources and Secondary Works

Haller — *Concilium Basiliense. Studien und Quellen zur Geschichte des Konzils von Basel*, ed. J. Haller et al., 7 vols. (Basle, 1896–1926).

Mansi — J. D. Mansi, *Sacrorum conciliorum collectio*, vols. xxix–xxxii, repr. (Paris and Leipzig, 1901–6).

Mon. Con. — *Monumenta conciliorum generalium saeculi XV. Concilium Basiliense. Scriptores*: vols. ii, iii, ed. E. Birk (Vienna, 1873–92).

Pérouse — G. Pérouse, *Le cardinal Louis Aleman, président du concile de Bâle et la fin du grand schisme* (Paris, 1904).

Reichstagsakten — *Deutsche Reichstagsakten*, vols. xiii (ed. G. Beckmann) and xiv (ed. H. Weigel), repr. (Göttingen, 1957).

Valois — Noel Valois, *Le pape et le concile*, 2 vols. (Paris, 1909).

R. Wackernagel, *Geschichte der Stadt Basel*, 3 vols. in 4 (Basle, 1907–24).

Aeneas Sylvius Piccolomini

Ady — Cecilia M. Ady, *Pius II, The Humanist Pope* (London, 1913).

Commentaries — *The Commentaries of Pius II*, trans. Florence A. Gragg, intro. and ed. Leona C. Gabel. Smith College Studies in History, vols. XXII (1–2), XXV (1–4), XXX, XXXV, XLIII (Northampton, Mass., 1937–57). Cf. R. Ceserani, *Gior. stor. della lett. ital.*, cxli (1964), 265–82; F. Gaeta (ed.), *Il primo libro dei 'Commentarii' di Pio II* (L'Aquila, 1966).

Paparelli — Gioacchino Paparelli, *Enea Silvio Piccolomini, Pio II* (Bari, 1950).

Voigt — G. Voigt, *Enea Silvio de' Piccolomini als Papst Pius der Zweite und sein Zeitalter*, 3 vols. (Berlin, 1856–63).

Wolkan — *Der Briefwechsel des Eneas Silvius Piccolomini*, ed. R. Wolkan. Fontes rerum Austriacarum, Abt. ii, vols. LXI, LXII, LXVII, LXVIII (Vienna, 1909–18). The first two parts of this collection are cited as I. i and I. ii and the third as II.

Other Works

Decr. — *Corpus Iuris canonici*, ed. E. Friedberg. Vol. I, *Decretum Gratiani* (Leipzig, 1879).

Mirbt — C. Mirbt, *Quellen zur Geschichte des Papsttums und des Römischen Katholizismus*, 3rd ed. (Tübingen, 1911).

P.G. — J. P. Migne, *Patrologiae cursus completus. Series graeco-latina*, 161 vols. in 166 (Paris, 1857–66).

P.L. — Idem, *Series latina*, 221 vols. (Paris, 1844–64).

Symbols used in the critical notes

B = Basle MS. E. II. 14
C = Basle MS. A. III. 38
D = Basle MS. A. IV. 16
V = Vienna MS. 5104
W = Vienna MS. 5080
α = *editio princeps*
β = consensus (in Book i) of BCDV
γ = consensus (in Book ii) of VW

COMMENTARII DE GESTIS CONCILII BASILIENSIS

AENEAE SYLVII PICCOLOMINEI SENENSIS[a] IN COMMENTARIOS SVOS DE GESTIS CONCILII BASILIENSIS

PRAEFATIO

NESCIO quae mea calamitas est quibusue urgeor fatis, ne me historiae furari sciam tempusque meum utilius consumere. Statui saepius ab iis me poëtarum et oratorum lenocinis sequestrare et aliquod sequi exercitium, unde aliquid tandem figerem, quo esset 'mihi tuta senectus a tegete et baculo,'[1] ne sicut aues feraeque in dies uiuerem. Nec deerant studia, quibus si forte uersari uoluissem, et opes cogere et amicos parare potuissem. Idque non mea solum sponte mihi suadebam, sed accedebant etiam necessarii, quorum illae assiduae uoces erant: 'Quid agis tandem Aenea? Tene quamdiu uiuis poëtica possidebit? Istuc aetatis non erubescis nihil habere agri, nihil pecuniarum? An nescis quia uigesimo grandem, trigesimo cautum, quadragesimoque diuitem anno esse oportet; qui has metas praeterierit, frustra conari?' Monebant igitur ut uenientis et iam propediem instantis quadragesimi anni cogitatum haberem, priusque aliquid tenere curarem quam id aetatis ingrederer. Dedi saepius manus facturumque me quod suasum erat spopondi; abieci oratorios codices, abieci historias, omneisque huiusmodi literas ut meae salutis inimicas pepuli. At sicut auiculae quaedam ignem candelae nequeunt dimittere, in eoque, priusquam fugiant, aduruntur, sic ego ad meum malum et ubi mihi pereundum est redeo; nec aliud mihi (ut uideo) hoc studium quam mors adimet. Sed postquam sic fata trahunt, nec quod uellem id possum, coniungenda est cum potestate uoluntas. Obiicitur paupertas, sed est tam pauperi quam diuiti usque ad mortem uiuendum.[2] Ac misera in senibus paupertas, miserior quippe

[a] B *adds in a different hand*: Hic factus fuit papa nomine Pius secundus

[1] Juvenal, ix. 139.

[2] Here and in the preface as a whole the author is presumably urging on Felix V his claims to support.

ERRATA

p. 2, line 3: for 'lenocinis' read 'lenociniis'
p. 6, note 1: for 'ignoscereter' read 'ignosceretur'
p. 42, line 8: for 'buorum' read 'quorum'
p. 46, note 9: for '*Manichaei*, *S*' read '*Manichaei*, 5'
p. 86, note 1: for '*Sentential*' read '*Sententiae*'

THE PREFACE OF AENEAS SYLVIUS PICCOLOMINI OF SIENA TO HIS COMMENTARIES ON THE PROCEEDINGS OF THE COUNCIL OF BASLE

IT is a misfortune of mine and a fate by which I am plagued that I cannot steal away from history and use my time more profitably. Again and again I have taken the decision to withdraw from the attractions of poets and orators and to practise some employment through which I might eventually get hold of something 'to preserve my old age from [the beggar's] mat and staff,'[1] so that I should not live, like the birds and beasts, from day to day. I did not lack interests which, if I had wished to devote myself to them, would have enabled me to amass wealth and acquire friends. That was not merely the prompting I gave myself, but I had acquaintances as well who constantly made remarks such as these: 'What in the world are you after, Aeneas? Is poetry going to claim you all your days? At your time of life are you not ashamed of owning no land and no money? Surely you are aware that a man at twenty should be grown up, at thirty cautious, at forty well-off, and that after passing these turning-points striving is in vain?' So they urged me to take thought for my fortieth year now approaching and almost upon me, and to care about getting hold of something before I entered upon that time of life. I gave in to them often enough and promised to act on their suggestions. I threw away my oratorical writings, my histories too, and I banished all literary efforts of that kind as hostile to my welfare. But just as some small birds cannot leave the flame of a candle and are burnt in it before they can escape, even so I come back to my own hurt and the place where I must perish, and nothing, I see, save death will take this interest from me. Yet since fate impels me thus, and I cannot do what I would, my wishes must be linked with my powers. I am taunted with poverty, but a poor man like a rich one must live until death.[2] Poverty is wretched for the old, but more

illiteratis. Sanum habere corpus et mentem integram non minus pauperi datur quam diuiti. Haec si teneam, nil ultra exposco. 'Frui paratis et ualido mihi' maximus atque optimus Deus donet, 'et, precor, integra cum mente, nec turpem senectam degere nec cithara carentem.'[1] Et quoniam sic animo sedet, ad commentarios nostros reuertamus, ac Basiliensis gesta Concilii ex ordine institutoque referamus.

[1] Horace, *Odes*, i. 31, 17–20.

wretched for the unlettered. To have a healthy body and a sound mind is granted as much to the poor man as to the rich. Provided I keep these I want nothing else. May God in his great power and goodness grant me 'to enjoy my possessions and to be of sound health, with a mind, I pray, unimpaired, and to pass an old age that is neither without honour nor lacking a lyre'.[1] As this is my fixed intention, let us return to our commentaries, and give an account of the proceedings of the Council of Basle in due order and according to plan.

COMMENTARIORVM AENEAE SYLVII PICCOLOMINEI DE GESTIS CONCILII BASILIENSIS

LIBER PRIMVS

APUD Hetruscos plerisque in locis, quoniam flumina sic tenuia sunt ut frumentarium molam nequeant rapere, ingenteis ducunt foueas, quibus fluuiorum cursum morantur biduanasque aut triduanas colligunt aquas; quae postea impetuosius exeuntes et molam trahunt et frumenti omnem quantitatem facile terunt. Haud secus mihi uidentur patres huius Synodi[a] facere, qui, tanquam nihil habeant aduersus Eugenium faciundum, diutius silent materiam tacite colligentes, exin una in die uno quoque impetu rem perficiunt. Sed quorsum haec forsitan quaeritur. Nempe ne quis me arguat negligentiae, qui plus solito plusque debito siluerim; nec enim scribere potui cum nihil fieret. Nunc uero cum res actae sint et relatu et cognitione dignissimae, accusationem, siqua paratur, scriptis praeueniam; nec patiar me argui negligentiae, quamuis potero nimiae forsitan audaciae reprehendi, qui rem arduam et grandem stilo inopi et arido sim complexus. In qua re nec mihi postulabo ignosci, qui sponte erro, et uenustatem scio reprehensionis a M. quondam Catone profectae in Aulum Albinum, qui cum Lucio Lucullo consul fuit.[1] Is Albinus res Romanas oratione Graeca scriptitauit; in eius historiae primo scriptum erat ad hanc sententiam, neminem succensere sibi conuenire, si quid in illis libris parum composite aut minus eleganter scriptum foret. 'Nam sum,' inquit, 'homo Romanus, natus in Latio, et eloquium Graecum a nobis alienissimum est;' ideoque ueniam gratiamque malae existimationis, si quid esset erratum, postulauit. Eaque cum legisset M. Cato: 'Nae tu,' inquit,

[a] huius Synodi BD; huiusmodi α

[1] 151 B.C. ; 'uenustatem . . . ignoscereter' Macrobius, *Satur.* pref. § 13.

THE FIRST BOOK OF THE COMMENTARIES OF AENEAS SYLVIUS PICCOLOMINI ON THE PROCEEDINGS OF THE COUNCIL OF BASLE

IN many parts of Tuscany, since the rivers there are so insignificant that they cannot turn a corn mill, the people dig huge dikes with which they hold up the flow of the rivers and gather the water of two or three days, which issuing later with greater force both turns the mill and grinds easily the whole amount of corn. The conduct of the Fathers of this Council seems similar. For long they hold their peace as though believing that no action should be taken against Eugenius, quietly gathering material, then on a single day with a single rush they accomplish their purpose. But perhaps you are asking the purpose of this. It is of course that nobody may charge me with negligence for being more reticent than was my habit and was proper. I could not write when nothing was happening. Now, however, when events have taken place well worth being reported and known, I shall by my writings anticipate any accusation that is in preparation, and shall not allow myself to be charged with negligence, though I may perhaps be criticized for rashness in tackling a difficult and large task with a poor and dry style. In this matter I shall not ask for any pardon, as I err of my own accord, and I realize the neatness of the rebuke once given by Marcus Cato to Aulus Albinus, who was consul with Lucius Lucullus.[1] This Albinus was the author of a history of Rome in Greek. At the opening of his account was a remark to this effect, that no one should be annoyed with him if any expression in those books lacked artistry and elegance. 'I am a Roman,' he said, 'born in Latium, and the Greek tongue is quite strange to me', and therefore he wanted to be pardoned and excused from criticism, if there were any mistake. On reading this Marcus Cato exclaimed, 'Really Aulus, you are too absurd! Why have you preferred to appeal against censure rather than to avoid it? For we usually ask

'Aule, nimium nugator es; cur maluisti culpam deprecari, quam culpa carere? Nam petere ueniam solemus aut cum imprudentes errauimus, aut cum noxam imperio compellentis admisimus. Te,' inquit, 'oro, quis perpulit ut id committeres, quod priusquam faceres, peteres ut ignosceretur?' Quod ne mihi quoque possit accidere, sine petitione ueniae rem aggrediar.

Frequens atque insigne Franconiae oppidum Norimberga est, et tam superis quam inferis Teuthonibus commune. Ibique paucis effluxis mensibus, oratores Alberti Romanorum regis[1] et aliorum Alemanniae principum conuenerunt, tum propter alias communis patriae causas, tum maxime ut eam quae inter Concilium et papam uigebat discordiam sopirent. Illuc[2] et oratores sacri Concilii accesserunt; et iussu papae uir magna hominum opinione sanctissimus, cardinalis Sanctae Crucis, [a][3] cum plerisque collegis peruenit. Vtque illic perfici res nequiuit, conuentus ipse Francfordiam ad calendas Marcias tunc proximas translatus est,[4] quod eo in loco Electores Imperii facilius conuenturi iudicabantur. Interim oratores Caesarei Electorumque Basileam petierunt, et contracta cum oratoribus aliorum principum qui Basileae degebant intelligentia, ac uocato praestantissimo uiro, cardinali Sancti Petri,[5] qui per id temporis exitum rerum Constantiae morabatur, maxime hortati sunt patres Concilii ut pacem amplecterentur quam ipsi offerent. Erat petitio principum, siue (ut uerius dicam) oratorum, ut sacro Concilio uidebatur, ardua, utque ipsi putabant, facilis; petebant nanque ut patres in alium se locum reciperent Conciliumque transferrent.[6] Quod unum semper Eugenius uisus est quaesiuisse ut sic uel patres Concilii dissiparet uel libertatem eis adimeret. Visum tamen est sanctae Synodo nec negandum esse quod principes poscerent, nec quod Eugenius cuperet permittendum; ideoque sic caute mutatio loci promissa est ut omnibus obuiatum periculis uideretur. Nequaquam tamen oratoribus principum accepta responsio fuit. Qui sic transferri Concilium postulabant ut magis dissolutio quam translatio diceretur

[a] Sanctae Crucis BV *in marg.*; crucifer α

---

[1] The Hapsburg successor of the Emperor Sigismund (d. 9 Dec. 1437), elected 18 March 1438, died 27 Oct. 1439 without papal coronation, hence was styled only 'king of the Romans'.

[2] The Diet met at Nuremberg in October and November 1438.

[3] Niccolò Albergati, cardinal 1426 (d. 1443).

[4] The decision to call a Diet at Frankfurt was taken between 15 and 19 Nov.: *Reichstagsakten*, XIII. 835.

[5] Juan Cervantes, cardinal 1426 (d. 1453), a former conciliarist and now papal legate.

pardon either when we have made a mistake unwittingly or when we have been guilty of a fault under compulsion. I ask you,' he said, 'who compelled you to commit what you wanted pardoned before you had done it'? So that this may not be my experience too, I shall come to my subject without any request for pardon.

There is a populous and famous town of Franconia called Nuremberg, belonging as much to the Upper as to the Lower Germans. There when a few months had passed, ambassadors of Albert, king of the Romans,[1] and of other princes of Germany held a conference on matters concerning the whole country and especially to lessen the discord raging between the Council and the pope. Thither[2] too came ambassadors of the holy Council, and on the pope's instructions the cardinal of S. Croce,[3] a person of the greatest holiness in the view of the majority of men, arrived with several colleagues. As the business could not be settled there, the meeting was transferred to Frankfurt for 1 March, then not far off,[4] because it was considered that the Electors of the Empire would more easily meet in that place. In the meantime the ambassadors of the emperor and of the Electors made for Basle. Reaching an understanding with the ambassadors of the other princes who were staying at Basle and summoning the very distinguished cardinal of St. Peter's[5] who throughout that time was awaiting the issue of affairs at Constance, they strongly urged the Fathers of the Council to grasp the peace they offered. The request of the princes, or more accurately of their ambassadors, was in the view of the holy Council difficult, but in their own view easy, for they asked that the Fathers should go to another place and transfer the Council.[6] This was the one thing that Eugenius seemed always to have wanted, that by this means he might either scatter the Fathers of the Council or take away their freedom. The Council, however, decided neither to refuse the request of the princes nor yet to allow what Eugenius wanted, and so the change of place was agreed, together with such precautions as made it seem that every danger had been avoided. However, the reply was not at all welcome to the ambassadors of the princes, who wanted the Council transferred in such a way that it could be described or at least regarded as a dissolution rather

[6] The attempted reconciliation would have made the emperor and the king of France arbitrators in the conflict between pope and Council and depended on a new council being convoked, the places suggested being Strasbourg, Constance, or Mainz: H–L. VII. 1063; *Reichstagsakten*, XIV. 61 (*c.* 12–14 Jan. 1439).

uel crederetur; ob quam causam inter deputatos Concilii et ipsos oratores pluribus diebus disceptatum est, plurimumque de concordia practicatum. Interque ipsas rerum difficultates Pataviensis[1] et Augustensis[2] episcopi, oratores Caesarei et admodum nobiles, ad ipsum regem abierunt, et cum his collega Ioannes Eich,[3] iurisconsultus plurimae lectionis, abscessit; prius tamen multum rogati multumque stimulati baronem magnanimum et apprime insignem, Conradum Vuinspergensem,[4] ex mandato regio protectorem sacro Concilio et omnium patrum defensorem dederunt. Qua ex re ut alienatum ab Eugenio aduersarii, sic patres sacri Concilii optimam erga se fore mentem Caesaris cognouerunt; quia nec protectorem misisset, nisi legitimum Concilium reputasset, nec rursus Concilium esse in Basilea putauisset, si Eugenio fidem habuisset.

Post illorum ergo recessum reliqui oratores Alberti Augusti, qui Basileae remanserant, episcopus Lubecensis,[5] uir recti consilii, ac Georgius,[6] tam literata quam armata insignis militia, cum aliis principum nuntiis nouam concordiae cedulam concluserunt, iuuante admodum et inter sepiusculas dissensiones arbitrante cardinali Sancti Petri, coram quo omnia peragebant; quam cedulam et sacrum Concilium ut insufficientem, et, sicuti postmodum relatum est, Eugenius ut erroneam respuit. Nec diu post responsio synodalis conclusa est, ipsisque oratoribus in generali contione reddita, cum iam propediem instaret conuentus Francfordiae celebrandus, qui tamen propter pestem ibi grassantem ad urbem metropolim, Maguntiam, haud amplius unius diei uia distantem, translatus fuerat. Visum est igitur oratoribus principum eo pergere, si forsitan pacis illic medium aliquod inuenirent, quo papam Concilio reunirent. Ex oratoribus Caesaris Lubecensis et Georgius miles; ex Gallicis archiepiscopus Turonensis[7] et Trecensis[8] episcopus ac collegae alii praeter Lugdunensem archiepiscopum;[9] ex Castellanis tantum Concensis episcopus[10] (nondum enim delitiae Hispaniarum, Burgensis,[11] ex legatione ad Caesarem

[1] Leonard von Layming (d. 1451).

[2] Peter von Schaumberg, cardinal 1439 (d. 1469).

[3] D.U.J., professor at Vienna (cf. *Mon. Con.* III. 181), bishop of Eichstätt 1445, d. 1464.

[4] Conrad von Weinsberg, imperial chamberlain, d. 1448. Albert had designated him as protector of the council earlier (13 Nov. 1438); he was installed at Basle on 15 Jan. 1439; *Reichstagsakten*, XIV. 6, 57–60.

[5] Johann Schele (d. 1439).

[6] Georg Fischel or Fischlin (Haller, VI. 304–95), Vischel (*Mon. Con.* III. 275); D.U.J. and a knight.

[7] Philippe de Coëtquis (d. 1441).

[8] Jean Léguisé (d. 1450).

[9] Amédée de Talaru (d. 1444).

[10] Alvaro Nuñez de Isorna, archbishop of Compostella 1445 (d. 1449).

than a translation; for this reason discussions took place for several days between the representatives of the Council and the ambassadors themselves, and there was much talk about a peaceful settlement. During these complicated negotiations the bishops of Passau[1] and Augsburg,[2] the emperor's ambassadors, men of high rank, left to go to the king himself, and with them went their colleague Johann von Eycke,[3] a learned counsel. But before they left, after many requests and under great pressure, on the king's instructions they appointed protector for the holy Council and defender of all the Fathers the noble and extremely distinguished baron, Conrad of Weinsberg.[4] Through this, just as the pope's enemies knew that [the emperor] was estranged from Eugenius, so the Fathers of the holy Council knew that the emperor's attitude was well disposed towards them; because he would not have sent a protector unless he had considered the Council lawful, nor again would he have recognized the Council's existence at Basle if he had believed Eugenius.

So after their departure the rest of the ambassadors of the Emperor Albert who had remained at Basle, the bishop of Lübeck,[5] a man of sound counsel, and George,[6] as distinguished in the service of letters as of arms, together with other spokesmen of the princes, drew up a new plan for peace with the full assistance and the mediation (amid the rather frequent disputes) of the cardinal of St. Peter's, in whose presence all their business took place. This plan was rejected by the holy Council as not going far enough and by Eugenius, so it was later reported, as mistaken. Not long afterwards the Council's reply was completed and handed to the ambassadors themselves at a plenary session on the eve of the assembly to be held at Frankfurt. This however, because of the plague raging there, had been transferred to the metropolitan city of Mainz, not more than a single day's journey away. The ambassadors of the princes resolved to go there in the hope of finding some peaceful compromise to reunite the pope and the Council. Of the emperor's ambassadors there were the bishop of Lübeck and the knight George; of the French the archbishop of Tours[7] and the bishop of Troyes[8] and other colleagues but not the archbishop of Lyons;[9] of the Castilians there was only the bishop of Cuenca[10] (for the bishop of Burgos,[11] the darling of Spain,

[11] Alfonso Garcia (d. 1456), who had been sent to Albert in Nov. 1438 (Valois, II. 146 n.) and returned in early April 1439 (Haller, VI. 358).

erat reuersus); ex Aragonensibus nemo. Postea tamen relatum est episcopum Albigaunensem[1] et Franciscum Barbauariam,[2] qui ex Mediolanensibus ibi fuerunt, regis quoque Aragonum[3] habuisse mandatum. Cardinalis autem Sancti Petri paucis ante diebus, siue quod pestem timuit iam paulatim crescentem, siue quod desperata pace in Basilea remanere non audebat, in Nidou, quod est Suitzerorum oppidum, se receperat. Vt tamen ire oratores Maguntiam accepit, in spem iterum pacis erectus, ex eo flumine,[4] quod Solodorum in duas diuidit partes, in Rhenum uenit. Eoque Maguntiam uectus est.

Fuit conuentus ipse admodum celeber.[5] Praesentes nanque Maguntinensis, Coloniensis, Treuerensis[6] archiepiscopi sacrique Romani imperii Electores, ac Coëlectorum[7] omnium nuncii affuerunt; ultimi uero omnium Patauiensis et Augustensis episcopi, abbas Scotorum Viennensium,[8] et Ioannes de Eich doctor comparuere, qui cum Lubecensi et Georgio Caesareum locum tenebant. Praecipuus tamen illo in conuentu fautor sacri Concilii habitus est Coloniensis archiepiscopus, qui summo studio summoque nisu rem bene dirigere conatus, se non minus uirtute animi quam genere atque opibus praestantem ostendit, eumque Maguntinus est imitatus. Rabanus uero Treuerensis aliquanto rigidiorem se praebuit. Censuit et sancta Synodus suos quoque ad ipsum conuentum oratores fore mittendos. Missique sunt Patriarcha Aquileiensis[9] cum auctoritate legati de latere, episcopi Vicensis[10] et Argensis;[11] theologi Ioannes Segouius[12] et Thomas de Corsellis;[13] iurisperiti Ioannes de Bachenstein,[14] auditor camerae, et Hugo,[15] Metensis archidiaconus, qui postea processum aduersus Eugenium habitum publice retulit; iisque adiuncti sunt Ioannes,[16] prior Traiectensis, et Nicolaus Aucupis,[17] Normannus, qui etiam

[1] Matteo del Carretto (d. 1448).

[2] A councillor of Filippo Maria, duke of Milan.

[3] On the attitude of Milan and Alfonso, king of Aragon and Naples, see Introduction, pp. xvii, xx.

[4] The Aar.

[5] The assembly at Mainz, March–April 1439, was not a Reichstag but a meeting of Electors or *Kurverein*; its proceedings are assembled in *Reichstagsakten*, XIV. 96–142.

[6] The holders of the three ecclesiastical electorates at this time were: Mainz—Dietrich von Erbach (d. 1459); Cologne—Dietrich von Mörs (d. 1463); Trier—Raban von Helmstadt (d. 19 May 1439).

[7] The lay Electors were the Count Palatine of the Rhine, the duke of Saxony, the margrave of Brandenburg and the king of Bohemia.

[8] John, abbot of the Schottenkloster (St. Mary's) at Vienna.

[9] Ludwig von Teck, who died of the plague, below, p. 194.

[10] Jorge de Ornos, promoted cardinal in 1440 by Felix V and deprived of Vich by Eugenius IV in 1445; he died in 1452 as bishop of Carpentras, to which see he had been translated by Nicholas V.

had not yet returned from his mission to the emperor); of the Aragonese there was no one. Afterwards, however, it was reported that the bishop of Albenga[1] and Francesco Barbavara,[2] who were there from the Milanese, had instructions too from the king of Aragon.[3] The cardinal of St. Peter's, either in fear of the plague that was now gradually increasing, or because, despairing of peace, he dared not remain in Basle, had gone a few days before to Nidau, a Swiss town. Yet when he learnt of the ambassadors' going to Mainz, he was buoyed up again by hopes of peace, and by the river[4] which cuts Solothurn in two he reached the Rhine. Down this he sailed to Mainz.

The meeting itself was quite well attended.[5] For there were present the archbishops of Mainz, Cologne, and Trier,[6] Electors of the Holy Roman Empire, and the delegates of all the other electors;[7] and last of all there appeared with them the bishops of Passau and Augsburg, the abbot of the Scots in Vienna[8] and Dr. Johann von Eycke, who were the emperor's representatives along with the bishop of Lübeck, and George. At that meeting the outstanding supporter of the holy Council was considered to be the archbishop of Cologne, who attempted with the greatest zeal and the greatest effort to handle the matter well, and showed himself no less pre-eminent in mental qualities than in descent and wealth. He was copied by the archbishop of Mainz. Raban of Trier showed himself rather inflexible. The Council too considered that it would have to send its ambassadors to the meeting. There were sent the patriarch of Aquileia[9] with the authority of a legate *de latere*, the bishops of Vich[10] and Ardjisch,[11] the theologians John of Segovia[12] and Thomas de Courcelles,[13] the lawyers Johann von Bachenstein,[14] auditor of the Camera, and Hugues,[15] archdeacon of Metz, who later publicly reported the process against Eugenius; to them were added Jean,[16] prior of Utrecht, and Nicolas Loiseleur,[17] a Norman,

[11] John Stojkovich of Ragusa, appointed to this see by the Council in 1438; Felix V made him a cardinal in 1440; d. 1443.

[12] See Introduction, p. xxviii.

[13] The Paris theologian and judge of Joan of Arc. Canon of Amiens, he refused the hat offered him by Felix.

[14] A canonist, archdeacon of Zagreb.

[15] Guillaume Hugues; made a cardinal by Felix in 1444 and also by Nicholas V in 1449; for his part in the process against Eugenius see below, p. 200 and Introduction, p. xxix, n. 2. He died in 1455.

[16] Jean Passart, prior of the convent of regular canons at Utrecht.

[17] Provost of Chartres. He is described as absent by Hugolin on 18 May 1439 but is present at Basle on 23 Nov. (Haller, VI. 428, 724).

usque in hunc diem non redierunt. Data quoque his est praeter spem aduersariorum facultas omnimoda ut quicquid ii agerent promitterentque pro bono uniuersalis ecclesiae et honore sacri Concilii, id ratum firmumque haberetur; qui et recepti Maguntiae honorifice, et legatione sua libere uti permissi sunt. Nemo illic erat qui Eugenii nuncium se uocitaret. Tarentinus,[1] in quem paulo ante lata erat sententia, cum collegis suis in remotis agebat, nec uenire Maguntiam audebat, siue quia congredi cum legatis conciliaribus uerebatur, siue quia mandatum illuc eundi nondum susceperat. Confluxerant tamen illuc plurimi fautores Eugenii tam ex Concilio quam ex Florentia locisque aliis. Fuerunt in sancta Synodo quamplures alii uiri incorporati iuratique, quorum semper animus a rebus quae Basileae gerebantur uisus est alienus; quique, licet laboraturos pro honore et statu sacri Concilii iureiurando se astrinxissent, ii nihilominus in omni negotio Eugenio magis quam sacro Concilio fauebant, quorum postea sectam Vuilhelmus Constantiensis[2] iurisconsultus 'Griseam' appellauit. Ex his quamplures Maguntiam perrexerunt, Eugenium, si qua in parte quirent, defensuri. Hercules tamen omnium Eugenianorum Nicolaus Cusanus[3] existimatus est, homo et priscarum literarum eruditissimus et multarum rerum usu perdoctus, cuiusque dolendum sit tam nobile ingenium ad illa schismatis studia diuertisse ut legatione ad Graecos uigore falsi decreti[4] fungeretur; hic omne studium suum omnemque conatum in defensione Eugenii collocauerat, atque ut est uersuti et callidi consilii, nunc una nunc alia impedimenta texebat.

Post uarios tamen multiplicesque tractatus uisum est Electoribus imperii aliisque Germanorum principum oratoribus decreta sacri Basiliensis Concilii in sua natione recipere atque obseruari mandare,[5] super decreto uero suspensionis deliberationem suspendentes, ne illo suscepto desperata pax cum Eugenio uideretur. Interim tamen duo missi[6] ab oratoribus papae Maguntiam peruenerunt, iunctique hominibus suae factionis turbare omnia satagebant; illud quoque sperare ausi ut suscepta semel decreta refutarentur. Quod ubi non successit, ad ultimum desperationis refugium

[1] Giovanni Berardi di Tagliacozzo (d. 1449). He had been a papal president of the Council. In 1437 he sided with the minority in associating the Council with Eugenius IV's negotiations with the Greeks and was charged with having illegally procured the official sealing of the decree passed by the minority (cf. below, p. 144, n. 2.). In his absence he was finally condemned by the Council 27 Feb. 1439: Valois, II. 62–69. Eugenius IV made him a cardinal.

[2] D.U.J., canon of Speyer.

[3] See Introduction, p. xxii.

[4] Nicholas of Cues was of the party that carried the minority decree (above, n. 1) to Eugenius in May 1437.

[5] The 'Acceptatio' of Mainz, 26 Mar. 1439; cf. Introduction, p. xx.

who have not returned to this very day. They were also granted, against the wishes of their opponents, complete powers, that their actions and promises for the good of the whole Church and the honour of the Council should be held to be valid and unalterable. They were worthily received at Mainz and allowed to act as plenipotentiaries. No one was there who styled himself an envoy of Eugenius. The archbishop of Taranto,[1] upon whom sentence had recently been passed, was living with his colleagues in seclusion and did not venture to come to Mainz, either because he was afraid of meeting the conciliar representatives, or because he had not yet been ordered to go there. Yet many partisans of Eugenius did gather there both from the Council and from Florence and other places. There were very many other men incorporated into, and sworn members of, the Council, whose attitude seemed always estranged from the proceedings at Basle, and who, though they had bound themselves by oath to work for the honour and authority of the holy Council, yet in every matter supported Eugenius more than the Council. This party the legal counsel, Wilhelm von Konstanz,[2] later called 'the Greys'. Very many of them came to Mainz in the hope of somehow or other defending Eugenius. The Hercules of all the followers of Eugenius was considered to be Nicholas of Cues,[3] a man both well versed in ancient literature and well informed through his wide experience. It is a matter for regret that his noble mind should have been diverted to schismatic ideas, so that on the strength of a false decree[4] he served on a mission to the Greeks. He had directed all his ardour and all his efforts to the defence of Eugenius and, being of versatile and shrewd counsel, contrived obstacles, now in one way, now in another.

Yet after varied and complicated debates the Imperial Electors and the other ambassadors of the German princes decided to accept within their nation the decrees of the holy Council of Basle[5] and to order their observance, suspending discussion upon the decree of suspension in case, if that were adopted, peace with Eugenius might seem beyond hope. However, in the meantime two persons[6] sent by the pope's ambassadors reached Mainz, and joining the members of their party busied themselves in causing confusion. They ventured even to hope that decrees already adopted would be repudiated. When this did not succeed, turning to the last refuge

[6] Tomasso de Aquila and Orlando de Cortino, both D.U.J.: *Reichstagsakten*, XIV. 102.

declinantes, inaudito papa non esse talia peragenda protestati sunt. Sed frustra omneis eorum conatus fuere. Receptis nanque decretis, oratores Conciliares ex licentia conuentus Basileam reuerterunt, solusque ibi sine mandato Vicensis episcopus ad paucos dies rogatu oratorum principum mansit. Recesserunt quoque Maguntinus, Coloniensis, et Treuerensis archiepiscopi, dimissis ibi Conciliariis, qui cum aliis principum oratoribus de pace transigerent.

Dum haec Maguntiae fiunt, inter theologos qui Basileae remanserant haud parua haesitatio suborta est dici ne posset haereticus Eugenius, qui tam rebelliter ecclesiae mandata contemneret; eamque ob causam congregati adinuicem diutius inter se disputarunt, aliis negatiuam, aliis affirmatiuam sententiam defendentibus, scientes hanc fuisse ueterem et Socraticam rationem contra alterius opinionem disserendi. Nam ita facillime quid uerisimillimum esset inueniri posse Socrates arbitrabatur. Inter disputandum autem triplex emersit opinio; alii nanque haereticum Eugenium affirmabant, alii non solum haereticum, uerum etiam relapsum,[1] tertii uero nec relapsum eum nec haereticum fateri uolebant. Erat inter ipsos theologos et autoritate et scientiae copia praecipuus Ebronensis episcopus,[2] serenissimi et potentissimi regis[3] Castellae orator, erat et abbas quidam Scotus;[4] qui tanquam acerrimi pugiles et in theatro pugnantes, aduersarios quoslibet prosternebant. Quorum argumentationibus aut acquiescebant alii aut cedebant; eorumque studio grauior tandem sententia uicit ut haereticus atque relapsus Eugenius diceretur, octo inter ipsos theologos conclusiunculis approbatis, quas ueritates appellitarunt, earum copiam in orbem diuulgantes. Quae res circa medium mensis Aprilis initium suscepit industria quidem ac solertia Nicolai[5] cuiusdam Burgundionis ex ordine Praedicatorum, uiri acuti et longe maioris animi quam corporis, qui nec deputationum nec congregationum aures unquam personare omisit, donec res capta et consummata est. Ne illud asserere dubitarim, rem hanc intactam remansisse, nisi istius homuncionis diligentia patres excitasset; quem si quis uideat, nunquam tanti existimet. Sed non sunt homines ex aspectu diiudicandi.

[1] The distinction made here and later between a heretic and a relapsed heretic was fundamental: the latter could not purge himself by further recantation.

[2] The Franciscan Bartolomeo de Pellegrini, whose death is mentioned below, p. 194.

[3] Juan II (1406–1453).

[4] Thomas Livingstone, abbot of Dundrennan; provided to Dunkeld by Felix V in 1440, died 1460. For his activity and that of other Scots at Basle see the article by J. H. Burns, *Innes Review*, XIII (1962), 3–53, 157–83, and his *Scottish Churchmen and the Council of Basle* (Glasgow, 1962).

[5] Nicolas Jaiquier; cf. below, pp. 92–94.

of despair they protested that such decisions should not be reached without the pope's being heard. Yet all their attempts were in vain. For the decrees were accepted, and the ambassadors of the Council with the leave of the assembly returned to Basle, and only the bishop of Vich remained there for a few days without instructions at the invitation of the ambassadors of the princes. On the dismissal of the conciliar party there left too the archbishops of Mainz, Cologne, and Trier, to confer about peace with other ambassadors of the princes.

While this was happening at Mainz no little uncertainty arose among the theologians who had stayed behind at Basle as to whether Eugenius could be called a heretic, seeing that he was showing such rebellious contempt of the instructions of the Church. Meeting together for that reason, they held a long discussion, some maintaining the negative, some the positive view, knowing that this was the old Socratic method of arguing against another's opinion. For Socrates thought that in this way what was closest to the truth could most easily be discovered. In the course of the discussion three views emerged; some maintained that Eugenius was a heretic, some that he was not only a heretic but relapsed,[1] and the third group was unwilling to admit that he was either relapsed or a heretic. Prominent among the theologians both in authority and knowledge was the bishop of Hebron,[2] ambassador of the serene and puissant king of Castile.[3] Prominent too was a certain Scottish abbot.[4] These, like active boxers putting on an exhibition fight, floored some of their opponents; others either accepted their pleas or gave way to them, and by their efforts the weightier view in the end prevailed: that Eugenius be called both a heretic and relapsed. Eight short resolutions were approved among these theologians, which they asserted to be truths; they published a copy of them. This affair began towards the middle of April, through the industry and shrewdness of a certain Nicolas,[5] a Dominican friar from Burgundy, an acute man with a mind far larger than his body, who did not stop dinning it in the ears of members of deputations and congregations until the matter was accepted and brought to a conclusion. I should not hesitate to assert that the matter would have remained unattempted had not this little man's diligence roused the Fathers, although to look at him you would not have considered him capable of so much. But men are not to be judged by their appearance.

Reuersis uero oratoribus ex Maguntia, habitaque certitudine de receptione decretorum, uisum patribus est conclusiunculas magistrorum[1] diligentius maturiusque discutere, uocatique sunt ex iussu deputationum magistri omneis ac doctores humani et diuini iuris in capitulum maioris ecclesiae, cum praelatis Eugenianam haeresim publice discussuri. Quae res Mediolanensi antistiti[2] magnae molestiae fuit timenti ne disputatio haec priuationem Eugenii secum traheret, quam ipse, ut dicebat, timore schismatis semper impedierat. Ea propter uocare alios, excitare torpentes, terrere[a] animatos omnique studio niti ut res ipsa turbaretur; et quamuis ex oratoribus ducalibus unicus ipse Basileae superesset, egregie tamen uices aliorum implebat. Ex animo nanque laboranti nihil uidetur esse difficile, itaque nec plus quicquam tres simul egissent quam solus ipse peregit; absentes namque suarum partium, ut potuit, literis, praesentes autem uerbis in defensionem Eugenii animauit. Ventum est tamen ad locum capituli, frequens quoque habita congregatio est; uenerant enim omnes aut dicendi aut audiendi studio illecti. Sexque omnino diebus et ante prandium et ante coenam protracta res disputando est. Medius erat inter omnes primoque loco ut iudex fidei[3] totiusque disputationis moderator et arbiter Ludouicus cardinalis et archiepiscopus Arelatensis,[4] praelatus cum multis uirtutibus insignis, tum praecipue fortis et constans. Nicolaus uero Amici,[5] qui et ipse procurator fidei[6] est et inter theologos Parisienses apprime clarus, quod quisque sentiret interrogabat. Suffragia quoque scriba publicus Ioannes Dieulifist[7] annotabat, plurimaque illic egregie disputata et prudenter examinata fuere; de quibus si facere uerba uoluerim, uereor ne me aliqui uitio mentis tantum opus ingressum iudicent, quia res est a mea professione meoque studio remotissima. Famulabor tamen mihi ipsi; nec me intra pomeria sacrorum eloquiorum ingressum, 'introspexisse in aedem Deae, a qua mares absterrentur'[8] existimabo. Atque ut de re ipsa dicere incipiam, conclusiones theologorum, tanquam disputationis fundamenta, ipso in exordio ponam. Nec ego iisdem utar uerbis

[a] terrere (te'rere) D; currere α

---

[1] Appointed on 15 Apr. 1439 to formulate the terms under which Eugenius could be termed a heretic.

[2] Francesco Piccolopasso (d. 1443), ambassador of the duke of Milan.

[3] The duties of the judge of faith, the determination of all matters concerning belief, heresy, witchcraft, etc., are set out in Pérousse, pp. 184–6.

[4] On Aleman see Introduction, p. xxii.

[5] Delegate of the University of Paris and canon of Amiens.

[6] The judge of faith had a procurator as his assistant for preparing relevant business.

[7] A canonist.

Now when the ambassadors had returned from Mainz, and certainty was felt about the acceptance of the decrees, the Fathers resolved to discuss with greater care and at greater length the short resolutions of the masters,[1] and there were summoned at the order of the deputations all masters and doctors of civil and canon law to the chapter-house of the cathedral to discuss in public with the prelates the heresy of Eugenius. This was a matter very troublesome to the archbishop of Milan,[2] who feared that this discussion might involve the deprivation of Eugenius, which he, as he said, had always opposed through fear of a schism. On that account he admonished some, stirred the sluggish, frightened the bold, and used all his energy to cause confusion in the matter, and though of the duke's ambassadors he alone remained at Basle, yet with notable success he acted for the others as well. For if one works with a will nothing seems hard, and three together would not have done more than he accomplished alone. For as far as he was able he inspired the absent members of his party by letters and those present by words to defend Eugenius. They came to the chapter-house and there was a crowded meeting, for all had been enticed by their eagerness to speak or listen. Discussion lasted for six days altogether, both morning and afternoon. In the midst of them all and occupying first place as judge of faith[3] and director and controller of the whole discussion was Cardinal Louis, archbishop of Arles,[4] a prelate notable for many virtues and in particular for courage and steadfastness. Nicolas Amici,[5] who too is a procurator of faith[6] and very well known among the theologians of Paris, asked each man for his opinion. The votes were recorded by the notary Jean Dieulifist,[7] and there was an excellent discussion and wise examination of several topics. If I were willing to make mention of these, I am afraid some would consider that my judgement was at fault when I entered upon so great a task, as this is very far removed from my promise and my aim. Yet I shall suit myself, and shall not consider that by trespassing within the bounds of holy writings I have 'peered into the temple of that goddess from whom males are scared away'.[8] Now in beginning to make mention of the actual subject I will state at the outset the resolutions of the theologians as being the foundation of the discussion. I shall not,

[8] A quotation (from 'introspexisse' to 'absterrentur') from Macrobius, *Satur.* i. 24, 12. Bona Dea, sometimes called Fauna, had a temple at Rome on the Aventine.

quibus illi; sententiam retulisse sat erit. Conclusiones huiusmodi fuerunt:[1]

1 Veritas est catholicae fidei, sacrum generale Concilium supra papam et alium quemuis potestatem habere.
2 Generale Concilium legitime congregatum sine ipsius consensu nec dissoluere nec transferre nec prorogare ad tempus ex auctoritate sua potest Romanus pontifex, idque ueritatis eiusdem est.
3 Qui pertinaciter iis ueritatibus se opponit, haereticus est censendus.
4 His ueritatibus Eugenius Papa IIII. repugnauit, cum primo ex plenitudine potestatis apostolicae Basiliense Concilium dissoluere siue transferre attentauit.
5 Errores his ueritatibus repugnantes monitus tandem per sacrum Concilium Eugenius reuocauit.[2]
6 Dissolutio siue translatio per Eugenium secundo attentata praedictis est obuia ueritatibus, inexcusabilemque circa fidem errorem continet.[3]
7 Eugenius iterato dissoluere seu transferre Concilium tentans in reuocatos errores prolabitur.
8 Commonitus per Synodum Eugenius ut dissolutionem siue translationem secundo attentatam reuocaret, post declaratam contumaciam in rebellione persistens, Ferrariaeque Conciliabulum erigens, seipsum pertinacem declarat.

Huiusmodi (sicuti arbitror) fuere conclusiones, quibus in capitulo coram patribus iterum atque iterum lectis, rogati sunt omnes uiritim sententiam dicere, pedibusque fere omnes in conclusiones ibant. Panormitanus tamen archiepiscopus,[4] uir inter omnes scientia eminens, plurima in aduersum disputauit. Plurima etiam praelatorum decus, Burgensis episcopus, ac eleemosynarius[5] regis Aragonum, non minus eloquentia quam doctrina praeclarus. Non tamen prioribus hi se conclusionibus opponebant, sed illis tantum quibus Eugenius tangebatur. Arguteque, ut est subtilissimus, aduersus posteriores conclusiones Panormitanus disseruit, ostendereque summo studio nitebatur Eugenium non esse relapsum; magnaque illi cum tribus uiris Argensi episcopo, Ioanni Segouio, ac Francisco de Fuxe[6] theologis concertatio fuit. Articulos

[1] Cf. Hugolin in Haller, VI. 370 and John of Segovia in *Mon. Con.* III. 240–1.
[2] See Introduction, pp. xvi, xvii.
[3] See Introduction, p. xix.
[4] On the archbishop of Palermo see Introduction, p. xxii.
[5] The Cistercian Bernard Serra, almoner to Alfonso V; for his death see below, p. 194.
[6] A theologian and Franciscan vicar; his name is also spelt Fuce and Fusce.

however, use the same words as they did. It will be sufficient to report the sense. The resolutions were of this nature:[1]

1 It is a truth of the catholic faith that the holy general Council holds power over the pope and anyone else.
2 The Roman pontiff of his own authority can neither dissolve nor transfer nor prorogue the general Council when lawfully assembled without its own consent, and that is part of the same truth.
3 Whoever obdurately opposes those truths must be deemed a heretic.
4 Pope Eugenius IV attacked these truths when first from the plenitude of his apostolic power he attempted to dissolve or transfer the Council of Basle.
5 Eugenius at the warning of the holy Council eventually renounced the errors at variance with these truths.[2]
6 Eugenius's second attempt at dissolution or transference is inimical to the aforesaid truths and contains unpardonable error as regards the faith.[3]
7 Eugenius in attempting a second time to dissolve or transfer the Council is relapsing into the errors he renounced.
8 Eugenius, when warned by the Council to renounce his second attempt at dissolution or transference, by persisting in rebellion after his evident contumacy and by upholding the Assembly of Ferrara, shows himself to be obdurate.

Of this nature, I think, were the resolutions, and when these had been read again and again in the chapter-house in the presence of the Fathers, all were asked individually to give their opinion, and almost all voted for the resolutions. The archbishop of Palermo,[4] however, a man eminent among all for learning, argued at length to the contrary. So too did that ornament of the prelates, the bishop of Burgos, and the almoner of the king of Aragon,[5] distinguished not less for eloquence than learning. These, however, did not oppose the earlier resolutions, but only those affecting Eugenius, and with the subtlety of a most astute mind Panormitanus held forth against the later resolutions, and worked energetically to show that Eugenius was not relapsed; and he had a great dispute with three theologians, the bishop of Ardjisch, John of Segovia, and François de Fuxe.[6] He made a threefold division of the

fidei trifariam diuidebat: stricte, ut in symbolo; large, ut in declarationibus per ecclesiam factis; largissime autem, ut in his quae ex praedictis resultant. Eugeniumque nullo istorum modorum uiolasse fidem in prima dissolutione quam fecit, quia nec in symbolo nec in ecclesiae determinationibus haberetur papam non posse concilia dissoluere; nec id sibi uideri ex determinationibus antea factis resultare, sed potius ex decretis Constantiensis Concilii. Hunc casum tanquam omissum dispositioni papae reseruari, cum in capitulo 'Frequens'[1] locus futuri concilii per papam approbante Concilio eligatur, et de hoc nihil omnino sit dictum. Quod si forsitan in prima dissolutione[2] peccasset Eugenius, excusatum tamen haberi debere, qui de consilio cardinalium egisset Romanam ecclesiam representantium, cuius tantam esse authoritatem dixit ut eius iudicium toti orbi praeponeretur, idque glossam[3] singularem astruere; nec inueniri unquam sacrum Concilium aduersus Eugenium tanquam haereticum processisse, idque signum esse quia non putarit eum a fide deuium; nec apud se momentum habere quod diceretur de adhaesione erroribusque reuocatis.[4] Legisse se totum adhaesionis textum, papamque non reuocasse dissolutionem ut fidei contrariam, sed ut scandala parturientem.[5] Vltimam quoque dissolutionem nihil habere huiusmodi, quoniam similiter ex consilio cardinalium dissoluisset, et propter unionem Graecorum fiendam, ac ne cogeretur in criminali causa per procuratorem respondere, cum personaliter mala ualitudine impeditus uenire non posset. Sicque cum ex prima dissolutione non fuisset in errorem fidei lapsus, persuaderi sibi non posse Eugenium nunc dici relapsum, qui nec prima nec secunda dissolutione fidem uiolarit.

Fuit oratio Panormitani apud omnes magis laudata quam probata. Id tamen habuit efficaciae ut postea uerbum 'relapsum' ex conclusionibus tolleretur, eiusque loco poneretur 'prolapsum.' Nec Panormitanus ipse omnino ab haeresi Eugenium audebat excusare, plusque in prima quam in secunda dissolutione uim faciebat, non tamen sine reponsione recessit. Assurgens nanque Ioannes Segouius, theologiae peritissimus, reuerenter submisseque,

[1] See Introduction, p. xiv.

[2] For the two bulls (12 Dec. 1431 and 18 Sept. 1437) cf. H–L. VII. 696–8, 951 and refs. The second of them, *Doctoris gentium* (cf. Introduction, p. xix) aroused controversy on the question of the consent of the cardinals, mentioned by Panormitanus: see Valois, II. 111.

[3] A reference to Johannes Teutonicus, gloss on C. 24 q.1 c.6.: Tierney, p. 253.

[4] Panormitanus at this point is pointing out that, since the Council has not earlier convicted Eugenius of heresy, it is illogical now to try to make out that he is a relapsed heretic.

[5] *Dudum sacrum*: cf. Introduction, p. xvii.

articles of the faith, precise as in the Creed, broad as in declarations made by the Church, very broad as in the consequences of the first two, holding that Eugenius had under none of these headings harmed the faith in the first dissolution that he made, because neither in the Creed nor in the canons of the Church was it maintained that the pope could not dissolve councils; nor did it appear to him that this was a consequence of the canons previously made, but rather of the decrees of the Council of Constance. Such an occasion had been, as it were, left out of account, and was reserved for the pope's ordering, since in the decree *Frequens*[1] the place for a future council was chosen by the pope with the Council's approval, and nothing at all was said about this. But if perhaps Eugenius had done wrong in the first dissolution[2] he ought to be considered excused, as he had acted in accordance with the advice of cardinals representing the Roman Church, the authority of which (he said) was so great that its judgement would be preferred to the whole world's, and which was affirmed by a singular gloss;[3] nor was it found that the holy Council had ever proceeded against Eugenius as a heretic, a sign that it did not think that he had turned aside from the faith. He himself attached no weight to what was said about adherence [to the Council] and about renounced errors.[4] He had read the whole text of [Eugenius's] adherence, and the pope had not renounced the dissolution as contrary to the faith, but as an occasion of scandal.[5] Moreover, in the last dissolution there was nothing of this kind, since in a similar way he had ordered the dissolution on the advice of the cardinals, and to facilitate union with the Greeks, and he should not be compelled to give answer in a criminal case through an agent when he could not put in a personal appearance owing to bad health. So, since from the first dissolution he had not fallen into an error of faith, he was persuaded that Eugenius could not now be called relapsed, seeing that he had not harmed the faith either by the first or the second dissolution.

The speech of Panormitanus met with more general praise than approval. It was, however, so far effective that later the word 'relapsed' was taken out of the resolutions, and in its place was put 'lapsed'. Panormitanus did not venture to clear Eugenius completely of heresy, and placed more weight on the first than the second dissolution, nor did he withdraw without a reply. For John of Segovia, who was very distinguished in theology, rose, and

ut tanto praelato conueniebat, respondit. Fateri se inquit quod de articulis fidei trifariam diuisis Panormitanus dixisset, idque ad suam causam facere, quia si ea pro articulis fidei tenenda essent quae ex determinationibus ecclesiae resultarent, manifestum foret conclusiones, de quibus agitur, ex determinationibus ecclesiae, hoc est Constantiensis Concilii redundare; quia si ibi Concilio generali papa subiicitur, quis est qui papam habere imperium in Concilium, quod est suum superius, dicat? Stareque Eugenium debuisse, quia Concilium, quod supra se est, eo inuito dissoluere non poterat; quem articulum sine dubio uiolauit. Et si omnino dici quis uelit in prima dissolutione hunc articulum non esse lesum, quia nondum facta esset declaratio, sciat ille qui sic opinatur Romanum pontificem non solum explicita fidei, sed implicita quoque scire oportere, qui uicarius Christi et caput omnium existens, docere atque instruere cunctos habet. At si omnino hoc effugiat, ex illo capite conuincetur, quia diutius in dissolutione sua post declarationem Concilii perstitit, nec determinationi ecclesiae acquieuit, ideoque si dissoluendo forsitan non errauit in fide, utique in permanendo errauit.[1] Idque bellissime ex dicto Clementis saepe per Panormitanum allegati concluditur dicentis quia qui rebelliter uiuit, et bona agere negligit, potius diaboli quam Christi membrum esse ostenditur, et magis infidelis quam fidelis esse monstratur.[2] Sicque non obediens ecclesiae, Eugenius infidelis dici haud absurde potest. Nec uerum id fore quod papa in fide non fuisset impetitus. Etenim in responsione tam illa quae incipit 'Cogitanti'[3] quam alia quae 'Sperant oratoribus papae deditis'[4] aperte illa uerba reperiri: 'Hic articulus fidem concernit, malumusque mori quam per ignauiam cedere'; quo dicto satis admonuisse Synodum patere[a] quia papa contra fidem ueniret. Ideoque cum postea adhaerendo[5] reuocasset Eugenius dissolutionem, errorem quoque fidei in ea contentum reuocasse uidetur; scandala quoque, de

[a] patere α; patet BV *in marg.*

[1] John of Segovia's argument is as follows: the pope is subject to a general council (the decree *Sacrosancta* of the Council of Constance) and this implies that he cannot dissolve or translate it. If the pope pretends ignorance of this implication of *Sacrosancta*, then he cannot ignore the decree enacted at the third session of the Council of Basle (29 Apr. 1432, Mansi, XXIX, cols. 23–27) in which the Fathers stated that the pope could not dissolve, translate, or adjourn the Council without their consent.

[2] Pseudo-Clement, *Ad Iacobum ep.* iii, *P.L.* 130, col. 46A. Cf. below, p. 70, n. 6.

[3] The 'responsio synodalis' of the general congregation held on 3 Sept. 1432; Mansi, XXIX, cols. 239–67.

[4] Presumably the conciliar reply of 16 June 1433 (Mansi, XXIX, cols. 267–73)

replied with reverence and modesty as befitted so great a prelate. He said he agreed with the remarks of Panormitanus about the threefold division of the articles of the faith, and that supported his own case, because if those things were to be held as articles of faith which were consequences of the canons of the Church, it would be obvious that the resolutions under discussion proceeded from the canons of the Church, that is, the Council of Constance; because if there the pope was in subjection to the general Council, who might say that the pope had any command over the Council which was his superior? Eugenius should have halted, because he could not dissolve against its will a Council that was superior to himself; and this article he certainly violated. If anyone wished it to be expressly stated that in the first dissolution this article was not infringed because the declaration had not yet been made, the holder of this view should realize that the Roman pontiff must know not only the explicit matters of the faith but the implicit ones too. For being the vicar of Christ and head of all, he had to teach and instruct all men. But if he should dodge this completely, he would be convicted under the head that he persisted in his dissolution for a long time after the declaration of the Council, and did not accept a canon of the Church, and therefore if he did not perhaps commit an error in faith in making the dissolution, he most certainly did in his obduracy.[1] That conclusion was very neatly drawn from a saying of Clement often quoted by Panormitanus to the effect that he who lived in rebellion and neglected to do what was right was shown to be a member of the devil rather than of Christ, and was revealed as being an unbeliever rather than a believer.[2] So it was not absurd to call Eugenius an unbeliever as not obedient to the Church. Nor was it true that the pope was not attacked on a matter of faith. For both in the reply beginning 'Considering',[3] and in the other, 'They hope, when the pope's ambassadors are given up'[4] these words were openly found: 'This article concerns the faith, and we prefer death to a cowardly surrender'; from which remark it was clear enough that the Synod had warned the pope that he was going against the faith. So when afterwards by his adherence[5] Eugenius had renounced the dissolution, he clearly renounced the error of faith contained in it as

where this phrase is indeed found (col. 272) but which begins 'sperauit hactenus haec sacra synodus'.

[5] *Dudum sacrum* (5 Feb. 1434); see Introduction, p. xvii.

quibus mentio fieret, propter errorem fidei esse suborta, quod aliqui subesse Concilio papam dicerent, negarent aliqui, ipsamque doctrinae diuersitatem scandala secum trahere. Expresse quoque in adhaesione papae reuocari assertiones nomine papae factas contra Concilii autoritatem. Et licet in huiusmodi reuocationibus non esset seruatus stilus et ordo iudiciorum, sufficere tamen in rebus talibus quod actum esset, cum Concilium contra papam ageret, quo in casu sola esset ueritas obseruanda; nec esse Concilium iuri positiuo subiectum ut seruare terminos, et iudicialem sequi strepitum debeat. Glossam autem illam singularem, quae Romanam ecclesiam orbi praeponeret,[1] se omnino contemnere, beneque singularem esse, quae tam fatua diceret; indignumque fore ut illam quispiam sequeretur. Mirarique se de Panormitano et aliis nostrorum temporum doctoribus, qui dum se glossarum extollere putant autoritatem, ipsam deprimunt, cum singularitatem adiiciunt; singularis enim est glossa quae sola est. Sed quis non pluris faciat glossam in omnibus locis idem sentientem, semperque constanter locutam, quam uno tantum in loco aliquid asserentem, quod sine dubio possit per errorem uideri assertum? Quantum uero ad ueritatem, habere se Hieronymum doctorem grauissimum glossa illi contrarium, qui orbem etiam quoad autoritatem urbe ipsa, id est Roma, maiorem esse non ambigit.[2]

Nec ista finire Segouius sine interpellatione potuit. Saepe namque Panormitanus uerba ipsius interrupit; et nunc unum nunc aliud dictum confutari satagebat. Surrexit Argensis etiam episcopus, uir non solum eloquens sed etiam animi plenus, acriterque Panormitani dicta et argumenta disturbauit; plus tamen inter eos processum est quam disputandi modus exigeret, neque enim a probris abstinuerunt. Veniam tamen Argensis postea petiit, licet forsitan minus errasset, ut fit, quia semper inferiores oportet succumbere. Dixerat forte Argensis Romanum pontificem ministrum ecclesiae fore, idque ferre Panormitanus non poterat; tantumque ea die seipsum et scientiam suam, quae utique maxima est, deseruit ut Papam ecclesiae dominum asseuerare non uereretur.

[1] Above, p. 22.
[2] Jerome, *Ep.* cxlvi; *P.L.* 22, col. 1194; cf. below, p. 44, n. 4; Tierney, pp. 40–41.

well; and the scandal moreover, of which mention was made, arose because of the error of faith, since some said the pope was beneath the Council, others denied this, and the very discrepancy of doctrine brought scandal with it. In the pope's act of adherence those assertions were also expressly renounced which had been made in the name of the pope against the authority of the Council. Though in retractions like these the style and order of legal documents were not observed, still what was done in such matters was enough since the Council was acting against the pope; in which case only the truth was to be respected; nor was the Council subject to positive law that it should keep [legal] terms and follow judicial procedure. Further that 'singular gloss' which 'preferred the Roman Church to the world',[1] he held in utter contempt; it was a good thing it was 'singular', since it made such a fatuous statement, and it did not deserve to have anyone following it. He was surprised at Panormitanus and other doctors of our times who, while thinking they praised the authority of glosses, actually lessened it by adding the 'singularity'. For a 'singular gloss' was one that stood alone; but who would not value more a gloss possessing the same meaning in all places, and always consistently expressed, than one making an assertion in only a single place, which could without doubt seem to have been made in error? As far as the truth was concerned he took Jerome, the most learned of doctors, to be in opposition to that gloss, for he had no doubt that as regards authority the world was greater than the city, that is than Rome.[2]

John of Segovia was not able to finish without interruption. For often Panormitanus broke in upon his words, and actively tried to confute now one remark now another. There rose also the bishop of Ardjisch, a man not only of eloquence but full of courage, who sharply demolished the remarks and arguments of Panormitanus, and matters between them went beyond the requirements of moderate discussion, for they did not refrain from abuse. Yet afterwards (though perhaps he was less at fault), the bishop of Ardjisch asked pardon, as usually happens because subordinates should always submit. The bishop of Ardjisch had happened to say that the Roman pontiff was the servant of the Church, which Panormitanus could not tolerate; and that day so far forgot himself and his learning, which is very great, as not to shrink from claiming that the pope was ruler of the Church. John

Cui Segouius: 'Vide quid ais Panormitane', inquit, 'honoratior titulus Romani pontificis ille est, quo seruum seruorum se Dei appellat. Id enim ex eo est sumptum quod Christus discipulis ait, cum quaererent quis eorum esset maior futurus. Scis enim respondisse illum quia "principes gentium dominantur eorum: uos autem non sic",[1] et reliqua, ubi dominatum omnino prohibuit; et Petrus, qui et ipse uicarius Christi primus fuit: "Pascite", inquit, "qui in uobis est gregem Dei prouidentes, non coacte, sed spontanee";[2] et paulopost: "Neque ut dominantes in clero".[3] Quod si filius dei, Christus, "non ministrari sed ministrare uenit",[4] quo pacto eius uicarius dominabitur, aut dici dominus, sicut uis, Panormitane, poterit? Cum "non" sit "discipulus supra magistrum, neque seruus supra dominum suum";[5] "neque uocemini magistri", inquit Dominus, "quia magister uester unus est, Christus", et: "qui maior est uestrum, erit minister uester".'[6]

Hac responsione inquietato paululum Panormitano, recessum est. Sequenti die generalis congregatio fuit, et post prandium ad capitulum omnes redierunt. Rogatusque sententiam Lugdunensis archiepiscopus, orator regius, uir inter omnes et probitate uitae et scientiae copia eminentissimus, postquam haereticum esse Eugenium pluribus rationibus comprobauit, amare conquestus est, illorum ignauiam plurimum detestatus, qui talem hominem Romano pontificio praefecissent; omnesque astantium animos commouit ut secum calamitates uniuersalis ecclesiae deplorarent. At Burgensis episcopus, orator Hispanus et inter praelatos apprime doctus, conclusiones bifariam diuisit, aliasque generales, aliasque personales appellans. Egregieque circa tres primas locutus est, nullatenus se de ipsis dubitare asseuerans, nisi quod illa sibi adiectio dubia uideretur, quae fidei faceret mentionem. Plurimumque illic immorari uoluit ut sacrum Concilium supra papam esse ostenderet. Idque postquam iure diuino humanoque probauit, physica etiam ratione asseruit, adductoque in testem summo omnium philosophorum Aristotele, dicebat in omni regno bene instituto illud in primis desyderari ut plus regnum posset quam rex; si contra reperiretur, id non regnum sed tyrannidem dici debere.[7] Sic etiam sibi de ecclesia uideri, quod eam

[1] Matt. 20: 25, 26; Luke 22: 25, 26.
[2] 1 Pet. 5: 2. [3] Ibid. 5: 3. [4] Matt. 20: 28.
[5] Matt. 10: 24. [6] Matt. 23: 10, 11.
[7] Aristotle, *Politics*, 1279[a], [b].

of Segovia replied, 'Watch what you are saying, Panormitanus. It is a very honourable title of the Roman pontiff when he calls himself "servant of the servants of God". For that is taken from what Christ said to his disciples when they were asking which of them would be the greatest. For you know he replied that "the princes of the Gentiles exercise lordship over them, but ye shall not be so"[1] and so on, when he completely forbade lordship, and Peter, who himself was the first vicar of Christ, says: "Feed the flock of God which is among you, taking the oversight thereof, not by constraint but willingly";[2] and a little later: "neither as being lords over [God's] heritage".[3] But if Christ, the son of God, "came not to be ministered unto, but to minister",[4] how will his vicar exercise lordship or be able to be called lord, as you wish, Panormitanus? For "the disciple is not above his master, nor the servant above his lord",[5] "neither be ye called masters", saith the Lord, "for one is your master [even] Christ", and "he that is greatest among you shall be your servant".'[6]

Panormitanus was rather perturbed by this reply, and the meeting broke up. On the following day there was a general congregation, and in the afternoon they all returned to the chapter-house. Being asked for his opinion, the archbishop of Lyons, an ambassador of the king, a man outstanding among all for his uprightness of life and store of knowledge, after proving on many grounds that Eugenius was a heretic, made bitter complaint, denouncing thoroughly the cowardice of those who had appointed such a man to the Roman pontificate, and he stirred the minds of all present so that they lamented with him the misfortunes of the universal Church. The bishop of Burgos, however, a Spanish ambassador and particularly learned among the prelates, divided the resolutions into two groups, calling some general and the others personal. He spoke excellently about the first three, stating that he had no doubts at all about them, except that the addition which made mention of the faith seemed doubtful to him. He wanted to dwell on this very much to show that the holy Council was superior to the pope. After proving this by divine and human law he claimed it by scientific reasoning too, and bringing as witness the greatest of all philosophers, Aristotle, he said that in every well-ordered kingdom it was particularly desirable that the kingdom should have more power than the king; if the opposite was found, it deserved the name not of kingdom but of tyranny.[7] Similarly his own view

plus suo principe, id est papa, posse oporteret; quem sermonem sic ornate, sic suauiter disputauit, sic docte atque mirifice[a] ut omnes ab eius ore auide dependerent, iam non, ut in aliis fit, orationis finem sed longam continuationem desyderantes, ipsumque unicum esse scientiae speculum praedicarent. Vt uero alias ingressus est conclusiones, opponereque hic se uoluit, uisus est aliquantisper a seipso discedere Burgensemque esse desinere. Nec enim ille in uerbis lepor, nec illa in oratione grauitas, aut in uultu hilaritas apparebat; ac si se ipse potuisset cernere, admirationem sui forsitan habuisset. Quis enim uim quandam ac potestatem ueritatis tunc non uiderit, quae homini pro se loquenti sententias et uerba suggessit; aduersus se autem praedicanti etiam ipsam, quae innata erat, surripuit eloquentiam? Illud tamen Panormitanus ac Burgensis modestiae ostenderunt, quia, etsi ueritates fidei esse non faterentur, in eo tamen non suae sententiae acquiescendum dicebant, qui sacris literis non essent imbuti, sed theologorum. Eleemosynarius uero Aragonum regis, ut est consilio callidus, nequaquam directe ad conclusiones disputabat, sed furtim quaedam argumenta collegerat, quibus nunc hic, nunc illic praestaret impedimentum. Aduersus quos et abbas de[b] Scotia,[1] uir subtilis ingenii, plurima disputauit; et Thomas de Corsellis, inter sacrarum literarum doctores insignis, quo nemo plura ex decretis sacri Concilii dictitauit,[c] uir iuxta doctrinam mirabilis et amabilis, sed modesta quadam uerecundia semper intuens terram et uelut latenti similis, pro conclusionibus late et clare disseruit.

Nimis (ut uideo) rem protraherem, si quid singuli dixerint explicare pergam, fiamque forsitan lectoribus taediosus hoc modo procedens; utilius, sicuti mihi uidetur, argumenta exponam quibus ratae conclusiones fuerunt. Nec ego de quinque posterioribus sermonem habebo, quae solum uidentur in facto consistere, dum Eugenii personam respiciunt; solum tres primas mea disputatio complectetur. Subiiciam igitur aliqua probationi accommoda, non quae ipse cogitarim, aut meo studio ex obscurissimis scripturarum tenebris elucubrauerim, sed quae ego in

[a] mirifice BV; uerifice α [b] de B (cf. p. 200); *om.* α [c] dictitauit B; dictauit α

[1] Livingstone; see above, p. 16, n. 4.

about the Church was that it should have more power than its prince, that is the pope. In this discourse he argued with such elegance, charm, learning, and excellence that all eagerly hung on his words, not as in the case of other [speakers] longing for the end of the speech, but for a long continuation of it, and they proclaimed that he was the sole mirror of learning. When, however, he touched upon the other resolutions, and here wished to show opposition, he seemed for a while to go out of character and to cease to be the bishop of Burgos. For that charm of word, that dignity of utterance, that cheerfulness of countenance were all missing, and if he had been able to see himself he would perhaps have felt surprise at the sight. For who has not beheld a force, as it were, and power of truth which has supplied phrases and words to a man when speaking for himself, but which, when he speaks against himself, has stolen away even his inborn eloquence? Yet Panormitanus and the bishop of Burgos did show this much moderation, in that, though they did not admit that they were truths of the faith, they did not expect agreement with their own views upon this point, by those filled not with Scripture, but with the learning of the theologians. The almoner of the king of Aragon, being shrewd in counsel, did not argue directly against the resolutions, but had got together some arguments on the quiet with which now here, now there, he put forward an objection. Against these three the abbot from Scotland,[1] a man of keen intelligence, argued at length; and broad and clear support for the resolutions came from Thomas de Courcelles, distinguished among the doctors of divinity, who spoke more than anyone in accordance with the decrees of the holy Council, a man who was astonishingly attractive as regards learning, but who through a certain modest bashfulness was always gazing at the ground and like a man in hiding.

I should make the story too long, I see, if I continue setting down the words of each person, and I shall become perhaps tedious to my readers if I go on in this way; it will be more useful, I believe, to give the arguments leading to the ratification of the resolutions. I shall say nothing about the five later ones, which seem only to consist of incidents concerning Eugenius as an individual. My discussion will include only the first three. So I will add some things that lend themselves to proof, not reflections of my own, nor discoveries brought to light by my researches in the obscurities of the records, but what I heard in the Fathers' discussion and

disputatione patrum audita memoriae commendaui. Quantum ergo illinc haurire mea paruitas quiuit, eius autoritatis est prima conclusio ut ea probata reliquae ueniant. In prima igitur uis maior eaque primitus dissertanda est, duoque circa ipsam inuestigatu examinatuque digna se offerunt, alterum, numquid generale Concilium autoritatem habeat supra Romanum pontificem, alterum, an id credere fides catholica iubeat. Quae duo si deduxerim, nihil est quod postmodum dubitare possimus.

Quod autem papa Concilio generali subesse debeat egregie ratio per Burgensem episcopum deducta superius probat. Est enim papa in ecclesia tanquam in regno rex,[1] regem autem plus posse quam totum regnum absurdum est; ergo nec papa plus posse debet quam ecclesia. Sed sicut nonnunquam reges male administrantes et tyrannidem exercentes a toto regno excluduntur eiiciunturque, sic etiam per ecclesiam, hoc est per generalia concilia, Romanos pontifices posse deponi non est ambigendum. Neque hic ego illos audio qui tam latam regibus attribuunt potestatem ut eos teneri legibus nullatenus uelint; genus est enim adulatorum, qui aliter garriunt quam ipsi sentiant. Etenim licet dicatur in sinu principis ἐπιείκειαν[a] semper fore, id ego intelligo, cum ratio suadet a uerbis legis esse recedendum. Rex enim ille dicitur qui est speculator ac procurator publici commodi, cui est cordi utilitas subditorum, qui, quaecunque agit, refert ad eorum quibus praeest commoditatem; quodsi secus fecerit, non rex sed tyrannus dicendus est, cuius est proprium uacare proprio emolumento. Hoc enim differt rex a tyranno, quod alter eorum quos regit commodis inuigilat, alter suis intentus est.[2]

Quod ut manifestius fiat, subiicienda causa est, quae reges ab initio introduxit. Et quidem, ut Cicero in *Officiis*[3] ait, certum est fuisse aliquod tempus quo sine regibus uiuebatur; at postquam iure gentium possessiones coeperunt diuidi, non alia de causa reges sunt instituti nisi 'iusticiae fruendae'. 'Nam cum premeretur initio[b] multitudo ab his qui maiores opes habebant, ad unum aliquem uirum confugiebant uirtute praestantem, qui cum[c] prohiberet iniuria tenuiores' aequitatem constituendo, 'summos cum

[a] ἐπιείκειαν α; epycheyam B; ephicheyam V [b] initio αBV *codex Bernensis of Cicero*; inops *inferior MSS. of Cicero*; in otio *others* [c] cum *Cicero*; *om.* α

---

[1] Cf. Aquinas, lib. 4 *Sent.* d. 20, q. 4, a. 3 ad 3, quaestiunc. 4, Sol. 3: quoted by O. Giercke, trans. Maitland, *Political Theories of the Middle Age* (Cambridge, 1900), p. 144, n. 131.

[2] Cf. Aristotle, *Politics*, 1311ᵃ.

[3] *De Off.* ii. 12, 41.

committed to memory. As far as I, in my insignificance, was able to gather from that source, the first resolution is of such authority that the rest follow when it has been established. So in the first one there is the greater force, and it must at the start be discussed. Regarding it, two things present themselves as worthy of investigation and examination; the one is whether the general Council has authority over the Roman pontiff, the other is whether the catholic faith orders that belief. If I settle these two points there is nothing else on which we may feel doubt.

As for the pope having to be beneath the general Council, the reasoning elaborated above by the bishop of Burgos proves that excellently. For the pope in the Church is like the king in a kingdom,[1] and for a king to have more power than the whole of the kingdom is absurd; therefore the pope should not have more power than the Church. But just as kings sometimes, when they administer badly and practise tyranny, are banned from the whole of their kingdom and turned out, even so there is no reason for doubt that Roman pontiffs can be deposed by the Church, that is, by general councils. Nor in this do I listen to those who assign such wide power to kings that they wish them to be in no degree bound by laws; for such men are a tribe of flatterers, whose chatter is at variance with their real feelings. For though it be said that equity always dwells in the bosom of a king, I take that to be when reason urges departure from the words of the law. For he is called a king who watches and looks after the public interest, who has the weal of his subjects at heart, who relates all his actions to the convenience of those over whom he is set, and if he acts otherwise, he must not be called a king but a tyrant, whose characteristic it is to attend to his own profit. For in this a king differs from a tyrant, that the one of them watches over the welfare of those whom he rules, the other is intent on his own welfare.[2]

To make this clearer, the reason must be given for the original introduction of kings. Now, as Cicero says in his *De Officiis*,[3] it is certain that there was a time when men lived without kings; but after by the law of nations possessions began to be divided, kings were instituted for no other reason than 'that justice should be enjoyed'. 'For when the masses were oppressed at the beginning by those who had greater means, they would take refuge with some individual outstanding for his virtue, who in guarding the weaker from harm', and by establishing equity, 'would keep the

infimis pari iure retinebat[a]'. Cumque adhuc regnantibus regibus debiliores nonnunquam opprimerentur, leges constitui placuit, quae ad iudicandum non odio aut gratia ducerentur, sed tales inopi, quales potenti praestarent aures; quo fit ut leges non solum populum sed regem quoque obligare sciamus. At si regem contemnere leges, rapere bona subditorum, uiolare uirgines, stuprare matronas, omniaque suae libidini et temeritati committere uideamus, nunquid, congregatis regni proceribus, illo summoto, alius sublimabitur, qui et bene gubernare iuret et legibus obtemperare? Nempe ut ratio suadet, sic etiam usus edocet. Idemque fieri in ecclesia, hoc est in Concilio, quod in regno consentaneum esse uidetur. Sicque satis apparet, quod diximus, papam subesse Concilio. Illud tamen negari non debet quia maior est papa quolibet alio Christiano. Et sicuti regi quilibet baro de regno subiicitur, sic Romano pontifici singuli ecclesiae praelati parere tenentur. Sed his praeteritis, cum Burgensi episcopo, uiro non minus docto quam eloquenti, ad diuina eloquia transeamus.

Fundamento autem rei quam petimus uerba sunt redemptoris nostri, Iesu Christi, cum in pluribus locis tum ibi, cum Petrum alloquitur, dicens: 'Tu es Petrus, et super hanc petram aedificabo ecclesiam meam, et portae inferi non praeualebunt aduersus eam.'[1] A quibus uerbis ideo placuit exordiri, quod aliqui uerba haec ad extollendam Romani pontificis autoritatem solent adducere; sed ut statim patebit, alius est uerborum Christi sensus quam aliqui opinentur. Ait ergo: 'Et portae inferi non praeualebunt aduersus eam', magna quippe promissio, magna etiam uerba Domini. Etenim quid dici grandius potuit quam portas inferi aduersus ecclesiam praeualere non posse? Portae utique inferi, ut inquit Hieronymus, peccata significant.[2] At si peccata expugnare ecclesiam nequeunt, certe nec maligni spiritus, qui nullam penitus in humanum genus nisi per peccata uim habent, aliquid aduersus ecclesiam possunt. Eamque ob causam, cum apud Iob dicatur: 'Nulla potestas super terram est, quae potestati maligni spiritus comparetur',[3] restat potestatem ecclesiae omnibus potestatibus esse maiorem. Possumus etiam ex hoc dicto aliter quoque argumentari,

[a] retinebat *codex Bernensis of Cicero*; pertingerent α; pertingeret BC; pertingetur V

[1] Matt. 16: 18.
[2] *Commentar. in Isaiam,* viii. 26, *P.L.* 24, col. 303.
[3] Cf. Job 41: 24.

highest and the lowest in equality of rights.' Since, even while kings were reigning, the weaker were at times oppressed, it was their will that laws be established which for passing judgement might not be guided by hatred or favour, but might listen to the powerless as to the powerful; the result is that we know that laws are binding not only on the people but on the king. If, however, we should see a king showing contempt of the laws, seizing the property of his subjects, violating maidens, debauching matrons, and subjecting everything to his own lust and licence, will not the leaders of the kingdom meet, and when he is removed will not another be promoted, who swears to govern well and obey the laws? Of course the prompting of reason is the same as the lesson of experience. It seems in keeping too that the same thing should happen in the Church, that is, in the Council, as in a kingdom. Thus it is clear enough, as we have said, that the pope is beneath the Council. Yet it should not be denied that the pope is greater than any other Christian; and just as any baron of the kingdom is subject to a king, so individual prelates of the Church are bound to obey the Roman pontiff. But passing over these things, let us go on with the bishop of Burgos, a man no less learned than eloquent, to the words of scripture.

As the basis of the matter under investigation there are the words of our Redeemer, Jesus Christ, in several places, as when he addresses Peter saying: 'Thou art Peter, and upon this rock I will build my church, and the gates of hell shall not prevail against it.'[1] It seemed desirable to begin from these words, as some are in the habit of citing them to magnify the power of the Roman pontiff; but it will straight away be clear that the meaning of the words of Christ is not what some think. He says then: 'and the gates of hell shall not prevail against it.' This is indeed a great promise, and great too are the Lord's words. For what could be said of more might than that the gates of hell cannot prevail against the Church? The gates of hell indeed, as Jerome says, mean sins.[2] Now if sins cannot take the Church by storm, then certainly neither can evil spirits, which have absolutely no power against the human race except through sins, have any effect against the Church. For which reason since it says in Job: 'No power is over the earth to be compared with the power of an evil spirit',[3] the conclusion is that the power of the Church is greater than all powers. We can also from this saying draw a different

quia si portae inferi, id est peccata, aduersus ecclesiam nihil queant, ecclesia ipsa impeccabilis esse monstratur; quod quidem de summo pontifice, qui homo et mortalis est, nemo dixerit, cum scriptum sit quia septies in die cadit iustus.[1] At si ecclesia immaculata est, quia nec peccato potest deturpari, quis est qui peccatorem hominem impeccabili ecclesiae praeferat? Nec illis praestemus aures, qui uerba illa Christi Iesu dicentis: 'Oraui pro te, Petre, ut non deficiat fides tua'[2] nolunt ad ecclesiam referri; quoniam, sicut Augustinus in expositione psalmorum[3] inquit, quaedam dicuntur, quae, si proprie ad Apostolum Petrum pertinere uideantur, non tamen habent illustrem intellectum, nisi cum referuntur ad ecclesiam, cuius ipse cognoscitur in figura gestasse personam. Vnde alibi in quaestionibus noui et ueteris testamenti de his quoque uerbis: 'Rogaui pro te, Petre'[4] quid ambigitur? Numquid pro Petro rogabat, pro Iacobo et Ioanne non rogabat, ut de caeteris taceam? Manifestum est in 'Petro' omnes contineri, quia et alio loco apud Ioannem dicit: 'Ego pro his rogo, quos mihi dedisti,' et 'Volo, ubi ego sum, et isti sint mecum.'[5] Quo fit ut ecclesiam frequentissime per 'Petrum' intelligamus. Idque hoc fieri in loco non ambigimus, aliter uero stare ueritatis uerba non possent; cum paulopost Petri fides ad tempus Christum negando defecerit, at fides ecclesiae, cuius personam Petrus gestabat, semper intemerata permansit. De Romanis uero pontificibus liceret exempla admodum multa referre, si tempus sineret, qui[a] aut haeretici aut aliis imbuti uitiis sunt reperti. Nec nos fugit Marcellinum[6] iussu Caesareo idolis thurificasse; alium uero, quod maius et horribilius est, diabolica fraude Romanum pontificatum ascendisse.[7] Nobis tamen illud Pauli ad Hebraeos sufficit testimonium, qui omnem pontificem infirmitate, id est prauitate peccandi, circumdatum esse dicit;[8] ecclesiam autem impeccabilem permanere etiam alia ipsius Christi testimonia comprobant. Apud Matthaeum ait: 'Ego uobiscum sum, usque ad consummationem seculi',[9] quae uerba non solum Apostolis (ipsi enim usque ad

[a] qui BV; quoniam α

[1] Prov. 24: 16. The Vulgate text has 'enim', not 'in die'.

[2] Luke 22:32, the Vulgate text having 'Rogaui'.

[3] *Enarratio in Ps.* 108. 1, *P.L.* 36, cols. 1431–2.

[4] Luke 22:32.

[5] John 17: 9, 24.

[6] Pope A.D. 296–304. The story, in the *Golden Legend*, 26 Apr., describes how the pope was compelled 'to sacrifice two grains of incense on the altar'.

[7] Sylvester II, pope A.D. 999–1003, as suggested in the margin of *ed. prin.* Gerbert of Aurillac's reputation as a scholar and scientist led to his being credited with diabolical powers: see Platina, *Vita Christi ac omnium pontificum*,

argument—that if the gates of hell, that is, sins, have no power against the Church, the Church itself is shown to be incapable of sin; which no-one will ever have said about the supreme pontiff, who is a man and mortal, since it is written that seven times in the course of a day the righteous man falls.[1] Now if the Church is without stain, since it cannot be defiled by sin, who could possibly prefer a man who is a sinner to the sinless Church? Nor let us listen to those who will not have it that the words of Jesus Christ when he says: 'I have prayed for thee, Peter, that thy faith fail not'[2] refer to the Church; since, as Augustine says in his exposition of the Psalms,[3] certain things are said which even if they appear to concern the Apostle Peter personally, are without clear meaning except when they refer to the Church, of which he is recognized as having been the symbol and personification. Hence elsewhere in discussions of the New and the Old Testaments what doubt is there about these words too: 'I have pleaded for thee, Peter'?[4] Surely it does not mean that he did plead for Peter but not for James and John, not to mention the others? It is clear that all are included in 'Peter' because in another place in John he says: 'I pray for them which thou hast given me', and: 'I will that they also be with me where I am'.[5] The result is that very often by 'Peter' we understand the Church. We are in no doubt about that happening in this place; otherwise indeed the words of the truth could not endure. Though shortly afterwards Peter's faith for a time failed by his denial of Christ, still the faith of the Church which Peter personified remained always unassailed. As for the Roman pontiffs it would be possible to recall very many instances, if time permitted, when they were either found to be heretics or tainted by other vices. We do not forget that Marcellinus[6] at the emperor's command offered incense to idols; that another rose to the Roman pontificate by diabolical trickery—a greater and more flagrant scandal.[7] For us Paul's words in Hebrews are sufficient evidence: 'Every high priest is compassed with infirmity',[8] that is, by the wickedness of sinning; but that the Church remains sinless is proved by other evidence too from Christ himself. For in Matthew he says: 'I am with you unto the end of the world',[9] words which were uttered not only to the Apostles, for they

ed. G. Gaida, *Rerum Italicarum Scriptores* (Città di Castello–Bologna, 1913–32), p. 177.

[8] Heb. 5: 1, 2.

[9] Matt. 28: 20.

seculi finem non permanserunt) sed etiam successoribus dicta fuerunt. Nec tunc uoluit Christus significare se Deum per omnia fusum, quomodo etiam in peccatoribus deprehenditur, sed speciale quoddam donum gratiae ostendere per assistentiam suam, qua sanctam ecclesiam in Apostolis eorumque successoribus consistentem seruaret immaculatam. Alibi quoque: 'Ego rogabo Patrem',[a] inquit, 'et alium paracletum dabit uobis, ut maneat uobiscum in aeternum, spiritum ueritatis, quem mundus non potest capere, quia non uidet eum, nec scit eum; uos autem eum cognoscetis, quia apud uos manebit.'[1] Quae uerba cum discipulis Iesu dicta sint, ad successores quoque et sic ecclesiae dicta intelliguntur; ac si in aeternum spiritus ueritatis in ecclesia est, nemo negare debet ecclesiam permanere incorruptam. Ex ea quoque autoritate, qua dicitur sponsus ecclesiae Christus,[2] quis non uidet incontaminandam fore ecclesiam? Sponsus nanque et sponsa (ut Apostolus inquit) duo sunt in carne una;[3] carnem autem suam, ut idem subiicit, nemo odio habet.[4] Eoque fit ut Christus ecclesiam odire non possit, quoniam sponsa est eademque caro cum ipso, ac se odire non potest; ergo non peccat ecclesia. Nam si peccaret, odio haberetur; peccatores nanque, ut alibi dicitur, Deus odio habet.[5] Quae autoritates ut inuicem connecti queant, fateri cum Apostolo debemus ecclesiam Dei non habere maculam neque rugam;[6] qui etiam ad Timotheum scribens, ecclesiam ipsam 'columnam et firmamentum ueritatis' fore asseuerat.[7] Vnde in Canticis sponsus: 'Tota pulchra es, amica mea, et macula non est in te.'[8]

Exterrere aliquos uerba haec possent, dum fore impeccabilem ecclesiam astruo. Nam cum in ecclesia contineantur omnes qui Christiano censentur nomine, quique in communi credentia articulorum fidei et sacramentorum participatione conueniunt, uereor ne qui me omnes homines impeccabiles dixisse opinentur; quae sententia tantum a mea abest, ut eius oppositum uerum putem. Existimo enim quia nullus sit in ecclesia impeccabilis mortali carne uestitus. Nec ista inter se pugnant, habet enim hoc ecclesia ut, licet singula membra peccare possint, totum tamen corpus non possit. Semper enim in ecclesia uiri sunt aliqui boni, qui, licet humanae fragilitati subditi sint, uirtutis tamen perfectae perfecto funguntur munere, domitisque carnalibus desyderiis[9] hostiam se Deo placentem exhibent.[10] Nec uulgari nonnullorum

[a] patrem BV *Vulgate*; *om.* α

[1] John 14: 16, 17, with future tense v. 17, as in Vulgate.
[2] Matt. 9: 15. [3] Eph. 5: 31. [4] Eph. 5: 29.
[5] Ecclus. 12: 3 and 7. [6] Eph. 5: 27. [7] 1 Tim. 3: 15.
[8] Song of Solomon 4: 7. [9] Cf. 1 Pet. 2: 11. [10] Rom. 12: 1.

themselves did not survive until the end of the world, but also to their successors. Christ did not then mean that he as God was spread through all things, as is found even in sinners, but that he was revealing a certain special gift of grace through his presence by which he might keep free from stain the holy Church consisting of the Apostles and their successors. Elsewhere too he says: 'I will pray the Father and he shall give you another comforter, that he may abide with you for ever; [even] the spirit of truth, whom the world cannot receive because it seeth him not, neither knoweth him: but ye will know him for he will dwell with you.'[1] These words, though they were uttered to the disciples of Jesus, are understood as uttered to their successors too and thus to the Church; and if 'the spirit of truth' is for ever in the Church, no one should deny that the Church remains uncorrupted. From that text too in which Christ is called the bridegroom of the Church,[2] who does not see that the Church is immune from contamination? For the bridegroom and the bride (as the Apostle says) are two in one flesh,[3] and no-one, he adds, hates his own flesh.[4] So it comes about that Christ cannot hate the Church, since it is his bride and the same flesh as himself and he cannot hate himself. So the Church does not sin. For if it sinned it would be hated, since, as is said elsewhere, God hates sinners.[5] To link together these texts we ought to admit with the Apostle that the Church of God has neither spot nor wrinkle.[6] He too when writing to Timothy maintains that the Church is the very 'pillar and ground of the truth'.[7] Hence the bridegroom says in Song of Songs: 'Thou art all fair, my love; there is no spot in thee.'[8]

Some people could find these words shocking when I maintain that the Church is sinless. For since the Church embraces all who are known by the name of Christians and who come together with a common belief in the articles of faith and with participation in the sacraments, I am afraid that some may think that I have said all men are sinless—a belief so far from being mine that I think its opposite true. For I consider that no-one in the Church is sinless as being clothed in mortal flesh. There is no contradiction here, for the Church has this quality that though individual members may sin, the whole body cannot. For there are always in the Church some good men, who though subject to human frailty, yet perform the perfect duty of perfect virtue and, taming their fleshly lusts,[9] present themselves a sacrifice acceptable unto God.[10] Nor do I agree

opinioni consentio, qui tempore Dominicae passionis solam Virginem aiunt in fide perstitisse, unde audent aliqui dicere, sic extenuari fidem[a] posse, ut ad unam solam aniculam reuertatur. Quorum sententiam, ne dicam insaniam, aperte mihi uidetur Paulus explodere, cum ad Romanos ait: 'An nescitis in Helia quid dicit scriptura, quemadmodum interpellat Deum aduersus Israël: "Domine, Prophetas tuos occiderunt, altaria tua suffoderunt, et ego relictus sum solus, et quaerunt animam meam." Sed quid dicit illi responsum diuinum? "Reliqui mihi septem milia uirorum, qui non curuauerunt genua sua ante Bahal."'[1] Etenim quid aliud ibi responsum diuinum indicat quam fatuam esse illorum opinionem qui ad tam paucos redigi ecclesiam arbitrantur? Oportet utique nos credere uerbis Christi, quae omnia illis repugnant qui solam Virginem perseuerasse in fide praedicant. Ait nanque ad Patrem Iesus: 'Pater sancte, serua eos in nomine tuo, quos dedisti mihi, ut sint unum, sicut et nos. Cum essem cum eis, ego seruabam eos in nomine tuo. Quos dedisti mihi custodiui, et nemo ex eis periit, nisi filius perditionis.'[2] Et: 'Non rogo ut tollas eos de mundo, sed ut serues eos a malo.'[3] Ecce quia orat Christus ne Apostoli cadant; orans autem Christus absque dubio auditur. Alibi enim dicit: 'Scio quia me audis.'[4] Sed quo pacto auditur, si omnes pro quibus orat, ut isti rabuli dictitant, in passionis tempore deuiarunt? Exemplum: quo pacto Iesus matrem suam charissimam in cruce pendens Ioanni commendasset, si is aut iam erat aut statim futurus erat alienus a fide? Centurio praeterea nunquid e uestigio clamat: 'Vere Filius Dei erat iste'?[5] Iudaei quoque illo in tempore, qui ab Hierosolymis longe aberant, et dici fideles poterant et in sua fide saluari, cum (sicut Apostolus ait) ad Euangelium homines obligentur, postquam eis innotuit.[6]

Relinquamus igitur istos, et, quod est uero similius, teneamus fuisse, esseque semper in ecclesia non paruum bonorum hominum numerum iudicemus; ab illisque, ut a parte digniori, sanctam et immaculatam denominemus ecclesiam, quae tam malos quam bonos complectitur. Ecclesia nanque sagenae missae in mari comparatur, ex omni genere piscium congreganti,[7] et rursus homini

[a] fidem α; Christianam fidem BV

---

[1] Rom. 11: 2–4 quoting 1 (3) Kings 19: 10, 14, 18. [2] John 17: 11, 12.
[3] John 17: 15. [4] John 11: 42. [5] Matt. 27: 54.
[6] Cf. perhaps Rom. 10: 8–14; the allusion in the text above is by no means clear. [7] Cf. Luke 5: 4–6.

with the view that some commonly hold that at the time of our Lord's Passion only the Virgin persisted in the faith, so that some venture to say that the faith can be so reduced that it goes back to a single old woman. Their view, not to call it their senselessness, Paul seems to me clearly to explode when he says to the Romans: 'Wot ye not what the scripture saith of Elias? how he maketh intercession to God against Israel [saying]: "Lord they have killed thy prophets, and digged down thine altars; and I am left alone, and they seek my life." But what saith the answer of God unto him? "I have reserved to myself seven thousand men, who have not bowed the knee to [the image of] Baal."'[1] For what else does the answer of God mean there than that it is a stupid opinion to think that the Church is reduced to so few. Especially should we believe the words of Christ, all of which are at variance with those who say that the Virgin alone persevered in the faith. For Jesus says to his Father: 'Holy Father, keep through thine own name those whom thou hast given me, that they may be one, as we are. While I was with them I kept them in thy name: those that thou gavest me I have kept, and none of them is lost, but the son of perdition.'[2] And: 'I pray not that thou shouldest take them out of the world, but that thou shouldest keep them from evil.'[3] Notice how Christ is praying that the Apostles may not fall; moreover Christ when praying is heard beyond a doubt. For elsewhere he says: 'I know that thou hearest me.'[4] But in what way is he heard if all for whom he prays, as those wranglers keep saying, turned aside at the time of his Passion? For example, how would Jesus, hanging on the cross, have commended his dear mother to John if John was either already or about to be estranged from the faith? Besides, did not the centurion cry forthwith, 'Truly this was the Son of God'?[5] Jews too at that time who were far away from Jerusalem could both be called faithful and be saved in their faith, since, as the Apostle says, men are bound to the Gospel after it has become known to them.[6]

Let us therefore leave such [wranglers] and, what is nearer the truth, let us hold that there was, and let us judge that there is always, in the Church no small number of good men, and from these, as from the worthier part, let us call holy and without stain the Church which includes bad men and good alike. For the Church is compared to a net cast in the sea collecting fish of every kind;[7] and again to a man who was a king, who made a marriage

regi, qui fecit nuptias filio suo, et misit seruos suos uocare inuitatos ad nuptias,[1] et subditur: 'Et congregauerunt bonos et malos, quotquot inuenerunt.'[2] Erronea enim est illorum opinio qui solos bonos contineri intra ecclesiam dicunt; quae si uera esset, omnia confunderet, nec ubi ecclesia foret scire possemus. Cum autem (sicut scriptura dicit) nemo sciat utrum sit dignus odio uel amore,[3] approbatior ueriorque illorum sententia est qui omnes fideles intra ecclesiam recipiunt; buorum, licet pars magna uoluptatibus et auariciae seruiat, aliqui tamen semper [separati] sunt a peccatis mundi mortalibus. Quae pars ut dignior denominationem dedit ecclesiae ut 'sancta' diceretur; quod tam frequens factum est ut in symbolo decantare[a] praecipiamur: 'Vnam sanctam catholicam et apostolicam ecclesiam,' quem articulum viii. Synodum Constantinopolitanam aliis adiecisse ferunt.[4] Quare si sancta est ecclesia, impeccabilis quoque est, ut ad institutum redeam. 'Sanctum' enim (ut Macrobio Trebatium referenti placet)[5] 'interdum idem est quod sacrum, idemque quod religiosum', interdum uero idem est quod incorruptum; unde et illud:

> '"Sancta ad uos anima, atque istius inscia culpae,
> Descendam."[6]

Non enim sacro aut religioso eius anima tenebatur, quam sanctam, hoc est incorruptam, uoluit ostendere.' Eoque modo sanctam praedicamus ecclesiam, quam Petrus Apostolus immaculatam dicebat, sicut in famosa Clementis epistola legimus.[7] Ad hoc etiam tendit, quod dicitur apud Paulum caput ecclesiae fore Christum.[8] Nam si ecclesia peccaret tota, nequaquam suo capiti conueniret, Christo, qui nulla unquam ex parte corruptus existit. Hoc itidem apud Matthaeum significare uoluit Christus, cum domum illam collaudat, quae fuerat supra firmam petram aedificata, cui nec uenti potuerunt officere nec pluuiae.[9] 'In domo Dei,' inquit Apostolus, 'quae est ecclesia',[10] 'aedificata supra firmam petram,' quae (sicut idem Apostolus praedicat) erat Christus.[11] Ecclesiam ergo supra Christum fundatam, quis est tam demens aut tam sui oblitus ut peccato subditam esse uelit? Quique non potius cum Propheta exclamet: 'Domine, dilexi decorem domus tuae.'[12] Hinc illa Ioannis aurea sententia, cui etiam aureum os fuisse praedicant,

[a] decantare BV; decenter decantare α

[1] Matt. 22: 2 ff. [2] Matt. 22: 10 (paraphrased). [3] Cf. Eccl. 9: 1.

[4] Until the late nineteenth century the so-called Council of Constantinople of 381 was credited with the addition of material to the Nicene Creed.

[5] *Satur.* iii. 3, § 5. [6] Virgil, *Aen.* xii. 648–9.

[7] Pseudo-Clement, *Ad Iacobum fratrem Donimi ep.* i, *P.G.* 1, col. 473 and *P.L.* 130 (Pseudo-Isidore), col 32 C; cf. below, p. 70, n. 5.

for his son, and sent his servants to call the bidden to the marriage,[1] and there is added: 'And they gathered good and bad as many as they found.'[2] For it is a mistaken belief that is held by those who say that only the good are included in the Church. If this were true it would cause general confusion, and we could not know where the Church was. Since, moreover, as the scripture says, no-one knows whether he deserves hate or love,[3] that view is more acceptable and truer of those who bring all the faithful within the Church, some of whom always, though the majority are slaves to pleasures and avarice, are [free] from the deadly sins of the world. This part as being the worthier has given the Church its appellation of 'holy'. This has happened so often that we are told to chant in the Creed, 'One holy catholic and apostolic Church', which eighth article they say the Synod of Constantinople added to the others.[4] So if the Church is holy, it is sinless also, to return to my theme. For 'Holy' (so Macrobius has it, quoting Trebatius)[5] 'is at times the same as sacred and the same as religious', at times the same as unspoiled; whence comes:

> '"A holy soul and free from such reproach,
> I shall come down to you."[6]

For his soul was not connected with what was sacred or religious, but the poet wished to depict it as holy, that is, unspoiled.' In that way we proclaim the Church holy, which the Apostle Peter called without stain, as we read in the famous letter of Clement.[7] Paul's words too, that the head of the Church is Christ, point the same way.[8] For if the whole of the Church sinned, it would not be in keeping with its head, Christ, who is in no wise corrupt. In Matthew Christ wished to give the very same meaning when praising that house built upon firm rock which neither the winds nor the rains could harm.[9] 'In the house of God,' says the Apostle, 'which is the Church',[10] 'built upon firm rock', which, as the same Apostle says, was Christ.[11] Who then is so senseless or so forgetful of himself that he would have the Church, founded upon Christ, subject to sin? Who would not rather cry out with the Prophet: 'Lord I have loved the glory of thy house.'[12] Hence that golden opinion of John, who, they declare, had a mouth of gold, who says:

[8] Eph. 1: 22, etc. [9] Matt. 7: 24, 25.
[10] 1 Tim. 3: 15. [11] 1 Cor. 10: 4. [12] Ps. 26(25): 8.

qui ait: 'Non cessat impugnari ecclesia, non cessat insidias pati, sed in nomine Christi semper superat, semper uincit: et quamuis alii insidientur, quamuis repercutiant eam fluctus, fundamentum tamen, quod supra petram est, non quassatur.'[1] Hilarius quoque: 'Proprium esse solet ecclesiae,' inquit, 'ut tunc uincat, cum laeditur: tunc intelligatur,[a] cum arguitur: tunc secura sit, cum deseritur: tunc obtineat, cum superata uidetur.'[2]

Multis (ut mihi uidetur) rationibus ac testibus probatum est ecclesiam non errare, quod de Romanis pontificibus non asseritur; quae ratio haud inepte summum pontificem ecclesiae subiicit. Conueniens enim est ut perfectioribus minus perfecti subdantur. Sunt tamen et alia testimonia aliaeque rationes, de quibus etiam hoc in loco aggrediar dicere. 'Si autoritas quaeritur', inquit Hieronymus, libenter enim in eius sententiis tanquam in agro fertili uersor,[3] 'orbis maior est urbe.'[4] Quid tum? Obsecro, Hieronyme, magnus est papa, quia Romanae praeest ecclesiae? Magna eius est autoritas, maior tamen est uniuersalis ecclesia, quae non urbem unam duntaxat sed totum complectitur orbem. Exhinc si mater omnium fidelium est ecclesia, Romanum etiam pontificem in filium habet; alias uero (sicut beatissimus praedicat Augustinus) nunquam habebit Deum patrem, qui ecclesiam noluerit recognoscere in matrem.[5] Quod Anacletus intelligens uniuersalem ecclesiam (ut canonistae sciunt) matrem suam appellat.[6] Et Calixtus: 'Sicut filius', ait, 'uenit facere uoluntatem patris, sic et nos implere uoluntatem matris nostrae, quae est ecclesia.'[7] Vnde apparet tanto superiorem esse ecclesiam Romano pontifice, quanto est matre inferior filius. Supra etiam diximus[8] ecclesiam Christi Iesu sponsam fore, papam uero uicarium esse scimus. At nemo sic uicarium suum instituit ut eius sponsam illi subiiciat. Quinimmo plus arbitrii in rebus arduis habere creditur sponsa quam uicarius, cum illa unum cum sponso corpus existat, uicarius non idem cum domino. Nec Pauli ad Romanos uerba praeteribo: 'Omnis', inquit ille, 'anima potestatibus sublimioribus subdita sit';[9] nec excipit animam papae. Quare cum nullus alius mortalium supra papam

[a] *So Hilary*; intelligat αβ

---

[1] There are many passages in Chrysostom very close to this; cf. *P.G.* 51, cols. 77–79.

[2] St. Hilary of Poitiers, *De Trinitate*, vii. 4, *P.L.* 10, col. 202; but Hilary reads 'tunc obtineat cum deseritur'.

[3] The author's frequent use of Jerome may be traced through the Index of Quotations and Allusions.

[4] *Ep.* cxlvi, *P.L.* 22, col. 1194; cf. above, p. 26, n. 2.

[5] *Sermo de Symbolo,* 13; *P.L.* 40, col. 668.

[6] *Ep.* i, *P.L.* 130 (Pseudo-Isidore), col. 66 D; *Decr.* C. 12, q. 2, c. 6 (Friedberg, I. 688).

[7] Ibid., col. 130 D; *Decr.* D. 12, c. 1 (Friedberg, I. 27).

'The Church does not cease to be assailed, it does not cease to suffer treacherous attacks but in the name of Christ it always prevails, always conquers. Though some lie in wait, though the waves buffet it, still its foundation, which is on rock, is not shaken.'[1] Hilary also says: 'It is the characteristic of the Church to conquer when it is harmed, to be understood when confuted, to be safe when it is deserted, to last when it seems overcome.'[2]

By many arguments and by the evidence of many witnesses it has been proved, I consider, that the Church does not err—a claim not made for the Roman pontiffs. This reasoning not unfittingly subjects the supreme pontiff to the Church. For it is proper that the less perfect be subjected to the more perfect. Yet there are other pieces of evidence and other arguments about which at this point I shall undertake to speak as well. 'If authority is needed', so says Jerome, for gladly do I dwell among his opinions as in a fertile field,[3] 'the world is greater than the city.'[4] Well then, I beg you, Jerome, is the pope great, because he is set over the Church of Rome? Its authority is great, yet greater is the universal Church, which embraces not merely a single city but the whole world. Hence if the Church is the mother of all the faithful, it has also the Roman pontiff as a son; for otherwise, as the blessed Augustine preaches, that man will never have God as father, who has been unwilling to recognize the Church as mother.[5] Anacletus aware of this calls the universal Church his mother, as the canonists know.[6] And Calixtus says: 'Just as a son comes to do the will of his father, so we too to fulfil the will of our mother, which is the Church.'[7] From this it is clear that the Church is as much superior to the Roman pontiff as the son is inferior to his mother. We have also said above[8] that the Church is the bride of Christ Jesus, and we know that the pope is his vicar. Yet no one appoints his vicar in such a way that he subjects his bride to him. No, the bride is believed to have greater power in difficult questions than the vicar since she forms one body with her husband, but the vicar is not one with his lord. Nor shall I leave out Paul's words in Romans: 'Let every soul', he says, 'be subject unto the higher powers';[9] nor does he except the soul of the pope. So though no other mortal is superior to the pope, it seems necessary that we should make him subject to the Church. Nor should he think he

[8] Above, p. 38. [9] Rom. 13: 1.

sit, necessarium uidetur ut illum ecclesiae subiiciamus. Nec ideo se putet exemptum, quod ei dictum a Christo fuerit: 'Quodcunque ligaueris',[1] et reliqua. In eo nanque (ut post dicemus) personam ferebat ecclesiae; cui etiam dictum reperimus: 'Quaecunque ligaueritis super terram, ligata erunt et in coelis.'[2] Vlterius, si omnis potestas a Christo concessa, ut ad Corinthios scribit Apostolus, data est 'in aedificationem' ecclesiae 'et non in destructionem',[3] cur non ecclesia summum pontificem clauibus abutentem et omnia destruentem corripere possit? Adde et aliud argumentum: Homo in hac uita minor est angelis. Legimus namque apud Matthaeum de Ioanne Baptista quia 'qui minor est in regno coelorum, maior est illo'.[4] Alibi tamen dixerat ueritas quod 'inter natos mulierum non surrexit maior Ioanne Baptista.'[5] Sed perge ulterius. Angelis credere homines (exemplo Zachariae) coguntur ne, sicut ille, caecitatis incurrant uitium non credentes.[6] Quid plus? Romanus pontifex homo est, ergo angelis minor, et angelis praestare tenetur fidem. At angeli ab ecclesia discunt, eiusque doctrinae reuerenter acquiescunt, ut ad Ephesios inquit Apostolus;[7] ergo et summus pontifex idem tenetur efficere, et qui minor est angelis, minor est ecclesia, quae illis est maior. Cuius nempe tanta est autoritas ut recte per Augustinum soli aequiparetur[8]; quoniam sicut caetera lumina sol unus euincit, sic omnes autoritates ecclesia superat. Vnde eiusdem Augustini legitur dictum: 'Euangelio non crederem, nisi me autoritas ecclesiae commoueret',[9] quae nusquam de Romano pontifice dicta reperiuntur, qui cum uicem gerat ecclesiae eiusque administrator existat, nequaquam putandus est aut domino maior aut aequalis. Maxime tamen Romanum pontificem subiectum esse ecclesiae uerba ipsius Christi, saluatoris et Domini nostri, ostendunt cum, sicuti post dicemus,[10] Petrum, futurum papam, ad ecclesiam remittit inquiens: 'Dic ecclesiae.'[11] Ad cuius autoritatem etiam illa pertinent uerba: 'Qui uos audit, me audit',[12] non solum Apostolis sed eorum quoque successoribus et toti ecclesiae dicta; quo fit ut, si ecclesiam Romanus pontifex non audiat, Christum quoque non audiat, et tanquam ethnicus et publicanus haberi debeat, quia (ut etiam asserit Augustinus)[13] cum excommunicat ecclesia, in coelo ligatur

[1] Matt. 16: 19. [2] Matt. 18:18. [3] 2 Cor. 10- 8. [4] Matt. 11: 11.
[5] Ibid. [6] Luke 1: 20, where, however, Zacharias is struck dumb.
[7] An error; there is no such statement in Ephesians.
[8] *Ep.* cxcix, 39; *P.L.* 33, col. 919.
[9] *Contra epistolam Manichaei*, 5; *P.L.* 42, col. 176.
[10] Below, p. 50. [11] Matt. 18: 17. [12] Luke 10: 16.
[13] *In Ioannis euangel.*, tract. *l*, 14; *P.L.* 35, col. 1763; (cf. *Decr.* C. 24, q. 1, c. 6; Friedberg, I. 968).

is exempt because it was said to him by Christ: 'Whatever thou shalt bind', and so on.[1] For then he was, as we shall later show, personifying the Church, to which we find was also said: 'Whatever things ye shall bind on earth shall be bound too in heaven.'[2] Further if all power granted by Christ, as the Apostle writes in Corinthians, is given 'for the edification' of the Church 'and not for destruction',[3] why should not the Church be able to reprove the supreme pontiff if he misuses his keys and destroys all things? Add too another proof. A man in this life is less than the angels. For we read in Matthew about John the Baptist that 'he that is least in the kingdom of heaven is greater than he'.[4] Yet elsewhere the Truth had said: 'Among them that are born of women there hath not risen a greater than John the Baptist.'[5] But continue further. Men are compelled to believe angels, warned by the fate of Zachariah, lest they incur, as he did, the injury of blindness through not believing.[6] In short the Roman pontiff is a man, therefore less than the angels, and is bound to believe angels. But angels learn from the Church, and reverently accept its teaching, as the Apostle says in Ephesians.[7] Therefore even the supreme pontiff is bound to do the same, and, as he is less than the angels, is less than the Church, which is greater than they. Its authority is certainly so great that it is rightly compared by Augustine[8] with the sun since, just as the sun alone surpasses all other lights, so does the Church surpass all authorities. Hence we read a remark by the same Augustine: 'I should not believe in the Gospel, did not the authority of the Church move me',[9] which is nowhere found to have been said of the Roman pontiff, who, since he is the representative and the administrator of the Church, is in no way to be thought of as either greater than his lord or as equal to him. Yet that the Roman pontiff is subject to the Church is particularly shown by the words of Christ himself, our Saviour and our Lord, when, as we shall say later,[10] he refers Peter, the future pope, to the Church, with the words: 'Tell [it] unto the Church.'[11] To [Christ's] words of authority these belong as well: 'He that heareth you heareth me',[12] said not only to the Apostles but to their successors too and the whole Church. So the result is that if the Roman pontiff does not listen to the Church, he does not listen to Christ either, and should be treated like a heathen and a publican, because, as Augustine maintains also,[13] when the Church excommunicates, the excommunicated person is bound in

excommunicatus, et cum soluit, soluitur. Quo dicto tam papa quam alii continentur. Ex eo tamen illorum maxime uesania confutatur, qui dari per synodum generalem remissionem plenariam inficiantur, cum synodus (ut postea ostendemus) uniuersalem ecclesiam repraesentet. Illos tamen haereticorum loco habendos censeo, quoniam si haereticus est qui Romanae ecclesiae primatum aufert, ut Constantiensis Concilii decreta demonstrant,[1] quanto magis haereticus erit qui eius[a] ecclesiae detrahit autoritati, in qua Romana et omnes aliae continentur?

Opinio (sicut iam liquet) omnium mortuorum est, si opinio uocari debet quae idoneis confirmatur autoribus, quia Romanus pontifex uniuersali ecclesiae subiectus existit, neque hoc uiuentes negare audent. Illud autem apud aliquos reuocatur in dubium an id quoque de generali concilio credi oporteat. Sunt enim aliqui, siue auidi gloriae, siue quod adulando praemia expectant, qui peregrinas quasdam et omnino nouas praedicare doctrinas coeperunt, ipsumque summum pontificem ex iurisdictione sacri Concilii demere non uerentur. Excaecauit nanque illos ambitio, a qua non solum hoc modernum, sed omnia usque in hanc diem schismata suborta reperiuntur. Nanque ut olim pestiferam illam bestiam, quae per Arrium[2] primo quasi de infernis extulerat caput, cupiditas episcopatus induxit, sic hodiernam haeresim illi praecipue nutriunt, quos iam mendicare suppudet,[3] quorum alius clamat subditorum facta iudicari a papa, Romanum uero pontificem solius Dei reseruari arbitrio. Alius dicit quia primam sedem[4] nemo iudicabit, quod neque ab Augusto, neque ab omni clero, neque a regibus, neque a populo ualeat iudicari. Alius asserit eiectionem summorum pontificum sibi Dominum reseruasse. Alius uero asserere non ueretur Romanum pontificem, quanuis animas cateruatim secum ad inferos trahat, nullius reprehensioni fore subiectum.[5] Nec consyderant miseri quia quae praedicant tantopere uerba aut ipsorum summorum pontificum sunt suas fimbrias extendentium,[6] aut illorum qui eis adulabantur. Et quia

[a] eius V; *om.* α

---

[1] *Sacrosancta* and *Frequens* again.

[2] Who denied the divinity of Christ or, in more technical language, denied that Christ was consubstantial with God the Father; d. 336.

[3] A reference to the parable of the unjust steward, Luke 16: 3? or to certain theologians from the mendicant Orders, such as the Dominican referred to below, n. 5.

[4] That is, Rome.

[5] The chief pro-papal writer of the mid-fifteenth century was the Spaniard, Juan de Torquemada (Turrecremata), died 1468. He had played a prominent role on the papal side in the discussions at Mainz (above, p. 12; *Reichstagsakten*

heaven, and when it looses, he is loosed; and by this saying the pope is just as much bound as others. From this above all comes the refutation of the senseless beliefs of those who deny that full remission is given by a general synod, since a synod, as we shall afterwards show, represents the universal Church. I consider that such persons should be regarded as heretics, for if he is a heretic who takes away the primacy of the Roman Church, and the decrees of the Council of Constance prove this to be so,[1] how much more of a heretic will he be who belittles the authority of that Church in which the Roman and all others are included?

The opinion, as is now clear, of all the dead, if 'opinion' is the right name for what is confirmed by the appropriate authorities, is that the Roman pontiff is subject to the universal Church, nor do the living venture to deny this. Some, however, do doubt whether this should be believed about a general council as well. For there are some, who either through eagerness for fame, or because they expect rewards for flattery, begin to preach certain foreign and entirely novel doctrines, and do not fear to exclude the supreme pontiff himself from the jurisdiction of the holy Council. For ambition has blinded them—ambition the cause not only of this modern schism, but of all others up to this day. For just as in the past that pestilential monster, which through Arius[2] had first as it were put forth its head from hell, was introduced by the greed of the episcopate, so this heresy of today is chiefly fed by those who are now somewhat ashamed to beg.[3] One of whom proclaims that the deeds of subjects are judged by the pope, but the Roman pontiff is reserved for the judgement of God alone. Another says that no one will judge the first see[4] because neither by the emperor nor by all the clergy nor by kings nor by the people may it be judged. Another maintains that the Lord has reserved for himself the casting out of the supreme pontiffs. Another indeed does not shrink from maintaining that the Roman pontiff, even if he should drag souls in crowds with him to hell, is subject to the reproof of no one.[5] Nor do these wretches consider that the words they are so fond of preaching are either those of the supreme pontiffs themselves as they 'enlarge their borders'[6] or of their

xiv. 99), and Eugenius IV made him a cardinal in the promotion of 18 Dec. 1439. For a brief survey of recent literature on papalist writers in the mid-fifteenth century see D.L.O., pp. 286–7.

[6] Cf. Matt. 23: 5.

huiusmodi dicta solutionem habent, recurrunt statim ad Euangelium, et uerba Christi non prout Spiritus Sancti sensus exposcit,[1] sed suopte ingenio interpretantur. Plurimumque illud extollunt quia Petro sit dictum: 'Tu uocaberis Cephas',[2] per quod eum caput ecclesiae faciunt: 'Tibi dabo claues regni coelorum',[3] et: 'Quodcumque ligaueris super terram',[4] et: 'Rogaui pro te, Petre, ut non deficiat fides tua',[5] et: 'Pasce oues meas',[6] et: 'Duc in altum rete,'[7] et: 'Noli timere, iam ex hoc eris homines capiens',[8] quodque soli Petro tanquam Apostolorum principi Christus mandauerit pro se et ipso staterem dare,[9] et quia Petrus traxit ad terram rete plenum piscibus magnis,[10] et quod solus Petrus ad Christi defensionem gladium euaginauit.[11] Quae omnia hi homines miro modo sublimant, expositionibus sanctorum doctorum omnino posthabitis; quas si ut par esset consyderarent, manifeste cognoscerent quia ex autoritatibus supradictis Romanus pontifex non coniunctim sed separatim omnibus praeest. Sed his modo praeteritis, quia responsio per infrascripta patebit, quid nos a doctissimis uiris de hac quaestione audiuerimus hora exposcit ut in medium afferamus.

Illudque in primis cupio notum quia Romanum papam omnes qui aliquo numero sunt Concilio subiiciunt.[12] Ad cuius rei probationem omnia fere repetunt, quae superius de ecclesia recitauimus. Competere nanque generali Concilio omnia putant quae ecclesiae. Primoque huc trahunt illud Euangelicum: 'Dic ecclesiae', quo in loco scire conuenit quia Petro futuro summo pontifici Christus loquebatur, instruens eum quid esset facturus circa fratris correctionem. Ait igitur: 'Si peccauerit in te frater tuus, uade et corripe eum inter te et ipsum solum, si te audierit, lucratus es fratrem tuum; si autem te non audierit, adhibe tecum unum uel duos ut in ore duorum testium uel trium stet omne uerbum: quod si non audierit, dic ecclesiae.'[13] Quid igitur hic per 'ecclesiam' intelligemus? An fidelium multitudinem ubique gentium dissipatam? 'Iugum meum', inquit Dominus, 'suaue est et onus meum leue';[14] at quomodo 'leue,' si praecipit Christus quod factu est impossibile? Quo enim pacto potuisset Petrus ecclesiam alloqui dispersam, singulosque Christicolas hostiatim per ciuitates et

[1] Cf. the reference in this connection to Jerome, below, p. 92.
[2] John 1: 42, 'which is by interpretation, A stone'; cf. Matt. 16: 18.
[3] Matt. 16: 19. [4] Ibid.
[5] Luke 22: 32. [6] John 21: 17.
[7] A conflation of the phrases in Luke 5: 4: 'Launch out into the deep and let down your nets for a draught'.
[8] Luke 5: 10.
[9] Matt. 17: 27. [10] John 21: 11. [11] John 18: 10.
[12] Cf. Introduction, pp. xii–xiii.
[13] Matt. 18: 15–17. [14] Matt. 11: 30.

flatterers. And because sayings of this kind are prone to evaporation, they run straight off to the Gospel, and interpret the words of Christ not as the sense of the Holy Spirit requires,[1] but by their own wit. They make very much of Peter being told: 'Thou shalt be called Cephas',[2] through which they make him head of the Church, 'I will give unto thee the keys of the kingdom of heaven',[3] and: 'Whatever thou shalt bind on earth',[4] and : 'I have prayed for thee, Peter, that thy faith fail not',[5] and: 'Feed my sheep',[6] and: 'Cast the net into the deep',[7] and: 'Fear not, from now on thou shalt be a fisher of men',[8] and that to Peter alone, as though to the leader of the Apostles, Christ gave orders to give for each of them a 'piece of money',[9] and that Peter brought to the land a net full of great fish,[10] and that Peter alone in defence of Christ unsheathed a sword.[11] All of which these men magnify surprisingly, neglecting entirely the interpretation of them by the holy doctors, for if they considered this as it deserves, they would learn quite clearly from the passages just quoted that the Roman pontiff is in charge of all not in a body but as individuals. But passing over these things now, because the reply will be clear in what is to come, the occasion demands that we should report what we have heard from the greatest scholars on this question.

This in particular I wish known, that all who are of some repute subject the Roman pontiff to the Council.[12] For the proof of this they repeat almost all the things which we have recited above about the Church. For they think all things belong to the general Council which belong to the Church. In the first place they apply that saying from the Gospel: 'Tell [it] unto the Church', where it is proper to know that Christ was speaking to Peter, who was to be the supreme pontiff, instructing him in what he was to do about the correction of his brother. He says then: 'If thy brother shall trespass against thee, go and tell him his fault between thee and him alone: if he shall hear thee, thou hast gained thy brother. But if he will not hear thee, take with thee one or two more, that in the mouth of two or three witnesses every word may be established. And if he shall neglect to hear them, tell [it] unto the Church.'[13] What then shall we understand here by 'the Church'? Is it the multitude of the faithful, scattered everywhere on earth? 'My yoke', the Lord says, 'is easy and my burden is light';[14] but how 'light' if Christ's bidding is impossible to perform? For in what way could Peter have addressed the scattered Church and tracked

oppida uestigare? Alius est profecto uerborum huiusmodi sensus, aliterque interpretationem fieri oportet; quae ut rite a nobis fiat, duplicis personae quam Petrus gestauit meminisse nos conuenit, summi pontificis et hominis priuati. Dum in Petro priuatum hominem recognoscimus, haud inepta illorum est expositio, qui per ecclesiam praelatum ecclesiae recipiunt. Docuit enim nos Christus ut ad episcopos nostros recurramus uel ad ipsum Romanum pontificem, cum fratres aduersus nos haberemus peccantes. At cum in Petro Romanum papam suscipimus, ridenda magis quam probanda expositio est huiusmodi. Nec enim ad papam, id est ad seipsum, uel ad praelatum alium, hoc est ad suum inferiorem, remittendus est papa. Fit nanque huiusmodi remissio ut qui papam non ueretur alium uereatur. Verum cum in ecclesia nemo sit eminentior papa, exploratum est quia qui Romanum papam non ueretur alium non uerebitur. Vt igitur uerus et sanus maneat intellectus, uim uerbis facere non oportet; planus est et per se lucidus horum sensus uerborum, nec suppletione nec alteratione hic textus indiget Euangelicus. Videndum nobis est quid hoc uerbum 'ecclesia' significet, quod bis tantum in ore Christi fuisse reperimus, hic scilicet et cum Petro dixit: 'Tu es Petrus, et super hanc petram aedificabo ecclesiam meam.'[1] 'Ecclesia' ergo conuocationem significat multitudinis. 'Dic, ecclesiae', id est 'Dic multitudini fidelium congregatae'; qui cum non soleant nisi in generali Concilio conuenire, bellissima interpretatio erit: 'Dic ecclesiae', id est 'Dic Concilio generali', libenterque hoc in passu audire uellem, si qui sint qui proprie magis exponi haec uerba in praelato existiment quam in Concilio, cum singularem hominem pro multitudine ponant. Quod si admitti in sacra scriptura debeat, nihil posthac firmum reperiemus.

Caeterum si de nostro sensu quisquam miretur, scrutari eum ueteres uolo codices; inueniet enim quia nec noua nec peregrina nec mea est interpretatio, sed sanctorum patrum ueterumque doctorum, qui primi ecclesiam illuminarunt; ut testimonio est Gregorius Papa, non minus sanctimonia uitae quam literarum

[1] Matt. 16: 18.

down single worshippers of Christ individually throughout countries and towns? The meaning of words like these is, of course, different, and the interpretation is bound to be made differently. That it may be made properly by us, it is as well for us to remember Peter's double personality as supreme pontiff and private individual. While we are recognising in Peter the private individual, the explanation of those who understand by 'the Church' the prelate of the Church is not unreasonable. For Christ taught us that we should have recourse to our bishops or to the Roman pontiff himself when we considered that our brothers were sinning against us. But when we take Peter as being the Roman pope, then this sort of explanation deserves ridicule rather than approval. For the pope cannot be referred to the pope, that is, to himself, or to any other prelate, that is, to his inferior. For any referring of this sort results in the person who does not fear the pope fearing someone else. Yet since in the Church no one is more eminent than the pope it is clear that he who does not fear the Roman pope will not fear anyone else. So that the meaning then may remain true and sensible we must not do violence to the words; the sense of these words is in itself straightforward and lucid, and this Gospel text needs neither addition nor alteration. We must see what this word 'Church' means, which we find was only twice on the lips of Christ, namely here and when he said to Peter, 'Thou art Peter, and upon this rock I will build my Church'. Then 'the Church' means 'the calling together of the multitude'. 'Tell [it] unto the Church', that is, 'Tell the multitude of the faithful gathered together'; and since they are not in the habit of meeting except in the general Council, the neatest interpretation will be, 'Tell [it] unto the Church', that is, 'Tell the general Council', and I should be glad to hear as regards this passage if there are any who think that these words are applied more appropriately to a prelate than to the Council since they set a single individual in the place of the multitude. If this must be admitted in holy Scripture, we shall find from now on nothing established.

However, if anyone is surprised at our meaning, I wish him to examine the old books, for he will discover that this interpretation is not new, not strange, and not my own, but belongs to the holy fathers and doctors of old time, who first shed light upon the Church. Proof of this is given by Pope Gregory, who deserves to be remembered no less for his holiness of life than for his skill in

peritia memorabilis, cuius ad Constantinopolitanum episcopum haec in registro uerba leguntur: 'Et nos quidem,' inquit, 'in quibus talis tantaque per ausum nepharium culpa committitur, seruamus quod ueritas praecipit dicens: "Si peccauerit in te frater tuus",[1] et reliqua.' Post subdit: 'Si in mea correptione despicior, restat ut ecclesiam debeam adhibere'; quae uerba satis manifeste ecclesiam pro generali Concilio suscipiunt.[2] Nec enim diffusam undique ecclesiam sed in unum collectam, id est generale Concilium, adhibiturum se Gregorius promittebat. Quod enim ubique diffusum est, adhiberi non possit, nisi congregetur. Nicolaus etiam Papa regem Lotharium de concubinatu redarguens: 'Quod si id non egeris', inquit, 'praecaue ne hoc sanctae ecclesiae dicamus';[3] quo dicto non se iturum per orbem omnesque uiritim certionaturum Nicolaus dicebat, sed conuocaturum ecclesiam, id est generale Concilium, ibique Lotharii crimen publicaturum, ut qui Romani iussa pontificis contempsisset, generalis Concilii reuerentiam pertimesceret. Possem in hanc sententiam infinitos pene citare testes, qui omnes idem saperent, sed unum pro omnibus ac prae omnibus sufficere debet Constantiensis Concilii testimonium. Eo nanque in loco, ubi aduersus Petrum de Luna[4] fertur sententia, de eo his uerbis habetur mentio,[5] eaque in generali Concilio locum habere dicuntur.[6] Quibus ex uerbis plus illud habemus quia non solum papa in correptione fratris ad Concilium remittitur, ubi per se non potest, sed etiam ubi de ipsius Papae correptione agitur, ad Concilium est recurrendum.

Vnde apparet uerissimam esse interpretationem nostram, quae nobis ecclesiam in generali Concilio exponit. Hinc est quod in Actibus Apostolorum congregationes quae tunc fiebant appellabantur ecclesiae. In Concilio quoque Niceno et in aliis, cum aliquis excommunicaretur, semper fere subiungitur: 'Hunc excommunicat catholica et apostolica ecclesia.' Atque ex hoc introductus est ille conciliorum titulus, quo sacrum generale Concilium uniuersalem ecclesiam repraesentare dicimus. Vnde et leges Concilii (ut canonistae uolunt et bene uolunt) leges ecclesiae nuncupantur. Nec enim alibi ecclesia quam in generali Concilio

[1] Gregory the Great, pope A.D. 590–604, *Ep.* v. 18, *P.L.* 77, col. 743.

[2] Ibid.

[3] *Ep.* cxlix, *P.L.* 119, col. 1150. The reference is to a lengthy episode (A.D. 860–5) during which Pope Nicholas I (858–67) ordered Lothair II of Lorraine to abandon the mistress he wished to marry and take back the wife he had repudiated.

[4] Benedict XIII; cf. Introduction, p. xiii.

[5] Mansi, XXVII, col. 1141: 'necesse fuit secundum praedictam Christi euangelicam doctrinam dicere Ecclesiae.' (The decree *De uultu*, session xxxvii, 26 July 1417; H–L. VII. 440–1.)

letters; his words to the bishop of Constantinople read thus in the Register: 'We too', he says, 'among whom this great wrong is being committed by a dastardly attempt, keep to the bidding of the Truth when it says: "If thy brother has sinned against thee"[1] and so on.' Later he adds: 'If in my giving of reproof I am despised, it remains for me to approach the Church', and these words obviously take 'the Church' to mean 'the general Council'.[2] For Gregory was not promising to approach the Church scattered everywhere, but gathered together in one body, that is, the general Council. For what is scattered everywhere cannot be approached, unless it meets together. Pope Nicholas too, when rebuking King Lothair for concubinage, says: 'If you have not done that, beware of our telling this to the holy Church';[3] in which remark Nicholas was not saying that he would go round the world and address all men individually, but that he would call together the Church, that is, the general Council, and would there make public Lothair's misdeed, so that he who had despised the orders of the Roman pontiff might fear the supreme power of the general Council. I could cite in support of this view an almost unending series of witnesses, who all had the same view, but one piece of evidence must suffice above all and before all, that of the Council of Constance. For in the passage where a sentence is passed against Pedro de Luna,[4] mention is made of him in these words,[5] and they are affirmed to have a place in the general Council.[6] From these words we gather all the more that not only in the giving of reproof to his brother is the pope being referred to the Council, when he cannot do this by himself, but also, when it is a question of reproving the pope himself, recourse must be had to the Council.

From this it appears that our interpretation is quite correct in defining for us the Church as the general Council. This is the reason why in Acts of the Apostles congregations that were then coming into being were called churches. In the Council of Nicaea too and in others, when anyone was excommunicated, there is almost always this addition: 'This man the catholic and apostolic Church excommunicates'. From this has been brought in that designation of the councils by which we say that the holy general Council represents the universal Church. For this reason too the laws of the Council, as the canonists hold, and rightly hold, are

[6] The meaning here is obscure. Perhaps a reference to the records of the Council has been omitted.

leges promulgat, nisi et leges ecclesiae appellemus Romanorum pontificum constitutiones; quod minus proprium est, quam in Concilio, ubi, licet non omnes ecclesiasticae personae conueniant, plurimae tamen interesse solent, et in illis quae ueniunt tota residet potestas ecclesiae. Vnde in Actibus Apostolorum legimus quia 'placuit apostolis et senioribus cum omni ecclesia'.[1] Etenim licet illic non essent cuncti fideles, quod eorum pars magna tunc Antiochiae moram trahebat, tota tamen ecclesia dicitur, quia tota potestas in Concilio residebat ecclesiae. Parique ratione edita per Nicenum Concilium tanquam per catholicam ecclesiam ordinata suscipimus, licet non omnes episcopi Niceae[2] fuerint. Nec ego minoris autoritatis Constantiense Concilium existimauerim quam Nicenum, licet illic maior episcoporum numerus conuenisset; quo tempore impletum erat illud propheticum quia 'in omnem terram exiuit sonus eorum, et in fines orbis terrae uerba eorum'.[3] Hodie uero si minores habentur synodi, minor quoque et arctior Christiana religio facta est, non tamen propterea minor est autoritas. Sed ne longius euagemur, illud nobis sat est, quod per 'ecclesiam' Concilium intelligimus generale. Vt ergo ad institutum redeamus, Redemptorem nostrum Petro dicentem audiamus: 'Si peccauerit in te frater tuus', usque ibi, 'Dic ecclesiae', Conciliumque per ecclesiam sumamus. Quis hic maior erit, isne qui remittitur ad Concilium, an Concilium ipsum ad quod Petrus remittitur? Remittit ueritas summum pontificem ad generale Concilium. Cur hoc? Nempe ut non dedignentur Romani Papae aliquam in terris potestatem supra se recognoscere, quam et in rebus praegrandibus consulant, et illius determinationibus acquiescant. Vnde et Petrus alio nomine Simon est appellatus, quod (ut Rabano placet in *Homiliis*)[4] Hebraica lingua interpretatur 'obediens' ut intelligerent omnes etiam in Romano pontifice necessariam esse obedientiam.

Sufficere nobis Constantiense Concilium posset, cuius non minor autoritas fuit quam illorum quatuor, quae doctor illustris Gregorius[5] ut quatuor Euangelia uenerari se dicit. Sed libet in hac re paululum immorari, nullumque omnino locum aduersariorum temeritati relinquere, qui, dum unius hominis libidinem sustinere conantur, dumque priuatum bonum communi anteuertunt,

[1] Acts 15: 22. [2] A.D. 325. [3] Ps. 19 (18): 4 (5).
[4] Rabanus Maurus, *Comment. in Matthaeum* iii. 10; *P.L.* 107, col. 888.
[5] Pope A.D. 590–604, *Decr.* D. 15, c. 2 (Friedberg, I. 35); cf. below, p. 78, n. 3.

called the laws of the Church. For nowhere else than in the general Council does the Church promulgate laws, unless we also call 'laws' the regulations of the Roman pontiffs. This is less appropriate than in the case of the Council, where, though not all ecclesiastical personages come together, yet the majority usually attend, and in those who come resides the whole power of the Church. Hence we read in Acts of the Apostles, 'Then pleased it the apostles and elders, with the whole Church'.[1] For though not all the faithful were there, because the majority of them were then delaying at Antioch, still the whole Church is named because the whole power of the Church resided in the Council. Similarly we regard the decisions of the Nicene Council as being ordained by the catholic Church, though not all the bishops were at Nicaea.[2] Nor should I consider the Council of Constance to be of less authority than that of Nicaea, though a greater number of bishops met there. At that time there was fulfilled the prophecy: 'Their sound has gone forth into every land and their words to the end of the world'.[3] Today indeed if smaller synods are held, and the Christian religion has become smaller too and narrower, its authority has not for that reason become less. Yet to go no further afield, it is sufficient for us that by 'the Church' we understand 'the general Council'. To return then to our theme, let us listen to our Redeemer saying to Peter: 'If thy brother has sinned against thee' and right on to: 'Tell [it] unto the Church', and let us take the Council for the Church. Who then will be the greater, he who is referred to the Council or the Council itself to which Peter is referred? The Truth refers the supreme pontiff to the general Council. Why is this? Surely it is so that the Roman popes may not disdain to recognise some power on earth over themselves, which they may consult on matters of very great weight, and so that they may agree with its canons. Hence Peter too had the other name of Simon, which, as Raban believes in the *Homilies*,[4] in the Hebrew tongue is interpreted as 'obedient', that all might understand that even in the Roman pontiff obedience is necessary.

The Council of Constance could suffice for us, whose authority was no less than that of those four which the distinguished doctor Gregory[5] says he reverences like the four Gospels. Yet it is pleasing to dwell a little on this matter and to leave no room at all for the irresponsibility of opponents who, in trying to uphold the licence of a single person, and in putting private interest before the

incredibile est quantas errorum nebulas excitent. Aduersus quos cum multi alii tum praecipue Zacharias, Chalcedonensis episcopus, uir et re et nomine excellens, armatus uenit. Qui cum in Constantinopolitana[a] sancta et magna Synodo[1] Romani pontificis sententia sibi obiiceretur, Nicolai Papae[2] et aliorum patriarcharum, principem esse canonem replicauit. At Zosimus[3] Papa sic de statutis generalium conciliorum ait: 'Contra statuta patrum condere aliquid uel mutare nec huius quidem sedis potest autoritas'; nec de statutis patrum aut in urbibus aut in eremis disgregatorum loquitur (illa enim papam non ligant), sed de his quae in generalibus conciliis per patres eduntur. Quod ut clarius liqueat, Leonis Papae, omnium Romanorum pontificum eloquentissimi,[4] subiicienda sunt uerba, qui editionem Niceni Concilii nulla unquam ex parte solubilem fore ad Anatholium scribit, quasi seipsum et sic summum patriarcham excludens. Damasi uero clarior in hanc sententiam est autoritas ad Aurelium Archiepiscopum scribentis, sicut in libro Conciliorum narrat Isidorus, cuius dignissima de autoritate Synodali haec uerba leguntur:[5] 'Quoniam blasphemare Spiritum Sanctum non incongrue uidentur qui contra eosdem sanctos canones non necessitate compulsi sed libenter' (ut praefixum est) 'aliquid aut proterue agunt, aut aliquid praesumunt, aut facere uolentibus sponte consentiunt.' Cuius blasphemiae an Gabriel, qui se dictitat Eugenium,[6] sit hodie particeps illi diiudicent qui eum audiunt asserentem tantum a se abesse, ut generalibus conciliis debeat obedire, ut se tunc maxime dicat mereri, cum Concilii decreta contemnit. Sed addit Damasus:[7] 'Idcirco norma sanctorum canonum, qui sunt Spiritu Dei et totius mundi reuerentia consecrati, fideliter a nobis est scienda et diligenter tractanda; ne quo modo sanctorum patrum statuta absque ineuitabili necessitate (Quod absit!) transgrediamur.' Hodie tamen passim in omnibus literis apostolicis nonobstantiae[8] reperiuntur, quas nulla induxit alia necessitas quam pecuniae cumulandae; sed de his ipsi uiderint qui talia struunt. Nos iterum ad Damasum redeamus. In epistolis nanque Ambrosii,[9] Mediolanensis episcopi,

[a] Chalcedonensi αβ

---

[1] A.D. 869: Mansi, XVI, col. 87.

[2] Cf. above, p. 54, n. 3.

[3] Pope A.D. 417–18. *Decr.* C. 25, q. 1, c. 7 (Friedberg, I. 1008).

[4] Leo I the Great, pope 440–61, *ep*, XVI, *P.L.* 84, col. 724.

[5] *Decr.* C. 25, q. 1, c. 5, from Pseudo-Isidore (see Friedberg, I. 1008).

[6] Gabriele Condulmaro was the personal name of Eugenius IV.

[7] Cf. above, n. 5.

[8] Prefacing passages in papal rescripts which contravened earlier legislation. This aside of the author refers to the sale by the curia of privileges such as the right to hold incompatible benefices.

[9] Bishop A.D. 374–97; *P.L.* 16, cols. 1222–4 with n. 51.

common good, stir up incredibly great clouds of errors. Against whom many came armed and in particular Zacharias, bishop of Chalcedon, a man outstanding both in deed and reputation. For when in the holy and great Synod of Constantinople[1] he was confronted with the opinion of the Roman pontiff, Pope Nicholas,[2] and of other patriarchs, in rebuttal he urged the supremacy of the canon. But Pope Zosimus[3] has this to say about the statutes of the general councils: 'It is not possible for the authority of this see to institute anything or make a change contrary to the statutes of the Fathers', and he is not speaking about the statutes of the Fathers scattered in either the cities or the deserts (for they do not bind the pope), but about those which are given out by the Fathers in general councils. That the matter may appear in a clearer light, the words should be added of Pope Leo, the most eloquent of all the Roman pontiffs,[4] who writes to Anatolius that the ordinances of the Nicene Council will never in any degree be capable of dissolution, as though excluding himself and thereby the supreme patriarch. The authority of Damasus is clearer still in favour of this view when he writes to Archbishop Aurelius, as Isidore relates in his book on the Councils, whose words[5] about the worthy authority of the Synod run thus: 'Since it is not inconsistent to suppose guilty of blasphemy against the Holy Spirit those who contrary to the same holy canons, without the compulsion of necessity but of their own free will', so the preface goes, 'either act wantonly or show presumption or of their own accord agree with those who wish to do so'. Whether Gabriel, who calls himself Eugenius,[6] is involved today in this blasphemy those may judge who hear him maintaining that he is so far from owing obedience to general councils that he is particularly deserving when he is defying the decrees of the Council. But Damasus adds:[7] 'Therefore the rule of the holy canons which have been consecrated by the Spirit of God and by the reverence of the whole world must be faithfully known by us and carefully observed, that we may in no way transgress the statutes of the holy Fathers save through unavoidable necessity, and far be that from us!' Yet today everywhere in all the papal letters 'Notwithstandings'[8] are found, introduced by no other necessity save that of amassing money, but this must be the concern of those who concoct such things. Let us return again to Damasus. For in the letters of Ambrose,[9] bishop of Milan, mention is found of a certain letter which

mentio inuenitur cuiusdam epistolae, quam ipse Damasus scripsisse fertur iudicibus a Capuana Synodo[1] deputatis, ubi ostendit sui officii non esse in causis manum apponere in quibus Synodus praeuenisset; quo dicto illos manifeste redarguit qui summum pontificem Concilii principem dicunt, quod si uerum esset, potuisset utique Damasus causam Bonosii episcopi[2] ad se recipere terminandam, quamuis per Concilium prius coeptam. Sed quoniam Synodus maior est papa, prohibitum se Damasus nouit. Vnde Hilarius Papa[3] sciens Synodum supra se fore, ut canonistas non fugit, decreta sua per Concilium[4] uoluit approbari. Neque in hac sententia doctorum omnium doctor Augustinus desyderatur, qui sic in epistola quam ad Glorium et Eleusium ac Felicem grammaticum scribit[5] casum enarrat. Accusabatur Cecilianus episcopus per Donatum et alios quosdam. Melchiades Papa cum quibusdam episcopis Cecilianum absoluit, et in episcopatu confirmauit. Illi hac sententia irritati scissionem in Africae partibus induxerunt. Increpat illos Augustinus, qui cum aliud haberent remedium aduersus papae sententiam, schisma potius eligissent. In eosque per hunc modum inuehitur: 'Ecce putemus illos episcopos, qui Romae iudicarunt non bonos iudices fuisse; restabat adhuc plenarium ecclesiae uniuersalis iudicium, ubi etiam cum ipsis iudicibus causa posset agitari, ut si male iudicasse conuicti essent, eorum sententiae soluerentur.' Vnde apparet non solum papae solius sed papae etiam cum adiunctis episcopis sententiam per Concilium posse rescindi; plenarium enim uniuersalis ecclesiae iudicium nusquam alibi quam in Concilio reperitur. Nec aliquem moueat quod Augustinus de solis episcopis mentionem facere uideatur. Nam si textus epistolae perlegatur, Romanus pontifex cum episcopis iudicasse inuenietur. Ex conciliis etiam Africanis prohibiti sunt Romani pontifices ne appellationes illorum audirent qui a Synodo appellassent; quae omnia superioritatem conciliorum ostendunt. Idque in Actibus Apostolorum liquidius demonstratur,[6] ubi Petrus per congregationem Apostolorum reprehenditur, quod ad Cornelium gentilem introisset, tanquam non liceret eum magni aliquid facere sine scitu Concilii; et tamen tam sibi quam aliis

[1] A.D. 391; cf. H–L. II. 808[2].

[2] Who had argued that the Virgin ceased to be such after giving birth to Christ.

[3] In synodo Romano, i; *Decr.* C. 25, q. 1, c. 4 (Friedberg, I. 1008).

[4] At Rome, A.D. 465 (cf. Friedberg, loc. cit.; H–L. II. 903).

[5] *Ep.* xliii; *P.L.* 33, cols. 166–9.

[6] Acts 11: 1–18.

Damasus himself is held to have written to the judges appointed by the Synod of Capua,[1] in which he shows that it does not fall within his duty to touch those cases in which the Synod had taken prior action. By this statement he clearly refutes those who say that the supreme pontiff is the head of the Council; for if this were true, Damasus could in particular have been able to take upon himself the case of Bishop Bonosius[2] to bring it to an end, though it had been started previously by the Council. Yet since the Synod is greater than the pope, Damasus recognized that he was prevented. Pope Hilary[3] likewise knowing that the Synod was superior to himself, as the canonists were well aware, wished his decrees to be approved by the Council.[4] In this view too Augustine, the doctor of all doctors, is not found wanting, who thus describes the occurrence in a letter that he writes to Glorius and Eleusius and Felix the grammarian.[5] Bishop Cecilianus was being accused by Donatus and certain others. Pope Melchiades together with certain bishops acquitted Cecilianus, and confirmed him in his bishopric. The others, stung by this verdict, caused division in Africa. Augustine rebukes men who, though they had another remedy against the pope's verdict, had chosen a schism instead. He inveighs against them like this: 'Behold are we to consider those as bishops, who judged that there were not good judges at Rome? There still remained the plenary judgement of the universal Church, where the case could have proceeded even against the judges themselves, so that if they had been convicted of judging wrongly, their verdicts would be set aside.' It appears from this that the verdict not only of the pope alone but of the pope even with the addition of bishops can be rescinded by the Council, for the plenary judgement of the universal Church is found nowhere else but in the Council. No one should be worried because Augustine seems to make mention only of bishops. For if the text of the letter be read, the Roman pontiff will be found to have been judge along with the bishops. Furthermore the Roman pontiffs were prevented by the African councils from hearing the appeals of those who had appealed against the Synod; all of which shows the superiority of the councils. This is more clearly pointed out in Acts of the Apostles,[6] when Peter is reproved by the assembly of the Apostles for entering the house of Cornelius, a Gentile, as it was not possible for him to do anything of great importance without an ordinance of the Council; and yet as much

dictum fuerat: 'Ite, et baptizate',[1] et reliqua. Plus tamen illud uidetur urgere quod ad Galatas scribit gentium doctor[2] Paulus, ubi se ideo restitisse Petro in faciem dicit, quod ad ueritatem Euangelii non ambularet.[3] Cuius uerba, si recte intelliguntur, nil aliud per ueritatem Euangelii suscipiunt quam canonem Concilii inter Apostolos editum, quoniam sic discipuli in unum congregati determinassent; unde ostendit Paulus quia oportebat Petrum generali Concilio obedire.

Caeterum ne ulterius haec disputatio nos teneat, subiicienda est Constantiensis Concilii determinatio, quod uolens ambiguitatem huiusmodi reserare certamque uiuendi legem elargiri, solenni decreto declarauit omnes homines cuiuscunque status aut conditionis, etiam si papatus existerent, statutis et ordinationibus sacrorum generalium conciliorum obedire teneri.[4] Et quamuis ibi quaedam restrictio sit, dum dicitur: 'In his quae pertinent ad fidem, extirpationem schismatis, et reformationem ecclesiae in capite et in membris', notanda est tamen ampliatiua clausula quae subiungitur: 'Et in pertinentibus ad ea'; quae adiectio adeo praegnans est ut omnia quae cogitari possunt in uentre claudat, nec immerito. Cum enim ait Apostolis Dominus: 'Euntes, docete omnes gentes',[5] non dixit in tribus tantum sed: 'Docentes eos seruare omnia quaecunque mandaui uobis',[6] et alibi non istud aut illud sed: 'Quaecunque ligaueritis',[7] inquit; quae omnia pro autoritate ecclesiae generaliumque conciliorum deducuntur. Ad quam extollendam illa etiam ueniunt: 'Qui uos audit, me audit',[8] et: 'Vobis datum est nosse mysterium Dei',[9] et: 'Vbi duo uel tres congregati fuerint in nomine meo',[10] et: 'Quaecunque petieritis',[11] et: 'Pater sancte, serua illos quos dedisti mihi',[12] et: 'Ego uobiscum sum usque ad consummationem seculi',[13] et ex Paulo: 'Dei adiutores sumus',[14] et: 'Qui nos fecit idoneos ministros noui testamenti',[15] et: 'Ipse dedit quosdam quidem apostolos, quosdam autem prophetas',[16] et reliqua. In quibus omnibus locis et Christus et Apostolus de autoritate plurium locuti sunt; quae omnia ad uniuersalis ecclesiae praeeminentiam afferuntur. Sed cum ipsa nihil sparsim statuere aut ordinare queat, necessario dicendum est supremam illam ecclesiae potestatem in generalibus conciliis, dum tamen illa conueniunt, residere. Ideoque obseruatum est in

[1] Cf. Matt. 28: 19. [2] 1 Tim. 2: 7. [3] Gal. 2: 11, 14.
[4] *Sancrosancta*, Introduction, p. xiii.
[5] Matt. 28: 19. [6] Matt. 28: 20.
[7] Matt. 18: 18, (cf. John 20: 23). [8] Luke 10: 16.
[9] Mark 4: 11. Cf. Matt. 13: 11; Luke, 8, 10. [10] Matt. 18: 20.
[11] Matt. 21: 22. [12] John 17: 11. [13] Matt. 28: 20.
[14] 1 Cor. 3: 9. [15] 2 Cor. 3: 6. [16] Eph. 4: 11.

to him as to others had been said: 'Go ye and baptize',[1] and so on. Yet that point seems to be put more forcibly in what Paul, the teacher of the Gentiles,[2] writes in Galatians, when he says that he withstood Peter to his face for not walking according to the truth of the Gospel.[3] These words of his, if rightly understood, mean by 'the truth of the Gospel' nothing but the canon of the Council determined among the Apostles, since this had been the decision of the disciples when gathered together; so Paul shows that Peter was bound to obey the general Council.

However, so that this discussion may not keep us any longer, there must be added the decision of the Council of Constance, which, in its wish to clear up ambiguity of this kind and to grant a fixed rule of living, in solemn decree declared that all men of whatsoever sort or condition, including even the popes, were bound to obey the statutes and ordinances of the holy general councils.[4] Though there is a certain limitation in this when the words come 'in those things which pertain to the faith, the rooting out of schism and reform of the Church in head and members', yet notice should be taken of the amplifying clause which is added: 'and in the things pertaining to them'. This addition is so comprehensive that it includes everything which can be imagined, and rightly so. For when the Lord said to the Apostles: 'Go ye and teach all nations',[5] he did not use three [words] only, but [continued]: 'Teaching them to observe all things whatsoever I have commanded you',[6] and elsewhere he said not this or that but: 'Whatever things ye shall bind',[7] all of which are adduced in support of the authority of the Church and general councils. In amplification come the following: 'He that heareth you heareth me',[8] and: 'Unto you it is given to know the mystery of God',[9] and: 'Where two or three are gathered together in my name',[10] and: 'Whatsoever ye shall ask',[11] and: 'Holy Father, keep those whom thou hast given to me',[12] and: 'I am with you even unto the end of the world',[13] and from Paul: 'We are the helpers of God',[14] and: 'Who hath made us able ministers of the new testament',[15] and: 'He himself gave some, apostles; and some, prophets',[16] and so on. In all these places both Christ and the Apostle spoke about the authority of several persons; and all of these are adduced to support the pre-eminence of the universal Church. Yet since itself it can determine or ordain nothing in a scattered fashion, the highest power of the Church must of necessity be said to rest in

primitiua ecclesia ut ardua negocia non nisi in generalibus conciliis, siue congregationibus expedirentur. Idem quoque postea factum reperimus. Cum enim diuisae forent ecclesiae, et aliter atque aliter de fide Christi sentirent, generalia concilia habita sunt, et in Niceno Arriana, in Constantinopolitano Macedoniana, in Ephesino Nestoriana, in Chalcedonensi uero Eutitiana haereses condemnatae reperiuntur;[1] quod ad rem tantam iudicium Romani pontificis non existimabant sufficere, longeque uim habere maiorem Concilii quam Romani papae sententiam arbitrabantur, quod istum ut hominem posse, illud autem, in quo tot simul homines Spiritu Sàncto directore conuenirent, errare non posse diiudicarent. Pulcherrimaque ad propositum Marciani Caesaris uerba narrantur in hunc modum: 'Vere impius atque sacrilegus est, qui post tot sacerdotum sententiam opinioni suae aliquid retractandum relinquit. Extremae quippe dementiae est in meridie et perspicuo die commentitum lumen quaerere; quisquis enim post ueritatem repertam aliquid ulterius discutit, mendacium quaerit.'[2]

Constare iam omnibus arbitror Romanum pontificem subesse Concilio. Subdubitare tamen aliqui solent an etiam deponi per Concilium possit, quia, etsi probatum est papam subesse Concilio, non tamen fateri uolunt idcirco posse deponi; de qua re non erit extra propositum pauca dissertare. In primisque de nostris rabulis aliqua dicere, qui pro defensione Romani pontificis adhuc instant, unoque uicti praelio aliud instaurant, ut qui pertinacia magis quam ignorantia contendunt. Hi hoc etiam loco repeti uolunt quae superius de Romani pontificis seu patriarchae retulimus eminentia; utque sunt nonnulli magis uerbosi quam eloquentes, plurimum in eo commorantur quod Petro ueritas dicit: 'Tibi dabo claues regni coelorum', et: 'Quodcunque ligaueris super terram, erit ligatum et in coelis';[3] quasi per illa uerba princeps fieret aliorum. Iterumque illud amplificant, dum dicitur: 'Pasce oues meas',[4] quod aliis minime dictum inueniunt, et quia dicitur Petrum fuisse uerticem et os collegii apostolorum. Ideoque

[1] The first four Ecumenical Councils and the doctrinal disputes with which they dealt: Nicaea (A.D. 325), Constantinople (A.D. 381), Ephesus (A.D. 431), Chalcedon (A.D. 451).
[2] Isidore, *Conc. Chalc.*, *P.L.* 84, col. 173.
[3] Matt. 16: 19.
[4] John 21: 16, 17.

the general councils, at any rate while they are in session. Therefore it was the observance of the primitive Church that difficult business was settled only in general councils or gatherings. We find that the same was the practice afterwards too. For when the churches had been divided, and had different views about the faith of Christ, general councils were held, and heresies are found to have received condemnation, the Arian at Nicaea, the Macedonian at Constantinople, the Nestorian at Ephesus, the Eutychian at Chalcedon.[1] This was because for so great a matter they did not consider that the judgement of the Roman pontiff was enough, and they thought that the view of the Council had far greater force that that of the Roman pope, since they judged that he as a man could err, but that it, where so many men met at the same time under the Holy Spirit's guidance, could not. Excellently to the point are the words recorded of the Emperor Marcian which run: 'He is truly impious and sacrilegious who after the considered view of so many priests leaves anything to be further examined by his own opinion. For it is the height of madness in the noonday and clear daylight to look for artificial light; for whoever, after the truth is discovered, discusses anything further is looking for a falsehood.'[2]

I think it is now agreed among all that the Roman pontiff is beneath the Council. Yet some are apt to have slight doubts whether the Council can go to the length of deposing him, because although it has been proved that the pope is beneath the Council, yet they do not wish to admit that he can therefore be deposed. It will not be alien to our purpose to discuss this briefly, and in particular to mention those wranglers of ours who are still so intent on the defence of the Roman pontiff and, who when beaten in one battle, start something else, being contenders rather from persistence than ignorance. These at this point too wish repeated what we have earlier related about the pre-eminence of the Roman pontiff or patriarch and, as some of them are more wordy than eloquent, they dwell long upon the words of the Truth to Peter: 'I will give unto thee the keys of the kingdom of heaven, and whatsoever thou shalt bind on earth shall be bound in heaven',[3] as if by those words he was becoming leader of others. Again they elaborate the saying: 'Feed my sheep',[4] which they discover was not said to others at all, and the description of Peter as the head and mouthpiece of the college of Apostles. Therefore they hold

recte dictum censent quia nemo iudicabit primam sedem, omnesque cum Bonifacio[1] sentiunt, qui ait nulla ex causa posse iudicari, nisi deprehendatur a fide deuius, etiam si cateruatim innumerabiles populos secum in Tartarum ducat perpetuo cruciandos; quasi non posset aliis aperire coelum, si alius illud sibi claudere quiret, nec rursus alios pascere, si ipse indigeret pastu. Nos autem his in rebus nihil momenti ponimus, nihil omnino difficultatis meminimus, namque quod in sermone natalis Petri et Pauli Augustinus in hunc modum ait: 'Dominus Iesus discipulos suos ante passionem suam (sicut nostis) elegit, quos fratres appellauit, inter hos pene ubique Petrus solus totius ecclesiae gestabat personam, et propterea audire meruit: "Tibi dabo claues regni coelorum". Has enim claues non ille ut homo unus sed unitas accepit ecclesiae.'[2] Et alibi *De agone Christiano*:[3] 'Huic enim', inquit, 'ecclesiae claues regni coelorum datae sunt, cum Petro datae sunt. Et cum ei dicitur, ad omnes dicitur: "Amas me, pasce oues meas".'[4] Et Ambrosius in principio Pastoralis: 'Quas oues et quem gregem', ait, 'non solus tunc suscepit beatus Apostolus Petrus sed et nobiscum eas suscepit, et nos cum illo eas suscepimus omnes.'[5] Quibus ex dictis rabulorum nostrorum fundamenta concutiuntur ac penitus euertuntur. Quoniam si personam ecclesiae Petrus ferebat, non Petro sed ecclesiae potius uim illorum uerborum debemus asscribere. Quae autem Bonifacius asserit, quo pacto subsistere queant non uideo, atque, ut mox dicemus, longe a ueritate uidentur, nisi aliter atque sonant intelligantur.

Magnum tamen alicui fortasse potest uideri quod dicitur Romanum pontificem caput esse militantis ecclesiae. Nanque ut in corpore humano nunquam suadent medici propter aliquam aegritudinem caput abscindi, quamuis et ulcerosum sit et quouis morbo infectum, sic in hoc mystico ecclesiae corpore semper uidetur caput esse custodiendum et, quamuis criminosum sit, nihilominus tolerandum. Sed conuerte hoc argumentum. Si posset humano corpori, uno submoto capite, aliud inueniri, sicut in ecclesiastico cernimus, nunquid saepissime ob uarias aegritudines capita mutarentur? Praeterea si sic uolumus agere ut sic se caput ecclesiasticum ad suum habeat corpus, sicut humanum ad suum, necessarium erit ut extincto capite corpus etiam extinguatur, sicut

[1] St. Boniface, *Decr.* D. 40, c. 6 (Friedberg, I. 146; cf. Tierney, p. 57).
[2] *Sermo* ccxcv; *P.L.* 38, col. 1349.
[3] *P.L.* 40, col. 308.
[4] John 21: 16.
[5] Pseudo-Ambrosius, printed as Gerbert, *De informatione episcoporum, P.L.* 139, col. 171.

that it was rightly said that no-one shall judge the first see, and all share the view of Boniface,[1] who says that [the pope] can for no reason be judged, unless he be caught departing from the faith, even though he leads countless peoples with him in crowds to hell and everlasting torture—as if he could not open the heaven to others, if another could close it against him, nor again feed others if he himself needed feeding! We however attach no importance to these matters, and are not conscious of any difficulty at all, for as Augustine says in his sermon about the birthday of Peter and Paul: 'The Lord Jesus before his Passion, chose, as you know, his disciples, whom he called brothers. Among these almost everywhere Peter alone personified the whole Church, and on that account deserved to be told: "I will give unto thee the keys of the kingdom of heaven". For these keys he received not as one person but as the oneness of the Church.'[2] Elsewhere in *On the Christian Struggle*[3] he says: 'For to this Church were given the keys of the kingdom of heaven when they were given to Peter. It is to all that the words are said which are said to him: "Thou lovest me, feed my sheep"',[4] and Ambrose at the beginning of his Pastoral says: 'Not alone did the blessed Apostle Peter take charge of these sheep and this flock, but along with us he took it, and all of us have taken it with him'.[5] Through these statements our wranglers have their premises shaken and completely overturned. Since if Peter was personifying the Church, we should assign the force of those words not to Peter but rather to the Church. In what way Boniface's assertions can hold good I do not see and, as we shall say shortly, they seem far from the truth, unless they be understood in a sense different from their apparent meaning.

Yet perhaps to someone it may seem an important saying that the Roman pontiff is the head of the Church militant. For just as in the human body doctors never advise in any illness that the head be cut off, even though it may have both ulcers and any other disease, so in this mystical body of the Church it always appears that the head must be kept safe, and though it be guilty must none the less be endured. Yet put this argument in a different form. If it were possible in the human body when one head had been removed for another to be found, as we see happening in the ecclesiastical body, would not heads be changed very often for ailments of various kinds? Besides, if we wish to argue like this, that the ecclesiastical head should be on the same terms with its

in humanis corporibus cernimus; sicque in absurdum uenies, quod, mortuo Papa, mortuam etiam ecclesiam confiteberis, quod quantum a ueritate absit non nos latet. Quicquid tamen dicant aliqui, ego cum illis non sentio qui Romanum pontificem caput ecclesiae dicunt, nisi forsitan ministeriale; legimus enim quia Christus est ecclesiae caput, non papa, et illud est uerum caput, immutabile, perpetuum, et aeternum. Romanus autem pontifex nihil plus est quam ueri capitis locum tenens; ecclesia uero ipsius Christi corpus, cuius etiam ipse papa est membrum, uicarius autem Iesu Christi non in destructionem sed 'in aedificationem corporis' eiusdem Christi,[1] quod est ecclesia.

Quo fit ut, si damnosus et destructor reperiatur, deponi et abiici queat, non enim id agit propter quod est institutus. Et oportet nos (sicut Leo inquit)[2] Euangelici meminisse mandati, ut si nos oculus aut pes aut dextera scandalizauerit manus, a compage corporis auferatur;[3] quoniam et alibi inquit dominus quia 'omnis arbor quae non facit fructum excidetur et in ignem mittetur'.[4] Et iterum dicitur nobis: 'Auferte malum de uobis ipsis'.[5] Iustum est enim et ualde iustum, ut in epistola Clementis ad Iacobum fratrem Domini scribitur, separari eum qui saluari uult ab eo qui non uult.[6] Sed ut clarius apertiusque rem aperiamus, referendum est quod apud Ioannem Dominus dicit: 'Ego sum uitis uera, et pater meus agricola est', inquit Dominus, 'et uos estis palmites: omnem palmitem in me non ferentem fructum, tollet'.[7] Verba sunt ad Apostolos dicta, inter quos etiam Petrus erat, quem etiam auferri uult, non afferentem fructum. Hieronymus quoque super illis Matthaei uerbis:[8] 'Sal infatuatum ad nihilum prodest, nisi ut proiiciatur foras, et conculcetur a porcis', sic in persona Petri et Pauli inquit: 'Non est facile stare in loco Petri et Pauli, et tenere cathedram iam cum Christo regnantium. "Infatuatum sal", id est stultus praelatus, insipidus in praedicando et fatuus in delinquendo, "ad nihilum prodest", nisi ut mittatur foras, id est deponatur; "et conculcetur a porcis", id est a daemonibus, qui

[1] Eph. 4: 12. [2] *Ep.* clv, *Decr.* C. 24, q. 3, c. 34 (Friedberg, I. 999).
[3] Cf. Matt. 5: 29, 30; 18: 8, 9; Mark 9: 42–46.
[4] Matt. 7: 19. [5] 1 Cor. 5: 13.
[6] Pseudo-Clement, *Ad Iacobum ep.* i. *P.G.* 1, cols. 478–80.
[7] John 15: 1, 2, 5. [8] Matt. 5: 13 (paraphrased).

body as the human head with its body, it will follow inevitably that on the death of the head the body dies too, as we see happening with human bodies; thus the absurdity will be reached of admitting that on the death of the pope the Church is dead too. We realize how far this is from the truth. Whatever some may say, I do not agree with those who term the Roman pontiff head of the Church, unless perhaps the administrative head, for we read that Christ is the head of the Church, not the pope, and that is the true head, unchangeable, perpetual, and eternal. The Roman pontiff is nothing more than the lieutenant of the true head. The Church is the body of Christ himself, of which the pope too himself is a member, but the vicar of Christ not for the destruction but 'for the edifying of the body' of the same Christ,[1] which is the Church.

In consequence if he should be found to be harmful and destructive, he can be deposed and cast out, for he is not doing that for which he was appointed. We ought, as Leo says,[2] to remember the Gospel instruction that if the eye or the foot or the right hand has been a cause of offence to us it should be removed from the structure of the body,[3] since elsewhere too the Lord says that every tree that does not bear fruit shall be cut down, and cast into the fire.[4] Again we are told: 'Put away from among yourselves that wicked person.'[5] For it is just and very just, as is written in the letter of Clement to James, the Lord's brother, for him who wishes to be saved to be separated from him who is unwilling.[6] To put the matter more clearly and more openly, one must recall what the Lord says in John: 'I am the true vine, and my father is the husbandman', says the Lord, 'and ye are the branches. Every branch in me that beareth not fruit he shall take away.'[7] The words were said to the Apostles, among whom was Peter too, whom he wishes to be taken away too if he bears no fruit. Jerome too comments upon those words of Matthew:[8] 'If the salt have lost his savour it is good for nothing but to be cast out and trodden under foot of swine', and speaks like this regarding the role of Peter and Paul: 'It is not easy to stand in the place of Peter and Paul, and to hold the Chair of those who now reign with Christ. Salt that has "lost his savour", that is a foolish prelate, savourless in preaching, and unsavoury in sinning, is "good for nothing" except that it should be cast out, that is, deposed, and "trodden under foot of swine", that is, by demons, who have the

dominantur malo praelato, tanquam pecori suo'. En clarum est Hieronymi[1] testimonium: '"Proiiciatur foras", id est deponatur,' exponit, et loquitur de praelato qui Petri locum tenet et sic de Romano pontifice, quem, in praedicando insipidum et fatuum in delinquendo, ex gradu suae dignitatis deponendum affirmat. Nec (ut aliqui delirant) propter solam haeresim. Apud Isidorum autem Ispalensem, in libro Conciliorum epistola quaedam Clementis,[2] successoris Petri, ad Iacobum fratrem Domini reperitur inserta, ubi Clemens beati Petri ad se uerba referens sic ait: 'Si enim mundialibus curis fueris occupatus, et teipsum decipies et eos qui te audient, non enim poteris quae ad salutem pertinent plenius singulis quibusque distinguere; et ex eo fiet ut et tu, tanquam qui non docueris quae ad salutem hominum pertinent, deponaris, et discipuli per ignorantiam pereant'. Alibi tamen pro[a] 'deponaris' inuenitur 'puniaris';[3] quae duo uerba, si bene intelligantur, non multum inter se differunt, depositio nanque punitionis loco fit. Nec hic obiiciat quispiam hanc epistolam non esse putandam Clementis, cum scripta dicatur ad Iacobum, qui (sicut *Scholastica* tradit *Historia*)[4] prius obiit quam Petrus occideretur; potuit nanque Clemens uiuum Iacobum existimare, cum scripsit, qui magno terrarum et maris spatio inter se distabant. Nec facile Christianorum nuncii Romam ueniebant. Praeterea huius epistolae in pluribus Decretorum locis[5] tanquam uerae fit mentio, ideoque non erit ab re etiam ipsius epistolae alia uerba referre; ait[6] enim quia qui rebelliter uiuit, et discere atque bona agere recusat, magis diaboli quam Christi membrum esse ostenditur, et potius infidelis quam fidelis esse monstratur. Super quibus uerbis glossa[7] quae singularis per Panormitanum dicitur[8] et plurimum approbatur, ait quod: 'si notorium sit quodcunque Romani pontificis crimen, ex quo scandalizatur ecclesia, quod potest de illo papa accusari,

[a] pro α; loco BV

---

[1] *Ep.* xiv. 9, *P.L.* 22, col. 353; *Decr.* C.2, q.7, c.29 (Friedberg, I. 492) but only as far as 'regnantium'.

[2] The letter, *ep.* i, is not included in the *Concilia*, *P.L.* 84, but is in Pseudo-Isidore (Isidorus Mercator), *Decretalium Collectio*, *P.L.* 130, col. 22A (which has 'audiunt'); cf. *Decretales Pseudo-Isidorianae et capitula Angilramni*, rec. P. Hinschius (Leipzig, 1863), p. 32 (which has 'decipias', 'audiunt').

[3] For the reading 'puniaris', see Hinschius, loc. cit., n. 10; and cf. *P.G.* 1, col. 466 and n. 59.

[4] Petrus Comestor, *Historia Scholastica*, *P.L.* 198, col. 1686.

[5] In fact two letters, i and iii, are being confused.

[6] *Ep.* iii, *Decr.* D. 38, c. 16; cf. above, p. 24, n. 2.

[7] Joannes Teutonicus, gloss on D. 40, c. 6, in Tierney, p. 251.

[8] Panormitanus's main work on the Council, *Tractatus super Consilio Basiliensi* (here quoted from the edition printed at Lyons, 1516) outlines the back-

mastery over a bad prelate as if over their herd.' You see that the witness of Jerome[1] is clear: '"He should be cast out", that is deposed', he explains, and speaks about the prelate who is Peter's deputy and thus about the Roman pontiff, who, if savourless in preaching and unsavoury in sinning, is, he maintains, to be deposed from the rank of his office. Nor is this, to quote the nonsense of some, for heresy alone. In Isidore of Seville too, in the book of the Councils, a certain letter of Clement,[2] Peter's successor, to James, the Lord's brother, is found inserted, in which Clement speaks like this, applying to himself the words of St. Peter: 'For if you are kept busy by worldly cares, you will deceive both yourself and those who hear you; for you will not be able to explain fully enough to individuals that which concerns salvation, and the result will be that you, as not having taught what concerns men's salvation, will be deposed and your disciples perish through ignorance.' Elsewhere, however, one finds 'punished' for 'deposed'.[3] These two words, if rightly understood, do not differ very much. For deposition takes the place of punishment. The objection should not be made that this letter must not be thought to be Clement's, as it is said to be written to James, who, as the *Historia Scholastica* tells,[4] died before Peter was put to death. It was possible for Clement to believe James to be still alive when he wrote, seeing that they were widely separated by lands and sea. Nor was it easy for the messengers of the Christians to come to Rome. Besides there is mention made of this letter in several passages of the decretum as though it were genuine, and so it will not be out of place to quote some more words from this very letter.[5] It says[6] that he who lives rebelliously and refuses to learn and practise good, is shown to be more a member of the devil than of Christ, and is revealed as unfaithful rather than faithful. Upon these words a gloss,[7] called 'remarkable' by Panormitanus[8] and much approved, runs: 'If any misdeed of the Roman pontiff gains notoriety so that the Church finds it a cause of offence, the pope can be indicted for this, should he be incorrigible.' If

ground history (ff. iia–iiib) and then considers (*a*) whether there has been and still is a legitimate general council in Basle (ff. iii^{v}b–ix^{r}b), (*b*) whether the Council has the right to try and to depose Eugenius (ix^{r}b–xiii^{r}a), (*c*) whether it can properly proceed to elect a new pope (xiii^{r}a–xiv^{v}b); with an affirmative conclusion in each case. The 'nobilissima uerba' of the gloss referred to above are quoted by Panormitanus at f. xi^{v}a and consist of the passage referred to in the previous note from Joannes Teutonicus (who is not named).

si sit incorrigibilis.' Si accusari, ergo et puniri ac exigente delicto deponi; alias frustra accusaretur.

Nullus iam superest aemulis nostris defensioni locus, quin papa deponi queat. Quod licet deductum sit, non tamen adhuc liquet an per Concilium, quam prouinciam nunc ingredimur; illudque nobis initio fatebuntur aduersantes quoniam ab ecclesia potest Romanus pontifex deponi, quia cum sit papa uicarius ecclesiae, nemo dubitat quin dominus uicarios suos possit ad nutum suum destituere, nec dubium est uerius dici papam ecclesiae uicarium quam Christi. At si ecclesia potest Romanum patriarcham destituere, ergo et Concilium potest. Nanque, ut supra ostensum est, uniuersalis ecclesia nihil statuit, nihil ordinat, nihil decernit, nisi cum est in generalibus conciliis congregata; tuncque licet non assint omnes, sat est quia uocati sunt omnes quos ratio exigit interesse. Sed hic quoque, ut fit, ex dubio dubium oritur. Nam cum ecclesia tam laicos quam clericos complectatur, cur soli clerici concilia gerant quaerendum uidetur; nec enim uidemus laicos interesse aut uocem habere in conciliis. Possetque aliquis arbitrari quia quod dicitur ecclesiam non errare, id ad utrunque statum atque utrunque sexum referri, ut errantibus clericis laici maneant, rursusque uiris errantibus foemellarum aliquae in fide ac ueritate persistant; sed est erroneum sic opinari.

Debemus nanque duplicem consyderare ecclesiam, alteram quae laicos cum clericis in se habet, alteram quae solos clericos, et ad secundum pertinet docere, purgare, illuminare, dirigere, corrigere, pascere, et perficere primam, quia supremum in terris tribunal apud clericos non apud laicos existit; quod tam ex ueteri testamento quam ex nouo comprobatur. In Deuteronomio nanque sic scribitur: 'Si difficile et ambiguum apud te iudicium esse prospexeris inter sanguinem et sanguinem, causam et causam, lepram et non lepram, et iudicum intra portas urbis tuae uideris uerba uariare, surge, et ascende in locum quem elegerit Dominus Deus tuus. Veniesque ad sacerdotes leuitici generis, et ad iudicem qui fuerit illo tempore, quaerens[a] ab eis, qui indicabunt tibi iudicii ueritatem. Et facies quodcunque dixerint qui praesunt loco quem elegerit Dominus, et docuerint te iuxta legem eius; sequerisque

[a] quaerens α; quaeres B; quaeresque *Vulgate*

'indicted,' he can therefore be punished too, and, if the fault requires it, deposed, otherwise indicting him would be in vain.

No scope for defence now remains for our foes to prevent the possibility of the pope being deposed. Though that is settled, it is not yet clear whether he can be deposed by the Council, and this domain we are now entering. One point our opponents will grant us at the outset, that the Roman pontiff can be deposed by the Church; since as the pope is the vicar of the Church, no one doubts that a lord can put down his vicars at his will, and it is not in doubt that the pope is called with greater truth the vicar of the Church than of Christ. Yet if the Church can deprive the Roman patriarch, the Council can too. For, as we have shown above, the Church as a whole decides nothing, ordains nothing, decrees nothing except when it is assembled in general councils, and then though not all are present, it is enough that all have been summoned whom reason requires should be present. Here too, as usually happens, doubt arises from doubt. For since the Church embraces the laity as much as the clergy, it seems necessary to inquire why only clergy hold councils, for we do not find the laity attending or having a voice at councils. Anyone might think that the saying that the Church does not err, refers to both conditions and both sexes, so that if the clergy err, the laity remains sound, and again if the men err, some of the women remain steadfast in faith and truth. This belief is mistaken.

We must consider the Church as twofold, one part containing both laity and clergy, and one the clergy only, and to the second belongs teaching, purifying, enlightening, directing, correcting, feeding, and perfecting the first part, because the highest court upon earth exists among the clergy not the laity. The proof of this comes as much from the Old Testament as the New. For in Deuteronomy it is written thus: 'If thou perceive that the judgement with thee be hard and doubtful between blood and blood, cause and cause, leprosy and not leprosy, and thou see that the words of the judges within the gates of thy city do vary, arise and go up to the place which our Lord thy God shall choose. And thou shalt come to the priests of the Levitical stock and to the judge that shall be at that time, and thou shalt ask of them, who shall show thee the truth of the judgement. And thou shalt do whatsoever they, that are presidents of the place which the Lord shall choose, shall say and teach thee according to his law; and thou shalt

sententiam eorum, nec declinabis ad dexteram uel ad sinistram. Qui autem superbierit, nolens obedire sacerdotis imperio, qui eo tempore ministrat coram Domino Deo tuo, et decreto iudicis, morte moriatur homo ille, et auferes malum de medio Israël, cunctusque populus audiens timebit, ut nullus deinceps intumescat superbia.'[1] Ecce ergo quia in ueteri testamento supremum tribunal apud sacerdotes fuisse monstratur, quod etiam apud Matthaeum[2] testatur Dominus, dum ait sacerdotibus Iudaeorum quod ipsi essent duces aliorum, et ad eos spectaret sedere in cathedra Moysi et docere populum, quodque in eis esset clauis scientiae. Ex quibus uerbis ostenditur supremum et maximum tribunal Iudaeorum in synagoga fuisse, quae res satis nos admonet idem quoque in nouo testamento debere seruari, cum uetus fuerit typus noui; et quae non inueniuntur mutata, stare non prohibentur. Sunt tamen et huiusmodi res in Euangelica lege, euidentissima testimonia, idque praecipue ex gestis Christi potest comprehendi, qui omnia uerba potestatem significantia ad Apostolos discipulosque direxit, quos fuisse omnes presbyteros constat, ut est illud: 'Venite post me, et faciam uos piscatores hominum',[3] ubi piscatoribus sacerdotes et laici piscibus equiparantur. Discipulos quoque 'operarios in messem suam',[4] id est in ecclesiam, constituit, et dedit illis autoritatem docendi et instruendi; unde apud Lucam mittens eos dicit: 'Qui uos audit, me audit: et qui uos spernit, me spernit.'[5] Apud Matthaeum uero inquit: 'Euntes, docete omnes gentes.'[6] Et alibi ad populum: 'Omnia quaecunque dixerint uobis, seruate, et facite',[7] de scribis loquens. Taceo illud quod est omnibus maius: 'Quaecunque ligaueritis',[8] et reliqua. Nanque id quoque solis sacerdotibus dictum reperitur. Voluit enim Christus ostendere quia sicut in ueteri testamento sacerdotum fuit suprema potestas, sic etiam in nouo seruari deberet; ideoque non inepte Apostolus Paulus magistrum se gentium[9] uocitat. Nec existimet aliquis id tunc illis tantum fuisse dictum qui perfecti erant et quorum lux omnibus lucebat. Nanque et successoribus dicebatur, quicquid Apostolis et discipulis dicebatur, quod autoritatem sonaret, sicut Ambrosius[10] super uerbo: 'Pasce oues

[1] Deut. 17: 8–13, in the 1609 Douay version, with which the text above corresponds rather than with the A.V. The Latin at this point does not correspond with the Vulgate.

[2] Matt. 23: 2. [3] Matt. 4: 19. [4] Matt. 9: 38; Luke 10: 2.

[5] Luke 10: 16. [6] Matt. 28: 19. [7] Matt. 23: 3.

follow their sentence, neither shalt thou decline to the right hand nor to the left hand. But he that shall be proud, refusing to obey the commandment of the priest which at that time ministreth before our Lord thy God and the decree of the judge, that man shall die, and thou shalt take away the evil out of Israel, and the whole people hearing shall fear, that none afterward swell in pride.'[1] Notice then that in the Old Testament the highest court is shown to have belonged to the priests, evidence of which is given in Matthew[2] by the Lord when he says to the priests of the Jews that they were the leaders of others, and that it was their concern to sit in Moses' seat and teach the people, and in them was the key of knowledge. From these words it is clear that the highest and chief court of the Jews lay in the synagogue. This circumstance is sufficient to remind us that the same arrangement must be retained in the New Testament too, since the Old was the prototype of the New, and things which are not found to have been changed are not prevented from persisting. There are, however, things of this kind in the Gospel law, very obvious pieces of evidence, and this can be understood particularly from the actions of Christ, who directed all words meaning power at his Apostles and disciples who, it is agreed, were all priests, as this shows: 'Follow me, and I will make you fishers of men',[3] when priests are compared to fishermen and laymen to fish. The disciples too he appointed as 'labourers in his harvest',[4] that is the Church, and gave them authority to teach and instruct: so in Luke, when sending them forth, he says: 'He that heareth you heareth me, and he that despiseth you despiseth me'.[5] In Matthew he says: 'Go and teach all nations',[6] and elsewhere to the people, speaking of the scribes: 'All whatsoever they say to you, [that] observe and do'.[7] I have not mentioned what is greater than all: 'Whatsoever ye bind'[8] and so on. For that too is found to have been said to priests alone. For Christ wanted to show that just as in the Old Testament the priests held the supreme power, so also in the New it must be retained; and therefore it is not out of keeping that the Apostle Paul calls himself the teacher of the Gentiles.[9] Nor should anyone think that this was only said to those who were perfect and whose light was clear to all. For whatever was said to the Apostles and disciples was said to their successors also, to have the sound of authority; as Ambrose[10] comments on the text: 'Feed

[8] Cf. above, p. 62, n. 7. [9] 2 Tim. 1: 11. [10] See above, p. 66, n. 4.

meas', et Augustinus de uerbo: 'Tibi dabo claues', quos supra retulimus.[1] Clarius tamen ad Ephesios Paulus, 'Et ipse dedit', inquit, 'quosdam quidem apostolos, quosdam autem prophetas, alios uero euangelistas, alios autem pastores et doctores; ad consummationem sanctorum in opus ministerii, in aedificationem corporis Christi, donec occurramus in unitatem fidei omnes, et agnitionis filii dei, in uirum perfectum, in mensuram aetatis plenitudinis Christi; ut iam non simus sicut paruuli fluctuantes, et circunferamur omni uento doctrinae in nequitia hominum, in astutia ad circunuentionem erroris.'[2] Quibus in uerbis ostendit Paulus Iesum Christum superna repetentem ecclesiae suae uoluisse consulere, ne in uiam erroris declinaret per nequitiam hominum seducta; constituisseque directorium quoddam, ad quod foret in dubiis casibus recurrendum, idque ex sacerdotibus ordinasse apostolis, prophetis, euangelistis, pastoribus, et doctoribus, nec eos solum qui tunc erant sed eorum etiam successores, quando dicitur: 'Donec occurramus ei', id est in fine seculi. Vnde apud Matthaeum dicitur: 'Ego uobiscum sum, usque ad consummationem seculi.'[3] Et Augustinus super Matthaeum, dum scribitur: 'Tibi dabo claues' etc., dicit per illa uerba datam esse iudiciariam potestatem non solum Petro sed toti ecclesiae in episcopis et presbyteris.[4] Sciendum est enim (ut Clemens asserit in epistola supradicta)[5] episcopos uicem apostolorum gerere, et reliquorum discipulorum uicem tenere presbyteros; sic enim praedicasse Petrum, qui a Domino didicisset, ait. Vnde apparet ecclesiae potestatem omnimodam in sacerdotibus consistere, eorumque determinationi et mandatis ex iussu domini omnes homines teneri parere, quia ab eo sit dictum: 'Omnia quaecunque dixerint uobis, facite'.[6] Quibus ex uerbis, illud mihi consequens uidetur, ut sicut uniuersalis ecclesia, quae omnes complectitur, nequit errare, sic etiam errore omni careat quae solos continet clericos; quoniam si illa tenetur huic auscultare atque obedire, sequeretur, ut hac errante illa erraret, quod tamen nequaquam admittimus.

Dicimus ergo uniuersali ecclesiae, quae omnes Christi fideles amplectitur, potestatem omnimodam fore concessam, Romanumque pontificem illi subiectum posse per ipsam non bene regentem

[1] Cf. above, p. 66, n. 2.
[2] Eph. 4: 11–14.
[3] Matt. 28: 20.
[4] Cf. above, p. 66, n. 2.
[5] Pseudo-Clement, *Ad Iacobum ep.* i, *P.L.* 130, col. 30D.
[6] Matt. 23: 3.

my sheep', and Augustine on the text: 'I will give unto thee the keys', which we have previously mentioned.[1] Yet more clearly did Paul say in Ephesians: 'He gave some, apostles; and some, prophets; and some, evangelists; and some, pastors and teachers; for the perfecting of the saints, for the work of the ministry, for the edifying of the body of Christ, till we all come in the unity of the faith and of the knowledge of the Son of God, unto a perfect man, unto the measure of the stature of the fulness of Christ: that we henceforth be no more like children tossed to and fro, and carried about with every wind of doctrine, by the sleight of men, and cunning craftiness, whereby they lie in wait to deceive.'[2] In these words Paul showed that Jesus Christ, when returning to the realms above, wished to take thought for his Church, that it should not turn aside into any path of error, led astray by the wickedness of men, and he instituted a certain directing body to which reference might be made in doubtful circumstances, and appointed it of priests who were apostles, prophets, evangelists, pastors, and teachers, not merely those who were alive at that time, but their successors too, for the words are: 'Till we come to him', that is at the end of the world. So in Matthew the words are: 'I am with you even unto the end of the world',[3] and Augustine, commenting on the passage in Matthew: 'I will give unto thee the keys' and so on, says that in those words the power of judgement was given not only to Peter, but to the whole Church in its bishops and priests.[4] For it should be known, as Clement maintains in the letter already mentioned,[5] that bishops represent apostles and that priests represent the other disciples: for he says this was the preaching of Peter, who learnt it from the Lord. From which it is clear that power of every kind in the Church lies in the priests, and that by the Lord's command all men are bound to obey their decisions and orders, because his words were: 'All whatsoever they say to you, do'.[6] From these words it seems to me to follow that just as the universal Church, which includes all, cannot err, similarly that assembly is free of all error which contains the clergy alone, for if the former is bound to listen to and obey the latter, it would follow that if the latter erred, the former would too, which we do not admit at all.

We say then that to the universal Church which enfolds all the faithful of Christ power of every kind is granted, and that the Roman pontiff is subject to it, and that by it, if he does not rule

deponi, abiici, excommunicari. Rursus adiicimus quia quaecunque illa uniuersalis ecclesia potest, haec etiam clericorum potest, et in hac potestatis supremae exercitium inueniri. Et cum illa ab hac dirigatur, illuminetur, pascatur, nephas est dicere hanc fore errori subiectam. Tunc enim non bene prouidisset ecclesiae, sponsae suae, Iesus Christus, nec utile directorium instituisset, quod est omnino absurdum; ueritasque illa manet quia clericorum ecclesia errori nequaquam subiicitur. Ipsi autem clerici soli habent in conciliis iudicare; quoniam in eis est (ut supra diximus) clauis scientiae, et ad eos spectat docere populum et sedere in cathedra Moysi. Iterum quoque sciendum est quoniam sacerdotes per orbem dispersi non statuunt canones nec iudicant, nisi quilibet plebem suam; tuncque papa omnibus maior est, et ipse est sacerdos, qui ministrat coram Domino, in eoque plenitudo potestatis existit. Vbi uero in Spiritu Sancto congregantur episcopi et sacerdotes concilium celebrantes, licet non omnes assint, quia tamen legitime uocatio facta est, iam non in papa sed in Concilio plenitudo potestatis consistit, statimque ut incipit Concilium esse, incipit papa superiorem habere. Nec scio quando ex plenitudine potestatis possit (stante Concilio) quicquam statuere, cum iam cesset in eo ipsa plenitudo. Sed (ut in proposito maneamus) illud omnino concludimus quia quod ecclesiae uniuersali permissum est, id quoque ecclesiae clericorum permittitur. Et quod permittitur ecclesiae clericorum, id etiam generale Concilium habet commissum sibi. Quo fit ut si uniuersalis ecclesia, prout nemo potest negare, Romanum pontificem deponere potest, generale quoque Concilium potest.

Possumus hanc sententiam euidentioribus firmare testimoniis. Glossa est quam suis in scriptis mirifice Panormitanus extollit,[1] cuius sententia est generale Concilium esse iudicem papae in omnibus casibus in quibus ille potest iudicari; sed est canon Synodi Constantinopolitanae octauae,[2] illius magnae et memorabilis, et quam Gregorius[3] inter quatuor uenerari se more quatuor Euangeliorum dicit, in haec uerba: 'Porro si Synodus uniuersalis fuerit congregata, et facta fuerit de sancta Romanorum ecclesia quaeuis ambiguitas et controuersia, oportet uenerabiliter et cum

[1] For canonist statements in this sense see Tierney, pp. 57 ff., 171 ff., 212 ff.; Panormitanus, loc. cit. above, p. 70, n. 8.

[2] Constantinople 869, can. 21; H–L. IV. 529. The authority of the Eighth Ecumenical Council was not generally accepted by the Greek Church, and raised controversy at this very time during the negotiation for reunion: Gill, pp. 150–1; H–L. IV. 543–4.

[3] *Ep.* XXV; cf. above, p. 56 and n. 5. The proceedings of the first Roman Council under Gregory VII made great use of Gregory the Great's letter. Perhaps this accounts for the confusion here.

well, he can be deposed, cast away, and excommunicated. Again we add that whatever the power of the universal Church is, the whole assembly of the clergy has it too, and in the latter is found the exercise of its highest power. Since the former is directed, enlightened, and fed by the latter, it is wrong to say that the latter is subject to error. For in that case Jesus Christ would not have taken good care for the Church, his bride, nor have set up a useful directing body, which is quite absurd; and the truth remains that the whole assembly of the clergy is not at all liable to error. For the clergy alone have the power of judging in councils since in them, as we have said above, is the key of knowledge, and it is their concern to teach the people and sit in Moses' seat. Again it should be known that priests scattered throughout the world do not decide the canons or give judgement, except each to their own diocese; and at such times the pope is greater than all, and himself is a priest who ministers in the presence of the Lord, and in him exists the plenitude of power. When, however, bishops and priests meet in the Holy Spirit holding a council, though not all are present, yet because the summons is lawful, the plenitude of power rests now not in the pope, but in the Council, and the moment the Council begins to exist the pope begins to have a superior. I do not know if there is an occasion when he can settle anything from his plenitude of power while the Council is in being, since the plenitude itself comes to an end in the Council. Yet to keep to our purpose, we conclude entirely that what has been permitted to the universal Church is permitted too to the whole assembly of the clergy. What is permitted to the whole assembly of the clergy, that too the general Council considers as entrusted to itself. The result is that if the universal Church can depose the Roman pontiff, as no one can deny, the general Council can too.

We can support this view with clearer evidence. There is a gloss to which in his writings Panormitanus gives high praise,[1] the sense of which is that the general Council is the judge of the pope in all circumstances in which he can be judged. But there is a canon of that great and memorable eighth Council at Constantinople[2] which Gregory[3] says he reverences among the four like the four Gospels, which runs thus: 'Further if the universal Synod has met and any doubt and dispute has arisen about the holy Roman Church, inquiry must be made reverently and with fitting respect about the point at issue, and the solution be accepted,

conuenienti reuerentia de proposita quaestione sciscitari, et solutionem accipere, non tamen audacter sententiam dicere contra seniores Romae summos pontifices.' Ecce ut sacrum illud Concilium Constantinopolitanum et ab omnibus approbatum seniores Romae pontifices iudicio Synodali supponit; nec aliquem moueat, quia non exprimitur depositio, dicitur enim: 'Quaeuis ambiguitas'. Si enim de quauis ambiguitate cognoscit Synodus, ergo uidebit utrum papa sit deponendus, quia id etiam potest in ambiguitatem uenire. At ne longius exempla petamus, Ioannes XXIII,[1] quem et maior Christianae religionis pars et ipsa Constantiensis Synodus pro Romano pontifice uenerata est, per Concilium a pontificio eiectus fuit. Nec haeresis in eo condemnata est ulla, sed quoniam scandalizabat ecclesiam aliis criminibus, sancta Synodus eum papatu abdicandum censuit; perpetuis exinde temporibus exemplo tali proficiens, ut cessaret illorum opinio qui tantum haeresim facere locum depositioni asserunt.

Vnum tamen hic non est omittendum quod quidam et boni (ut mihi uidentur) et docti (ut reputantur) disputando solent tueri. Asserunt enim generalia concilia nullius esse penitus efficaciae nulliusque omnino momenti, nisi Romanus pontifex illa indixerit, eiusque autoritas perseuerauerit in eisdem. Vnde Pascasium, Siciliensem episcopum et sanctissimi Leonis Papae nuncium, in magna Synodo Chalcedonensi increpasse aiunt Dioscorum, quod ausus esset facere sine autoritate sedis apostolicae concilium in Epheso, quod nunquam rite factum est, neque fieri licuit.[2] In omnibus nanque Synodis apocrisiarii apostolici decretas sententias primo propter summam autoritatem eiusdem sanctae sedis confirmabant et subscribebant; quia aliter nullum habebant robur, ut credit Isidorus.[3] Adducunt et aliud eiusdem Synodi Chalcedonensis testimonium, ubi cum facta esset mentio Ephesini Concilii, omnes episcopi clamauerunt: 'Illud concilium dicere non debemus, quoniam nec apostolica autoritate coactum est, neque rite peractum.'[4] Ex quibus autoritatibus mirum in modum se putant armatos qui fieri sine consensu papae concilia negant. Quorum sententia, si (ut ipsi uolunt) inuiolata persistat, ruinam secum ecclesiae trahit. Quid enim remedii erit, si criminosus papa perturbet ecclesiam, si animas perdat, si peruertat exemplo malo populos, si denique contraria fidei praedicet, haereticisque

[1] See Introduction, p. xiii.

[2] Fourth Ecumenical Council, A.D. 451; H–L. II. 649–834.

[3] 'Praefatio' to the *Concilia*, *P.L.* 84, col. 91; *Decr.* D. 16, c. 1 (Friedberg, I. 41).

[4] Cf. H–L. II. 670 and for the Council of Ephesus, A.D. 449, dominated by Dioscorus, ibid. II. 584–621; its acts were annulled by the Council of Chalcedon.

yet without boldly delivering an opinion against the older chief pontiffs of Rome.' Notice how this holy Council of Constantinople, approved by all, subjects the older pontiffs of Rome to the Synod's judgement, nor should anyone be disturbed because there is no mention of deposition, since the words used are 'any doubt'. For if the Synod takes note of any doubt, then it will see whether the pope should be deposed since that too can enter into doubt. Without looking further for instances, John XXIII,[1] whom the greater part of the Christian faith and the Synod of Constance itself respected as Roman pontiff, was turned out of his papal office by the Council. No heresy was condemned in him, but, since he caused offence to the Church by other crimes, the holy Synod decided that he should resign the papacy, hence gaining this advantage for perpetuity from such a precedent that this was the end of the belief of those who claim that heresy alone gives a ground for deposition.

One point, however, must not here be overlooked, which is maintained in debate by certain persons who are in my view good and in the general opinion learned. They claim that general councils are of no efficacy and importance at all unless the Roman pontiff has called them into being, and his authority has continued in them. So they say that Paschasinus, bishop of Sicily and the envoy of the holy Pope Leo, at the great Synod of Chalcedon attacked Dioscorus for venturing without the authority of the apostolic see to hold a council at Ephesus, which never happened or could happen legally.[2] For in all the Synods apostolic legates first confirmed and subscribed to the resolutions passed because of the supreme authority of the same holy see, since otherwise, so Isidore believes,[3] they had no validity. They bring forward other evidence too from the same Synod of Chalcedon, at which when mention had been made of the Council of Ephesus, all the bishops exclaimed, 'We ought not to call that a council, since it was not summoned by apostolic authority nor carried out legally'.[4] From these texts those who deny that councils can be held without the pope's agreement think they have obtained splendid weapons. Their view, if (as they wish) it continued unimpaired, involves the ruin of the Church. For what remedy will there be if a pope who is a criminal should upset the Church, destroy souls, and by his evil example lead peoples astray, and finally preach things contrary to the faith and fill those set under him with heretical

dogmatibus imbuat subditos? Nullumne hic parabimus obstaculum? Sinemusne cum ipso cuncta ruere? Quis est, qui existimet Romanum pontificem ad sui emendationem Concilium congregare? Nempe, ut peccant homines, sic etiam impune peccare uolunt.

At ego dum ueteres lego historias, dum Actus perspicio Apostolorum, hunc equidem usum non inuenio ut soli papae concilia congregauerint. Primumque omnium Conciliorum, ubi Matthias substitutus est Iudae, non iussu Petri sed iussu Christi congregatum inuenio; qui Apostolis praecepit ne ab Hierosolymis discederent, sed promissionem Patris expectarent.[1] Secundum, de electione diaconorum, non solus Petrus sed duodecim Apostoli congregarunt, quia scriptum est: 'Conuocantes duodecim multitudinem'.[2] Tertium, de sublatione circuncisionis et aliorum legalium, communis inspiratio congregauit, scribitur enim: 'Conuenerunt Apostoli et seniores'.[3] Quartum uero, ubi quaedam legalia permissa sunt, uidetur per Iacobum fratrem Domini coadunatum,[4] et sic discurrendo per omnia nihil in primitiua ecclesia reperiretur, per quod autoritas haec congregandi concilia solis Romanis pontificibus pateat. Nec post, tempore magni Constantini et aliorum Augustorum, ad congreganda concilia quaesitus est magnopere Romani assensus papae, ideoque Chalcedonensis Synodus sic de se ait: 'Sancta et magna uniuersalis Synodus, quae secundum gratiam Dei et sanctiones piissimorum Christianissimorumque imperatorum Valentiniani et Martiani Augustorum congregata est apud Chalcedonem, metropolim Bithyniae prouinciae';[5] nec de Romano pontifice efficit Synodus mentionem, quamuis eius illic consensus fuerit. In hac re tamen distinguendum putarem, nec absolute negarem papae consensum necessarium, nec absolute requirerem; immo nunquam eo uolente refutarem, dicerem tamen quia ad congreganda concilia requirendus sit papae consensus, ne summa illius sedis autoritas et dignitas uideatur contemni. Si tamen ille resistat, congregarique concilium omnino nolit, et maior pars praelatorum iudicet necessarium esse concilium, etiam si papa nolit, concilium congregari posse putabo. Eoque modo intelligo uerba Concilii Chalcedonensis. Dioscurus enim concilium in Epheso[6] congregans apostolicam

[1] Acts 1: 4–26.
[2] Acts 6: 2.
[3] Acts 15: 6.
[4] Acts 21: 18.
[5] Isidore, *Conc. Chalc. P.L.* 84, col. 163.
[6] See above, p. 80, n. 4.

doctrines? Shall we do nothing to stop him at this point? Shall we allow everything to go to ruin along with him? For who could imagine the Roman pontiff summoning a council for his own correction? As men sin so they wish, of course, to sin without penalty.

Yet as I read the old accounts and scan Acts of the Apostles, I do not find this practice of the popes alone summoning councils. The first of all the Councils, when Matthias was put in the place of Judas, I find, was summoned not by the order of Peter but by that of Christ, who told his Apostles not to leave Jerusalem but to await the Father's promise.[1] The second, about the choosing of deacons, not only Peter but the twelve Apostles summoned, because the wording is: 'The twelve calling together the multitude'.[2] The third, about the abolition of circumcision and other legal matters, common inspiration summoned, for the words are: 'The Apostles and elders came together'.[3] The fourth, when certain legal practices were permitted, seems to have been called together by James the Lord's brother.[4] On running through all of them in this way nothing would be found in the early Church conferring this right to summon councils on the Roman pontiffs alone. Later, in the time of Constantine the Great and other emperors, the agreement of the Roman pope was not particularly sought for the summoning of councils, and therefore the Synod of Chalcedon speaks thus about itself: 'The holy and great universal Synod, which has been summoned in accordance with the grace of God and the sanction of the most pious and Christian emperors Valentinian and Marcian at Chalcedon, metropolis of the province of Bithynia'.[5] The Synod makes no mention of the Roman pontiff, though it was held with his agreement. In this matter I should consider that a distinction should be drawn, and I should not completely deny that the pope's agreement is necessary, nor should I completely insist upon it. No. If he were willing I should never reject it, but I should say that the pope's agreement should be sought for summoning councils, so that the highest authority and dignity of that see may not seem to be slighted. If, however, he should resist, and be quite unwilling that a council be summoned, and the majority of the prelates should judge a council necessary, I shall think that a council can be summoned even if the pope should disagree. That is the manner in which I take the words of the Council of Chalcedon. For Dioscurus in summoning a council in Ephesus[6] had shown contempt of the apostolic see,

sedem contempserat, quod nullatenus licuit. Praeterea si aliqui praelati (inuito papa) uellent concilium facere, existimo habendum respectum ad summam sedis apostolicae dignitatem ut non sit ei paucorum praelatorum iudicium anteponendum. Vbi uero communiter inspiratio est praelatorum, unius hominis iudicium cedat oportet, etiam si Petri successor existat. Nec illud uideo semper obseruatum ut sine autoritate papae concilium non sit habitum. Nec enim Pisanum Concilium papae alicuius autoritate aut consensu congregatum fuit, cum et Gregorius illud abhominaretur, et Benedictus execraretur.[1] Idem quoque de Constantiensi Concilio dici potest, quod autoritate Ioannis conuenit, qui quantum ad Hispanos papa non fuit.[2] Et si Pisanum Concilium uerum non fuit concilium, Ioannes papa uerus non fuit; unde etiam consensus eius ad congregandum Constantiense Concilium nihil operatus fuisset. Sed dicunt aliqui, quia cardinales fuerunt Pisis, qui pars sunt apostolicae sedis, etiam autoritatem fuisse apostolicam; quod quam uerum sit facile potest percipi, quia plus est solus papa quam omnes cardinales. Ille est enim uicarius Christi illeque Petri successor, non cardinales, in illoque plenitudo residet potestatis, et ad eum ligare et soluere pertinet; utcumque est, mihi non consonat idcirco negari concilium, si papa, quotiescunque papa dissentit, nisi eius spreta sit autoritas. Cur enim in generali Concilio alia exigitur potestas, in quo est praesens diuina maiestas? Illud autem plus quam fatuum est dicere, ut postquam semel consensus papae fuerit, si reuocetur, cessare Concilium; quoniam non est amplius arbitrii papae reuocare consensum. Necessariumque habet Concilio parere, cuius ipse pars maiori parti cedere habet. Et si se a consensu maioris partis segregat, ab unitate ecclesiae recedens schismaticum sese facit.

Longius forsitan quam res exposceret uideor esse digressus, multaque praeter intentionem contexuisse; fit tamen saepius ut uerbum ex uerbo fluat. At si recte pensitemus, nihil est ab re dictum; omnia nanque eo tendunt ut Romanum pontificem generali Concilio subiiciant, quod prima conclusio theologorum habuit. Quae quoniam ex superioribus dictis satis explicata uidetur, iam tempus est ut ad secundam uela tendamus; quam

[1] See Introduction, p. xii.

[2] See Introduction, p. xiii.

which was not at all lawful. Besides, if any prelates wished to hold a council against the pope's will, I think respect should be paid to the supreme dignity of the apostolic see, so that the opinion of a few prelates should not be preferred to it. But when there is a general inspiration of the prelates, the opinion of one man ought to give way, even if he is the successor of Peter. Nor do I find that it has always been the practice that a council has not been held without the pope's authority. For the Council of Pisa was not summoned with the authority or agreement of any pope, as Gregory detested it and Benedict cursed it.[1] The same too may be said about the Council of Constance, which met by John's authority who, so far as the Spaniards were concerned, was not pope.[2] If the Council of Pisa was not a true council, John was not a true pope; and consequently his agreement with the summoning of the Council of Constance would have been of no avail. Yet some say that because there were at Pisa cardinals, who are part of the apostolic see, its authority too was apostolic. What truth there is in this can easily be seen, as the pope alone is more than all the cardinals. For he and not the cardinals is the vicar of Christ and he is the successor of Peter, and in him lies the plenitude of power, and to him it belongs to bind and to loose. However one looks at it, to me it does not seem proper that a council should be refused if and when the pope disagrees, unless his authority has been scorned. For why in the general Council, at which there is present God's majesty, is any other power required? Yet it is more than stupid to say that, after the pope has once given his consent, if this be revoked the Council comes to an end, since it is no longer within the discretion of the pope to revoke his consent. He is bound to obey the Council in which as a part he must give way to the majority. If he withdraws from agreement with the majority then, leaving the unity of the Church, he makes himself schismatic.

I seem perhaps to have digressed at greater length than the topic demanded, and to have included much beyond my intention. Yet it frequently happens that word runs on from word. And if we think it over correctly, nothing irrelevant has been said. For everything points towards putting the Roman pontiff beneath the general Council, which was the first resolution of the theologians. Since this seems to have received sufficient explanation in the earlier discussion, it is now time to set our sails towards the

primis adhuc spirantibus uentis facile absoluemus. Nanque si uerum est, ut est, papam subesse Concilio, quo pacto poterit ipse papa inuitum Concilium dissoluere, mutare, aut transferre? Quoque uultu dicemus quia ius habeat in suum superiorem, qui est inferior? Quomodo corrigere papam sancta Synodus poterit, si solui Synodus uel inuita per papam potest? Sit papa libidini seruiens, sit auri et pecuniae cupidus, sit bellorum ac tumultuum auidus, sit hostis ecclesiae et Christiano infestissimus nomini, quo pacto illum redarguere Concilium poterit, si illi facultas pateat dissoluendi? Nempe, ut agi de sua correptione in Concilio Romanus pontifex audiet, mox ad dissolutionis remedium properabit. Quoniam sicut pulchre Macrobius inquit:

'Cui plus licet quam par est, plus uult quam licet,'[1]

at si dissoluendo uel transferendo potest se Romanus pontifex a correptione Concilii eximere, iam sequitur ut supra eum Concilium non sit; aut igitur negandum est quod supra probauimus papam subesse Concilio, aut dissoluere inuitum Concilium negandum est papae. Nanque ut uera est prima conclusio, sic utique falsae sunt quae illam impedire possunt omnes conclusiones. Maneat igitur et secunda conclusio theologorum; quam, licet aliqui in certis admittant casibus, in certis excludant, ego illam ubique recipio, nec unquam aut ullo pacto dissolutionem Concilii papae concedo, nisi etiam concedat Concilium. Habeat papa quascunque causas, quascunque rationes, omnia cassa, omnia uana sunt nolente Concilio. Nanque si causae dissoluendi sunt, non papa de illis sed Concilium iudicabit, eiusque non papae iudicio stabit. Nanque si admittimus ex certis causis inuitum Concilium posse papam dissoluere, id est papam iudicem Concilii facere, quod esset primae conclusioni omnino contrarium.

Ex duobus quae supra proposui declaranda[a] alterum iam est absolutum, alterum e uestigio trutinabimus; probatum nanque est et Concilium supra Romanos esse pontifices et ab eis inuitum non posse dissolui. Videndum est modo an ita credere ex fide sit, quae res tertiam intuetur conclusionem. Fuerunt autem plurimi qui, licet conclusiones has duas faterentur ueras, dubitare tamen se dicerent an id esset fidei catholicae ueritas. Est igitur nobis

[a] declarandis αβ

---

[1] *Satur.* ii. 7, 11. Macrobius is here quoting from the *Sentential* of Publilius Syrus (though this line is not found in any of the manuscripts of Publilius).

second, which, while the first breezes are still blowing, we shall easily accomplish. For if it be true, as it is, that the pope is beneath the Council, in what way will the pope himself be able to dissolve, change, or transfer the Council against its will? In what fashion shall we say that he has a right over his superior, being himself inferior? How will the Council be able to correct the pope, if the Council, even against its will, can be dissolved by the pope? Suppose the pope be licentious, desirous of gold and money, eager for wars and disturbances, the enemy of the Church, and the bitter foe of Christianity, how will the Council be able to rebuke him, if he should have the ability to dissolve it? Of course, as soon as the Roman pontiff hears of discussion in the Council about reproving him, he will rush quickly to the remedy of dissolving it, since, as Macrobius nicely puts it: 'He who has more power than he should, wants more than he should'.[1] If by dissolving or translating it the Roman pontiff can rid himself of the Council's reproof, then it follows that the Council is not superior to him. So either we must deny what we previously approved, that the pope is beneath the Council, or we must deny the pope the right to dissolve the Council against its will. For just as the first resolution is true, so are all resolutions false which can obstruct it. So the second resolution of the theologians should hold good as well, which, though some admit it in certain cases and reject it in others, I accept everywhere, and I do not ever or in any way grant the pope the right of dissolving the Council, unless the Council should grant it too. Whatever grounds and reasons the pope has, all is futile and vain if the Council is unwilling. For if there are grounds for dissolving it, the Council not the pope will judge them, and its judgement, not the pope's, will be decisive. For once we admit that on certain grounds the pope can dissolve the Council against its will, that is making the pope judge of the Council, which would be quite opposed to the first resolution.

Of the two subjects which I previously suggested for discussion one has now been fully handled, the other we shall examine forthwith. It has been proved both that the Council is superior to the the Roman popes and that it cannot be dissolved by them against its will. We must now see whether this belief accords with the faith, which has a bearing on the third resolution. There were very many who though they admitted these two resolutions to be true, yet said they doubted whether that was the truth of the catholic

secunda pars confirmanda, uidendumque est an ex fide sit papam subesse Concilio; quo probato ex fide etiam esse patebit quia papa non potest inuitum Concilium dissoluere, quam consequentiam nemo ex disputantibus refutauit. Quaerendum ergo in primis est quid ipsa fides sit, ut sic facilius quid ad eam pertineat cognoscamus. Atque ut Tullianam praetereamus definitionem, qui ait fidem esse dictorum conuentorumque constantiam et ueritatem, atque ideo fidem appellari, quod fiat quod dictum est,[1] nihil enim de uero Deo sensit, fides (ut theologi definiunt) est firma adhaesio rebus creditis ex autoritate dicentis. Si igitur credimus (ut supra est dictum) Romanum papam subesse Concilio, certe aliqua nos autoritas ad id credendum impellit, sicque fides illius est qui hoc credit; sed non quaerimus utrum ex fide tantum, sed utrum ex fide catholica sit. Rursus ergo quaerendum est quid sit fides catholica. Estque 'catholica' Graecum uerbum, quod latine 'uniuersale' significat. Catholica igitur fides, id est uniuersalis fides; nec ideo dicitur uniuersalis, quod uniuersi eam habeant, sed quod uniuersi habere eam tenentur. Nec enim incarnatum Deum omnes credunt, credere tamen omnibus est debitum. Nec ideo desinit fides nostra esse catholica, licet quamplurimi aduersentur eidem. 'Quid enim', inquit Apostolus ad Romanos, 'si quidam illorum non crediderunt? Nunquid incredulitas ipsorum fidem Dei euacuabit? Absit! Est autem Deus uerax, omnis homo mendax.'[2] Credere igitur papam subesse Concilio non minus erit fidei catholicae, quamuis aliqui aliter sentiant.[3] Id enim credere omnes astringimur, siquidem ex codice Euangelico sumitur.[4] Nanque non solum quae in symbolo sunt annotata nos ligant, sed omnia quoque quae sacris continentur scripturis et maxime in Euangelio et Paulo, ex quibus nec unum apicem negare nobis permittitur.

At ea quae dicimus de superioritate Concilii generalis ex dictis Christi Iesu, nostri Redemptoris, atque ex magistri gentium[4] epistolis colliguntur. Ergo ad credendum omnes astringunt. Quod autem ista ex Euangelio recipiantur, testimonio est Constantiense Concilium, quod autoritatem suam super illis uerbis: 'Dic

[1] Cicero, *De Off.* i. 7, 23, where the etymology is advanced that *fides* derives from *fio*.

[2] Cf. Rom. 3: 3, 4.

[3] The doctrine of conciliar supremacy had been made a dogma by the Council of Basle in May 1439: see Introduction, p. xix.

[4] 2 Tim. 1: 11.

faith. So there is a second part to be confirmed, and we have to see whether it accords with the faith that the pope is beneath the Council. When this is proved, it will be obvious that it accords with the faith too that the pope cannot dissolve a Council against its will, a consequence none of the disputants rejected. Inquiry must in particular be made about what the actual faith is, so that we may learn more easily what belongs to it. We must indeed pass over the definition given by Cicero, who says faith is the steadfastness and truth of promises and agreements, and is for this reason called faith, that what has been promised becomes fact,[1] because Cicero has no understanding of the true God. Faith, as the theologians define it, is a firm adherence to things believed because of the authority of the speaker. If then we believe, as has previously been said, that the Roman pope is beneath the Council, truly some authority drives us to believe this, and thus it is the faith of him who believes it. Yet we are not inquiring whether it accords with faith only, but whether with the catholic faith. Again then we must inquire what is the catholic faith. 'Catholic' is a Greek word meaning 'universal' in Latin. The catholic faith then is the universal faith. It is not called universal because all people universally possess it, but because all people universally are bound to possess it. For it is not all people that believe in God incarnate, yet it is binding on all to believe this. Our faith too does not cease to be catholic though very many oppose it. 'For what,' says the Apostle in Romans, 'if some did not believe? Surely their unbelief shall not make the faith of God without effect? God forbid! God is true, though every man is a liar.'[2] Believing then that the pope is beneath the Council will not belong any the less to the catholic faith even if some think otherwise.[3] We are all bound to believe anything taken from the text of the Gospel. For not only things which are set down in the Creed are binding upon us, but all things too contained in holy Scripture and particularly in the Gospel and Paul, from which we are not permitted to reject even a single stroke.

What we say about the superiority of the general Council is gathered from the sayings of Christ Jesus, our Redeemer, and from the letters of the teacher of the Gentiles.[4] Therefore they oblige all to believe. As evidence that those things are received from the Gospel is the Council of Constance, which wishes its authority to be founded on the words: 'Tell [it] unto the Church',

ecclesiae', et: 'Vbi duo uel tres', et: 'Quaecunque ligaueritis', et huiusmodi[1] fundatam uult. Caeterum si haec ab Euangelio descendit ueritas, utique catholicae fidei ueritas est, omnesque sub poena damnationis aeterne obligatos facit. Plus etiam (si licet) dico. Omnia equidem quae generale Concilium definit sub simili poena tenemur credere, idque pulcherrime uidetur Augustinus astruere.[2] Ait enim quod Euangelio non crederet, nisi autoritas ecclesiae se commoueret. Ecclesiamque pro Concilio nominauit; nec enim ecclesia ubique diffusa, sed in concilio congregata de receptione Euangeliorum statuit. Eoque fit ut quemadmodum strinxit nos Concilium ad credulitatem illorum, sic et alia nobis credenda offerre possit. Vnde Martinus quintus,[a] dum adhuc Constantiae degeret, sacro approbante Concilio, literas sub plumbea bulla emisit,[3] quae articulos enumerat super quibus interrogari deberent, qui in suspicionem haeresis incidissent, inter quos etiam illum ponit, an credat sacrum generale Concilium potestatem habere immediate a Deo, eiusque ordinationes ab omnibus Christifidelibus esse recipiendas; quod si negaret, haereticus haberetur.[4] Quare cum sancta et magna Constantiensis Synodus ueritatem illam praedicauerit de superioritate Concilii generalis, quid obstat quo minus hanc esse ueritatem catholicae fidei fateamur? Ecclesia quippe catholica Constantiae congregata illam fidem recepit, id est sic credidit ex autoritate dicentis, scilicet Christi, et aliorum sanctorum. Ad hoc etiam perpulchre faciunt uerba Synodi Chalcedonensis in hunc modum: 'Non licet illum qui condemnatus est ab omni synodo episcopum nominare. Definitio omnibus placet; haec fides patrum est. Qui praeter ista sapit, haereticus est.' Et iterum regula est ut 'ab electa synodo non liceat appellare; haec est fides patrum. Qui praeter ista sapit, haereticus est.'[5] En amplissimum magnae et sanctissimae Synodi testimonium haereticum dicit qui aliter sapit quam Concilium sapiat. At haereticus nemo est, nisi qui catholicam fidem respuit, ergo catholica fides fuit credere quod ab electa synodo non liceat appellare. Verum quo pacto id fidei erat catholicae? Nempe quia sancta Synodus Euangelica et sacra scripta peruoluens

[a] quintus CDV; quartus α B

[1] Matt. 18: 17; 18: 20; 18: 18.

[2] Cf. p. 46, n. 9.

[3] *Inter Cunctas*, 22 Feb. 1418, Mansi, XXVII, col. 1196 ff.; H–L. VII. 511–28.

[4] The passage in question forms part of the questions to be put to persons suspected of Wycliffite or Hussite heresy and expressly refers not to *all* acts of the Council of Constance, but to those 'in fauorem fidei et ad salutem animarum'. For the important problem, how far the popes from Martin V onwards accepted Constance as an ecumenical council, see the long footnote by Leclercq in H–L. VII. 585–94, largely rehearsing the conclusions of Valois.

and: 'Where two or three', and: 'Whatsoever ye shall bind', and the like.[1] However, if this truth comes down from the Gospel, it is assuredly the truth of the catholic faith, and places all men under an obligation on pain of eternal damnation. I go, if possible, even further. We are bound to believe under a like penalty everything that the general Council determines, and Augustine seems to state this very neatly.[2] For he says he would not believe the Gospel unless the authority of the Church moved him, and he named the Church meaning the Council, for the Church, not when scattered everywhere but when met in council, decides about the receiving of the Gospels. Therefore it comes about that just as the Council binds us to believe them, similarly it can offer us other things to believe. Hence Martin V, whilst he was still staying at Constance, with the approval of the holy Council sent out a bull[3] which sets forth the articles on which those should be questioned who had fallen under the suspicion of heresy, among which he includes this one, whether [the man interrogated] believes the general Council has power directly from God, and whether its ordinances should be accepted by all the faithful of Christ; if he denied this, he should be considered a heretic.[4] So since the holy and great Synod of Constance preached that truth about the superiority of the general Council, what prevents us admitting that this is the truth of the catholic faith, seeing that the catholic Church, gathered at Constance, accepted that faith, that is, it held this belief in accordance with the authority of the speaker, namely Christ, and other saints? This receives fine support also from the words of the Council of Chalcedon that run like this: 'It is not lawful to name as a bishop a man condemned by the whole synod. This restriction has general approval. This is the faith of the Fathers. He who has understanding other than this is a heretic.' Again it is a rule that 'there is no appeal from an elected synod. This is the faith of the Fathers. He who has understanding other than this is a heretic.'[5] You see the very ample evidence of the great and most holy Synod in calling him a heretic who has views different from the views of the Council. Yet nobody is a heretic but he who rejects the catholic faith; therefore it was the catholic faith to believe that there is no appeal from an elected synod. But in what way was that part of the catholic faith? Why, because the holy Synod, perusing the Gospel and sacred scriptures, accepted

[5] Cf. H–L. II. 711.

eandem conclusionem ex uerbis Christi aliorumque sanctorum patrum recepit. At sicut illud Chalcedonensis Synodus ex sacra scriptura resumpsit, sic hoc quod disputamus Constantiense Concilium excerpsit. Et sicut illud catholicae fidei est, sic etiam istud; et praeter utrunque sentiens haereticus est.

Delirare illi praeterea mihi uidentur qui has ueritates fassi ueritates fidei non fatentur. Nanque si ueritates sunt, unde obsecro ueritates sunt? Nempe non ex grammatico, minusque ex logico aut astronomico, a physico quoque aliena haec sunt. Nec alius mihi quam theologus ueritatem fatebitur istam, cui necessitatem sacra scriptura imponit; qui nec Christo incredulus nec Apostolo rebellis erit. Est igitur ex fide catholica haec ueritas, eamque omnes amplecti debent, cui qui resistit pertinaciter haereticus, ut tertia conclusio asserit, censendus est. Nec durum alicui uideatur haereticum dici qui generalis Concilii potestati derogat, quae tam multis testimoniis autoritatibusque firmatur, cum etiam haereticus habeatur qui Romanae ecclesiae primatum aufert; qui unus est ex Graecorum damnatis erroribus.[1] Refert etiam noster Panormitanus Hieronymum dicentem quia qui aliter scripturam intelligit quam Spiritus Sancti sensus efflagitat, licet ab ecclesia non recesserit, tamen haereticus appellari potest.[2] Ex quo sequitur ut qui ex uerbis Christi, cum ait Petro: 'Dic ecclesiae', non intelligit per 'ecclesiam' generale Concilium, aliter intelligit quam Spiritus Sancti sensus exposcit, sicque possit haereticus notari. Quod autem sensus Spiritus Sancti alius sit quam ille putet Constantiensis declarat Synodus, quae per Spiritum Sanctum directa, uerba illa: 'Dic ecclesiae', de Concilio generali est interpretata.[3] Hisce igitur et aliis maioribus rationibus admodum multis uisae theologis sunt tres supradictae conclusiones uerae, et per ipsas etiam reliquas approbarunt, studio maxime ac diligentia fratris Nicolai Gallici[4] ex ordine Praedicatorum, uiri et ingenio et solicitudine ad modum praestantis, cui nimirum huiusce rei expeditionem attribuo; quem si quis (ut supra diximus) uideat, nequaquam tanti efficiat. Sed preciosiora nonnunquam sunt parui

[1] The other issues with the Greeks were: use of leavened bread; the doctrine of purgatory; and the additions in the Latin creed of the word 'filioque', the procession of the Holy Ghost; see Gill.

[2] Panormitanus (see above, p. 70, n. 8) f. xiiib refers to *Decr.* C. 24, q. 3, c. 27 (Friedberg, I. 998) quoting Jerome on Galatians 4: 25–26 (*P.L.* 26, col. 417).

[3] Cf. above, p. 54.

[4] Cf. above, p. 16.

the same resolution from the words of Christ and of other holy Fathers. Just as the Synod of Chalcedon adopted that from holy Scripture, even so did the Council of Constance extract that which we are discussing; and just as the former is part of the catholic faith, so is this latter too, and he who believes differently from either is a heretic.

Besides, those seem to me to be talking nonsense who admit these truths and do not admit that they are truths of the faith. For if they are truths, from what source, I ask, do they come? It is not, of course, from the grammarian, and still less from the logician and astronomer, and these things too do not belong to the natural scientist. No one will display that truth to me, except the theologian, on whom holy Scripture puts the obligation, who will be neither an unbeliever in Christ nor rebellious against his Apostle. This truth then comes from the catholic faith, and all must embrace it, and only one who stubbornly resists it is to be considered a heretic, as the third resolution maintains. Nor should it be thought hard that the name of 'heretic' is given to anyone who diminishes the power of the general Council, which is supported by so much evidence and authority, since even he is held to be a heretic who denies the primacy of the Roman Church, which is one of the errors of the Greeks that have been condemned.[1] For our Panormitanus recalls Jerome's saying that he who takes Scripture in a meaning other than that required by the sense of the Holy Spirit, though he has not left the Church, can be called a heretic.[2] From which it follows that whoever in the words of Christ to Peter: 'Tell [it] unto the Church', does not take 'the Church' in the sense of the general Council, understands this otherwise than the sense of the Holy Spirit requires, and thus could be branded as a heretic. That the sense of the Holy Spirit is other than he thinks is made plain by the Synod of Constance, which, under the direction of the Holy Spirit, has interpreted the words: 'Tell [it] unto the Church', as referring to the general Council.[3] For these then and other greater reasons, that are quite numerous, the three resolutions previously mentioned seemed true to theologians, and through them they approved the rest too, in particular through the zeal and diligence of Brother Nicolas, a French Dominican friar,[4] a person of quite unusual talent and carefulness, whom I credit with the completion of this matter, though anyone seeing him, as we have said already, would

corporis uascula, ut lapilli gemmaeque testantur, et ille[a] de quo apud Statium:

'Maior in exiguo regnabat corpore uirtus.'[1]

Satisfactum iam arbitror (quantum ingenioli mei suppetunt uires) his quae promisimus, nec aliquem modo existimo de tribus primis conclusionibus addubitare. Nunc ad historiam repedandum est, quaeque[b] post conclusiones theologorum intercesserint, referre est animus. Sunt enim plurima digna relatu, et quae posteris forsitan aliquando proderunt. Vt igitur res est a theologis comprobata, examen deputationum successit, quarum tres sine magno negotio cum theologis consenserunt. Quarta uero, cui 'de communibus'[2] nomen est, admissis tribus primis conclusionibus de reliquis titubare uidebatur. Obexque ibi maximus erat Georgius, Vicensis episcopus,[3] cui nouiter ex Maguntia redeunti, qui nec in disputatione capitulari fuerat, persuaderi non poterat absque noua uocatione Eugenium declarari posse haereticum; fauebatque sibi plurimum Amadeus, Lugdunensis archiepiscopus,[4] non quod ita sentiret, palam nanque in disputatione capitulari Eugenium haereticum atque relapsum praedicauerat, sed quia timebat depositionem papae nimium festinari. Erantque illa in deputatione complures, qui non modo nunc sed semper Eugenii partibus fauerant; haec deputatio, ne secundum ueterem Concilii consuetudinem a tribus deputationibus concluderetur, omnem deliberationem suspendit. Plus enim suspendendo quam denegando praestabat impedimenti, remque sic ad longum trahebat. Ea de causa missi sunt aliarum deputationum nuncii, quorum hortatu deputatio de communibus suspensionem super tribus conclusionibus reuocauit.

Iamque aderat (ut ueteribus placuit) Veneri sacratus dies,[5] in quo solet ex consuetudine generalis congregatio haberi fierique conclusio negotiorum extrema. Interim tamen Mediolanensis[6] et Panormitanus archipontifices, quique cum eis uel regis Aragonum uel ducis Mediolani cooratores erant, magnopere ad impediendum

[a] ille B; illo α [b] quaeque V; quaeue αBCD

---

[1] *Theb.* i. 417.

[2] See Introduction, pp. xvii–xviii for the deputations or committees into which the Council of Basle was divided.

[3] Cf. above, p. 12, n. 10.

[4] Cf. above, p. 10, n. 9.

[5] Friday, 24 Apr. 1439.

[6] Cf. above, p. 18, n. 2.

not judge him to be of such importance. Yet at times the vessels of smaller size have the greater value. This is shown by precious stones and gems, and by that man of whom Statius says 'greater virtue reigned in a small body'.[1]

I think I have now fulfilled my promises as far as is within the scope of my modest talent, and I do not consider that anyone still is in any doubt about the first three resolutions. Now we must turn back to narrative. I propose to tell what happened after the resolutions of the theologians. For there are many things worth telling and which perhaps will at some time benefit posterity. Well then, when the theologians had given their approval, the examining by the deputations followed, three of which without any great fuss agreed with the theologians. The fourth, which was entitled 'On general business',[2] admitted the first three resolutions but seemed shaky about the rest. The greatest obstacle there was Jorge, bishop of Vich.[3] Recently returned from Mainz, and not having been present at the discussion in the chapter-house, he could not be convinced that without a further summons Eugenius could be declared a heretic, and he was warmly supported by Amédée, archbishop of Lyons.[4] Not that this was [Amédée's] opinion, for at the discussion in the chapter-house he had openly declared Eugenius a heretic and a relapsed heretic, but he was afraid that the deposition of the pope was being rushed. There were in that deputation several who not only now but always had taken Eugenius's side. This deputation, to prevent a resolution being passed by three deputations according to the long-standing practice of the Council, held up the whole discussion. For it was more obstructive to hold things up than to reject them outright, and thus [the deputation] dragged out the affair to great length. For that reason spokesmen of the other deputations were sent, at whose request the deputation on general business cancelled its postponement over the three resolutions.

Now it was nearly the day sacred to Venus[5]—to use the expression of the ancients—on which in accordance with custom the general congregation was usually held and the final passing of business took place. However, in the meantime the archbishop of Milan,[6] and Panormitanus, with their colleagues, the other ambassadors of the king of Aragon and of the duke of Milan, armed themselves thoroughly to be obstructive, and encouraged all the members of their party to offer ready and resolute resistance; by

se armabant; omnesque suae partis homines hortabantur, ut praesenti fortique animo resisterent, aliosque qui pestem[1] in municipiis fugerant, missis nunciis ac literis reuocabant. Vocatus est cardinalis Terraconensis,[2] qui tunc Solodori moram trahebat. Vocatus est Lodouicus protonotarius de Roma,[3] qui Balnea[4] petierat non tantum ualetudinis causa, quantum ne contra mentem suam tueri Eugenium cogeretur; uocati sunt alii complures episcopi Aragonum, qui omnes pridie quam fieret congregatio remearant praeter cardinalem, qui post congregationem rediit. Vt igitur ad generalem deuentum est concionem,[5] e uestigio principum oratores affuerunt, et quasi facta conspiratione in unam sententiam consonarunt, conclusionem pro uiribus impedituri. Primus igitur Burgensis episcopus, inter omnes consilio et facundia praestans, differri conclusionem expectarique alios principum oratores ex Maguntia propediem redituros suadebat. Post eum Panormitanus archipraesul, uir summo ingenio et scientiae copia praeditus, primusque inter sui regis[6] oratores, huiusmodi fere orationem exorsus est.

Praeceptum se inquit a prophetis habere sine intermissione clamandi, qui aiunt: 'Clama, ne cesses, quasi tuba exalta uocem tuam'.[7] Quod si unquam in re quapiam fuit clamandum, haec praecipue quae in manibus esset clamore indigeret et uociferatione, cum ageretur de statu uniuersalis ecclesiae aut praeseruando aut penitus prosternendo; se uero in ea re tantum clamasse ut minime dubitaret impletum a se illud Dauidicum fore, quo ait: 'Laboraui clamans, raucae factae sunt fauces meae'.[8] Velle tamen et nunc et quoties opus ingrueret sine ulla requie clamitare, et maxime modo in negotio perdifficili et omnium maximo, in quo petebat sacrum Concilium sibi et aliis principum oratoribus benignas praebere aures; addens in omni re quae ab aliquo postulatur quatuor esse consyderanda quae nunc quoque rogabat patres ut animaduerterent, quis peteret, quid peteretur, cur peteretur, et qui demum effectus ex petito denegato uel concesso proueniret. Ad primum dicebat clarissimos reges et potentissimos principes cum suis praelatis esse petentes, regem Castellae, regem Aragonum, ducem

[1] Below, p. 192.

[2] Domingo Ram, cardinal 1426, administrator of Tarragona 1434, archbishop 1440, died 1445.

[3] Lodovico Pontano or di Roma, D.U.J. For Aeneas's admiration of him and for his death see below, pp. 100–2.

[4] Probably the Swiss town of that name, 41 miles from Basle, famous from Roman times for its hot mineral springs.

[5] Friday, 24 Apr. 1439: *Mon. Con.* III. 264; Haller, VI. 373.

[6] Alfonso V; for Panormitanus's role at Basle see Introduction, p. xxii.

[7] Isa. 58: 1.

[8] Ps. 69 (68): 3 (4).

sending messengers and letters they recalled others who in the small towns had fled from the plague.[1] There was summoned the cardinal of Tarragona,[2] who was dallying at Solothurn at that time. There was summoned Lodovico di Roma,[3] the protonotary, who had gone to Baden[4] not so much for the sake of his health as in case he should be compelled to support Eugenius against his better judgement. There were summoned too several other Aragonese bishops, who had all come back the day before the congregation took place, except the cardinal, who returned after the congregation. So when the general congregation assembled,[5] the ambassadors of the princes attended at the start, and, as though they had entered into a conspiracy, were all of the same voice, wanting to prevent with all their might the passing of the resolution. First of all then the bishop of Burgos, outstanding among all for his resourcefulness and eloquence, advised that the passing of the resolution be put off, and that they should wait for the other ambassadors of the princes, who were due back soon from Mainz. After him Panormitanus, the archbishop, a man gifted with the highest intellect and a store of knowledge, leader among his king's[6] ambassadors, began a speech which went very much like this.

He said that he had an order to cry aloud unceasingly from the prophets who say: 'Cry aloud, spare not, lift up thy voice like a trumpet.'[7] If in any matter crying aloud was needed, this one before them deserved crying aloud and shouting, since they were concerned with either the preservation or the complete abasement of the position of the universal Church. He himself had cried aloud so much in that matter that he had no doubt that he had fulfilled David's saying: 'I am weary of my crying: my throat is dried.'[8] Yet he wished both now and whenever the need was upon them to keep on crying aloud without any rest, and especially now in a business of very great difficulty and the most important of all, in which he asked the holy Council to listen sympathetically to himself and the other ambassadors of the princes; adding that in every matter when a request was made by anyone, four things needed to be considered, which now too he asked the Fathers to notice: who was asking, what was being asked, why it was being asked, and lastly what result followed from the request being refused or granted. With regard to the first he said that the most famous kings and most powerful princes along

Mediolani, eorundemque principum episcopos; meritaque tam regum praefatorum quam ducis Mediolani erga ecclesiam numerabat. Nec continere se potuit, cum de praelatis mentio incidit, quin aliquantisper calefieret, diceretque apud se fore maiorem praelatorum partem. Nanque si episcopi et abbates tunc computarentur, nemini dubium esse quin maior pars differri praesentem rem uellet. Cumque totius potestas Concilii in episcopis resideret, haud ferendum esse ut eis spretis, quod maiori parti inferiorum placeret, id concluderetur. Apostolis nanque et eorum successoribus, qui episcopi sunt, datas fuisse a Domino claues dicebat, triaque synodorum genera inueniri, episcopalem, prouincialem, et generalem, nullamque sine episcopis fieri synodum; indignumque sibi uideri morem hunc praesentis Concilii, ubi non qua quisque dignitate polleret, sed quam multas haberet secum uoces, pensitaretur.[1] Episcopos tamen iuxta famosam Clementis epistolam columnas esse et claues coeli;[2] inferiores uero cum eis non decisiuam sed consultiuam tantum habere uocem, futurumque hac uice scandalum, si sine episcopis res fidei terminum sumeret, in quo non solum episcopi sed etiam seculi principes admitti deberent.[3] Et cum ipsi nomine principum suorum cuperent ad examen praesentis rei admitti, uelleque maturius singula cognoscere, haud dignam esse rem quaerebatur se contemni.

Post multaque in hanc sententiam dicta ad secundam suae orationis partem transiuit, quid esset quod peteretur exponens. Non aurum aut argentum, non lapides preciosos, non prouincias aut regna, non rem denique factu difficilem, ocium tantum sacri Concilii exposci, ut quiescerent patres in processu papae inque conclusione rerum quae agerentur; neque id diu sed usque ad reditum oratorum ex Maguntia, quos breui uenturos certo sciret, rem paruam et sine magno rogatu concedendam, tum quia nihil periculi secum ferret, tum quod ipsis oratoribus principum Maguntiae existentibus iniuriosum esset non expectari, cum non suas ob commoditates sed reipublicae tantum causa et pro bono

[1] On the membership of the Council see Introduction, p. xviii. Panormitanus is drawing the familiar distinction between a numerical majority and a minority which might be *sanior*.

[2] Pseudo-Clement, *Ad Iacobum ep.* i, *P.L.* 130, col. 32C and *P.G.* 1, col. 478.

[3] Ambassadors of princes were not normally allowed to participate in conciliar discussions on matters of a doctrinal nature. See below, p. 108.

with their prelates were making the request, the king of Castile, the king of Aragon, the duke of Milan and the bishops of the same princes; and he recounted the benefits received by the Church from the kings mentioned and the duke of Milan. He could not refrain, when mention was made of the prelates, from becoming heated for a while, and saying that the majority of the prelates was with him. For if the bishops and abbots were counted, it was clear to all that the majority wanted the present matter postponed. Since the power of the whole Council rested in the bishops, it was intolerable that they should be scorned and that what pleased the majority of the lower orders should be passed. For he said that the Apostles and their successors, who were the bishops, were given the keys by the Lord. Three kinds of synods were found, episcopal, provincial, and general, and no synod was held without the bishops. The practice of the present Council seemed to him unfitting in which each person was assessed not by the weight of his rank, but by the number of votes at his disposal.[1] Yet according to the well-known letter of Clement the bishops were the pillars and keys of heaven;[2] along with them the lower orders had not the right to vote but only to be consulted, and there would be on this occasion a scandal if a matter of faith reached its conclusion without the bishops. In this not only the bishops but the secular princes too should be admitted.[3] Since they themselves wished in the name of their princes to be admitted to the examining of the present topic, and wanted longer time for learning the details, he complained that it was not fitting that they should be treated with contempt.

After saying a good deal in support of this point of view, he passed on to the second part of his speech, explaining what it was that was being asked. The request was not for gold or silver, not for precious stones, not for provinces or kingdoms, not finally for anything difficult to accomplish, but merely for the inactivity of the holy Council, that the fathers should do nothing in the process against the pope and about passing the resolution on the matter under discussion; and that not for any long time, but only until the return of the ambassadors from Mainz (these, he knew for certain, would arrive soon)—a small matter and one to be granted without much asking, both because in itself it involved no danger, and because it was unfair to the princes' ambassadors themselves now at Mainz if they did not wait for them, seeing that they were away

pacis abessent. Nec oblitum se fore quod ipsis abeuntibus nomine omnium supplicassent ne quid in eorum absentia in rebus Eugenium concernentibus innouaretur. Moxque tertiam orationis partem subiiciens, quamobrem dilatio peteretur, absoluit; quia non propter priuatam alicuius utilitatem sed propter commune bonum, non ad perturbandam sed ad rem melius examinandam, ut omnia cum pace et tranquillitate transirent, utque tanto esset res firmior et stabilior, quanto plurium foret consensu probatior. Sicque ad ultimum uenit, rogitans patres ut utranque partem sequuturos effectus mente conciperent, siue concederent, siue negarent quod posceretur. 'Etenim si negabitis', inquit, 'petitiunculam principum, omnes indignabuntur, omnes hanc repulsam molestissime ferent, dicent in re parua a uestro coetu se fore spretos, non obedient uobis, non recipient uestra mandata, frustra leges efficietis, nisi principes exequantur, inuanumque omnes editiones uestrae transibunt; tolerandumque hoc putarem, nisi etiam maiora timerem. Quid enim si illi Eugenio se coniungant, qui non solum uestra beneficia sed uitam quoque uobis eripere cupit? Heu quas strages, quasque occisiones oculi mentis intuentur meae! Vtinam uana sit opinio mea! At si facilem petitionibus principum assensum praestabitis, obligatos se uobis illi existimabunt, praecepta uestra recipient; quicquid ab eis petieritis, obtinebitur; aduersarium uestrum relinquent, illum uituperabunt, illum abominabuntur; uos extollent, uos magnificient, uobis se totos dabunt; sequeturque optimus ille, quem quaeritis, fructus reformationis et tranquillitatis ecclesiae.' Sicque omnibus ex capitibus rogabat supersederi. Tandem uero, nisi exaudirentur principum oratores, habere se inquit scriptam protestationem, quam legi coram iuberet.

Finitis Panormitani uerbis, Ludouicus, Romanus protonotarius, totius humani iuris gnarus, assurrexit, cuius tanta memoria fuit ut nulli ueterum cedere putaretur, siue Simonidem siue Theodecten, siue illum qui a Pyrrho missus ad senatum uenit Cyneam, siue Carneadem Seriphium, Metrodorum, Hortensium, siue qui horum ultimus fuit, Lucium Senecam,[1] de diuinitate memoriae

[1] A list of prominent Greeks and Romans celebrated for their eloquence or memory: Simonides (d. 468 B.C.), Theodectes (d. 334 B.C.), Cineas (*fl.* 280 B.C.), Carneades (d. 128 B.C.), Metrodorus a follower of Carneades, Hortensius (d. 50 B.C.), Seneca (d. A.D. 65).

not for their own benefit, but solely on government business and for the sake of peace. Nor did he forget that when they were leaving they had begged in the name of all that no new step be taken in matters concerning Eugenius during their absence. Passing on quickly to the third part of his speech, he stated why they wanted delay, that it was not for anyone's private advantage, but for the common good, not to confuse the issue but to give it a closer examination, so that everything should proceed in peace and quiet, and lead to a surer and more settled result because of the wider approval gained. In this way he reached the last point, asking the Fathers to imagine the effects in either case of their granting or rejecting the request. 'If you refuse to grant this small plea of the princes', he said, 'all will feel indignation and great annoyance at this rebuff, and will say that in a small affair they have been treated by your gathering with scorn. They will not obey you, they will not accept your orders, you will pass laws in vain unless the princes make them effective, and all your declarations will come to nothing. This I should think tolerable if I did not fear worse. For suppose they should join Eugenius, who wishes to take away not only your privileges but also your lives! Alas! What visions I have of slaughter and killing! I wish that this were mere imagination. If, however, you give a ready assent to the princes' requests they will consider themselves under an obligation to you, and will accept your orders. Whatever you ask from them you will get; they will abandon your enemy, will disparage and hate him, will praise and glorify you, will place themselves entirely at your service, and the result will be that excellent reward, which you want—the reformation and tranquillity of the Church.' So on all these grounds he asked for a postponement. Finally, if the ambassadors of the princes were not given a hearing, he said he had the text of a protest which he would order to be read out publicly.

When the words of Panormitanus had ended, Lodovico the Roman protonotary rose, a man versed in the whole range of human law, whose memory was so good that he was not considered as yielding precedence to any of the ancients, whether we honour for the god-like quality of his memory Simonides or Theodectes or Cineas, the envoy of Pyrrhus to the senate, or Carneades of Seriphus, or Metrodorus, or Hortensius, or (the latest of them) Lucius Seneca.[1] For he remembered everything he had ever read

commendemus. Erat enim memor omnium quae ipse unquam aut legisset aut audisset, nec oblitus erat eorum aliquid quae ipse uidisset. Nec ut caeteri iurisconsulti principia legum in disputando allegabat, sed quasi codicem legeret, sic textum memoriter referebat.[1] Vir non Roma tantum sed coelo dignus, et cui nemo mortalium comparandus uideretur, non admirationi sed stupori futurus omnibus populis, si (ut aequum uidebatur) aetatis tempora duplicasset. Sed inuidit fortuna Italiae, nec tantum scientiarum lumen crescere passa est. Immisit pestiferum morbum, uirumque uix trigesimum egressum aetatis annum abstulit.[2] Nec plus horis sex et triginta sinit egrotare, uisusque non transitus ille hominis sed furtum. Quis enim uirum adeo iuuenem, adeo robustum, tam breui morula expirare putasset? Sed fuit mors damnosior morte cuiusuis regis, quippe quod regi haeres succedit in regno, uiro autem adeo docto nullus superest in literis haeres. Sed dum cardinalari uir benemeritus manet, apud Cartusiam[3] tumulatur.

Is ergo laudatis Panormitani dictis, uenisse se pridie ex Balneis[4] dicebat, rem sibi nouam uideri quae tunc in medium deduceretur. Cupere in ea audire se alios, et audiri ab aliis, suique principis[5] nomine interesse discussioni. Eos qui Maguntiae fuissent expectandos esse, et ad rei examen admittendos, qui et praelati essent magni precii, et potentissimorum principum oratores; nec abhorrere se quod Panormitanus dixisset de uocibus inferiorum, nec a ueritate sibi alienum uideri solos episcopos decisiuam uocem habere in conciliis. Et licet aliqui suum Achillem[6] in hac disputatione arbitrarentur quod Actuum quintodecimo scribitur, se tamen nihil exinde moueri, nec momentum in eo facere, quamuis dicatur: 'Visum est Spiritui Sancto, et nobis',[7] ubi et Apostoli et seniores fuerunt; per quod uidetur alios cum Apostolis habuisse uocem decidentem. Dicebat enim non esse argumentum ex gestis Apostolorum sumendum, quorum exempla miranda essent magis quam imitanda, nec ibi patere quod Apostoli uocassent seniores ex debito, solumque narrari eos interfuisse, ex quo nihil inferretur;

[1] Lawyers in speaking and writing habitually cited authorities by the first words of the law or the section of the commentary.

[2] Below, p. 194.

[3] Situated in Klein-Basel across the Rhine.

[4] Cf. above, p. 96, n. 4.

[5] The king of Aragon.

[6] In Roman literature Achilles is the paragon of warriors.

[7] Acts 15: 28.

or heard, and had not forgotten anything he had himself seen. Unlike other legal experts he did not merely quote the first words of laws in debate but, as though he were reading the book, would recall the [whole] text from memory.[1] He was a man worthy not only of Rome but of heaven, one to whom no mortal seemed comparable. He was marked out to be an object not of admiration but of astonishment to all peoples if, as seemed fair, the length of his life had been doubled. Yet fortune had a grudge against Italy and did not permit further distinction to such an ornament of all learning. It sent upon him a pestilential disease, and carried him off when he had barely passed his thirtieth year.[2] It did not allow him to be ill for more than thirty-six hours, and it seemed to be not so much the passing as the theft of a human life. For who would have thought that a man so young and strong would breathe his last in so short a time? His death was a greater calamity than the death of any king, since in a kingdom an heir succeeds the king, but no heir in letters survives a man so learned. At a time when he was well qualified to be made a cardinal, he was buried in the Charterhouse.[3]

He then, after praising the words of Panormitanus, said he had come the previous day from Baden,[4] and that the matter which was then under discussion seemed to him to be a new one. He was anxious to hear others upon it and to be heard by others, and to take part in the discussion in the name of his prince.[5] They should wait for those who had been at Mainz, and admit them to the examination of this matter, as they were both prelates of high esteem and ambassadors of powerful princes. He did not reject what Panormitanus had said about the votes of the lower orders, and it did not seem remote from the truth that only bishops had the right to vote in councils. Though some considered as their Achilles[6] in this discussion what is written in Acts 15, he was not influenced by it, nor did he attach importance to it, though the words were: 'For it seemed good to the Holy Ghost and to us',[7] when there were both Apostles and elders; from which it was clear that others along with Apostles possessed a vote. For he said that they should not take as evidence the actions of the Apostles, whose example called for wonder rather than imitation, and that it was not obvious there that the Apostles had summoned the elders because they were obliged to do this. All that the account said was that they were taking part, from which nothing

uideri autem sibi inferiores in Basiliensi Concilio tantum ex gratia fore ad decidendum admissos cum episcopis, quia potuissent episcopi autoritatem suam aliis communicare, in his tamen quae gratiae forent uno contradicente, nihil fieri posse. Adducebatque uirum maxime autoritatis, Concensem episcopum,[1] in testem, qui nullam incorporationem inferioris populi aequo animo sustinuisset, ideoque nec alios inferiores nec seipsum, qui nondum esset praelatus, uocem habere decidentem in Concilio. Quare cum esset res magna quae tractaretur et praelati tunc contradicerent, rogabat Concilium ut oratores principum ex Maguntia expectando faceret de necessitate uirtutem. Fuit eius oratio eo molestior, quo plures erant suis contacti uerbis, maximeque in eo sibi est adclamatum, quod dixerat Apostolos non esse imitandos; id enim quasi blasphemiam omnes impugnarunt. Mirari tamen hic aliquis possit quod uir tantus et tanta scientia fretus non plura dixerit, nec adduxerit meliora; sed est ignoscendum memoriae hominis, qui nec libens nec laetus in hac re loquebatur, quique nihil magis cuperet quam quod peteret non impetrare.[2]

Cathaniensis[3] exinde ac Bosianus[4] episcopi, qui et ipsi regii oratores erant,[5] paucis habitis uerbis in sententiam Panormitani declinarunt. Vicem autem magni et potentissimi ducis Mediolani solus tunc archiepiscopus Mediolanensis gerebat, uir et literis et consilio promptus. Albigaunensis enim episcopus et Franciscus Barbauaria nondum ex Maguntia repedauerant. Is ergo, ut est Hieronymianus et illius facundissimi doctoris imitator, adductis magistri sui plerisque autoritatibus, supersederi magnopere suadebat, omnem praecipitationem inimicam consilio omnemque festinantiam detestatus; maximeque uultu et gestibus rem praesentem abominari se ostendebat. Tandemque nisi exaudiretur, et suo et prouincialium suorum nomine protestari in aduersum se dixit. Mox secuti sunt Dertusensis[6] et Gerundensis[7] episcopi, ac Segobricensis electus.[8] Abbas montis Aragonum[9] et nonnulli alii eiusdem dignitatis homines[10] Panormitani sententiam comprobauerunt. Parmensis[11] uero episcopus ad Mediolanensem accessit. Eleemosynarius[12] quoque qui postea Basiliensem fugiens pestem

[1] Above, p. 10, n. 10.

[2] The implication is that Lodovico was expressing what he believed to be Aragonese policy rather than his own opinion.

[3] Giovanni Pesci, a Franciscan; translated to the titular see of Philippopolis in 1447.

[4] Giuliano de Tallada, O.P., died 1445. Bosa is in Sardinia.

[5] Of the king of Aragon.

[6] Otón de Moncada, promoted cardinal by Felix V in 1440, died 1473.

[7] Bernardo de Pau, died 1457.

[8] Gisberto Pardo.

[9] An Augustinian house at Huesca.

[10] Cf. *Mon. Con.* III. 265.

[11] Delfino Angeli de Pergula, translated to Modena 1463, died 1465.

was to be inferred. It seemed to him that only as a favour were the lower orders at the Council of Basle admitted to make decisions along with the bishops, because the bishops had been able to share their authority with others, but where it was a matter of favours, if one person spoke against them, nothing could be done. He brought forward as a witness a man of the greatest authority, the bishop of Cuenca,[1] who had not readily tolerated any incorporation of the lower people, and for that reason, he said, neither the lower orders nor he himself, who was not yet a prelate, had a deciding voice in the Council. Since the matter under discussion was an important one and the prelates were at present in opposition, he asked the Council by waiting for the ambassadors of the princes from Mainz to make a virtue of necessity. His speech was the more irksome as several were shocked by his words, and there was loud disapproval of his saying that the Apostles were not to be imitated, for all attacked that as though it were blasphemy. One might feel surprise that a man of such worth, with such learning at his command, did not say more or make a better contribution. Yet one must pardon the memory of a man who did not speak willingly or gladly on this matter, and who was only anxious not to be granted his request.[2]

Next the bishops of Catania[3] and Bosa,[4] who were royal ambassadors[5] themselves, said a few words, and inclined to the view of Panormitanus. Moreover the great and puissant duke of Milan was represented at that time by the archbishop of Milan alone, a man of ready learning and counsel, for the bishop of Albenga and Francis Barbavara had not yet returned from Mainz. He then, being a follower of Jerome and an imitator of that eloquent doctor, produced many authoritative passages from his master and was strongly in favour of a postponement, denouncing all hurry and all haste as inimical to counsel; and by his looks and gestures he made very clear his dislike of the present matter. Finally he spoke of making a protest to the contrary in his own name and in that of the members of his province, unless his words were regarded. Soon his lead was followed by the bishops of Tortosa[6] and Gerona,[7] and the elect of Segorbe.[8] The abbot of Montearagón[9] and some others of the same rank[10] approved of the view of Panormitanus. The bishop of Parma[11] joined the archbishop of Milan. The almoner[12] too, who afterwards, to avoid the plague at Basle, took

[12] Bernard Serra; cf. above, p. 20, n. 5.

Zofingen confugit, ibique in oppido Suitzerorum intra Lucernam et Basileam obiit,[1] uir in omni hominum numero recipiendus, et Martinus de Vera,[2] doctus et constans, ambo regis Aragonum oratores, collegae sui Panormitani dictis se confirmarunt. Tunc alii Aragonenses et Cathalani fere omnes, quisque pro se loqui uolentes (facta praefatiuncula) regis se sui uotis annuere dicebant. Videbaturque res astutia praeordinata, ut uel sic tempus redimerent[3] conclusionemque differrent.

Vbi autem complures sunt auditi, et Cathalanorum longus ordo finiuit, Ludouicus, cardinalis Arelatensis, uir omnium constantissimus, et ad gubernationem generalium conciliorum natus, oratorum omnium qui locuti fuerant uerba resumpsit. Versusque primitus ad Castellanos, plurima de ipsorum erga sacrum Concilium deuotione disseruit, similiterque de Cathalanis ac Lombardis.[4] Post rem ingressus, 'Negotium', inquit, 'istud, reuerendissimi patres, nouum non est nec hodie aut pridie inchoatum. Iam plures hebdomadae sunt quibus conclusiones huiusmodi inter magistros disputatae, et Maguntiam aliasque in orbis partes destinatae sunt. Post in capitulo huius ecclesiae iterum sex continuis diebus uiritim et mature discussae, ex hinc non sine magno interuallo in sacris deputationibus approbatae.[5] Et sicut ueritas non quaerit angulos, omnia palam et publice gesta sunt. Nec potest aliquis ignorantiam praetendere; nec praelati aut principes contempti sunt. Omnes qui aderant Basileae uocauimus, omnes ut interessent sumus hortati. Et quoniam de magno illo et potentissimo rege Castellae mentio facta est, quis est qui nesciat ipsius regis oratores interfuisse, Burgensem ac Ebronensem episcopos, uiros tum prudentissimos, tum scientiae atque eloquentiae copia praestantissimos? Tu quoque, Panormitane, qui regis Aragonum serenissimi uicem geris, bis in capitulo affuisti, bis egregie atque acerrime disputasti, bis quod sentires in hac re aperuisti. Quid est quod amplius expectari desyderas? Ex territorio ducis Mediolani archiepiscopus Mediolanensis affuit, qui, licet orator non sit, qualis tamen quantusque praelatus habeatur non ignoratis.' Cumque ita dixisset, commotus aliquantisper archiepiscopus:

[1] Below, p. 195. [2] A canonist. The name is so spelt by Hugolin and Segovia.
[3] Cf. Eph. 5:16.
[4] That is, subjects respectively of Alfonso V and the duke of Milan.
[5] Cf. Introduction, p. xvii.

refuge at Zofingen and died in that Swiss town between Lucerne and Basle,[1] a man worthy of admission to every circle of men, and the learned and steadfast Martin de Vera,[2] both ambassadors of the king of Aragon, gained courage from the words of their colleague Panormitanus. Then other Aragonese and almost all the Catalans, each wishing to speak for himself, after a short preface said they agreed with the wishes of their king. The matter seemed to have been cleverly pre-arranged so that even in this way they should redeem the time[3] and put off the passing of the resolution.

When, however, several had been heard, and the long succession of Catalans came to an end, Louis, cardinal of Arles, the most steadfast person of all, with an innate ability to direct general councils, took up the words of all the ambassadors who had spoken. Turning at the start to the Castilians, he said a good deal about their devotion to the holy Council, and likewise about the Catalans and Lombards.[4] Then coming to the matter, 'Most reverend fathers', he said, 'this business is not new, nor put in hand today or yesterday. For several weeks now resolutions of this kind have been discussed among the masters and have been sent to Mainz and other parts of the world. Afterwards, in the chapter-house of this church on six days running they were again discussed one by one and at some length, and thereafter, not without a long interval, they were approved in the holy deputations.[5] As truth does not seek the crannies, everything has been done openly and publicly. No man can make ignorance his excuse, nor have the prelates or princes been held in contempt. We summoned all who were present at Basle, and encouraged them all to take part. Since mention has been made of the great and puissant king of Castile, everyone is aware that the ambassadors of the king himself took part, namely the bishops of Burgos and Hebron, persons both of great wisdom and pre-eminent for the extent of their knowledge and eloquence. You too, Panormitanus, who represent his Serene Highness the king of Aragon, were twice present in the chapter-house, and twice effectively and shrewdly intervened in the debate, twice revealed your views on this matter. What is your reason for wanting further delay? From the territory of the duke of Milan there has been present the archbishop of Milan and, though he is not an ambassador, you all know what a great prelate he is considered.' At these words the archbishop was roused momentarily

'Haud melius', inquit, 'praesidentis locum tu tenes, Arelatensis, quam ego oratoris ducalis.' Pluribusque lacessere eum uerbis pergebat. At cardinalis, ut est patientissimus iniuriarum, nullaque prorsus contentione prouocabilis: 'Hoc est', ait, 'quod mox uolebam. Nanque si orator est archiepiscopus, nulla omnino superest suo duci querela, qui oratorem suum in rerum discussione habuit. Taceo de reliquis principibus, quoniam nec ipsi conqueruntur. Rex tamen Christianissimus Francorum Lugdunensem inter disputantes, uirum maximum et grauissimum, habuit; caeteri uero principes cur hac in re debeant expectari non uideo, qui Concilium ad ea quae sunt fidei congregatum scientes, nequaquam absurdum putant dubia fidei in Concilio declarari, ad quae si uoluissent adesse, iam dudum uenissent.

'Quanquam nec illud est omnino uerum quod Panormitanus dicit, seculares principes admitti debere ad rem fidei, si ad decidendum intelligit. Et licet Martianus imperator dicat: "Nos autem ad fidem confirmandam uolumus interesse Synodo",[1] quae uerba totiens Panormitanus in medium adducit, subiungendum tamen est quod ille subiungit ut uerborum perfectus habeatur intellectus, ait enim: "Nos ad fidem confirmandam, non ad potentiam exercendam uolumus Synodo interesse", ut eo uel maxime dicto metum adimeret iis qui eius praesentiam uiolaturam Concilium[2] arbitrabantur. Quod si nostri hodie principes facerent, iam utique res esset quam quaerimus expedita. At moderni aliqui principes, cum nequeant per se minari, qui absunt, per oratores inferunt metum; sed uiderit de his Deus. Res autem praesens cur tanta discussione indigeat (ut aliqui uolunt) non intelligo. Etenim si rite memini, saepe hoc idem quod conclusiones sonant Panormitanus hoc in loco asseruit, saepe etiam Ludouicus. Si quis eorum contradicere pergat, eueniet ei quod Didymo, "quo nemo" ut Quintilianus ait[3] "plura scripsit". Qui "cum historiae cuidam tanquam uanae repugnaret, oblatus est liber eius, qui eam continebat"; sic et hi duo uiri, quamuis doctissimi atque acutissimi sint, suis tamen scriptis poterunt confutari.[4] Sunt praeterea epistolae

[1] Isidore, *Conc. Chalc. P.L.* 84, col. 162.
[2] At Chalcedon, A.D. 451.
[3] *Inst. Or.* i. 8, 20.
[4] Cf. Introduction, p. xxii, and above, p. 70, n. 8.

and said, 'You are no better at holding the position of president, cardinal of Arles, than I at being the duke's ambassador', and he went on to attack him at great length. The cardinal, however, being most tolerant of affronts, and completely above provocation by any dispute, replied 'That is just what I was wanting. For if the archbishop *is* an ambassador, his duke has no ground left to him at all for complaint, seeing that he has had an ambassador present at the discussion. I make no mention of the other princes, since they do not themselves complain. Now the most Christian king of the French had [the archbishop of] Lyons, an important and influential person, present among the disputants. As for the rest of the princes I do not see why we should wait for them. Aware that the Council has been called to discuss matters of faith, they do not think it at all absurd that doubtful points of faith are made clear in the Council, and if they had wished to be present for them, they would have come long ago.

'Yet what Panormitanus states is not entirely true, that secular princes should be admitted for matters of faith, if he means for giving their votes. Although the Emperor Marcian says: "We wish to attend the Synod to maintain the faith"[1]—words which Panormitanus so often quotes in public—yet one must add what he adds to reach a complete understanding of the words, namely: "We wish to attend the Synod to maintain the faith, not for the exercise of power", and this is said above all to quieten the fears of those who thought his presence would harm the Council.[2] If our princes would do this today, then the purpose of our search would be completely achieved. Yet some modern princes, since they are unable through their absence to utter threats in person, inspire fear through their ambassadors—but may God attend to such actions! Why the present matter needs so much discussion, as some hold [that it does], I do not understand. For if my memory is correct, the apparent meaning of the resolutions is what Panormitanus has often maintained in this place and Lodovico too. If either of them should persist in contradicting, the same thing will happen to him as happened to Didymus, the most voluminous of writers, according to Quintilian.[3] For when Didymus objected to a certain story as being false he was confronted with his own book containing it. Even so these two men also, though of the greatest learning and perception, can still be refuted by their own writings.[4] There are as well the synodal

Synodales et decreta huius Concilii huiusmodi referta conclusionibus. Quid igitur est, quod quaeat difficultari? Quid est quod impugnari possit? An nunc ponemus in dubium quod est toties praedicatum, asseueratum, decretum?

'Verum aiunt oratores abesse principum, qui episcopi sunt, et quorum praesentia autoritatem maiorem redderet. Sed absunt non solum qui Maguntiam perrexerunt, immo et alii pene infiniti per orbem ubique dispersi, quos si expectare omnes oporteat, nihil unquam poterit expediri. Vocati sunt omnes ad Concilium, uenire potuerunt si uolebant; qui assunt iis est commissa potestas, hique tractare negotia debent. At si dicitur hos reipublicae causa abfuisse, nempe nos eos non misimus, potiusque inuito quam uolente Concilio illuc[1] iuerunt; quod si etiam a Concilio missi fuissent, non tamen ita ligatae manus essent nostrae, quin reformare possemus ecclesiam, aliter uero nihil unquam in Concilio fieri posset. Cum enim semper sint per Concilium missi aliqui, semper essent expectandi aliqui; ideoque aut nihil agere oporteret aut nullos extra destinare praelatos. Quod autem praelati et praesertim episcopi contemnantur, id est a uero remotissimum. Nanque ut cernitis, ii primi sedent, primi loquuntur, primique ad omnia uocitantur. Et si scite ueraciterque loquantur, facile inferiorum omnium ad se trahunt sententiam. Nec forsan absonum fuerit dicere nullam unquam fuisse Synodum, quae magis quam ista potestatem episcoporum ampliauerit. Etenim quid hodie erant episcopi, nisi umbrae quaedam? Quid plus eis restabat quam baculus et mitra? Nunquid pastores sine ouibus dici poterant, cum nihil in subditos statuere possent? Nempe cum esset in ecclesia primitiua episcoporum summa potestas, hodie ad id uenerant ut solo habitu et redditibus superarent presbyteros. At nos eos in statu reposuimus pristino, nos beneficiorum collationem ad eos reduximus, nos eis confirmationem electionum restituimus, nos causas subditorum eisdem reddidimus audiendas, nos eos qui iam non erant episcopi fecimus episcopos.[2] Quid est quod episcopi ab hac se Synodo contemni asserant? Quidue unquam molestum

[1] To Mainz; cf. above, p. 12.

[2] References to the limitation of papal power made by the earlier reform legislation at Basle.

letters and decrees of this very Council crammed with resolutions of this same kind. What is it then that can be made into a difficulty? What is it that can be opposed? Can it be that we shall now call in question what has been so often proclaimed, asserted and decreed?

'But they say the ambassadors of the princes are absent, who are bishops, and whose presence would give an increase of authority. But there are absent not only those who have gone to Mainz, but others almost beyond number, scattered everywhere through the world; if we had to wait for all of them, nothing could ever be settled. All have been summoned to the Council, and could have come if they wanted. Those who are present are entrusted with power, and these must handle the business. But if it is being said that these have been absent on government business, we certainly did not send them, and it was rather against the wish of the Council than by it that they went there.[1] Even if they had been sent by the Council, our hands would not have been so tied that we could not reform the Church, otherwise nothing could ever be done at the Council. For since there have always been some sent out by the Council, there would always be some for whom there had to be waiting, and therefore inevitably either nothing would be done or no prelates would be sent away. That prelates and especially bishops are being held in contempt is very far from the truth. For as you all perceive they are the first to take their seats, the first to speak, and the first to be summoned to everything. If they speak with skill and truth, they easily sway in their direction the view of all the lower orders. Perhaps it will not be out of keeping to say that there has never been a Synod which increased the power of the bishops more than this one. For what were the bishops today, but mere shadows? What else was left to them but a staff and a mitre? Could they be called shepherds without sheep, since they could decide nothing regarding their subjects? Though in the early Church the power of the bishops had been supreme, today they had come to such a pass that only in their dress and revenues did they surpass priests. We, however, set them back in their previous position, we restored to them the collation of benefices, we returned to them the confirmation of elections, we gave back to them the hearing of their subjects' pleas, we made bishops those of them who were not bishops.[2] Why then do the bishops claim that they are being held in

eis aut iniuriosum fecimus? At dicit Panormitanus quia cum sint plurimi episcopi secum, pauci uero contra, non est a multitudine inferiorum habenda conclusio. Meminerit tamen ipse Panormitanus quoniam non est nouus hic procedendi modus; ordinem procedendi ipsum sibi Concilium ab initio dedit, nec unquam postea immutauit. Tibique hoc alias, Panormitane, placuit, cum multitudo te sequeretur; nunc quia non sequitur, displicet. Sed non sunt decreta conciliorum ut uoluntates hominum mutabilia. Scias praeterea quia illi ipsi episcopi qui uerbo tecum sentiunt, mente non sentiunt, nec illud in angulis dicunt, quod publice dicunt. Timent quod eis domi dixisti displicere se regi, nisi tuam sequerentur sententiam. Timent uim principis, spoliarique temporalibus formidant, neque (ut in conciliis fas est) liberam habent uocem. Quamquam et ipsi si ueri essent episcopi, si ueri animarum pastores fuissent, animam ponere pro suis ouibus non dubitarent, nec largiri ecclesiae matri suae suum sanguinem uererentur. Sed est hodie (proh dolor!) rarus in terris praelatus qui temporalia spiritualibus[1] non praeponat; quorum amore detenti principibus magis quam Deo placere student, et Deum quidem in angulis, principes uero in publico confitentur, de quibus in Euangelio Dominus: "Omnis ergo", inquit, "qui confitebitur me coram hominibus, confitebor et ego eum coram Patre meo, qui in coelis est",[2] et econuerso non confitebitur illum coram Patre suo Dominus qui ueritus est coram hominibus Dominum confiteri. Nec etiam id uerum est, quod ait Panormitanus, plures episcopos secum fore. Sunt enim plures hic procuratores episcoporum, quos ipse non dinumerat, quia secum non sapiunt.

'Neque in Concilio (ut ipse ait) dignitas patrum sed ratio spectanda est; nec aliquid est quod in singulis rebus spectari magis quam ueritatem conueniat. Nec ego cuiusuis episcopi mendacium, quamuis ditissimi, ueritati praeponam pauperis presbyteri. Nec dedignari episcopus debet, si aliquando ignarus et rudis sequacem non habeat multitudinem, et si uox inopis sacerdotis, docti tamen et acuti, suae praeponitur; habitat nanque saepius in sordido palliolo quam in pictis uestibus sapientia. Nec, uos rogo, episcopi,

[1] That is, the revenue of his see before spiritual matters.
[2] Matt. 10: 32.

contempt by this Synod? What have we ever done that was harmful or unjust to them? Panormitanus says that, since there are very many bishops with him and few against, a resolution must not be passed by a crowd of lower clergy. Yet Panormitanus himself should remember that this method of procedure is not new; the Council at the beginning imposed on itself this method of procedure, and did not change it afterwards. You liked this on other occasions, Panormitanus, when the crowd followed you, but now you do not like it because it does not follow you. The decrees of councils, unlike the wills of men, are not changeable. You should realize too that those very bishops who agree with you in word do not agree in intention, and they do not say in private what they say in public. They are afraid because you told them they were incurring the displeasure of their king at home unless they followed your view. They are afraid of the violent reaction of their prince, and terrified of being deprived of their temporalities. They have no free vote as they should have at councils. Yet they themselves, were they true bishops, had they been true shepherds of souls, would not hesitate to lay down their lives for their sheep, nor would they fear to bestow their blood upon the Church, their mother. But today, sad to say, rare upon the earth is the prelate who does not set *temporalia* before *spiritualia*.[1] Occupied by their love of the former, they are eager to please princes rather than God, and in fact they confess God in private and the princes in public. Of such the Lord says in the Gospel: "Whosoever therefore shall confess me before men, him will I confess also before my Father, which is in heaven",[2] and conversely the Lord will not confess before his Father him who has feared to confess the Lord before men. Nor is it true as Panormitanus says that the majority of bishops is with him. For there are several bishops' proctors here, whom he does not count, because they do not share his views.

'In the Council it is not the rank of the Fathers, as he says, but their reasoning that deserves attention, and nothing in the details should properly receive greater attention than the truth. Nor will I prefer the falsehood of any bishop, however wealthy, to the truth of a poor priest. No bishop should be scornful if, ignorant at any time and unskilled, he has not got a crowd at his back, and if the view of some priest, penniless yet learned and clever, is preferred to his own, for wisdom more often dwells within a mean and slender cloak than in embroidered garments. Do not, I beg you,

tantopere inferiores contemnite. Primus enim qui pro Christo obiit, quique uiam aliis ad martyrium aperuit, non episcopus sed tantum leuita fuit.[1] Quod uero Ludouicus et ipse Panormitanus astruunt de uocibus episcoporum, id nescio unde habeant, neque id usquam solutum inuenio; ipsi sicubi repererunt, me ut commoneant, obsecro. Atque (ut ueterum Conciliorum referamus exempla) in omnibus illis interfuisse minores cum episcopis inueniemus. Et licet Ludouicus Apostolorum exempla nobis interdixerit, ego illorum potissime in Actibus sisto. Quid enim est quod magis sequi nos deceat quam ecclesiae primitiuae doctrinam atque consuetudinem? Dicitur ergo in Actibus Apostolorum quintodecimo: "Visum est Spiritui Sancto et nobis",[2] quod uerbum "nobis" ad eos quippe refertur, qui fuerant antea nominati, Apostolos et seniores. Nobis ergo Apostolis scilicet et senioribus. Neque hoc uerbum, "uisum est", consultationem illic sed decisionem significat. Vnde apparet alios quam episcopos habuisse uocem decidentem. Alibi quoque in eisdem Actibus, cum essent Apostoli magnum aliquid tractaturi, nequaquam ausi sunt per se definire, sed uocauerunt duodecim multitudinem.[3] Dicit tamen Ludouicus non patere illic quod Apostoli ex necessitate uocassent alios. At ego ad eum dico: "Vnde tu scis quia non ex necessitate uocarunt?" Sed cum utrunque incertum sit, nihil prohibet imitari Apostolos, quia cum omnia "ad nostram doctrinam scripta"[4] sint, apparet uoluisse Apostolos nobis exemplum dare ut in rebus arduis inferiores admitteremus; ideoque in Conciliis postea celebratis reperimus interfuisse presbyteros. Atque in Concilio Niceno, quod est omnium famosissimum, Athanasius tunc tantummodo presbyter fuit, ipseque fere solus argumentationes disturbauit Arrianas; fuerunt et alii presbyteri. Et cum scribitur de trecentis et duodeuiginti episcopis, non tamen negatur de inferioribus, quos ideo puto obmissos, quod essent pene innumerabiles, fitque (ut scitis) denominatio plerunque a magis dignis. In Synodo uero Chalcedonensi, quae et ipsa ex quatuor prioribus censetur, sexcenti sacerdotes fuisse dicuntur; quae appellatio tam presbyteris est quam episcopis communis. In aliis uero Conciliis saepe omisso nomine episcoporum sacerdotumque sola fit mentio patrum, qui idem significant quod in Actibus

[1] Stephen; Acts 7. [2] Acts 15: 28. [3] Cf. Acts 21: 22. [4] Rom. 15: 4.

ye bishops, despise so greatly the lower orders. For he who first died for Christ, and who opened the way to martyrdom for others, was not a bishop but only a deacon.[1] As for what Lodovico and Panormitanus himself maintain about the votes of the bishops, I do not know whence they derive it nor do I find it anywhere laid down. I beg them to tell me if they have found it anywhere. To go back to the precedents of the ancient Councils, in all of them we shall find that the lower orders took part along with the bishops. Though Lodovico forbade us to use the Apostles as examples, I take my stand chiefly on their Acts. For what is there that we ought to follow rather than the teaching and custom of the early Church? Now in Acts of the Apostles 15 it says: "It seemed good to the Holy Ghost and to us",[2] and this expression "to us" refers actually to those who had been previously named, the Apostles and elders. "To us" then means to the Apostles and elders. This expression too, "It seemed good", does not point to consultation there but decision. From which it is clear that others besides bishops had the right to vote. Elsewhere also in the same Acts, when the Apostles were going to handle a major problem, the twelve on no account ventured to settle it on their own, but called together the multitude.[3] Yet Lodovico says that it is not obvious from this that the Apostles called others together of necessity. But I say to him, "How do you know that they did not call them together of necessity?" Since it is uncertain either way, nothing prevents our imitating the Apostles, for since all things are "written for our learning",[4] it is clear that the Apostles wished to set us an example, that in difficult questions we should admit the lower orders. Therefore in the Councils held later we find that priests took part. At the Council of Nicaea, the most famous of all, Athanasius was then only a priest, and almost single-handed confounded the Arian theses. Other priests were there too. When mention is made of 318 bishops, there is no denial of [the presence of] the lower orders, who, I suppose, are passed over because they were almost beyond count and, as you realize, for the most part it is the persons of higher rank who receive mention. At the Synod of Chalcedon, which is reckoned as one of the four major ones, there are said to have been 600 *sacerdotes*, a description belonging to priests as much as to bishops. At the other Councils there is often no reference to bishops and *sacerdotes* as such, but mention only of "Fathers", which means the same as "elders" in Acts of

Apostolorum seniores. Habemus etiam *Ecclesiasticae* testimonium *Historiae*, Romae aduersus Nouationes, qui se superbo nomine "Catharos" appellabant, Concilium fuisse congregatum sexaginta episcoporum et totidem sacerdotum et aliorum diaconorum.[1] Cumque Paulus, Antiochenus episcopus, qui fuit Galieno imperante, Christum communis naturae hominem praedicaret, Concilium aduersus eum in Antiochia conuenit. Ad quod uenerunt episcopi ex Caesaria Capadociae, ex Ponto, ex Asia, ex Hierosolymis, et multi alii episcopi et presbyteri ac diaconi. Et dicitur propter hoc pluries celebratum esse Concilium ultimumque in eodem loco Aureliano imperante, ubi Paulus damnatus est ab omnibus quae sub coelo sunt ecclesiis Christi, nec ullus magis elusit atque confudit Paulum quam Malchion, presbyter Antiochenus, qui oratoriam artem in Antiochia docuerat.[2]

'Sed quid ego in hac re diutius inmoror? Concilii Toletani quinti[3] hec sunt uerba: "Post ingressum omnium episcoporum atque consessum uocentur deinde presbyteri, quos causa probauerit introire, nullus se inter eos ingerat diaconorum, post hos ingrediantur diaconi probabiles, quos ordo poposcerit interesse; et corona facta de sedibus episcoporum, presbyteri a tergo eorum resideant, quos tamen sessuros secum metropolitanus elegerit, qui utique et cum eo iudicare uel definire aliquid possunt." Nec aliquis concilium illud prouinciale tantum asseueret fuisse. Ipsum enim Concilium de se loquens: "Quoniam", inquit, "generale Concilium agimus"; fueruntque ibi episcopi sexaginta ex Hispaniis Galliisque. Sed mouent forsitan Panormitanum et Ludouicum Chalcedonensis Concilii uerba, ubi episcopi de Constantinopolitana quadam congregatione, quae Flauianum et quosdam alios deposuerat, dicunt: "Nam milites magis eos deposuerunt quam nos, quia quicquid egimus, terrore compulsi fecimus; ipsi primi subscripserunt clerici";[4] quare clamant: "Synodus episcoporum est, non clericorum." Quae uerba, si sane intelligantur, inferiores nequaquam excludunt. Duo nanque ibi quaeruntur episcopi, alterum quod in Constantinopoli non erat libertas, alterum quod primi subscripserant clerici; quorum utrumque mali exempli fuit. Quare nimirum, si illud negatur fuisse concilium, at dicitur

[1] Eusebius, *Hist. Eccles.* vi, *P.G.* 20, col. 615 (A.D. 251).

[2] Eusebius in vii is also the source of this reference to Paul of Samosata, patriarch of Antioch, and his condemnation in A.D. 269: *P.G.* 20, cols. 706–19.

[3] In fact the fourth Council, A.D. 633. This was regarded as constituting an authoritative directive on conciliar procedure; cf. H–L. I. 93.

[4] H–L. II. 673. The stormy antecedents of the Council of Chalcedon (A.D. 451) are discussed ibid. II. 423–639. Flavian was archbishop or patriarch of

the Apostles. We have also the evidence of the *Ecclesiastical History* that there was summoned at Rome against the Novatians, who called themselves by the proud name of "the Pure", a Council of sixty bishops and the same number of priests and some deacons.[1] When Paul, bishop of Antioch, who lived when Gallienus was emperor, preached that Christ was a man of common human nature, a Council met to oppose him at Antioch. To this there came bishops from Caesarea in Cappadocia, from Pontus, Asia, and Jerusalem, and many other bishops and priests and deacons. It is said that the Council met on account of this several times, and lastly in the same place in the reign of Aurelian, when Paul was condemned by all the churches of Christ which are under heaven, and no one did more to parry and confound Paul than Malchion, a priest of Antioch, who had taught the art of rhetoric in Antioch.[2]

'Yet why do I dwell longer on this matter? These are the words of the fifth Council at Toledo:[3] "After the entry of all the bishops and their sitting down, next let the priests be summoned, whose entry the business justifies, and let none of the deacons take his place among them, and after these let deacons worthy of approval enter, whose presence their order has requested; and when a ring is made of the seats of the bishops, let priests sit behind them, but only those that the metropolitan has chosen to sit with himself, who in particular are capable of judging or settling anything along with him." No one would maintain that this was only a provincial council. For the Council's own words about itself are: "Since we are holding a general Council", and there were present sixty bishops from Spain and Gaul. Perhaps Panormitanus and Lodovico are stirred by the words spoken at the Council of Chalcedon, when the bishops say about a gathering at Constantinople which had put down Flavian and certain others: "The soldiers put them down rather than we, because our actions were carried out under the compulsion of terror, and the clergy added their names first."[4] So they exclaim: "A synod is [a meeting] of bishops and not of clergy." These words, if understood correctly, do not exclude the lower orders at all. For the bishops complain there of two things, first that there was no freedom at Constantinople, secondly that the clergy had added their names first, each of which set a bad precedent. So doubtless if it be said

Constantinople until his deposition in 449 at a synod at Ephesus, not at that held in Constantinople in 448 as suggested by Aeneas.

synodus episcoporum non clericorum, nempe hoc non excludit omnes inferiores, sed eos tantum qui solius primae tonsurae sunt clerici, quos etiam nos excludimus, seruantes quod Toletanum praecepit Concilium, duodecim uiros ad examen incorporandorum statuentes;[1] praeterea non dicitur ibi quod illa sint uerba Concilii sed episcoporum, quod illic aliqui, ut hic Panormitanus et Ludouicus, loquebantur.

'Sed ne per deuia longius peregrinemur, habemus ad tutelam inferiorum apertissima testimonia. Maximus ille quidem et omnium theologorum Aristoteles, Augustinus episcopus, super literam Matthaei Euangelistae, dum ait Christum dixisse Petro: "Tibi dabo claues regni coelorum", "Nimirum", ait, "per illa uerba iudiciariam potestatem datam esse non solum Petro, sed aliis etiam apostolis et toti ecclesiae in episcopis et presbyteris."[2] Si ergo iudiciariam potestatem habent presbyteri in ecclesia, quid eos prohibet in conciliis uocem habere terminatiuam? Augustino autem etiam consonat elegantissimus doctor Hieronymus, cuius super epistola Pauli ad Titum haec sunt uerba: "Antequam diaboli instinctu studia in religione fierent, et diceretur in populis: 'Ego sum Pauli, et ego Apollo, ego autem Cephae',[3] communi presbyterorum concilio ecclesiae gubernabantur; idem[a] enim presbyter qui et episcopus. Vnde episcopi cognoscere debent se magis consuetudine quam dispensatione Dominicae ueritatis presbyteris esse maiores, et in commune debere ecclesiam regere."[4] Alibi autem idem Hieronymus in ea quae est ad Damasum de gradibus ecclesiasticis epistola, in episcopis Dominum, in presbyteris Apostolos repraesentari dicit.[5] Atque ubi rationem Hieronymus nullam afferret, uidete quid homini tribuam; ipsa autoritate me frangeret.[6] Sed hoc etiam ex Paulo colligimus ad Titum, qui tantam inter episcopos et presbyteros conuenientiam facit ut ipsos presbyteros appellet episcopos.[7] Ex quibus lucide constat non esse presbyteros a conuentu episcoporum ac determinatione rerum arcendos. Et si (prout Hieronymo placet) episcopi sunt sola consuetudine praelati presbyteris, utique fieri potest ut consuetudinem contraria tollat consuetudo. At si presbyteri debent ecclesiam dei cum episcopis in communi regere, satis notum est quod ad eos quoque decidere res spectat ecclesiae dubias; unde

[a] idem enim *Jerome*; id enim α

---

[1] For the Twelve, elected (four by each deputation) each month, see *Mon. Con.* II. 261, and Introduction, above, p. xvii. [2] Cf. p. 66, n. 2.

[3] Cf. 1 Cor. 3: 4. [4] *Comment. ad Tit.* 1: 5, *P.L.* 26, col. 598.

[5] Pseudo-Jerome, *Ep.* xii, seu Opusculum de septem ordinibus ecclesiae, *P.L.* 30, col. 163. [6] Cf. Cicero, *Tusc. Disp.* i. 21, 49. [7] Tit. 1: 5–7.

that this was no council, but a synod of bishops and not of clergy, this does not of course exclude all the lower orders, but only those who are clergy merely of the first tonsure, whom we too exclude, keeping to the instructions of the Council of Toledo and appointing twelve men to consider those to be incorporated.[1] Besides it is not said there that those are the words of the Council, but of the bishops, because some spoke there as Panormitanus and Lodovico did here.

'Yet not to roam further afield, we have, for the protection of the lower orders, the clearest testimony. For that greatest of all theologians and their Aristotle, Bishop Augustine, on a passage of the Evangelist Matthew, relating that Christ said to Peter: "I will give unto thee the keys of the kingdom of heaven", comments: "Assuredly by those words judiciary power was given not only to Peter, but to the other Apostles too, and to the whole Church in the bishops and priests."[2] If then the priests have judiciary power in the Church what prevents them having a decisive voice in councils? In agreement with Augustine is the brilliant doctor Jerome, whose words on the Epistle of Paul to Titus are these: "Before by the implanting of the devil partisanship existed in religion, and among the peoples was said: 'I am of Paul, and I of Apollos, I too of Cephas',[3] churches were governed by a common council of priests. Now a priest was the same as a bishop. So the bishops must realize that it is rather by custom than by the ordering of the Lord's truth that they are greater than priests, and are bound to rule the Church for the common weal."[4] Elsewhere too the same Jerome in the letter to Damasus about rank in the Church says that in bishops there is a representation of the Lord and in priests of the Apostles.[5] Seeing that Jerome brought forward no reasoning, see what weight I give to him. He would crush me by his authority alone.[6] The same thing we infer from Paul's [Epistle] to Titus, who makes bishops and priests correspond so much, that he calls the very priests bishops.[7] From this it is plainly established that priests should not be excluded from the meeting of bishops and the settlement of business. If, as Jerome has it, bishops are merely by custom preferred to priests, it is definitely possible that an opposite custom may remove this custom. If priests are bound to govern the Church of God in common with the bishops, it is well enough known that it concerns them too to settle matters of the Church

est apostoli Pauli clarissimum testimonium. Nanque si (ut ipse ad Ephesios inquit)[1] Christus instituit apostolos, prophetas, pastores, et doctores ad opus ministerii, in aedificationem ecclesiae, usquequo sibi occurramus, hac ratione, ut non sit fluctuatio in diuersitate doctrinae, quis dubitat aliis quoque cum apostolis ecclesiae gubernationem esse concessam? Taceant, obsecro, hi nostri satrapae, nec plus sapere uelint quam oporteat sapere. Constantiensis Concilii recens memoria extat, ubi et plurimi ex nobis fuerunt, et ego etiam, qui nondum cardinalis nec episcopus sed tantum doctor eram, interfui; uidique sine difficultate inferiores cum episcopis ad decisionem rerum admitti arduarum.[2] Nec pudere nos debet maximam illam et sanctissimam Synodum[3] imitari, quae et Pisanum Concilium, et illud amplissimum Lateranense[4] secuta fuit, in quibus iudicasse cum episcopis presbyteros non est ambiguum. Praeterea si abbates (ut in omnibus conciliis obseruatum uidemus) uocem habent decisiuam, qui tamen non fuerunt a Christo instituti, cur non presbyteri, quorum ordinem Christus per discipulos instituit? Ex hinc si soli episcopi uocem habeant, id demum fiet, quod nationi placebit Italicae, quae sola nationes alias in numero episcoporum aut superat aut aequat.[5]

'Vtcunque est, opus Dei hac uice fuisse autumor ut inferiores ad decidendum reciperentur. Reuelauit enim ea nunc Dominus paruulis, quae sapientibus abscondit. En horum inferiorum zelum, constantiam, rectitudinem, magnanimitatem uidetis. Vbi nunc Concilium, si soli episcopi, solique cardinales uocem habuissent? Vbi nunc conciliorum autoritas? Vbi fides catholica? Vbi decreta? Vbi reformatio? Nempe omnia libidini Eugenii ac temeritati iam diu commissa fuissent, uictorque nephandissimi propositi sui ille fuisset, nisi quos modo spernitis inferiores sibi restitissent. Hi sunt qui priuationem ab Eugenio factam contempserunt; hi sunt qui minas, qui spolia, qui persecutiones ipsius flocci[a] fecerunt; hi sunt qui capti, qui incarcerati, qui fustibus caesi pro ueritate Concilii non timuerunt; hi sunt qui, licet dati praedae per Eugenium forent, remanere tamen in sacro Concilio uoluerunt;

[a] flecti αBCD; fleri V *in marg.*

---

[1] Eph. 4: 11.

[2] For Aleman's early career and presence at Constance see Pérouse, pp. 1–50.

[3] That is, the Council of Constance.

[4] The council of 1412–1413: H-L. VII. 88, 93–96.

[5] According to the 'Provinciale' in Eubel, *Hierarchia Catholica*, II, the number of bishoprics in the fifteenth century was: Italy (including the islands but excluding the see of Rome itself and the cardinal bishoprics) 294; elsewhere in Europe (France, Spain, England, Scotland, Ireland, Scandinavia, Prussia,

that are doubtful; whence comes the Apostle Paul's clear testimony. For if, as he himself says in Ephesians,[1] Christ instituted apostles, prophets, pastors, and teachers for the work of the ministry, for the edifying of the Church until we meet him, with this purpose that there should not be tossing to and fro with diversity of teaching, who doubts that to others too along with the Apostles was granted the governing of the Church? Let these satraps of ours, I beg, keep silence, and not wish to know more than they ought to know. The recollection of the Council of Constance is fresh, where most of us were present, and I too took part, who was not yet a cardinal or a bishop, but only a doctor, and I saw that the lower orders without any trouble were admitted with the bishops to settle difficult affairs.[2] We should not be ashamed either to imitate that great and holy Synod[3] which followed the Council of Pisa and the comprehensive one at the Lateran,[4] in which there is no doubt that the priests gave judgement with the bishops. Besides if, as we find is the practice at all councils, the abbots have a right to vote, though not instituted by Christ, why should not priests, whose order Christ did institute through his disciples? Then if only bishops should have a vote, the outcome will be favourable to the Italian nation, which by itself either surpasses or equals other nations in the number of bishops.[5]

'However that is, I maintain that God's hand has now brought it about that the lower orders should be admitted to make decisions. For the Lord has now revealed to babes what he hides from the wise. Behold you see the zeal, steadfastness, rectitude, and nobility of these lower orders. Where now would the Council be if only bishops and only cardinals had had a vote? Where now would be the authority of councils? Where would be the catholic faith, its decrees, and its reformation? I suppose everything would long have been entrusted to the pleasure and rashness of Eugenius, and he would have succeeded in his foul purpose, had not those lower orders whom now you despise withstood him. These are they who scorned the deprivation inflicted by Eugenius; these are they who made light of his threats, plunderings, and persecutions; these are they who when arrested, put in prison, beaten with rods for the truth of the Council, felt no fear. These are they who, though

Germany, Poland, and Hungary) 374. It was partly to avoid the consequences of this that voting at Constance was by 'nations'.

hi sunt qui famem, qui bellum, qui pestem[1] saeuissimam non formidarunt. Quid tandem est quod hi homines pro iustitia sacri Concilii non aequo animo tulerunt? Audire potuistis medias inter tribulationes inferiores istos alta uoce dicentes: "Et si omnes deuastatori ecclesiae obediunt Eugenio, et discedunt unusquisque a ueritate fidei et sanctorum patrum institutionibus, et consentiunt mandatis Eugenii, nos quidem et fratres nostri constantes erimus, et pro ueritate fidei et sanctorum patrum traditionibus mori non dubitamus"; quod et uere fecerunt. Nec enim aut minis territi aut spoliis mutati sunt; nec eos metus nec spes ulla a sancto proposito diuertit. Quod utrum cardinales effecerint (ut meo de ordine loquar) uos cernite. Episcopi autem, quos solos Panormitanus habere uult uocem, uidetis quam pauci nobiscum sunt; et illi ipsi qui praesentes adsunt, haudquaquam uirtute ualent irrumpere iniquitatem, extimescunt terrenam faciem potentis, et ponunt scandalum in agilitate sua. Audistis hodie uota praelatorum, audistis quod omnes uoluntati regis dixerunt se acquiescere, nullus Dei. At ipsi inferiores ipsi sunt qui iustitiam, qui ueritatem, qui denique ipsum Deum prae oculis habuerunt; habendaque his gratia est, quod tales se Dei ecclesiae praestiterunt.

'Sed quid ego inferiorum defendo causam? Ipsos quoque episcopos uolunt nonnulli a nostro consortio excludere, qui sine possessione ecclesiae sunt, quos uocitant titulares,[2] nescientes miseri quia, dum istos repellunt, ipsum quoque Petrum et alios Apostolos damnant, quos diu sine magna plebe fuisse constat. Nec unquam aut tota Roma Petro aut tota Hierosolyma Iacobo paruit; quo tempore non plebes, sed plebeculae in Christo credebant. Etenim per immortalem Deum, quid est quod ab iis episcopis requiramus? Non habent populum, at hoc sine culpa ipsorum est. Non habent redditus, sed non pecunia facit episcopum; et "beati" sunt (ut inquit Dominus) "pauperes spiritu".[3] Nec diuites prima ecclesia uidit episcopos, nec suis expulsos sedibus Dionysium Mediolanensem, Eusebium Vercellensem, aut Hilarium Pictauiensem uetera Concilia respuissent, quamuis et pauperes et exules et sine plebe manerent.[4] At si uerum fateri uolumus, aptiores pauperes quam abundantes iudicio sunt faciendo, quod horum

[1] For the plague at Basle see below, p. 190.

[2] Those, that is, with a see 'in partibus infidelium', ordained largely in order to act as suffragans to bishops absent from their dioceses.

[3] Matt. 5: 3.

[4] Three fourth-century bishops and saints, who suffered persecution at the hands of Arian rulers.

treated as prey by Eugenius, wished to remain in the holy Council, these are they who dreaded neither hunger, nor war, nor the direst plague.[1] What finally is there which these men did not endure readily for the probity of the holy Council? You could hear those lower orders amid the tribulations saying in a loud voice, "Even if all obey Eugenius, the destroyer of the Church, and they forsake, every one of them, the truth of the faith and the institutions of the holy Fathers, and agree to the orders of Eugenius, yet we and our brothers will be steadfast, and for the truth of the faith and the traditions of the holy Fathers we do not hesitate to die", as in fact they did. They were neither terrified by threats nor warped by plunder, nor did any fear or any hope turn them aside from their sacred purpose. Notice now whether the cardinals acted thus, to speak of my own order. The bishops, whom Panormitanus wishes alone to have a vote, you see how few there are with us. Those that are present here are quite unable by their virtue to demolish iniquity, they are in fear of their ruler's earthly countenance, and cause a scandal by their instability. You have heard today the depositions of the prelates, you have heard them say that they all give assent to the king's will, none to God's. Yet the lower orders are the very persons who kept before their eyes probity, truth, and finally God himself, and thanks should be paid to them for showing themselves as such to the Church of God.

'Yet why do I defend the cause of the lower orders? Some wish to bar from our company those very bishops also who lack the possession of a church, the so-called "titulars",[2] not knowing, poor wretches, that in rejecting them they condemn Peter too and the other Apostles, who, as is well known, were long without a large community. At no time did the whole of Rome obey Peter, or the whole of Jerusalem, James; at that time not dioceses but only small congregations believed in Christ. For by immortal God, what is it that we expect from those bishops? They have no flock, but that is through no fault of theirs. They have no revenues, but it is not money that makes a bishop, and, as the Lord says, "blessed are the poor in spirit".[3] Neither did the early Church behold rich bishops, nor when they had been thrust from their sees would the early Councils have rejected Dionysius of Milan, Eusebius of Vercelli, or Hilary of Poitiers, though they remained both poor and exiles and without a community.[4] If we are willing to admit the truth, poor men are more suited than the affluent to the giving

diuitiae timorem, illorum paupertas libertatem afferunt. Nec illi pauperes tyrannidem timent, ut nostri diuites, qui umbris, delitiis, ocio ac desidiae dediti, negare potius Christum uolunt quam assuetis carere uoluptatibus; quosque non populus, sed redditus facit episcopos, quique amantes diuitias omnes pauperes existimant infelices. Sed nihil melius interuenire sapienti potest (ut Cicero ait) quam fortuna exigua.[1] Vnde et ueritas in Euangelio dicit quia "facilius est camelum per foramen acus transire quam diuitem intrare regnum coelorum".[2]

'Sed, ut ad Panormitani uerba maturius explicanda descendam, omittere statui duo illa, quae in prima orationis fronte proposuit, qui petant et cur petant.[3] Fatemur nanque maximos esse, potentes, et de ecclesia (ut ipse asseruit) optime meritos; nec dubitamus syncera eos intentione ad petendum moueri. Vtrum autem paruum[a] sit quod petitur, et an effectus quos ipse dixit resultare debeant, inquirendum est. Supersessio (inquit) petitur, dilatio ad paucos dies poscitur, res leuis, res modica, res concessu admissioneque facilis. Attendat hic tamen Panormitanus, aliquantisper dilationem in re fidei postulat. Iam declaratae sunt ueritates, iam discussae, iam ordinatae; paululum si supersedeatur, longissima fiet mora, saepe enim momenti transitus anni est transitus. Multa hic nobis exempla suppetunt. Hannibal apud Cannas uictoria potitus, si e uestigio urbem petisset, omnium iudicio coepisset Romam; quia tamen in crastinum distulit, restituto Romanis uigore exclusus est, et audire meruit: "Vincere scis, Hannibal, uti uictoria nescis".[4] Galli quoque Senones, Roma capta Capitolium obsidentes, dum tenacius aurum exposcunt, moramque in paciscendo trahunt, a Camillo inuasi turpiter expelluntur.[5] Sed quid ego uetera euoluo, cum nostra nobis exempla sufficiant? Scitis uos ipsi, quoties hae uobis dilationes nocuerint, quotiesque paucorum mora dierum longissimum traxit spatium, qui iam octauum annum in dilationibus

[a] paruum CDV (cf. 'rem paruam' p. 98); parum αB

[1] *De Fin.* i. 19, 63. (quoting Epicurus) [2] Matt. 19: 24; Mark 10: 24.
[3] Above, pp. 96 ff. [4] Livy, xxii. 51. 4. [5] Cf. Livy, v. 43–49.

of judgements, because the wealth of the latter brings fear and the poverty of the former freedom. Those who are poor do not fear the rule of a tyrant, as our rich do, who, given up to semblances, pleasures, ease, and sloth, are willing to deny Christ rather than be without their customary enjoyments. These not the people but their revenues make bishops, and they in love with their riches consider all the poor unhappy. Yet, as Cicero says, nothing better can happen to a sage than a slender fortune.[1] Wherefore the Truth also says in the Gospel that "it is easier for a camel to go through the eye of a needle than for a rich man to enter into the kingdom of heaven".[2]

'Yet to come down to the words of Panormitanus that need a longer discussion, I have decided to omit the two questions which he placed in the forefront of his speech, namely who are asking, and why they are asking.[3] We admit that they are great, powerful, and have deserved very well of the Church, as he claimed. We do not doubt that their motives for asking are honourable. We must, however, inquire whether it is little that is asked, and whether those consequences which he mentioned are bound to follow. He says they ask for a postponement and request an adjournment for a few days—a slight and ordinary thing, one easy to grant and permit. However let Panormitanus consider this. He is requesting an adjournment in a matter of faith to last for a time. The truths have already been made clear, discussed, and promulgated. If there should be even a short postponement, the delay will be very long. For often the passing of a moment is the passing of a year. There are many examples of this available to us. Hannibal after winning his victory at Cannae, if immediately he had marched on the city, would in the judgement of all have captured Rome. Yet because he put it off till the morrow, he was kept out when the strength of the Romans had been restored, and he deserved the criticism, "You can win victories, Hannibal, but you cannot make use of them".[4] The Senones too from Gaul, when they had taken Rome and were besieging the Capitol, whilst they persisted too long in demanding gold and in prolonging the delay by bargaining, were attacked by Camillus and shamefully driven out.[5] Yet why do I unfold ancient examples when our own are enough for us? You yourselves know how often these adjournments have harmed you, and how often the delay of a few days has prolonged a very lengthy interval, you who now are spending

agitis, semper dilationes ex dilationibus uidistis emergere. Illud tamen consyderare cupio Panormitanum quia, conclusione hac die turbata, uix scio an unquam amplius haberi queat; multa possunt oriri impedimenta, multa nasci obstacula. Nec ipse Panormitanus dicit, hac mora obtenta, uelle se cum collegis huiusmodi conclusionibus adhaerere, mandatumque ad id habere se negat. Et quod est magis ponderandum, oratores ex Maguntia reuersuros talia posse afferre dicit propter quae conclusiones huiusmodi omittantur, quasi aliquid esse possit ueritate praestantius, et propter quod a ueritate discedamus. Quae res manifestissime ostendit quia non moram ad examinandas melius, sed ad impugnandas ualidius conclusiones exposcunt. Nec circa effectus, quos ipse commemorat re negata siue concessa emersuros, cum Panormitano conuenio. Nec uideo cur principes hanc dilationem tantopere quaerant. Nullae super hac petitione sunt literae principum. Nemo est qui nouiter ab his ueniat, nec ipsorum interest, nisi ut res fidei terminetur.

'Illa autem perniciosa conclusio est, quam Panormitanus retulit, et ab illis religiosissimis principibus minime expectanda, dum ait si ipsis complaceamus, eos nobiscum futuros; si minus ad Eugenium defecturos, nobisque omnino rebellaturos.[1] Mirum uerbum, mira conclusio, et prorsus indigna, quae a tanto uiro dici debuerit! Constantiensis decreta Concilii sunt, omnes homines, cuiuscunque status aut conditionis existant, statutis et ordinationibus generalium alligari Conciliorum. Ad id Panormitani uerba non sonant; non enim Concilio principes, sed principibus uult obedire Concilium. Heu tempora, heu mores,[2] heu reuerendissimi patres, quo iam miseriarum sumus redacti! Quo pacto unquam obtinebimus papam, Christi uicarium et alium in terris Christum, Christianorum subesse Concilio, si Concilium ipsum mundanis debet obedire principibus? At ne, obsecro, talia de principibus illis sperate, ne credite illos matrem suam suppeditaturos ecclesiam. Non putate eos tantopere a ueritate alienari ut iustitiam supprimi uelint. Conclusiones de quibus agitur uerissimae sunt, probatissimae sunt, sanctissimae sunt. Si eas respuant principes, non nobis,

[1] Above, p. 100.

[2] Cf. Cicero, *In Catilinam*, i. 1. 2.

the eighth year in adjournments, and have seen adjournments ever arising out of adjournments. Yet I would like Panormitanus to consider this, that if the passing of the resolution is prevented today, I hardly think it can ever in the future be effected. Many hindrances can arise, many obstacles come into being. Panormitanus himself does not say that, if this delay is conceded, he is willing with his colleagues to abide by such resolutions, and he denies that he has instructions to that effect. A point that needs further pondering—he says that the ambassadors when they return from Mainz may bring messages with them that would cause resolutions of this kind to be abandoned, as if anything can be more excellent than the truth, and make us depart from the truth. This shows very plainly that they want delay not for a better examination of the resolutions but for a more vigorous attack upon them. I am not in agreement either with Panormitanus about the consequences which he states will follow if the request is denied or granted. Nor do I see why the princes want this adjournment so much. There is no letter from the princes about this proposal. There is no one who has recently come from them, nor have they any concern except that a matter of faith should be settled.

'Panormitanus, however, mentioned what is a harmful conclusion, and least of all to be expected from those most religious princes, when he said that if we pleased them, they would be with us; if not, they would go over to Eugenius in complete revolt against us.[1] This is a strange utterance, a strange conclusion, and one completely unworthy of being spoken by so great a man. The decrees of the Council of Constance are that all men, whatever their position and condition may be, are bound by the general Council's decisions and ordinances. The words of Panormitanus are not in accord with this. For he does not want the princes to obey the Council, but the Council the princes. Alas for the times! Alas for manners![2] Alas most reverend fathers, to what a wretched state we are now reduced! In what way shall we ever maintain that the pope, the vicar of Christ, and another Christ upon earth, is beneath a council of Christians, if the Council itself must obey worldly princes? Yet, I beg you, do not expect such things of those princes, do not believe that they will trample on their mother, the Church. Do not imagine that they are so greatly estranged from the truth that they wish justice to be suppressed. The resolutions under discussion are true, approved, holy. If the

sed sacrae scripturae et ipsi Christo se opponent; quod nec uos credere, nec Panormitanum dicere decebat. Durissima enim (ut pace tua dicam, Panormitane), uerba fudisti, nec aliud uisus es quaerere quam patribus istis timorem incutere. Nisi enim principibus pareamus, pericula et discrimina admodum magna commemoras. Vos autem, reuerendissimi patres, eos nequaquam timebitis qui occidunt corpus, animam autem non possunt occidere.[1] Nec ueritatem relinquetis, etiam si oporteat uestrum sanguinem ecclesiae elargiri. Nec enim remissiores aut tepidiores pro matre nostra ecclesia, et fide catholica esse nos decet quam martyres illos Dei sanctissimos, qui ecclesiam in suo sanguine fundarunt. Etenim cur nobis mori pro Christo sit graue, qui tam diram tamque acerbam pro nobis sustulit mortem? Qui cum esset immortalis atque impassibilis Deus, mortalem induit hominem, et, ut nos redimeret, crucis subire tormentum non formidauit. Ponite ante oculos uestros ipsum Apostolorum principem Petrum, ponite Paulum, Andream, Iacobum, Bartholomaeum; et, ne de solis loquamur episcopis, quid Stephanus, quid Laurentius, quid Sebastianus, quid Fabianus? Alii cruci affixi, alii truncati capite, alii lapidibus obruti, alii exusti carbonibus, alii aliis tormentis et durissimis cruciatibus excarnificati pro Christo obierunt. Hos, obsecro, imitemur, nec, si uolumus episcopi esse, et in honore succedere, martyrium formidemus. Heu nostrum effoeminatum animum, heu pusillanimum populum! Illi olim mortem contemnendo gentilem mundum et idolorum cultorem Christianum fecerunt; nos ignauia nostra et nimia uitae cupiditate Christianam religionem ex orbe toto ad angulum redegimus,[2] et timeo ne hoc quod restat modicum pusillanimitate amittamus, si principibus (ut Panormitano placet) defensionem et regimen ecclesiae committamus.

'Sed estote uos uiri fortes ac robusti in hoc tribulationum tempore, nec mortem pro ecclesia repudiate, quam pro Roma Curtius, pro Thebis Menoeceus, pro Athenis Codrus libenti et cupido animo tulit.[3] Excitare enim nos non solum martyres possunt sed ipsi etiam gentiles ut mortis timorem abiiciamus. Quid Theramenes ille Atheniensis, quam laeto animo, quamque ridenti uultu uenenum bibit? Quid Socrates, sanctissimus ille

[1] Cf. Matt. 10: 28. [2] A reference to the advance of the Ottoman Turks.
[3] Cicero, *Tusc. Disp.* i. 48, 116.

princes should reject them, they will set themselves in opposition not to us, but to holy Scripture and Christ himself. That was neither a proper thing for you to believe nor for Panormitanus to say. With all respect, Panormitanus, the words you have uttered are very hard, and you seem to have had no other object than inspiring fear in these Fathers. For you talk about the seriousness of the perils and dangers if we do not obey the princes. Yet you, most reverend Fathers, will not fear at all those that kill the body but cannot kill the soul.[1] You will not abandon the truth even if your blood has to be bestowed on the Church. For we ought to be no slacker or more lukewarm for the sake of our mother, the Church, and for the catholic faith than those most holy martyrs of God, who founded the Church upon their blood. For why should it be a hard thing for us to die for Christ, who endured for us so dreadful and harsh a death? Who, though he was God immortal and impassible, put on mortal man and to redeem us feared not to undergo the torture of the Cross. Picture to yourselves Peter, the leader of the Apostles, also Paul, Andrew, James, and Bartholomew, and not to speak only of bishops, the sufferings of Stephen, Laurence, Sebastian, Fabianus. Some by being nailed to a cross, some by being beheaded, some stoned, some burnt on coals, some tormented in other ways and racked to death by the cruellest tortures, gave up their lives for Christ. These, I beseech you, let us imitate, and let us not, if we wish to be bishops and succeed them in honour, fear martyrdom. Alas for our womanish mind! Alas for this faint-hearted people! They of old by despising death made Christian the gentile world that worshipped idols; we by our cowardice and excessive love of life have driven the Christian religion out of the whole world into a corner,[2] and I am afraid of our losing by faintheartedness even the modest remnant if, as Panormitanus wants, we entrust to the princes the defence and direction of the Church.

'But be brave and firm in this time of tribulations and do not reject death for the Church, which with a willing and eager mind Curtius endured for Rome, Menoeceus for Thebes, and Codrus for Athens.[3] For we can receive inspiration not only from the martyrs, but even from the Gentiles to cast away the fear of death. Take the famous Theramenes of Athens, with what a glad heart and a smiling face he drank poison! Take Socrates, that most righteous of philosophers, did he utter a groan or a lament when

philosophorum, nunquid aut gemens aut plorans sorbillauit aconitum?[1] Sperabant illi, quod nobis est quidem exploratissimum, non quippe moriendo mori, sed uitam praesentem cum meliori commutare. Erubescere profecto ipsi debemus, tot exemplis commoniti, tot literis imbuti, tam precioso Christi sanguine redempti, tantopere mortem fugere. Non duos aut tres tantum homines, sed legiones (scribit Cato)[2] saepe alacres in eum locum profectas, unde redituras se minime arbitrarentur; parique animo Lacedaemonii in Thermopylis occiderunt, de quibus Simonides:

"Dic, hospes, Spartae nos[a] te hic uidisse iacentes,
Dum sanctis patriae legibus obsequimur."[3]

Nec credite Lacedaemonios non ex proposito ad mortem iuisse, quibus dux Leonida: "Pergite", ait, "animo forti Lacedaemonii; hodie fortasse apud inferos coenabimus."[4] At ego, optimi patres, non ad inferos ut ille, sed ad ipsos coelites et infinita Paradisi gaudia uos inuito, si mortem pro ueritate sustinere potestis, uosque iis principum minis, si minae sunt ullae, obicere; uos ad illam aeternam gloriam accerso, ubi nihil unquam deest, nihil a suo statu tollitur aut declinat, ubi omnia bona atque perpetua exuberant, ubi nemo eget, nemo inuidet, nemo furatur, nemo rapit, nemo proscribit, nemo iugulat, nemo moritur; ubi omnes felices, omnes unanimes, omnes immortales, omnes sunt semper aequales; ubi quod unius est omnium est, et quod omnium singulorum. Quae si praesenti animo consyderabimus, nimirum Panormitano respondebimus omnes quod Cyrenensis Theodorus respondisse traditur Lysimacho regi crucem minitanti,[b] qui: "Istis, quaeso", inquit, "ista horribilia minitare[c] purpuratis tuis; Theodori quidem nihil interest humine an sublime putrescat."[5] Sic et nos principibus, si qui minentur, nec enim suos timebimus cruciatus. Quid ad nos uita longior? Nemo parum diu uixit, qui uirtutis perfectae perfecto functus est munere. Et si clarae mortes pro patria oppetitae non solum gloriosae rhetoribus sed etiam beatae uideri solent, quid de his dicemus, quae pro patria omnium patriarum ecclesia sustinentur? Nimium est quod aemuli nostri, reuerendissimi patres, sibi de uobis suadent, uos enim timidos,

[a] Spartae nos *Cicero*; Spartanos αβ [b] minitanti BCV; minitant α
[c] minitare BCV; minitari α

---

[1] Ibid. i. 40, 97 ff.
[2] Cato the censor (234–149) in his *Origines* according to Cicero, *De Senectute*, 20. 75.
[3] Cicero, *Tusc. Disp.* i. 42, 101, trans. after J. E. King (Loeb ed.).
[4] Ibid. i. 42, 102.
[5] Loc. cit.

swallowing the hemlock?[1] They were merely hoping for what we have as a certainty, not indeed to die by dying, but to exchange the present life for a better. Reminded by all these examples, steeped in all this literature, redeemed by the precious blood of Christ, we ought indeed to blush at being so anxious to avoid death. Not merely two or three men but whole legions, so writes Cato,[2] often eagerly set out for a place from which they little thought they would return; the Spartans who fell at Thermopylae were of like resolution, of whom Simonides says:

> "Stranger, at Sparta tell that here in the grave you beheld us
> Keeping the laws of our land by an obedience due."[3]

Do not believe that those Spartans went to death without a purpose, to whom their leader Leonidas said: "Go with a brave mind, Spartans, today perhaps we shall dine among the shades."[4] I, however, excellent Fathers, invite you not to the shades, as he did, but to the dwellers in heaven, and the unending joys of Paradise, if you can bear death for the truth and face the threats of the princes if they make any. I summon you to that eternal glory, where nothing is ever lacking, nothing is lifted from its position, or leaves it, where all things good and lasting abound, where no one is needy, no one is envious, no one steals, no one plunders, no one outlaws, no one murders, no one dies; where all are happy, all of one mind, all deathless, all ever equal; where what is of one is of all, and what is of all is of each. If we consider this in our present state of mind, we shall surely all make the reply to Panormitanus, said to have been made by Theodorus of Cyrene to King Lysimachus when he threatened him with the cross, namely: "I beg you to make those horrible threats to those courtiers of yours. Theodorus does not care whether he rots on the ground or in the air."[5] This shall be our answer too to the princes, if any should threaten us, for we shall not fear their tortures. How does a longer life matter to us? No one's life has been too short who has carried out the perfect task of perfect virtue. If instances of death nobly encountered for one's country seem not only glorious to teachers of rhetoric but also blessed, what shall we say of death suffered for the sake of that country of all countries, the Church? Our foes, most reverend Fathers, go too far in their self-persuasion about you, for they think you fearful, cowardly, lazy, and spiritless. The reason why they threaten you with the princes is because

ignauos, desides, ac uecordes arbitrantur; uobisque ideo principes obiectant, quod uos famem, sitim, exilium, mortemque pro ecclesia non iudicant sublaturos. Sed non erit uobis (ut existimo) durum pro uita aeterna facere, quod pro diuitiis transitoriis faciunt nautae, qui se uentis et mari committunt, incredibilesque procellas perferunt. Pernoctant uenatores in niue, in montibus, in syluis, et uri se frigoribus patiuntur, nec aliud eis est praemium quam uilis fera. Quid uobis, obsecro, faciendum, quibus laborum merces est Paradisus? Pudet me nostrae ignauiae, cum lego foeminas et ipsas quidem iuuenculas coelum martyrio rapere, nos autem solo mortis nomine exterreri. Vndecim millia uirginum, qui nostram alluit urbem, ad martyrium Rhenus euexit.[1] In India (ut inquit Cicero)[2] cum est uir aliquis mortuus, mulieres quae eius fuerunt, in certamen iudiciumque ueniunt quam plurimum ille dilexerit (plures enim singulis solent esse nuptae); quae est uictrix, laeta prosequentibus suis una cum uiro in rogum imponitur. Illa uicta moesta discedit, ut quae mori quam uiuere praeoptasset. Quem animum nos hodie pro Christo sumentes, Panormitano haud secus respondebimus quam Philippo Lacedaemonii, qui cum per literas minitaretur omnia se prohibiturum quae ipsi molirentur, quaesierunt num esset etiam mori prohibiturus.[3] Namque ut estis uiri prestantes, sic uirtute uestra utemini, quae semper libera est et semper inuicta. Cognoscitis enim quia "data est a Domino potestas uobis et uirtus ab altissimo, qui interrogabit opera uestra, et cogitationes sciscitabitur";[4] cui ut rationem reddatis bonam curabitis, iudicantes recte et custodientes legem iustitiae, et in omnibus non secundum hominum sed secundum Dei uoluntatem ambulabitis.[5] Cumque oratores ubique Eugeniani nouam doctrinam praedicent, Romanum pontificem supra uniuersalem ecclesiam extollentes, ne ignorantium animae capiantur conclusiones tres primas publicare non omittetis, apostolum Paulum imitati, qui Petro ad ueritatem Euangelii non ambulanti neque ad horam cessit.[6] Caeteras uero quae ipsum solum respiciunt Eugenium, ne Panormitanus, neue alii principum oratores plus debito clament, in praesentia[a] differetis.'

Hic cum Arelatensis fecisset loquendi finem, omnes in eum affixis uultibus admirationem stupore prodebant; deinde laudare

[a] praesentiarum αβ

---

[1] A reference to the story of St. Ursula; *Golden Legend*, 21 Oct. Basle was closely associated with the legend.

[2] Cicero, *Tusc. Disp.* v. 27, 78.

[3] Ibid. v. 14, 42.

[4] Wisdom 6: 4. The translation is from R.V.

[5] Cf. Wisdom 6: 5.

[6] Cf. Gal. 2: 11.

they consider that you will not endure hunger, thirst, exile, and death for the Church. Yet it will not be hard for you, so I believe, to do for eternal life what sailors do for transient riches, entrusting themselves to the winds and sea, and enduring storms past all belief. Hunters spend the night amid snow, on the mountains, in forests, and permit themselves to be blasted with the cold, their only reward being a worthless wild animal. What should you do, I beg you, when the reward of your toils is Paradise? I am ashamed of our cowardice when I read of women, and young ones at that, who grasped heaven by martyrdom; but we are terrified at the mere name of death. The Rhine, which flows past our city, carried eleven thousand virgins away to martyrdom.[1] In India, so Cicero tells us,[2] when a man is dead, his wives compete and are judged to see which he loved best. (The custom is for each man to have several wives.) The winner rejoicing, with her relatives accompanying her, is set upon the pyre along with her husband. The loser goes sadly away, as if she would have chosen to die rather than live. We, adopting this attitude of mind for Christ's sake, shall make exactly the same reply to Panormitanus as the Spartans made to Philip; for when he threatened in a letter to put a stop to all their activities, they asked whether he was going to stop them dying as well.[3] For just as you are outstanding persons so will you use your virtue which is always free and always unconquered. For you know that: "dominion was given you from the Lord, and your sovereignty from the most high, who shall search out your works, and shall make inquisition of your counsels",[4] to whom you will see that you give a good account, judging aright and keeping the law of justice, and in all things you will walk not according to men but after the counsel of God.[5] Since the ambassadors of Eugenius are preaching everywhere a new doctrine and raising the Roman pontiff above the universal Church, to prevent the souls of the ignorant being deceived you will not refrain from publishing the first three resolutions in imitation of the Apostle Paul, who when Peter was not walking according to the truth of the Gospel yielded not for an hour.[6] The others, which concern only Eugenius himself, so that Panormitanus and his fellow ambassadors of the princes may not protest excessively, you will for the present put off.'

When at this point the cardinal of Arles had finished speaking, all gazed at him in silent admiration. Then they praised one

hic memoriam, ille doctrinam, hunc esse unum qui dignissime praesideret, qui et confutare obiecta nosset, et (ut praesidentem decet) impenetrabilem se conuiciis exhiberet. At Cathalani, quoniam negari sibi dilationem uiderant, ne concordata duodecim uirorum legerentur, strepitu ac uociferatione obstabant, magno conatu studentes ut lecturam concordatorum protestatio quam Panormitanus effecerat praecederet. Nec res sine uiolentia fuit, cum nec mandata praesidentis reciperentur, nec ordo in rebus agendis solitus custodiretur. Erat nanque ubique clamor, ubique strepitus, ubique iurgia effundebantur. Nunc Panormitano nunc Ludouico sermo erat. Nulli tamen sine festinantia loqui licuit. Episcopi cum episcopis, inferiores cum inferioribus uerbales habebant rixas, omniaque contentionibus et probis insonabant. Quae cum uidisset, Ludouicus,[1] patriarcha Aquileiensis, uir non minus animi constantia quam generis (qui dux est)[2] nobilitate praestantissimus, ex eo zelo, quem ad ecclesiam gerit uniuersalem, uersus ad Panormitanum et Ludouicum protonotarium: 'Ne credite', inquit, 'rem sic abire. Germanorum nescitis mores; nempe si sic proceditur, nequaquam fas erit integris hanc prouinciam exire capitibus.'

Quo uerbo ueluti coelesti fulmine tacti, Panormitanus, Ludouicus ac Mediolanensis, uno impetu assurgentes: 'Libertas', inquiunt, 'nobis eripitur. En quid est quod frangenda nobis capita patriarcha minatur?' Versique ad Ioannem, comitem de Tierstein,[3] qui tunc locum protectoris tenebat, sciscitati ab eo sunt an protegere Concilium uellet omnesque in libertate tutari. Aderant etiam ciues ex senatu urbano, prouisuri ne quid scandali oriretur. Seruauerunt enim semper hunc morem ciues ut in omni negotio adesse curarent quod pariturum dissensiones arbitrarentur, illud praecipue adcauentes ne qui tumultus fierent, neue aliae quam uerbales rixae. Miraque adeo sapientia sunt ut nemo usque hodie querelam aduersus eos habuerit uiolatae per eos fidei. Seruarunt enim, dum fuere praesidentes Eugenii, quod publica fides continuit; et rursus Concilio nulla in parte defuerunt. Quare si

[1] Cf. above, p. 12, n. 9.

[2] A passage written before the patriarch's death (referred to below, p. 194)?

[3] Or Dierstein, vice-protector as lieutenant to Conrad von Weinsberg, cf. above, p. 10, n. 4.

his memory, another his teaching, saying that he alone was a worthy president who knew how to confute objections and, as befits a president, to show himself unshakable by abuse. Since, however, they had seen that they were not being granted their adjournment, the Catalans, to prevent the reading of the proposals approved by the Twelve, showed their opposition by noise and shouting, making a great attempt to secure that the protest made by Panormitanus should precede the reading of the approved proposals. The affair did not end without violence, since neither were the president's rulings accepted, nor was the customary order of procedure kept. For everywhere there was shouting and noise and the hurling of abuse. Now Panormitanus spoke, now Lodovico. Yet no one was allowed to speak without haste. Between bishops and between the lower orders alike there were wordy quarrels, and disputes and taunts resounded everywhere. Seeing this, Ludwig,[1] patriarch of Aquileia, a person outstanding no less for his steadfastness of mind than for his nobility of descent (he is[2] a duke), from the zeal which he bears to the universal Church turned to Panormitanus and Lodovico the protonotary and said, 'Do not imagine that the matter is passing off like this. You do not know the character of the Germans. If this is the way of things, we shall not be allowed to leave this province without getting our heads broken.'

At this remark, as though struck by a thunderbolt from the sky, Panormitanus, Lodovico, and the archbishop of Milan rose in a single movement saying, 'Our freedom is being taken from us. Why does the patriarch threaten us with the breaking of heads?' Turning to Johann, count of Thierstein,[3] who at that time was deputising for the protector, they inquired of him whether he was willing to protect the Council and keep all safe in freedom. Citizens too from the city council were present to see that no offence should take place. For the citizens always observed this practice of taking care to be present at every piece of business which they thought might cause dissensions, taking precautions in particular against any disturbance happening, or any quarrels other than verbal ones. They showed amazing discretion, so that no one right up to now has ever had a complaint against them that they had broken trust. For they preserved the continuity of public confidence while the presidents of Eugenius were there, and now again they did not fail the Council in any particular. So if citizens

usquam sunt ciues quippiam de uniuersali ecclesia bene meriti, ea profecto laus Basiliensium fuerit. Hi ergo cum Ioanne comite praesentes in conuentu patrum signum seruandae libertatis dederunt. Comes autem, tametsi erat rerum nouitate permotus, nec enim arbitrari poterat tam multas esse inter prudenteis homines contentiones, per interpretem tamen respondit bono ut animo essent omnes, quoniam Imperialem saluum conductum ad unguem seruari faceret. Nec patriarcham nec alium quenquam aut uiolare libertatem aut auferre securitatem promissam a Caesare ausurum. Rogare tamen se inquit patriarcham ut uerba reuocaret sua, utque nihil deinceps tale admitteret. At illustris ille pater, omnique in negotio sui generis praesagium ostendens, nihil turbatus, nihilque irritatus, Ioanni de Bachenstein,[1] auditori Camerae, uiro et graui et facundo, et cuius opera in multis legationibus Concilium saepe est usum, utiliter intentionem suam explicandam commisit. Is mentem patriarchae illam fuisse asseruit non ut alicui comminaretur, aut Conciliarem perturbaret libertatem, sed ut commoneret patres ad constantiam, utque recordarentur promissae toti mundo reformationis, neue unum hodie, aliud cras dicerent; quoniam si sic agerent, periculum esset ne laici reformationem sperantes in clerum delusi surgerent. Ideoque monere ut periculum patres praecauerent, nec sic Concilium re infecta desererent, petereque ipsum ueniam, si dicendo, uel in Concilium, uel in Panormitanum, uel in alium quempiam deliquisset. Quo facto uerum esse ostendit quod uulgo dicitur, nobilitatis sororem fore humilitatem; quae duo illo in homine pulcherrime apparuerunt. Nequaquam tamen patriarchalis humilitas clamores extinxit, sed quoties legendi concordati fiebat mentio, toties maior strepitus ac uociferatio impedientium extollebatur.

Eamque ob causam uenerandae autoritatis Amadeus, Lugdunensis archiepiscopus Galliarumque primas, zelo fidei tactus, quam tunc impediri supprimique cernebat: 'Habeo', inquit, 'reuerendissimi patres, non paruam loquendi occasionem. Septem namque aut eo plus annis apud uos sum nec unquam rem sicuti nunc miraculo similem uidi. Nunc autem stupenda cerno miraculorum signa; parumne est claudos ambulare, mutos loqui, et pauperes

[1] Above, p. 13, n. 14.

anywhere have ever deserved well of the universal Church, that can be reckoned as the particular merit of the people of Basle. Consequently the presence of these and of Count Johann at the meeting of the Fathers was an indication that freedom would be maintained. The count, though taken aback by these unprecedented events, for he could not imagine so much strife existing among men of wisdom, yet gave the reply through an interpreter that all should be of good courage, since he would see that the imperial safe-conduct was observed in every detail. Neither the patriarch nor anyone else would venture to harm their freedom, or take away the security promised by the emperor. He was asking the patriarch to withdraw his words, and not to repeat his action in the future. This noble Father, displaying in everything the perceptiveness of his race, was not at all confused or annoyed; he left it to Johann von Bachenstein,[1] an auditor of the Camera, a man of dignity and eloquence, whose services the Council has often used on many missions, to give a helpful explanation of his purpose. [This Johann] stated that the patriarch's aim had been not to threaten anyone or disturb the freedom of the Council, but to warn the Fathers to be steadfast, to remember the reformation promised to the whole world, and not to say one thing today and another tomorrow since, if they did, there was a danger of the laity, in their hope for reformation, rising against the clergy when frustrated. So he was warning the Fathers to beware of danger, not to abandon the Council in this way with nothing accomplished, and he was asking pardon if by his speech he had wronged the Council, Panormitanus, or anyone else. By this act he showed the truth of the common saying that humility is the sister of nobility, since both were beautifully evident in that man. Yet the patriarch's humility did not put an end to the shouting, but whenever there was talk of reading the approved proposals then there rose a greater noise and outcry from those who were obstructing it.

For that reason a man of respected authority, Amédée, archbishop of Lyons and primate of France, moved by zeal for the faith, which he considered was then being thwarted and suppressed, said, 'I have, most reverend Fathers, no small occasion for speaking. It is now quite seven years or even more that I have been with you, and I have never seen anything resembling a miracle, as I do now. I now perceive the astonishing signs of miracles. Is it a small thing that the lame walk, the dumb speak,

euangelizare? Vnde, obsecro, tam repens mutatio? Vnde tam cito qui domi iacebant surrexerunt? Quis auditum surdis, quis mutis sermonem praebuit? Quis euangelizare pauperes docuit? Video hic nouam turbam pluribusque inuisam mensibus. Nouos aspicio praelatos; qui usque in hanc diem tacuerunt, nunc loquaces sunt facti. Nunquid hoc est miraculo simile? Vtinam tamen ad ueritatem defendendam non ad iustitiam impugnandam uenissent. Illud autem maius omni miraculo uidetur quoniam uiros omnium doctissimos conclusiones nostras impugnare uideo, quae certae et uerissimae sunt, et ab illis, qui eas nunc reprobant, alias approbatae. Nec nos fugit Ludouicum protonotarium has ueritates Louanii ac Coloniae praedicasse, easque illinc uniuersalis studii autoritate firmatas reportasse.[1] Quare si ipse nunc mutatus est, ueritas tamen non est mutata. Ideoque uos rogo obtestorque, ne aures iis praebeatis qui quamuis doctissimi sunt, eam tamen quae omnes uirtutes decorat constantiam non habent.'[2] Quo finiente illico Ludouicus assurgens: 'Verum est', ait, 'illas me apportasse ueritates; uos tamen eas fidei ueritates nuncupatis, quae adiectio mihi subdubia est.' Cumque hoc dixisset, quaerebat Arelatensis, ut concordatum uirorum duodecim legeretur, pluresque sibi in auribus sibilabant ne sententia flecteretur.

Panormitanus uero, ut coeptum est legi concordatum, assurgentibus secum collegis et aliis Aragonensibus, altissime clamans, quoniam plane et mo[de]rate[a] loquens exaudiebatur nemo, 'Vos', ait, 'patres, nostras contemnitis preces, reges et principes contemnitis, praelatos contemnitis; at cauete ne, dum omnes despicitis, ab omnibus despiciamini. Vultis concludere, sed uestrum non est concludere; nos praelatorum maior pars sumus, nos Concilium facimus, ad nos concludere spectat. Egoque nomine praelatorum supersedendum esse concludo.' Quo uerbo tantus exortus est clamor, quantus solet in praeliis turbarum clangor et equorum fremitus audiri, cum signis collatis duo inuicem concurrunt exercitus. Alii quod Panormitanus effecisset execrantur, alii probant, faciuntque diuersa studia, diuersas contentiones. Tumque Nicolaus Amici,[3] ex Parisiensi schola theologus, cui id ex officio uidebatur incumbere: 'Appello a tua ista conclusione', inquit, 'Panormitane, ad praesens sedensque pro tribunali Concilium;

[a] morate αBCD; mature V

---

[1] In the summer of 1438. On this mission see *Reichstagsakten*, XIII. 406, 567–8 and nn., 830.

[2] The different approach of the French should be noted; cf. Introduction, p. xix.

[3] Cf. above, p. 18, n. 5.

and the poor preach the gospel? What, I beseech you, has caused so sudden a change? What has made those rise up so quickly who were lying down at home? Who has given hearing to the deaf, and speech to the dumb? Who has taught the poor to preach the gospel? I see here a new crowd, not seen for several months. I behold new prelates; those who have been silent up to this very day now have become full of talk. Surely this resembles a miracle. Yet I only wish they had come to defend the truth, not to make an onslaught upon righteousness. Moreover what seems even greater than any miracle, I see the most learned of all making an onslaught upon our resolutions which are definite and very true, and were approved on other occasions by those who now condemn them. We have not failed to notice that Lodovico, the protonotary, preached these truths at Louvain and Cologne and brought them thence confirmed by academic authority.[1] So even if he has himself now changed, the truth has not. Therefore I ask and beseech you not to lend ear to those who, though very learned, do not possess that steadfastness which adorns all virtues.'[3] As he ended Lodovico at once rose. 'It is true', he said, 'that I was the bearer of those truths; yet you call them truths of the faith—an addition which to me is rather doubtful.' After this remark, the cardinal of Arles asked that the approved proposals of the Twelve should be read, and many whispered to him not to change his mind.

When the reading of the approved proposals began, Panormitanus rose with his colleagues and some from Aragon, and shouted at the top of his voice, since no one was audible who spoke in a low or normal voice, 'You, Fathers, are showing your contempt of our requests, of the kings and princes, and of the prelates, but take care that while you look down on all, all do not look down on you. You wish to pass resolutions, but you have no right to pass them. We are the majority of the prelates, we compose the Council, it belongs to us to pass resolutions. In the name of the prelates, I move that there should be a postponement.' At this remark there arose a noise like the blare of trumpets heard in battle and the neighing of horses when combat is joined and two armies engage. Some condemned the action of Panormitanus, some approved of it; their inclinations and viewpoints were conflicting. Then Nicolas Amici,[3] a theologian from the University of Paris, who thought it his duty to pay attention to this point said, 'I appeal against that resolution of yours, Panormitanus, to the Council now present and

nec aliquid censendum esse quod fecisti affirmo, probareque, si expediat, praesto sum.' Videbatur iam pars obstantium meliori esse loco. Ipsi enim iam concluserant. Pro parte uero alia nec conclusum erat, nec concludi posse inter tam multos clamores sperabatur. Inter tot tamen strepitus turbulentasque uociferationes non defuit spectato et optimo uiro, Ioanni Segouio,[1] ex gymnasio Salamantino theologo, audientia, quoniam et illum conciliares auidi audiebant, quasi ex suis unum, et alii uirtutem hominis summamque bonitatem etiam inuiti uenerabantur. Tanta est enim uirtuti innata autoritas ut etiam in hoste colatur.[2] Verumque illud Vergilianum in eo fuit:

> Tum pietate grauem ac meritis si forte uirum quem
> Conspexere, silent arrectisque auribus astant.[3]

Omnes nanque, ut assurrexit Ioannes, silentium tenuerunt. Ille autem postquam desyderari sua uerba cognouit, sic exorsus est:

'Cogit me', inquit, 'uiri patres, zelus domus Dei ut loquar, uellemque hodie aut caecus fuisse ne ista quae fiunt cernerem, aut surdus ne quae dicuntur audirem. Quis enim uel tam saxeus uel tam ferreus esse potest ut a lachrymis temperet, cum sic autoritas ecclesiae laceratur, cum sic nobis et huic sacro Concilio libertas eripitur, cumque nullus iam uideatur locus ueritati relictus? O bone Iesu, cur sic tuam dereliquisti sponsam? Aspice iam tandem populum tuum, iuua nos, si iusta petimus; uenimus huc necessitati ecclesiae consultari. Nil nobis exposcimus, studium nostrum est ut ueritas elucescat. Veritates in sacris deputationibus approbatas nunc concludere sperabamus. Adsunt principum oratores, differri conclusionem exposcunt; nos autem memores eorum quae ad Valentinianum imperatorem scribit Ambrosius[4] in hunc modum: "At certe si uel diuinarum seriem scripturarum, uel uetera tempora retractemus, quis est qui abnuat in causa fidei, in causa inquam fidei solere episcopos de imperatoribus Christianis, non imperatores de episcopis iudicare?" ex urgentissimis causis petitionem[5] non admittimus. Eos tamen ut libuit longissime sermocinantes benigne et patienter audiuimus. Nunc si nostrum uelit aliquis loqui, interrumpitur, impeditur, perturbatur; quae ista honestas, quae modestia, quae grauitas? Licetne sic in

[1] Cf. above, p. xviii. For his own account of these proceedings see *Mon. Con.* III. 264–9.

[2] Cf. Ovid, *Met.* iv. 428: 'fas est et ab hoste doceri'.

[3] Virgil, *Aen.* i. 151-2.

[4] *Ep.* xxi, *P.L.* 16, col. 1046.

[5] For a postponement, put forward by the ambassadors of the princes, above, pp. 98, 100–6.

sitting as a court, and I claim that nothing you have done should be approved, and I am ready to justify this if necessary.' The opposition now seemed to be in the stronger position. For they had proposed a motion. On the other side no motion had been proposed, nor was there hope that one could be proposed amid so much shouting. Yet amid so many noises and so stormy an outcry, a hearing was granted to that experienced and excellent person, John of Segovia,[1] a theologian of the University of Salamanca, since both the conciliarists heard him with eagerness as being one of themselves, and the others even unwillingly respected the man's virtue and great goodness. For such influence is inherent in virtue that it is honoured even in a foe.[2] That saying of Virgil was true of him: 'Then, if perchance they behold a man honoured for noble character and deeds, they stand by silent with attentive ears.'[3] For all of them kept silence as John stood up, and he, when he knew that his words were wanted, began like this:

'My zeal for the house of God, Fathers, forces me to speak, and I would have wished today either to have been blind, so that I could not see what is happening, or deaf so that I could not hear what is being said. For who can be so made of stone or steel that he refrains from tears when the authority of the Church is thus torn asunder, when freedom is thus snatched from us and from this holy Council, and when there seems now no room left for truth? Good Jesus, why have you thus abandoned your bride? Behold now your people, help us if we ask what is just. We have come here to take thought for the needs of the Church. We require nothing for ourselves, our desire is that the truth may shine forth. The truths approved in the holy deputations we were now hoping to pass. There are present ambassadors of the princes, who request that the passing of the resolution be postponed. Remembering, however, that Ambrose writes[4] to the emperor Valentinian as follows: "If we review the unbroken canon of holy Scripture or look again at early history, who can possibly deny that in the cause of the faith, I repeat, in the cause of the faith, bishops usually pass judgement on Christian emperors, not emperors on bishops?"—for such compelling reasons we do not admit their request.[5] We listened with kindness and patience to them when they spoke—and they spoke as long as they liked. Now if any of us should wish to speak, he meets with interruption, obstruction, and disturbance. What fairness, what restraint, what dignity is there in this? Is it

Concilio facere? Vbi nunc Toletani decretum Concilii? Vbi nostra decreta, nedum tumultus sed confabulationis minimas prohibentia? Dicunt quia contemnimus eos, et ipsi sunt qui non solum contemnunt Concilium sed colaphizant. Minimum uerbum contra eos locutus est patriarcha idque non mala intentione, et statim de libertate fracta queruntur; se autem, cum uim Concilio faciunt, cum loqui praesidentem prohibent, cum legi ordinationes impediunt, non iudicant libertati contraire. Aiunt se esse Concilium, et tamen Concilio supplicant. Haec ego nequaquam intelligo. Si sunt Concilium, cur supplicant sibi; aut si non sunt Concilium, cur ipsum Concilium loqui non patiuntur? Cur responsum eius a quo petitur non expectant? Nimia est haec uiolentia. At certe nimia est patientia nostra, qui tales excessus in facie sustinemus ecclesiae, nos utique non ipsi. Nos sumus quibus est ablata libertas. Sed aiunt quia non debent inferiores aliquid iudicare, et quia non licet nobis cum minori episcoporum parte aliquid agere, quamuis Concilii maior pars simus. Quod si uerum esset, plurima ex uestris decretis ruerent, illud praesertim quod de prouincialibus et episcopalibus synodis promulgastis.[1] Quod cum non placeret praelatis, cardinalis Sancti Angeli,[2] tunc praesidens, uix quinque associatus episcopis, cum maiori parte inferiorum conclusit, licet episcopi admodum multi obstarent; quod tamen decretum et uos reputatis ualidum, et una cum aliis Eugenius in adhaesione recepit, sic et in omnibus fere decretis contigit quae pompam aut ambitionem episcoporum refrenant. Habetis praeterea in aduentu Alexandri, abbatis Vergiliacensis, qui primus omnium huc uenit, incepisse Concilium, quamuis nullus adhuc comparuisset episcopus;[3] idque fatetur in adhaesione Eugenius. Id ergo quod isti aiunt nil aliud est quam funditus hoc Concilium euertere; sed est satis huic parti ab Arelatensi responsum. Illud tamen ab episcopis cupio impetratum ut, si fateri nos uelint eos Apostolis succedere, et claues regni coelorum habere,[4] fateantur etiam ipsi quod per Apostolum dicitur,[5] Christum superna repetentem, alios apostolos,

[1] Passed in the fifteenth session, 26 Nov. 1433, H–L. VII. 838–40; Mansi, XXIX, cols. 74–77.

[2] Cesarini, see Introduction, p. XVI.

[3] On the date when the Council should have opened only the abbot of Vézelay had arrived. His protestation before the clergy of Basle, dated 31 Mar. 1431, is in *Mon. Con.* I. 68–69; cf. H–L. VII. 674.

[4] Cf. above, p. 98.

[5] Eph. 4: 11; cf. above, pp. 62, 76, 120.

permitted to behave like this in the Council? Where now is the decree of the Council of Toledo? Where are our own decrees, that forbid even the least chattering, let alone disturbances? They say we hold them in contempt, and yet they are the very people who not only hold the Council in contempt but knock it about. The patriarch uttered merely the lightest of words against them, and without evil purpose at that, and at once they complain of their freedom being impaired. Yet when they use violence towards the Council, when they prevent the president from speaking and hinder the reading of the ordinances, they do not judge that they are opposing freedom. They say they are the Council, and yet they make requests to the Council. This I do not understand at all. If they are the Council, why do they make requests to themselves? Or if they are not the Council, why do they not allow the Council to speak? Why do they not await the reply of the body to which they have addressed the question? This violence goes too far. Yet so assuredly does our patience, when we in particular and not they endure such irregularities in the sight of the Church. We are the persons from whom freedom has been taken. They say that the lower orders ought not to do any judging, and that it is impossible for us to pass anything with a minority of bishops, though we are the majority of the Council. If this were true, most of your decrees would be invalid, especially that which you promulgated about provincial and episcopal synods.[1] When this did not please the prelates, the cardinal of S. Angelo,[2] who was at that time president, with hardly five bishops to support him, but with the majority of the lower orders, passed this resolution, though quite a large number of bishops opposed it. Yet this decree you consider valid, and along with others Eugenius accepted it in his adherence, and so it has happened too with almost all the decrees that restrain the pomp or ambition of bishops. Moreover you accept that on the arrival of Alexander, abbot of Vézelay, who was the first to come here, the Council began, though no bishop had so far appeared.[3] This too Eugenius admits in his adherence. What then they are saying amounts to the complete overthrow of this Council, but the cardinal of Arles has made an adequate reply to this part of the argument. However, I want the bishops to grant this, that if they wish us to admit that they are the successors of the Apostles and hold the keys of the kingdom of heaven,[4] they too should admit what is said by the Apostle,[5] that Christ, on his return to the

alios prophetas, alios euangelistas, et alios pastores atque doctores instituisse ad opus ministerii, in aedificationem ecclesiae. Nanque sicut episcopi Apostolis succedunt, ita et nos theologi succedimus doctoribus, et presbyteri pastoribus, atque aliis alii, uoluitque Saluator noster per istos in communi ecclesiam gubernari. Vnde apparet uanum esse quod isti praedicant de inferiorum exclusione.

'Illud uero me magis angit, illudque mihi molestissimum est, quod singularis ingenii et admirandae doctrinae Panormitanus, sine ullo deputationum discussu conclusit, sine duodecim uirorum examine, sine scrutinio, sine ullo ritu conclusit. Quod nisi oculi mei essent indices, nunquam alteri referenti de tanto uiro existimassem. Nec adhuc scio an mihi satis credam, ita est mihi res uisa horribilis. Nec enim uideo, conclusio sua qua subsistat autoritate, nisi forsitan sui regis, quem ait sic uelle. Vos tamen, patres, cauete ne talem consuetudinem introducatis; quia periculosior esset quam perniciosum illud decretum, quod uos soletis paruum appellare. Illud enim legati apostolici et alii complices in deputationibus proposuerunt; uotorumque certum numerum habuerunt, scientes qui secum et qui contra se forent.[1] Hoc autem in confusione fit, quod si transeat impunitum, maiora admodum scandala suscitabit quam illud, fietque ut in omni negotio pauculi discrepantes praelati unum habeant qui pro eis concludat. Scitis praeterea quia solius praesidentis est concludere, solumque uno in casu ad alios successiue conclusio deuoluitur, quando qui praesunt iuxta uoluntatem quatuor aut trium deputationum et concordata uirorum duodecim nolunt concludere; quod an modo contingat uos cernitis, et ipse etiam, qui conclusit, optime noscit Panormitanus. Qui licet differendam ueritatem multis (ut sibi uidetur) rationibus astruat, ego uos rogo, patres amplissimi, ut Apostolum imitemini, qui sicut Arelatensis pulchre retulit,[2] neque ad unam horam Petro cessit ueritatem Euangelii deserenti. Succurrendum est subito in facto fidei, nec ulla res maius discrimen ex negligentia

[1] The reference is to the stormy debates in the spring of 1437 over a town within which union could be negotiated by the Council with the Greeks. At session xxv (7 May 1437, Mansi, xxix, cols. 133–6) the majority passed a decree that the venue of a council of union should be either Basle itself, Avignon, or a town in Savoy. In the tumult the minority also read and passed a decree that the union should take place at a council at Florence, Udine, or some other agreed Italian town. The minority's decree was known as the 'little decree'; it was authenticated surreptitiously with the Council's seal (cf. above, p. 14, n. 1) and confirmed by the pope on 30 May. At session xxvii (27 Sept. 1437, Mansi, xxix, col. 144) the Council declared the 'little decree' null and anyone who obeyed it liable to excommunication. On the episode cf. H–L. vii, 924–39 and Valois, ii. 34–63.

[2] Above, p. 132.

realms above, instituted some as apostles, some as prophets, some as evangelists, and some as pastors and teachers for the work of the ministry for the edifying of the Church. For just as bishops are the successors of the Apostles, so we theologians are the successors of the teachers, and the priests of the pastors and others of others, and our Saviour wished the Church to be governed by them in common. From which it is clear that what they say about excluding the lower orders is false.

'I am very pained and find it hard to bear that Panormitanus, with his outstanding intellect and admirable learning, should have proposed his motion without any discussion in the deputations, without examination by the Twelve, without a ballot, and without observing due form. Had not my own eyes witnessed it, I should never have believed this about so great a man on another's report. Even yet I do not know whether I can quite believe myself, so dreadful has it seemed. Nor do I see on what authority that motion of his rests, unless perhaps on that of his king who, he says, wishes it. You, Fathers, beware of introducing such a practice, because it would be more dangerous than that destructive decree which you usually call the small one. For that was a proposal by the papal legates and others associated with them on the deputations; they had a fixed number of votes, and could be sure who were with them and who against.[1] This, however, is happening amid confusion and, if it should go unchecked, it will stir up greater scandals than the other, and the result will be that in every matter of business a handful of bishops who dissent will have some one to propose a motion on their behalf. You are aware besides that only the president can put a motion, and that only in one circumstance does the putting of a motion go to others in succession, when those who are presiding in accordance with the will of three or four deputations and the approved proposals of the Twelve are against a motion being put. Whether this is now happening you can see for yourselves and Panormitanus, who proposed the motion, knows perfectly well himself. Though he maintains that the truth should be postponed for many reasons, as he believes, I ask you, noble Fathers, to imitate the Apostle, who, as the cardinal of Arles neatly recalled,[2] yielded not for one hour to Peter when he was abandoning the truth of the Gospel. We must give instant aid of a practical kind to the faith, for nothing suffers greater danger from neglect than the faith. Unless heresies are

quam fides patitur. Haereses nanque, nisi in ipso ortu extirpentur, haud facile tandem adultae tolluntur. Quare, obsecro, succurrite festinanter, ferte cito auxilium, date uela, impellite remos. Quid hic aut praelatos expectemus aut principes? Quaerenda non est alia potestas, ubi praesens est diuina maiestas. Praedicant ubique terrarum haereses Eugeniani, nec illis aliquis dicit ut supersedeant. Vobis autem, qui ueritatem publicare intenditis, mille susurrant ut sileatis; magnum est hoc uestrae bonitatis indicium. Benedictum olim, sanctissimum monachorum patrem, aiunt monasterium quoddam sanctorum uirorum uisitantem, infinitas daemonum uidisse cateruas, qui, cum sanctis patribus conflictantes, bona quae illi patrabant opera, perturbare conabantur; mox nundinas in permultis mercibus multisque contractibus frequentes adeuntem, unicum duntaxat daemonem, eumque tristem et otiosum in specula quadam constitutum aspexisse, miratumque Benedictum, quod locum sanctum et orationi deditum daemonibus plenum, locum autem prophanum et periuriis aliisque delictis occupatum, ab uno tantum daemone custoditum inuenisset, adiurasse daemonem, ut sibi causam proderet; illumque respondisse locum sanctum expugnatione daemonum indigere, qui autem sua sponte peccarent, iis non esse opus fraude diabolica.[1] Quod mihi uidetur Eugenianis contingere; uos autem in conflictu estis. Tantum rogo ut ad uictoriam festinetis, nec curetis has principum minas hasque hominum aduersantium contumelias. Quia "beati estis", inquit Dominus, "cum maledixerint uobis homines, et persecuti uos fuerint, et dixerint omne malum aduersum uos mentientes, propter me; gaudete et exultate, quoniam merces uestra copiosa est in coelis."[2] En quid nobis, oro, tantopere obiiciuntur principes, an non potens est Dominus "Deus noster eripere nos de camino ignis ardentis, et de manibus" principum "liberare"?[3] Ne obsecro, patres, ne obsecro, fratres, minorem habete in Christo Iesu fidutiam quam Sidrach, Misach, et Abdenago, qui senem Nabuchodonosor regem minime timuerunt. Sciantque ipsi principes quia "dominatur excelsus in regno[a] hominum, et cuicunque uoluerit, dabit illud."[4] Est desuper Deus cuncta prospiciens.[5] Est, est, inquam, in medio nostrum; quid trepidatis? Estote uiriles, et praebete uos murum pro ecclesia Dei. Ne sinite, obsecro, fidem sub uestris manibus deperire. Adest Deus omnipotens, adest qui uos protegat; nolite timere qui corpus tantummodo quaerunt

[a] regno *Vulgate*; regnum αBCV

---

[1] See the *Golden Legend*, 21 Mar. [2] Matt. 5: 11, 12. [3] Dan. 3: 17.
[4] Dan. 4: 17(14). [5] Cf. Ps. 14(13): 2; 53(52): 2(3). [6] See n. 1 on p. 148.

nipped in the bud, they are not easy to remove when fully grown. So, I beg you, hasten to lend aid, quickly bring help, set your sails, ply your oars. Why in this matter should we wait for either prelates or princes? We need not seek any other power when the divine majesty is present. The followers of Eugenius preach their heresies all over the world, and no one tells them to pause. To you, however, who intend to publish the truth, a thousand persons whisper that you should be silent. This is a great proof of your goodness. They say that once St. Benedict, father of monks, while visiting a monastery of holy men, saw endless crowds of demons, who, in conflict with the holy Fathers, tried to upset the good works they accomplished; later as he went to a market filled with many wares and much business, he caught sight of only a single demon, and a sad and idle one at that, posted on a watch tower, and Benedict marvelled at finding a place that was holy and given up to prayer full of demons, but one that was profane and filled with falsehood and other misdeeds guarded by only a single demon, and entreated the demon to tell him the reason. He replied that a place that was holy needed the assault of demons, but those who sinned of their own accord needed no deceit of the devil.[1] This seems to me to apply to the followers of Eugenius. You, however, are in conflict. I only ask you to hasten to victory, and not to worry about these threats of the princes, and these insults of your opponents. For "blessed are ye", says the Lord, "when men shall revile you, and persecute you, and shall say all manner of evil against you falsely, for my sake. Rejoice and be exceeding glad, for great is your reward in heaven."[2] Now why, I ask, are we threatened so much with the princes? Is not our Lord God "able to deliver us from the burning fiery furnace and to free us from the hands"[3] of princes? Do not, I beseech you, Fathers and brethren, have any less trust in Christ Jesus than Shadrach, Meshach, and Abednego, who were not at all afraid of old King Nebuchadnezzar. Let the princes themselves realize that "the most high ruleth in the kingdom of men, and giveth it to whomsoever he will".[4] There is a God who looks down upon all things.[5] He is here, here I tell you, in the midst of us. Why are you fearful? Act like true men, and show yourselves a bulwark of God's Church. Do not allow the faith, I beseech you, to perish in your hands. Almighty God is here—here to protect you. Do not be afraid of those who only seek to kill the body.[6] Do "judgement and

occidere,[1] facite "iudicium et iustitiam", ac confidite quia non tradet uos Dominus "in manus calumniantium".[2] Iterum dico uobis, estote uiriles, ecclesiamque matrem uestram defendite. Tibi autem, praesidens, dico quia oportet te magis Deo quam principibus complacere. Quare si hinc sine conclusione abeas, rationem te huius rei in districto Dei iudicio redditurum scito.' Nec plura locutus resedit.

Interea complures grauissimi uiri Panormitanum exhortabantur ut sua conclusione discederet. Instabatque magnopere Burgensis episcopus[3] ut, si posset, inter discordes patres concordiam sereret, et qua ipse sibi perpetuo fruitur, elargiri pacem aliis satagebat. Sed neque patribus conciliaribus sine conclusione discedere, neque Panormitano mutare sententiam cordi erat. Nec minus cessurum sibi Concilium Panormitanus opinabatur quam si ipse Concilii locum teneret, Concilium uero suum. Quam inter contentionem paululum nactus audientiae Lugdunensis conclusionem Panormitani nullius esse momenti, nec reuocatione indigere, quod foret omnino nulla, dixit; utilem tamen sibi uideri dilationem, si forsitan, uti Burgensis dixerat, agi de concordia patrum posset. Fuitque ipsius oratio haud grata collegis Panormitani, qui, ut audiuerunt, uilipendi suam conclusionem illico assumentes, asseuerabant illam ualere, seque Concilium facere; fiebatque continuo maior strepitus, nec audiri lectio ulla poterat. Maximusque illa die omnium bonorum uirorum timor fuit ne plus impedientes possent quam ipsum Concilium. Resque magno in periculo uidebatur ne perseuerantes aduersarii usque ad noctem uerba protelarent; quod unum moliri uidebantur ut ea saltem die uincerent. Iuuit tamen Deus ecclesiam suam, nec plus Eugenium in Concilio quam ipsum Concilium posse uoluit.

Erant turbata omnia, nec ut solebant suis subselliis praelati insidebant, sed ut quenque trahebat affectio illi Arelatensem, isti Panormitanum adibant, et quasi principem quique suum aut exercitus imperatorem adhortabantur. Iamque in uesperum dies ferebatur. Cum assurgentes ex locis suis Lausanensis episcopus,[4] uir inter omnes oculatus et prudens, Nicolausque Grossetanus,[5]

[1] Cf. Matt. 10: 28. [2] Cf. Ps. 119 (118): 121. [3] Cf. above, p. 10, n. 10.

[4] Louis de La Palu, created a cardinal by Felix V in 1440 and confirmed as such by Nicholas V in 1449, died 1451.

[5] N. di S. Geminiano, a Dominican theologian, provided to the see of Grosseto by the Council in March 1439: *Mon. Con.* III. 237; Haller, VI. 341 (where he is called 'N. de Senis').

justice", and trust that the Lord will not give you "into the hands of oppressors".[2] Again I say to you, be like true men, and defend the Church, your mother. To you, president, I say that you should please God rather than the princes. So if you should go away without passing a resolution, be assured that you will give account for this in the stern judgement of God.' Without further words he sat down.

In the meantime several of the most influential Fathers were begging Panormitanus to abandon his motion. The bishop of Burgos[3] was very pressing, so that, if possible, he might establish harmony among the inharmonious Fathers, and he was active to bestow on others the peace always enjoyed by himself. The conciliarist Fathers did not like going away without passing a resolution, nor did Panormitanus like changing his mind. Panormitanus believed that the Council would give way to him no less than if he were in the place of the Council and the Council in his. Amid this dispute the archbishop of Lyons gained some kind of a hearing and declared that the motion of Panormitanus was of no importance, and did not need to be withdrawn, because it was quite valueless. An adjournment seemed a good idea to him, in the hope, as the bishop of Burgos had said, of discussion taking place about the harmony of the Fathers. His words were not well received by the colleagues of Panormitanus who, when they heard it, assuming at once that their motion was being held in contempt, asserted that it was valid and that they composed the Council; and the result immediately was a greater uproar, and no reading could be heard. That day there was the greatest fear among all good men of the objectors having greater power than the Council itself. There seemed in this matter to be a great danger of the opponents persisting and prolonging their words until nightfall. Their sole aim seemed to be that on this day at least they should be successful. Yet God gave aid to his Church, and willed that Eugenius should not have greater power in the Council than the Council itself.

Everything was in a state of confusion. The prelates were not sitting, as they usually did, on their own benches, but as each was drawn by his loyalties. One party clustered round the cardinal of Arles, the other round Panormitanus, and each as it were encouraged his chief or his general. It was already nearly evening when, rising from their places, the bishop of Lausanne,[4] a man discerning among all and wise, and Niccolò of Grosseto,[5] who

plus Concilio quam sibi prospiciens, Arelatensem petierunt territantes ipsum, si sine conclusione assurgeret. Nuncque Franciscus de Fuxe,[1] nunc Andreas Hispanus,[2] professione minores et gradu theologi, auribus Arelatensis iminebant, in tantumque illum praemebant ut nec animum resumere paterentur. Laurentius quoque Rotella[3] infestus Arelatensi: 'Quid dormis nunc, praesidens?' ait, 'Vbi animus tuus? Vbi uersutiae tuae? Quid times, quid somnias?' Ille autem, ut agnouit rem in periculo esse, nec rectam conclusioni uiam patere, utendum astu censuit; utque tumultum aliquantisper componeret: 'Habeo,' inquit, 'sanctissimi patres, nouas ex Francia literas, quae mihi auditu stupenda enarrant; incredibiles illic nouitates sunt, eas, si aures mihi praestatis benignas, mox uobis exponam.' Qua re et silentium subitum impetrauit, et artificio miro attentos animos audientium reddidit. Vtque liberum sibi dicendi campum patere uidit, sine fabula sine ulla historia fuit, literarum sibi missarum seriem reserauit; exinde (prout oratoria exigit insinuatio) pedetentim ad causam rediens, Eugenianos nuncios implesse Galliam dixit, qui nouam doctrinam praedicantes, autoritatem Romani pontificis supra generalia Concilia magni facerent. Quibus, nisi cito occurreretur, fore ut pluribus fidem facerent; idcirco oportuisse sacrum Concilium de remedio cogitare, necessarioque iam ueritates de quibus ageretur[a] examinatas ut per eas Eugenianorum temeritas retunderetur, quae licet essent numero bis quatuor, non tamen fuisset intentio patrum omnes concludere, sed tantum priores tres, prout se inquit in nomine Patris, et Filii, et Spiritus Sancti concludere. Atque iis dictis laetus alacerque consurgens, ab omnibus suae partis hominibus summe probatus et laudatus recessit. Et alii quidem eum, alii uestimentorum fimbrias deosculabantur, secutique ipsum complurimi prudentiam eius magnopere commendabant, qui, licet origine esset Gallicus, Italos tamen hac die summa homines astutia superasset. Communis tamen omnium opinio fuit hoc Spiritus Sancti magis quam ipsius Arelatensis opus fuisse. Caeteri uero alterius factionis homines mente[b] alienati inclynatisque capitibus domum quisque suam perrexerunt, nec insimul recedentes, nec seinuicem salutantes, ut eos uictos cuiuslibet

[a] ageretur BC; agetur α [b] homines mente CDV; homines qui mente αB

[1] Cf. above, p. 20, n. 6.
[2] Called a Franciscan of Louis de La Palu's household by Pérouse, p. 280.
[3] A notary of the papal camera.

was taking more thought for the Council than for himself, sought out the cardinal of Arles threatening him if he rose without passing a resolution. Now too François de Fuxe[1] and now Andrew of Spain,[2] of the order of St Francis and graduates of theology, poured threats in the ears of the cardinal of Arles, and used such pressure that they did not allow him to recover his composure. Lorenzo de Rotella[3] too, an enemy of the cardinal cried, Why are you sleeping now, president? Where is your courage? Where is your ingenuity? Why are you fearful, why are you dreaming?' He, however, when he realized that things were dangerous, and that there was no straight way open to passing a resolution, thought fit to make use of subtlety, and to quieten the disturbance for a while cried, 'Holy Fathers, I have letters newly arrived from France which give me news that I am astonished to hear. There are fresh developments there beyond belief. If you give me your kind attention, I will soon tell you about them.' So he both gained a sudden silence, and by a surprising trick caught the attention of his hearers. When he saw that he had a clear field for speaking, he gave no narrative and no account, but opened a series of letters sent to him; then, as the orator's practice of insinuation requires, gradually returning to the subject, he said that France was full of messengers from Eugenius. Preaching a new doctrine, they were laying great stress on the authority of the Roman pontiff over general Councils. Unless they were quickly opposed, the result would be that they would convince the majority. It was therefore advisable for the holy Council to think of a remedy, and of necessity to think of the truths under discussion that had been examined, so that the effrontery of the followers of Eugenius might be checked by them. Though the truths were eight in number, it had not been the purpose of the Fathers to pass them all, but only the first three, even as he now declared them passed in the name of the Father, Son, and Holy Spirit. With these words he rose with gladness and happiness, and amid the great approval and praise of all his party withdrew. Some kissed him, others the fringe of his clothing, and very many followed him, greatly commending his practical ability. For though a Frenchman by birth, he had that day by his supremely sharp wits outdone the Italians. The general view was that this had been the work of the Holy Spirit rather than of the cardinal of Arles. The rest, belonging to the other party, bewildered and with bowed heads, went each to his own house, not going away together

uultus ostenderet. Plus quoque in uulgus de Panormitano relatum est, illum scilicet, postquam domum uenit, in cubiculum se recepisse, secumque de rege suo questum, quod eum aduersus ueritatem pugnare compelleret, et suam famam suamque animam ire perditum; mediasque inter lachrymas obdormiuisse, nec usque ad uesperas prae moestitia sumpsisse cibum, ut qui nec ignorans nec uolens ueritatem oppugnasset.

Eadem die reuersus est cardinalis Terraconensis,[1] uir et animo et consilio quam corpore maior, scientia uero literarum admodum tritus, qui eo tempore quo Armeniaci aduenerunt ad duas dietas,[2] se sequestrauerat. Cumque is generali congregationi interesse non potuisset, subito ad eum Cathalani Lombardique perrexerunt, diuersa cum eo consilia trutinantes. Aliis nanque deserendum[a] Concilium uidebatur, aliis persistendum, omnique nisu resistendum ne quid ulterius aduersus Eugenium fieret. Eaque inter eos sententia mansit. Die autem sabbati, quae fuit Aprilis quinta et uigesima, Lugdunensis archiepiscopus et Burgensis episcopus, accersitis in capitulo maioris ecclesiae praelatis multa de pace exorditi sunt, fiendasque illo die deputationes Burgensis episcopus suadebat, quibus Lugdunensis facultatem componendi committeret. Quibus responsum est, ut ipsi iudicarunt, duriter, ut alii estimarunt, suauiter. Iuste tamen, dixerunt nanque patres Concilii nullam esse ante concordiam posse quam aduersarii errati sui ueniam peterent, sicque finem fecerunt. Sequenti dominica idem Burgensis cum aliis ex Lombardis et Cathalanis Germanicam adiit nationem,[3] exinde senatum urbanum, et utrobique de prohibendo schismate sermonem fecit. Natio, ut postea intellexi, retulit se ad ea quae deputationes deliberarent. Senatus urbani, ut sunt homines praematuri et qui nihil sine consilio faciunt diligenti, rem illam ad se minime pertinere dixerunt, sed ad Concilium, cuius patres prudentissimi forent, nec ignorare, quid in rem esset fidei Christianae; si quid instaret periculi, id esse Concilio non consulatui suo monstrandum. Credere se, maiores Concilii ubi essent praemoniti, nihil mali admissuros; ad senatum uero urbanum nihil aliud pertinere quam tutari patres

[a] deserendum αBCD; deferendum (= differendum) V

[1] Cf. above, p. 96 n. 2.

[2] Bands of Armagnac mercenaries, out of work as a result of a peace concluded between the count of Vaudemont and René of Anjou, duke of Lorraine, menaced Alsace from the late autumn of 1438 to the spring of 1439: *Reichstagsakten*, XIV. 272 ff. The 'two diets' refer to Nuremberg (Nov. 1438, above, p. 8) and the assembly or congress (not strictly a diet) at Mainz (Mar. 1439, above, p. 10).

[3] For 'nations' at the Council see Introduction, p. xvii.

and not greeting one another, so that defeat could be read in the face of each. It also became generally known that Panormitanus, when he came to his house retired to his bedroom and after complaints to himself about his king for compelling him to fight against the truth and to endanger his reputation and his soul, in the midst of his tears he fell asleep, and through his melancholy took no food until evening, seeing that knowingly and unwillingly he had attacked the truth.

On the same day there returned the cardinal of Tarragona,[1] a man of greater mind and counsel than size, very polished in his knowledge of literature, who, when the Armagnacs approached the two diets,[2] had removed himself. Since he had not been able to attend the general congregation, the Catalans and Lombards of a sudden came and weighed up with him various plans. For some thought they should abandon the Council, others that they should continue and resist with every effort the passing of anything further against Eugenius. That was the view which prevailed among them. However on Saturday 25 April the archbishop of Lyons and the bishop of Burgos, summoning the prelates in the chapter-house of the cathedral, made many overtures about peace and the bishop of Burgos advised the convoking of deputations that day, to whom the archbishop of Lyons should entrust the power of making it. To this the reply given was a stern one in their judgement, but mild in the view of others. Yet it was a just one, for the Fathers of the Council said that it was impossible for harmony to exist before their opponents asked pardon for their error; and so they ended. On the Sunday following the bishop of Burgos again, accompanied by some of the Lombards and Catalans, approached the German nation,[3] and then the city council, and in both places held forth on preventing schism. The nation, I learnt later, applied itself to what the deputations were discussing. The members of the city council, who are experienced and who do nothing without careful reasoning, said that the matter was not their business, but the Council's, whose Fathers were of great wisdom, and that they realised what was in the interests of the Christian faith; if any danger threatened, that needed to be referred to the Council not to the city magistrates. They believed that the chief members of the Council, once they were warned, would allow no harm. It was the city council's business only to give the Fathers protection, and to guard the public

et fidem ciuitatis publicam custodire. Eoque responso Burgensem dimiserunt.

Interea patres Consilii formam decreti superioribus conclusionibus conscripserant, eamque in sacris deputationibus approbauerant. Sola communium deputatio limandum magis decretum censuit. Iamque[1] principum oratores ex Maguntino conuentu redierant omnes, habitisque inter se consiliis, impedire decretum statuerant. Nona igitur Maii die, quae et ipsa ut Iudaei seruarunt sabbati, ut gentiles Saturni, ut nos Virginis fuit,[2] ad generalem concionem deuentum est, quae admodum frequens fuit, utraque parte ad conflictum se exhibente. Ipsi autem principum oratores uocati per Lubecensem episcopum et Conradum de Vuinsperg, protectorem, in choro ecclesiae detinebantur, ibique de pace, si qua posset haberi, agitabatur, plusque ibi morati sunt quam alicuius ferret opinio; quae res praeter spem omni bene gerendae rei occasionem attulit. Erat tantummodo illa die forma decreti concludenda;[3] ideoque ut uidit Arelatensis concionem esse plenissimam, uiros duodecim concordasse, maximamque omnium cum silentio expectationem fore, haud expectandam esse turbationem censuit. Legique e uestigio concordata publica iussit; inter quae illud etiam erat, ut posset ipse Arelatensis, quando sibi uideretur, sessionem indicere. Quibus lectis, rogatus a promotoribus ex more conclusit, oratoribus principum adhuc in choro persistentibus. Qui, ut rem gestam intellexerunt, turbati admodum colloquia dimiserunt, Lubecensi omnia imputantes, qui eos ex industria tenuisset in choro, uerbaque protelasset. Ingressique concionem totum templum querimoniis impleuerunt.[4]

Primus tamen omnium et suo et protectoris nomine Lubecensis de conclusione conquestus est, eamque ut Concilium reuocaret minus libenter quam efficaciter postulauit; id si concederetur, tractaturum se pacem et protectorem inter Concilium et oratores principum pollicitus. Turonensis autem archiepiscopus uideri sibi dicebat usque ad sessionem liberam esse dicendi omnibus

[1] 7 May 1439.

[2] Saturday, 9 May; liturgical traditions had for long involved the celebration of the Virgin Mary on Saturdays. This was especially the case in Cistercian monasteries and among Franciscans; at the General Chapter at Assisi in 1269 it was enacted that a mass should be sung in her honour every Saturday. Cf. below, p. 180. The cult of Mary was very much in the minds of the Fathers of Basle at this time; a decree of the thirty-sixth session, 17 Sept. 1439, ordered acceptance of the doctrine of the Immaculate Conception, cf. H–L. VII. 1071.

[3] Decrees adopted in the general congregation were later formally enacted at a plenary session; cf. Introduction, p. xviii, and below, pp. 178–86.

[4] For the ensuing debate see Haller, VI. 411–15.

security of the state. With that reply they sent the bishop of Burgos away.

In the meantime the Fathers of the Council had drafted the form of the decree for the earlier resolutions, and had approved that in the holy deputations. Only the deputation on general business thought that the decree needed more revision. By now[1] all the ambassadors of the princes had returned from the meeting at Mainz, and holding discussions together had determined to obstruct the decree. So on 9 May, which was a sabbath by the Jewish reckoning, a Saturday by that of the Gentiles, and the Virgin's day by ours,[2] they came to the general congregation, which was quite well attended, as both sides were presenting themselves for conflict. Now the ambassadors of the princes, summoned by the bishop of Lübeck, and Conrad of Weinsberg, the Protector, were kept back in the choir of the church, and a discussion was held there on the possibility of gaining peace, and they stayed there longer than anyone expected—a circumstance which presented an unexpected chance of settling the whole affair successfully. Only the form of the decree had to be passed that day.[3] Therefore when the cardinal of Arles saw that it was a very full meeting, that the Twelve had given their agreement, and that all showed the greatest expectation in silence, he did not consider that any disturbance was to be expected. He ordered the publicly approved proposals to be read out forthwith, among which one was included that the cardinal of Arles himself, when he saw fit, could convene a [plenary] session. After these were read, he passed the resolution in the usual fashion at the request of the promoters, with the ambassadors of the princes still remaining in the choir. When they realized what had happened, they were quite distressed, and made an end to their discussions, blaming the bishop of Lübeck entirely for keeping them in the choir on purpose and prolonging the talk. Entering the general congregation, they filled the whole church with their complaints.[4]

First of all the bishop of Lübeck in his own name and in that of the Protector complained strongly about the passing of the resolution, and requested that the Council revoke it effectively even if not willingly. If that were granted he promised he and the Protector would handle the matter of peace between the Council and the ambassadors of the princes. Then the archbishop of Tours said that he considered that right up to the [plenary] session there

facultatem aduersus eam quae promulgari deberet legem, cum tunc canones consecrarentur, tuncque reciperent animam, cum infulati episcopi post lecturam decreti in sessione placere sibi respondissent, secus uero inanem esse interrogationem quae a promotoribus in sessione fieret;[1] ea de causa, cum nondum essent conclusiones in sessione approbatae, impune se circa eas pauca locuturum; rem esse grandem arduamque, nec tam breui spatio comprehensibilem, se solum nunc earum habuisse notitiam. Quia tamen archiepiscopus esset, oportere eum rem bene nosse ut domum rediens et informare regem et instruere subditos quiret; uelleque se atque collegas ante consessum fiendum et audire alios et audiri ab aliis. Nec uideri sibi ante relationem gestorum quae oratores principum Maguntiae egissent sessionem hanc fiendam; quae forsitan talia forent ut patrum possent intentionem mutare. Concensis uero episcopus, orator regis Castellae, qui et ipse nuper ex Maguntia reuenerat, uir plura intelligens quam explicare sciat, grauiter questus est contemni praelatos. Nec fuisse rem magnam ait, si expectati fuissent qui Maguntiam non uoluptatis sed necessitatis causa et cum grauibus periculis et sumptibus petiissent; postque quasi subridens: 'Ah demens,' inquit, 'ego, qui expectari praelatos ex Maguntia uolo, cum nec etiam ex choro huius ecclesiae expectati sint! Facite ergo ut libet. Si quid hinc scandali, si quid mali euenerit, neque nos oratores Castellae inculpandi sumus, neque serenissimo regi nostro quisquam iure imputauerit.' Mediolanensis quoque archiepiscopus, quod eius rei periculosissimum exitum iudicabat, in autorem Arelatensem acerbissime conuiciatus est: ipsum esse, qui copistarum paedagogorumque gregem nutriret, remque cum eis fidei concluderet, alium eum Cathelinam uocitans ad quem desperati et perditi omnes confugerent; illorumque ipsum esse principem et cum illis ecclesiam regere, nec in re omnium maxima magnis praelatis et magnorum principum oratoribus auscultare. Albigaunensis quoque, uir nobilissimus, et ex Caesarum sanguine descendens,[2] quamuis nunquam animum

[1] That is, the question whether the Fathers approved the decree, to which the affirmative 'Placet' was the answer; cf. below, p. 226.

[2] A reference to the romantic tradition that the lords of Carretto were descended from Widukind 'King of Saxony' and from Emperor Otto I. Cf. F. Sansovino, *Origine e fatti delle famiglie illustri d'Italia.* (Venice, 1670), pp. 317–8.

was complete freedom for everyone to argue against a law due to be promulgated since it was only then that the canons were given ultimate sanction, only then that they had force when the bishops in their mitres expressed their assent after the reading of the decree in the session; otherwise the question posed by the promoters at a session was meaningless.[1] For this reason as the resolutions had not yet been approved in the session, he would say without penalty a few things about them. It was an important and difficult matter, not to be understood in so short a space of time. He had only now got a full grasp of it. Yet since he was an archbishop, he ought to be fully aware of the matter, so that on his return home he could both inform the king and instruct his subjects. He and his colleagues wished before the holding of the meeting to hear other views and have their own heard. He did not consider that this session should take place before a report had been given of the actions of the ambassadors of the princes at Mainz, which perhaps would be of a nature to cause the Fathers to change their purpose. The bishop of Cuenca, ambassador of the king of Castile, who himself had just returned from Mainz, a person of greater understanding than power of expression, made a serious complaint that the prelates were being held in contempt. 'It would not have been a great matter', he said, 'to have waited for those who had gone to Mainz not for their pleasure but of necessity, and at great danger and expense.' Then with the hint of a smile, 'How senseless I am to want any waiting for the prelates [returning] from Mainz, since there was none [while they merely came] from the choir of this church! Do then as it pleases you. If any cause of scandal or trouble comes from this, we, the ambassadors of Castile, are not to blame, and no one will rightly attribute it to our most noble king.' The archbishop of Milan too, because he thought the outcome of this matter most dangerous, made a bitter attack upon the cardinal of Arles as responsible for it. He alleged that the cardinal gave a living to a flock of secretaries and tutors, and was determining with them a matter of the faith. He called the cardinal another Catiline, with whom all the desperate and abandoned characters took refuge. The cardinal was their leader, and with them ruled the Church, and in a matter of the greatest importance of all did not listen to the great prelates and the ambassadors of the great princes. The bishop of Albenga also, a man of the highest nobility,[2] descended from the blood

a Concilio alienasset, ne tamen ab aliis principum oratoribus[a] uideretur discrepare, haud absimilem querimoniam habuit de neglectu praelatorum. Exhinc ad Panormitanum oratio defluxit, qui ut uim dicendi maiorem habuit, sic etiam concitatiorem ostendit animum.

In exordio suae orationis Panormitanus, non ut oratores praecipiunt beneuolentiam, sed odium captare ab auditoribus uisus est. Dicebat enim Saluatorem nostrum signa in Euangelio quatuor ostendisse, quibus bonos cognosceremus a reprobis. Quoniam 'qui est ex Deo', inquit, 'uerba Dei audit, propterea uos non auditis, quia ex Deo non estis.'[1] Rursus quoque: 'Qui male agit, odit lucem.'[2] Alibi etiam: 'A fructibus eorum cognoscetis eos';[3] et: 'Non potest arbor bona malos fructus facere.'[4] Quae omnia in patres Concilii retorquebat, qui uerba Dei, id est uerba pacis, quae ipsi oratores proferrent non audirent, quique lucem fugissent, oratoribus absentibus et clanculum concludentes, quodque in sua deputatione diem festum non celebrassent, sed feriata die[5] conclusissent, et quod in praecedenti conclusione non ratione sed deceptione[6] uicissent. De fructibus dicebat ut ipsi patres meditarentur, quoniam si fructus eorum non essent boni, ipsi etiam boni non essent; se autem uidere in foribus concilium aliud, ubi timeret ne huiusmodi conclusiones reuocarentur, tanquam malae fructus arboris. Ideoque non esse sic repente in rebus maximis procedendum, uelleque se adhuc plenius ante sessionem audiri, tam suo qui archiepiscopus esset, quam sui principis nomine, qui non tantum unius sed plurium regnorum[7] rex haberetur. Se quoque antehac et uerbis et scriptis ac etiam factis autoritatem sacri Concilii magnificasse, uererique ne per tales modos autoritas ipsa conculcaretur. Ignoscique sibi tandem petiit, si patres Concilii offenderet, quoniam eum sic eloqui dolor moerorque cogeret.

Voluisset abbas Vergiliacensis ad ea responsum dare quae Panormitanus de sua deputatione tetigerat. Arelatensi autem prius dicere omnes placuit qui ex aduerso erant. Inter quos ultimo loco legistarum Homerus fuit Ludouicus protonotarius, qui, licet inuitus loqueretur, ubi tamen occeperat, retinere uerba nesciebat,

[a] oratorum principibus αβ

---

[1] John 8: 47. [2] John 3: 20. [3] Matt. 7: 20. [4] Matt. 7: 18.
[5] Friday, 24 Apr.; cf. above, p. 94. [6] Cf. above, p. 150.
[7] The Spanish lands of the Crown of Aragon, Sicily, Naples.

of the Caesars, though his attitude had never been at variance with the Council, yet so that he should not seem to stand apart from the other ambassadors of the princes, made a very similar complaint about the prelates being ignored. Next the word passed to Panormitanus, who matched his great forcefulness in speaking with the display of unusual emotion.

At the beginning of his speech Panormitanus did not appear to invite the good will of his audience as orators advise, but their hatred. For he said that our Saviour pointed out four signs in the Gospel for distinguishing the good from the wicked. He says: 'He that is of God heareth God's words, ye therefore hear them not, because ye are not of God.'[1] Then again: 'Every one that doeth evil hateth the light.'[2] Elsewhere too: 'By their fruits ye shall know them.'[3] And: 'A good tree cannot bring forth evil fruit.'[4] All these he turned against the Fathers of the Council, alleging that they did not hear the words of God, that is, the words of peace which the ambassadors were offering, and had fled from the light by passing a resolution when the envoys were away and in secret, and had not celebrated a festival in their deputation but had passed a resolution on a holiday,[5] and in the previous passing of a resolution had gained a victory not by reasoning but by deception.[6] He mentioned the fruits so that the fathers should reflect upon them, since if their fruits were not good they themselves were not good. He saw at the door another council at which he was afraid of resolutions of this kind being withdrawn as fruits of a bad tree. So in matters of the greatest importance it was not advisable to make a sudden advance, and he wished for a fuller hearing before the [plenary] session, as much in the name of himself, an archbishop, as in that of his prince, who was held to be king not only of one but of several realms.[7] He himself also had previously enhanced the authority of the holy Council in words and writings and actions as well, and so was afraid of that authority itself being trampled down by such methods. Finally he asked pardon if he offended the Fathers, as the pain and grief compelled him to speak in this way.

The abbot of Vézelay would have liked to make a reply to the references by Panormitanus touching his deputation. However, the cardinal of Arles preferred that all who were on the other side should speak first. Among whom in the last place was that Homer of the legists, Lodovico the protonotary, who, though he spoke

et cupiens doctus uideri bonum se fore obliuiscebatur. Is ergo debere Concilium aduertere dicebat ne inuitis praelatis materiam fidei agitaret, ne scandalum sequeretur, quod rem inualidam aliqui dicerent; nanque licet Christus duodecim Apostolos et septuaginta discipulos elegisset, in editione tamen symboli soli Apostoli interfuissent, quasi exemplum darent rem fidei ad solos Apostolos et sic ad solos episcopos pertinere. Nec esse in materia fidei cum festinantia procedendum, quae limpidissima esse debet, cum exigat Petrus probationem fidei preciosiorem esse auro, quod per ignem probatur;[1] quod si spretis episcopis huic rei daretur terminus, qui columnae et claues coeli dicuntur,[2] non posset bene probata fides uideri nec bene examinata. Fassusque tandem inferiores cum episcopis definire posse, minorem episcoporum partem cum maiori inferiorum parte aliquid posse terminare negauit. Exinde transiens ad ipsam fidei materiam dixit ueritates illas, de quibus erat quaestio, articulos fidei fore, si ueritates essent fidei; cumque articulos fidei quisque teneretur credere, has quoque omnes teneri credere ait, ideoque uelle se instrui et maturius edoceri in re quam esset pro fide crediturus, nec decere id sibi denegare Concilium quod promptissimum esse deberet iuxta normam Apostoli cuique poscenti de ea quae in eo est fide reddere rationem.[3]

Postquam uero dicendi finem omnes fecerunt, Arelatensis seipsum colligens, orationem multifariam habuit, nunc iis nunc illis respondens. Imperialiumque primo nunciorum desyderia laudauit, qui pacem et concordiam tractare se obtulissent; reuocari autem quod esset conclusum nec necessitatem urgere, nec honestatem pati. Oratorum uero Franciae petitionem iustissimam esse respondit, quod informari de re fidei poscerent, eorumque precibus Concilium annuiturum, missurumque ex magistris aliquos, qui eos domi edocerent; rem uero iam esse conclusam, nec amplius reuocari posse in dubium, sessionem uero non ad roborandum sed ad honestandum tantummodo actum fieri. Quod autem Concensis

[1] 1 Pet. 1: 7. [2] Cf. above, p. 98. [3] Cf. 1 Pet. 3: 15.

unwillingly, when he had begun could not control his words, and in desiring to seem learned forgot that he was good. He then said that the Council should be careful not to discuss the substance of the faith against the will of the prelates, so that the sequel should not be a cause of scandal through some saying this procedure was invalid. For though Christ had chosen twelve Apostles and seventy disciples, at the publishing of the Creed only the Apostles took part, as though establishing a precedent that a matter of the faith concerned only the Apostles, and thus only the bishops. In the substance of the faith progress must not be hurried, as the faith must be crystal clear, since Peter required that the trial of the faith should be more precious than gold, which is tried by fire,[1] but if an end should be put to this matter by scorning the bishops, who are called the pillars and keys of heaven,[2] the faith could not seem well tried or well examined. Though admitting at length that the lower orders could make decisions along with the bishops, he denied that a minority of bishops along with the majority of the lower orders could finally settle anything. Next passing to the actual substance of the faith he said that those truths which were in question were articles of the faith if they were truths of the faith; and since each person was bound to believe articles of the faith, he said all were bound to believe these too, and therefore he wanted to receive instruction and information at greater length about a matter that he was going to believe on behalf of the faith. It was not right for the Council to deny him what should be readily available according to the Apostle's standard, the giving of an account to anyone who asked for it of the faith that was in him.[3]

When all had ended speaking, the cardinal of Arles composed himself and made a comprehensive speech, replying now to one group now to the other. First he praised the intentions of the imperial envoys in offering their services to discuss peace and harmony. The withdrawal, however, of what had been passed was neither demanded by necessity nor compatible with honour. He replied that the plea of the ambassadors of France in requesting information about a matter of faith, was very reasonable and the Council would give assent to their prayers, and would send some of the masters to enlighten them privately. The matter was now passed, and could not further be called into question. The session was being held not to confirm but only to dignify what had been

tantopere quereretur, id sibi non esse admirationi, non enim sciret Concensis rerum processum, qui absens fuisset; quem melius instructum minime dicturum talia arbitraretur, quoniam uir iustus nihil postularet iniustum. Protestationem autem ipsius nihil mali habere quod nec regi suo nec sibi imputari uellet, si[a] quid ex conclusionibus factis proueniret scandali; non tamen id esse formidandum ut ex bonis operibus mala suboriantur. Mediolanensi uero, quod eum nimis turbatum uidebat, nimiumque commotum, nihil respondit ne forte ex grauibus uerbis grauiora suscitarentur. Panormitanum uero ad ultimum reseruabat. Ludouico uero protonotario instructionem petenti per uerba ad Turonensem dicta uoluit satisfactum, id tamen intactum non praetermisit quod de Apostolis et symbolo dixerat Ludouicus. Etenim quamuis soli Apostoli in symboli editione nominentur, id tamen non constare ait an soli in edendo fuerint; fierique id saepe ut soli principes adnotentur rerum autores gestarum, quamuis alios coadiutores habuerint. Idque in praeliis patere, quae, licet omnium militum gerantur manibus, paucis tamen asscribi solent; ut hac nostra aetate imperatori omnium praestantissimo, Nicolao Picenino,[1] quem continuus tot uictoriarum cursus illustrat, cuncta quae suus exercitus uel feliciter agit uel prudenter asscribunt, tametsi alii saepe et consilii inuentores et propositi executores fuerint; scireque Ludouicum debere articulos fidei non solum esse qui symbolo continentur, sed omnes quoque generalium conciliorum factas circa fidem declarationes. Nec ignorare ipsum aliquos esse ipsius symboli, quo nunc in ecclesiis utimur, articulos non ab Apostolis sed postmodum in generalibus Conciliis additos, portionemque illam de processione Spiritus Sancti mentionem habentem Lugdunense Concilium adiecisse,[2] in quo iudicasse cum episcopis inferiores non esset ambiguum. Cumque rem ipsam in proxima congregatione dilucidasset, haud amplius circa eam fore immorandum.

Sicque ad Panormitanum descendens uerba eius repetiit: 'Qui ex Deo est, uerba Dei audit.' Idque bene sumptum ex Euangelio, in Concilium autem non bene flexum dixit; se nanque firmiter

[a] si V (cf. p. 156); sed α

[1] The celebrated condottiere (d. 1444), who was much in the news in 1438–9 as commander of Milanese forces against Venice.

[2] In 1274, in which an abortive union with the Greek Church was negotiated.

completed. As for the serious complaints of the bishop of Cuenca he was not surprised. The bishop was not aware of the course of events as he had been absent, and he thought that if he had received fuller information, he would not have spoken like that, since a just man made no unjust request. There was no harm in his protestation that he wanted no blame assigned to his king or himself if any scandal should be caused by the passing of the resolutions. Yet, it was unnecessary to feel fear of evils arising from good works. To the archbishop of Milan, because he saw that he was overcome by his strong feelings and emotions, he made no reply, so that hard words should not provoke harder ones. He kept Panormitanus to the end. Lodovico the protonotary, who wanted instruction, he hoped would be satisfied by the words addressed to the archbishop of Tours, but he did not pass over and leave untouched what Lodovico had said about the Apostles and the Creed. For though only the Apostles were mentioned at the publishing of the Creed, he said it was not agreed whether they alone were involved in publishing it, and it often happened that only princes were recorded as responsible for achievements though they had others to help them. That was obvious in the case of battles, which, though fought by the hands of all the combatants, were ascribed only to a few. (As for instance in this age of ours men ascribe to the most distinguished general, Niccolò Piccinino,[1] who is famous for such an unbroken run of victories, all the success and skill of his army, though often others originated strategy and carried it out.) Lodovico should know that the articles of the faith were not only those contained in the Creed, but all those declarations of general councils made regarding the faith. Nor was he unaware that some articles of the actual Creed now used by us in church were added not by the Apostles but afterwards in the general Councils, and that part containing mention of the Procession of the Holy Ghost was added by the Council of Lyons,[2] at which beyond all doubt the lower orders gave judgement along with the bishops. Since he had cleared up this matter at the last congregation, there was no need to dwell upon it any longer.

Thus he came to Panormitanus, and recalled his words: 'He that is of God heareth God's words.' He said that though it was well quoted from the Gospel, it was not well directed against the Council, for he firmly believed that the ancients thought that the

credere quod ueteres existimarunt Spiritum Sanctum in medio esse conciliorum, ideoque uerba Concilii uerba esse Spiritus Sancti, quae si aliqui respuerent, ex Deo se utique fore negarent. Nec Concilium lucem odire, quod palam omnia et in publico faceret, et cuius congregationes omnibus essent apertae, nec ut aliquae aduersariorum conuenticulae, istos admitterent, illos excluderent. Rem quae nunc in manibus esset, duobus iam mensibus incoeptam agitari; primo in schola theologorum late diffuseque disputatas esse conclusiones, post Maguntiam et in alias orbis partes transmissas. Exinde uocatos in capitulo maioris ecclesiae patres uiginti circiter et centum numero fuisse, illic inter alios etiam ipsum qui nunc conquereretur Panormitanum, suoque more acute diserteque disputasse, nec ulli dicendi locum defuisse. Rursus quoque in deputationibus dixisse omnes liberrime quae uoluissent. In ea uero deputatione ubi Panormitanus esset, triduo rem fuisse discussam. Post duodecim uiros concordasse, mox generalem congregationem conclusisse; nullam rem unquam aut maturius aut diligentius fuisse expeditam, nec aliquid aut dolo aut clam factum. Quod autem die festo deputatio sedisset, id nihil mali habere, nec nouum esse, cum et saepe dominicis diebus et aliis in festiuitatibus sessum esset, ubi res indigeret celeritate, et maxime quia res fidei non habet ferias. Se uero in superiori congregatione neque dolose aut fraudulenter, ut Panormitanus dixisset, sed publice requirentibus promotoribus, et uia (ut aiunt) regia. Nec esse ulli iustam de se querimoniam, qui assumptus ad praesidentiam iurasset se semper conclusurum, ubi aut quatuor aut tres deputationes concurrerent. Cumque in pluribus causis papam tangentibus conclusisset, non uidere se nunc, cur in re fidei non concluderet, quia et cardinalis esset et ideo rubeum galerum gestaret, quoniam etiam sanguinem ad tutelam fidei deberet effundere, nec se nunc aliquid aduersus papam fecisse, qui, dimissis quinque conclusionibus Eugenium tangentibus, solas tres generales conclusisset;[1] quod nisi fecisset, habituros patres in eum iustissimam querimoniam, qui eius fidem secuti eum praesidentem legissent, a quo nunc in re fidei et in re maxime necessaria desererentur. Versusque ad

[1] Cf. above, pp. 20, 150, 154.

Holy Spirit was in the midst of their councils, and so the words of the Council were the words of the Holy Spirit; and if anyone rejected them, they said he was not of God. The Council did not hate the light, as it did everything openly and publicly, and its meetings were open to all, unlike certain gatherings of his opponents that admitted some and shut out others. The matter now in hand had been under discussion for two months already. The resolutions had first been widely and amply discussed among the professional theologians, and afterwards sent to Mainz and other parts of the world. Next in the chapter-house of the cathedral about 120 Fathers had been summoned, and among them Panormitanus himself who was now making the complaint, and in his usual fashion he had debated shrewdly and eloquently, and no one had been without the chance of speaking. Again in the deputations all had said what they wished with great freedom. In the deputation attended by Panormitanus the matter had been discussed for three days. Afterwards the Twelve had given their agreement, and the general congregation had passed a resolution. No matter had ever been investigated at greater length or more carefully, nor had anything been done with deception or secrecy. As for the sitting of a deputation on a holy day, that was not wrong nor an innovation, since there had often been a session on Sundays and other festivals, when the business required speed, especially as a matter of faith did not keep holidays. In the previous congregation they had acted not with trickery or deceit as Panormitanus alleged, but publicly at the request of the promoters and, as the saying was, on the king's highway. Nor was there any justification for a complaint about himself. When he had been adopted as president he had taken oath that he would always pass a resolution when three or four deputations were in agreement. Since in several cases concerning the pope he had passed resolutions, he did not see why he should not pass one now in a matter of faith, because he was a cardinal and therefore wore the red hat, since he was even bound to shed his blood to protect the faith, and he had not now done anything against the pope when, dismissing the five resolutions that concerned Eugenius, he had passed only the three general ones.[1] If he had not done this, the Fathers who in consequence of their faith in him had chosen him as president, would have good reason for complaint against him, by whom now in a matter of faith and a most essential

multitudinem bono animo esse patres rogauit, quia nunquam eos dimitteret, etiam si oporteret mori eum; dedisse se suam Concilio fidem, illamque uelle obseruare, nec eum ex suo proposito aut minas aut preces cuiuspiam posse deiicere; paratum se ad omnia fore quae sacrum sibi Concilium praeciperet, nec unquam mandatis se deputationum aliquo pacto defuturum. Quod autem Panormitanus Concilii autoritatem magnificasset, gracias sibi habendas ait, scire tamen eum debere autoritatem sacri Concilii tantam esse ut et nullius laudibus crescere et nullius uituperatione minui possit; atque his peroratis, formam decreti legi iussit.

Panormitanus uero et qui eum sequebantur caeterique protestationem quandam prius legi contendebant; diuque hinc atque hinc uociferatum est. Obtinuit tamen demum Arelatensis, lectaque forma decreti usque ad uerbum 'decernimus,' assurgens Panormitanus nihil passus est ulterius audiri. Indecorumque esse clamabat episcopus Cathaniensis solum Arelatensem cum paucis et titularibus episcopis rem concludere. Clamabant et omnes qui Panormitano fauebant. Cardinalis quoque Terraconensis, qui usque ad eam horam siluerat, grauiter suos castigabat, qui ueluti dormientes et somnolenti protestationem non legerent; familiaribusque illico uni ex suis ut protestationem perlegeret mandauit. At sicut antea lecturam concordatorum aduersarii perturbabant, sic nunc patres Concilii aduersariorum protestationi locum non admittebant.[a] Quod ubi Albigaunensis perpendit, scripturam sibi lecturae afferri praecepit. Iamque sonare uox coeperat, cum subito Arelatensis admonitu patriarchae assurrexit, cum multitudine patrum recessurus. Quae res apprime cardinali Terraconensi Panormitanoque placebat, sperantibus se cum suis in ecclesia remansuros. Reuocare conclusionem Arelatensem et aliam facere, iamque suos ut remanerent adhortabantur. Erat in concione suoque loco Georgius protonotarius de Bardaxina,[1] paulo inferius sedens quam suus auunculus, cardinalis Terraconensis, aetate admodum iuuenis, prudentia uero senex, et humanitate pernobilis, qui ut

[a] demittebant $\alpha\beta$

[1] D.U.J., archdeacon of Jativa S. Felipe in the diocese of Valencia.

matter they were deserted. Turning to the throng, he asked the Fathers to be of good heart because he would never send them away, even if he were bound to die. He had pledged his faith to the Council and wished to keep it, and neither the threats nor the prayers of anyone could turn him aside from his purpose. He was ready for everything which the holy Council gave him as an order, and would not in any way fail to carry out the instructions of the deputations. He said thanks were due to Panormitanus for enhancing the authority of the Council, yet he was bound to know that the authority of the holy Council was so great that it could not increase through anyone's praise, or decrease through anyone's abuse. After this peroration he ordered the wording of the decree to be read.

Panormitanus and his followers and the rest maintained that a certain protestation should be read first, and there was much shouting from both sides. In the end the cardinal of Arles prevailed, and when the wording of the decree had been read as far as 'We decree . . .', Panormitanus rose, and would not let anything else be heard. The bishop of Catania shouted that it was unfitting that only the cardinal of Arles with a few bishops, and titular ones at that, was passing a resolution. All those who supported Panormitanus shouted too. The cardinal of Tarragona, who had kept silence up to that moment, gave a stern reproof to his followers for their sleepy and slumbering attitude in not reading the protestation, and straightway he ordered one of his retinue to read it. Yet just as the opponents the previous time threw into confusion the reading of the approved proposals, so now the Fathers of the Council did not give an opportunity for the protestation of their opponents. When the bishop of Albenga realized this, he ordered a copy of the text to be brought to him. Already his voice had begun to sound, when suddenly the cardinal of Arles at the prompting of the patriarch rose to retire with the main body of the Fathers. This suited the cardinal of Tarragona and Panormitanus very well, as they hoped to remain in the church with their followers. They begged the cardinal of Arles to revoke the resolution, and to frame another, and their followers to stay behind. There was at the meeting and in his own place Jorge de Bardaxino,[1] the protonotary, sitting a little below his uncle, the cardinal of Tarragona, in years quite young, but grown old in wisdom, and well-known for his culture. Now when he saw the

uidit Arelatensem surgere, ipse quoque recedendum sibi statuerat, uocantique se auunculo et ut maneret praecipienti: 'Absit a me', inquit, 'pater, ut uestro in conuenticulo maneam, aut aliquid agam quod iureiurando a me praestito sit aduersum.' Quo dicto et praestantem uirtutem generositatemque suam patefecit, et nostros eorum quae facturi fuerant remanentes admonuit. Vox eius uox Spiritus Sancti fuit, uox plus quam credi posset necessaria; nisi enim uox eius sic sonasset, abissent forsitan conciliares, aliique[a] in ecclesia remanentes contrariam habuissent conclusionem, eamque ualidam asseuerassent, quod ultimam conclusionem dicerent inspiciendam. Nec unquam ut aliquibus in maiori, ut mihi uidetur in simili discrimine Concilium fuit. At plerique uiri admoniti uoce protonotarii, antiquorumque conciliorum et similium casuum reminiscentes, abscedentem iam multitudinem partim nutibus, partim uocibus reuocarunt, ipsisque ut sederent Arelatensis et patriarchae inclamitarunt, ne uacuam aduersariis et quietam dimitterent ecclesiam; unde et subito multitudo resedit, et fores obseratae fuerunt. Interea Matthaeus, Albigaunensis episcopus, protestationem nulli alteri quam sibi legebat. Nec enim prae strepitu poterat audiri. Quo finiente, tam Longobardi quam Cathalani protestationi adhaeserunt. Cardinalis quoque Terraconensis adhaerere se illi dissensioni dicens admirationem sui reddidit, et subridentibus aliquibus: 'Quid irridetis me', ait, 'insani? Oratores mei regis a uobis dissentiunt. Quid mirum est, si me inquam ipsorum consentire dissensioni?' Atque cum hisce sermonibus et ipse et omnes fere Aragonenses Longobardique et Castellani discesserunt. Caeteri omnes restiterunt. Et licet hora esset admodum tarda, iam enim duae post meridiem effluxerant horae, uidens Arelatensis quietum esse conuentum, priuatarum, ut moris est, personarum legi negotia iussit; quibus finitis, publica quoque iterari praecepit. Iterumque et legi conclusiones et formam decreti uoluit. Remanserant in congregatione oratores Imperii cum oratoribus Franciae, inuicemque de rebus gestis confabulabantur, nec quid legeretur magnopere aduertebant. Audiuit tamen uerbum de conclusionibus Turonensis, uersusque ad Lubecensem: 'En', inquit, 'res iterum fidei agitur; abeamus hinc, obsecro, ne scandalum

[a] aliique V; alii α

cardinal of Arles rising, he too decided to withdraw, and, when his uncle called him and told him to stay behind, he replied, 'Far be it from me, Father, to stay at your meeting, or do anything which is opposed to the oath I have taken'. By this remark he both revealed his own great and noble virtue, and reminded our party of what those who stayed were going to do. His voice was the voice of the Holy Spirit. It was a voice more needed than could be believed, for, if his voice had not spoken like this, the conciliar party perhaps would have gone away, and the others, staying behind in the church, have passed an opposite resolution, and asserted that it was valid, because they said the last resolution needed examination. The Council was never in greater danger according to some; to my mind never in such danger. Warned by the voice of the protonotary and remembering former councils and similar situations most people called back the throng now departing, partly by gestures partly by cries, and they shouted even to the cardinal of Arles and the patriarch to sit down and not to leave an empty and quiet church to their opponents. So the throng suddenly sat down and the doors were fastened. Meanwhile Matteo, bishop of Albenga, was reading the protestation to nobody but himself, for he could not be heard for the noise. As he ended both the Lombards and the Catalans gave their adherence to the protestation. The cardinal of Tarragona also, saying that he gave adherence to this dissent, caused some astonishment, and when several smiled he cried, 'Why do you laugh at me, you madmen? The ambassadors of my king dissent from you. Why is it surprising if I say that I assent to their dissent?' With remarks like this he and almost all the Aragonese, Lombards, and Castilians left. The rest all stayed behind. Though the hour was quite late, for already two hours had passed since midday, the cardinal of Arles, seeing the meeting quiet, ordered, as the practice is, the business of private individuals to be read. When this was over, he gave instructions that public business be resumed. He wanted both the resolutions and the wording of the decree to be read. There had stayed behind in the congregation the ambassadors of the Empire with those of France, and they conferred together about the events and did not pay particular attention to what was being read. Yet the words about the resolutions were heard by the archbishop of Tours, who turned to the bishop of Lübeck, and said, 'Look, a matter of faith is again being discussed. Let us go away, I beg

simus aliis, neue a caeteris oratoribus dissentire dicamur.' Cui Lubecensis: 'Mane', inquit, 'pater, mane hic; nunquid uerissimae huiusmodi conclusiones sunt? Quid tu hic timeas pro ueritate fuisse?' Nec ista a multis audita sunt; submissa nanque inter sese uoce sermones serebant. Audiui tamen ego, qui ad pedes eorum sedens quae ipsi dicerent uerba cupide obseruabam. Arelatensis autem lectis omnibus quae necessaria reputauit, petentibus promotoribus conclusit; et facto fine concionem dimisit.

Bis igitur, sicuti monstratum est, magnis in difficultatibus conclusit Arelatensis, quoniam nec materia nec forma potuit sine concertatione concludi; fuitque utraque miraculosa conclusio et praeter spem omnium, uel Arelatensis industria uel Spiritus Sancti munere habita. Ideoque relatum est postea Panormitanum, cum ex ecclesia abiret, uersum ad suos Italica nostraque lingua dixisse, 'E due', uolens significare quoniam aut bis pars sua succubuisset, aut bis fuisset decepta. Id nanque non sine indignatione pronunciauit.

Post haec deliberatum est inter Longobardos et Aragonenses aliquantisper a deputationibus abstinere; quod nec diu nec omnes seruarunt. Pluribus tamen diebus tranquilliores habitae sunt deputationes; nec usque ad quintam et decimam Maii lucem relatu dignum est quicquam actum. Quaesitaque interim concordia inter patres nusquam potuit reperiri. Vt ergo illuxit Veneris dies, quae fuit idibus Maii,[1] uocatus in concionem Nicolaus Amici promotor fidei, quae acta essent superioribus diebus succincte repetiit; utque indicere sessionem Arelatensis posset, explicauit.[2] Quare cum esset periculi plena in rebus fidei dilatio, in crastinum sessionem indici postulauit, requirens et cardinalem ipsum ob dignitatem suam, qui cardo ecclesiae diceretur, et reliquos episcopos, quoniam sic in consecratione promitterent, ne nunc in tanto negotio deforent ecclesiae, neue fidem opprimi paterentur. Alios uero minores sub iuramento praestito requisiuit. Iterum ergo ob haec uerba concertatum est. Arelatensis nanque, ut requisitus fuerat, sessionem

[1] That is, 15 May.

[2] See above, p. 154. Aleman had been given authority to decide when the session should be held. This discussion took place at the congregation normally held on a Friday. Cf. Haller, VI. 420–4.

you, so that we are not a cause of scandal to the others, and are not said to be dissenting from the other ambassadors'. To whom the bishop of Lübeck replied, 'Father, wait here. Surely resolutions of this kind are very true? Why should you fear having stood here for the truth?' This was not heard by many, as they conversed in a low voice. Yet I heard what they said, as I was sitting at their feet, and eagerly noted it. The cardinal of Arles, when everything had been read that he thought essential, at the request of the promoters put the resolution and with this ending dismissed the meeting.

Twice therefore, as has been shown, a resolution was put by the cardinal of Arles in the midst of great difficulties, since neither the content nor the wording could be carried without controversy. The putting of the motion came as a surprise on both occasions and was effected contrary to the expectation of all; it was thought to be due either to the efforts of the cardinal of Arles or to the working of the Holy Spirit. So it was related afterwards that Panormitanus, on leaving the church, turned to his followers and cried in Italian (my language), 'E due,' meaning that twice his party had failed, or twice it had been tricked. He uttered this with great indignation.

Afterwards a decision was taken among the Lombards and Aragonese to withdraw for a time from the deputations, a decision which they did not all observe or for very long. Yet for several days the meetings of the deputations were quieter, and up to 15 May nothing was done worth noting. Meanwhile the harmony that had been sought between the Fathers was not anywhere in evidence. When Friday, the Ides of May,[1] came, Nicolas Amici, promoter of the faith, was called to the congregation, and gave a short account of what had happened on the previous days, and explained how the cardinal of Arles could convene a session.[2] So since in matters of faith an adjournment was risky, he requested the convening of a session for the following day, asking the cardinal himself by reason of his rank, as he was called the Church's pivot, and the other bishops, since such was their promise at their consecration, not in so important a matter now to fail the Church, or allow the faith to be overthrown. He asked other lesser persons on the strength of the oath they had taken. So once again there was controversy over these words. For the cardinal of Arles, as he had been asked, convened a session, and appealed to all to be present

indixit, utque omnes adessent cum ornamentis est exhortatus. Lubecensis autem assurgens suo et protectoris[1] nomine protestatus est se sessioni fiendae minime assentiri, siqua in parte intelligentiae per oratores principum Maguntiae habitae derogaret. Eiusque protestationi accessit Georgius miles,[2] coambasiator eius. Protector uero Caesareus, ut se nominari per Lubecensem agnouit, miratus aliquantisper quid esset, ac per interpretem certior factus, nequaquam se inquit Lubecensis protestationi accedere, nec se actorum Maguntinorum aliquid nosse; se missum per imperatorem ad sacrum Concilium habere sua mandata, quorum recte recordaretur, illisque obediturum se esse. Post quem Concensis protestationis solitae tenorem repetiit, atque exinde ad Panormitanum sermo descendit.

Cuius antequam uerba refero, nemo ut admiretur cupio, quod totiens cadat in meum Panormitanus calamum, necessarium enim habeo rem, ut gestum est, sic narrare. Et euenit in huiusmodi rebus haud secus quam in bellicis actibus. Vt enim ibi qui uiribus corporis alios praestant et qui plura faciunt pluries nominantur, ueluti in bello Troico Achilles et Hector, sic in huiusmodi spiritalibus praeliis, qui plurimum eloquentia ac scientia pollent plus aliis agunt, plusque ut nominentur oportet. Erat nanque alterius partis princeps Panormitanus, alterius Arelatensis, sed illum non quippe uoluntas sed sola necessitas principem fecerat, eumque obedire principi suo oportebat. Vbi tamen ueritas esset non ignorabat, nec libenter ei resistebat; saepiusque illum ego in sua bibliotheca de suo principe uidi conquestum, qui aliorum monita sequeretur. Is ergo, ut locum dicendi habuit, mirari se supra modum ait quia procurator fidei[3] praelatos ad sessionem requireret, quod esset a suo officio alienum, nec debere illum praesidentis uicem usurpare. Iterumque de contemptu praelatorum conquestus addidit rem praesentem statum apostolicae sedis tangere, eamque ob causam debere, priusquam sessio fieret, sedem ipsam audiri. Nec curandum esse quod id Constantiense concilium uideretur decreuisse quod modo ageretur, quia Constantiae non fuisset auditus Ioannes,[4] nec alius pro ipsa sede locutus; quo uerbo omnia illius magnae et sanctae Constantiensis Synodi decreta reuocare in

[1] Conrad of Weinsberg, above, p. 10, n. 4.

[2] Georg Fischel, above, p. 10, n. 6.

[3] Each of the deputations had a proctor or promoter to co-ordinate its business.

[4] Pope John XXIII; cf. Introduction, p. xiii.

in solemn vestments. But the bishop of Lübeck rose, and made a protestation in his own name and that of the Protector,[1] saying that he did not agree with the holding of a session if it in any way impaired the understanding reached by the ambassadors of the princes at Mainz. His protestation was supported by the knight George,[2] his fellow-ambassador. The emperor's Protector, however, when he realized that his name was being mentioned by the bishop, wondered for a time what it was all about, and when informed by an interpreter, said that he did not support the bishop's protest, nor did he know anything about the proceedings at Mainz. He had been sent by the emperor to the holy Council, and had his orders which he remembered perfectly and was going to obey. Next the bishop of Cuenca made once again in substance his usual protestation, and the word then passed to Panormitanus.

Before I report his words, I want nobody to wonder why my pen is so often concerned with Panormitanus. I consider it necessary to relate the events just as they occurred, and the sequel in matters of this kind is the same as in warlike actions. Just as those who surpass others in bodily strength and who achieve more receive more frequent mention, as for instance Achilles and Hector in the Trojan War, so in spiritual contests of this kind those who have most power in eloquence and knowledge do more than others, and must be mentioned more often. For the leader of the one side was Panormitanus, of the other the cardinal of Arles. The former had been made leader not through his wish, but by necessity alone, and he was bound to obey his prince. He was not ignorant of where the truth lay, and did not resist it of his own free will. I often observed him complaining in his library about his prince for following the advice of others. He now, when he had a chance to speak, said he was surprised beyond measure that the proctor of the faith[3] was summoning the prelates to a session, which was no part of his duty, nor should he usurp the function of the president. After complaining again about the prelates being held in contempt he added that the present matter had a bearing upon the position of the apostolic see, and for that reason before the session took place a hearing should be given to the see. They should not worry that the Council of Constance seemed to have decided what was now being discussed, because at Constance John[4] had not been heard, and no-one else had spoken on behalf of the see. By this remark he seemed to be casting doubt upon and making light

dubium et paruifacere uidebatur. Ideoque tumultus pergrandis et clamor omnium factus est, una uoce dicentium sanctam esse Constantiensem Synodum, eiusque fore intemerandam autoritatem. Ille tamen adhuc instans magno elatoque animo, rem ipsam sine oratoribus principum perfici nequaquam posse asseruit, oportereque in re fidei principes audiri. Rursusque oratores ipsos consentire non posse, quod in Maguntina dieta[1] nihil se recepturos promisissent ex his quae, durante pacis tractatu per eos incepto, uel papa contra Concilium uel Concilium contra papam fecisset. Nec se dubitare quin tres primae conclusiones haereticum Eugenium declararent, quoniam notorium foret primis duabus Eugenium pertinaciter contraire. Eapropter, cum nondum esset sessio celebrata, et liceret ante sessionem cuique uolenti dicere, rogare se iterum atque iterum dixit ne sessio adhuc fieret.

Cui Arelatensis nil dubii fore respondit, quin ex officio suo promotor fidei ad rem fidei praelatos accerseret, et maxime quia sic deputatio fidei et ipsum totum Concilium sibi mandasset. Ad materiam praelatorum ait quia episcoporum absque ullo dubio maxima esset autoritas, in conciliis tamen introductum esse non nomine episcoporum sed Concilii fieri conclusionem. Vniuersalem ecclesiam certas sibi leges in hoc Concilio dixisse, quae usque hoc temporis inuiolatae manerent; nec grauem episcopis inferiorum praesentiam esse debere, cum et sub palliolo sordido sapientia, et sub preciosis uestibus saepe dementia delitesceret. Debere quoque illius Domitii episcopos meminisse, qui (ut Hieronymus refert) 'Cur te habeam', inquit, 'ut principem, si me non habes ut senatorem?';[2] oportet nanque ut episcopi presbyteros habeant ut presbyteros, si sibi ab eis ut episcopis honorem cupiunt exhiberi. Nec expectari principes ad huiusmodi rei decisionem debere, quia non hic principum sed Christi nomine congregata esset ecclesia; quae potestatem a Deo non a principibus recepisset, ad quam tutandam non minus inferiores quam ipsos episcopos cerneret

[1] Cf. above, p. 12, n. 5.

[2] *Ep.* lii. 7, *P.L.* 22, col. 534, (attrib. to L. Licinius Crassus in Cicero, *De Or.* iii. 1. 4).

of all the decrees of that great and holy Synod at Constance. Therefore there was a loud disturbance, and a general outcry that the Synod of Constance was holy, and there must be no tampering with its authority. He, however, with his great and lofty intellect still insisted and asserted that the matter could not be completed without the ambassadors of the princes, and that the princes ought to be heard in a matter of faith. [He maintained that] once again the ambassadors themselves had no power to give their agreement, because in the Diet[1] at Mainz they had promised they would accept nothing that had been done either by the pope against the Council or by the Council against the pope, during the discussions about peace which they had originated. He was in no doubt that the first three resolutions declared Eugenius to be a heretic, since it was well known that Eugenius obstinately opposed the first two. For that reason, as the session had not yet been held, and it was allowable for anyone who wished to speak before the session, he said that he begged again and again that the session should not take place yet.

In reply the cardinal of Arles denied that there was any doubt about it being in the competence of the promoter of the faith to call together the prelates for a matter of faith, particularly as this instruction had been given to himself by both the deputation on faith and the whole Council. With regard to the prelates he said that though the bishops' authority was the greatest beyond all doubt, at councils the practice had been introduced that a resolution was framed not in the name of the bishops but of the Council. The universal Church had in this Council fixed definite rules for itself which remained untouched right up to this time. The presence of the lower orders should not be grievous to the bishops, since wisdom often lay in hiding beneath a mean and slender cloak, and madness beneath costly vestments. The bishops should also remember a remark of the famous Domitius quoted by Jerome, 'Why should I regard you as a leader, if you do not regard me as a senator?'[2] For the bishops must regard priests as priests if they wish to be shown honour as bishops by priests. They should not wait for the princes to take a decision in this kind of thing, because the Church had gathered here not in the name of the princes but of Christ, and had received power not from the princes but from God. He observed that the lower orders were not less disposed than the bishops themselves to protect this power,

animatos, cum illos non solum bona temporalia sed uitam quoque ad defensionem ecclesiae daturos cognosceret. Episcopos uero aliquos nequid temporalitatis amitterent, libertatem ecclesiae principibus uenditeros, eosque iudices et dominos supra Concilium erecturos. De gestis uero Maguntiae nihilum se curare, quia (ut aiunt) sine hospite computassent.[1] Illud autem quomodo stare posset se minime intelligere, quod neque Concilio neque Papae obedituros se statuissent, quoniam aut illi parendum esset aut isti; tertium nullum esse tribunal, cui foret obediendum in his quae uel fidem uel animarum salutem respicerent. Nec passuram tandem ecclesiam ut iudicio principum res suae resque fidei terminentur. Nec enim Spiritum Sanctum principibus, sed ipsos principes illi subesse, seque pro hac conclusione nec fortunarum amissionem nec martyrii poenam formidaturum. Quod autem Panormitanus tam acerrimum Eugenii defensorem se exhiberet, id sibi stupori esse, quoniam nemo illius errata magis quam Panormitanus alias publicasset, cuius maxime opera et suasu et decretum monitorium aduersus Eugenium fuisset, et suspensio admissa;[2] unde ista mutatio nunc esset se poenitus ignorare, cum nec uitam Eugenius mutasset, nec stare in tanto schismate ecclesia posset.[3] Rogare tamen Panormitanum ut bene aduerteret an ex conscientia loqueretur. Conclusiones enim quae modo decretari deberent fore admodum generales, nullamque summi pontificis mentionem habere, in eisque ueritatem fidei contineri; si contra eas sentiret Eugenius, Papam corrigi aequius esse quam ueritatem omitti. Sicque facto fine admoniti omnes sunt die crastino ad sessionem uenire. Rogauit quoque protector sacrum Concilium ne qui familiares afferre arma in sessionem permitterentur, quia paratus esset saluum conductum Imperatoris seruare, et cum senatu ciuitatis quoscunque rixantes ab iniuriis prohibere.

Vt sabbati dies illuxit, quae fuit Maii sexta et decima, omnes ad horam uenerunt quibus sessio[4] cordi erat. Ludouicus quoque, Lausanensis episcopus, magni consilii magnique animi pater, missam incepit. Oratores autem principum adhuc tentaturi aliquid in chorum ecclesiae uenerant, mittentesque Lubecensem ac

[1] In the margin of the first edition this proverb is given in Gothic type and in German. 'Sy hatten die ürten on den wirt gemacht.'

[2] Mansi, XXIX, col. 165; H–L. VII. 953.

[3] For the political reasons see Introduction, p. xxii.

[4] The thirty-third plenary session.

since he knew that they would give up not only their temporal property, but their lives too to defend the Church; while some bishops, so as not to lose any of their temporal power, would sell the freedom of the Church to the princes, and would set them up as judges and rulers over the Council. With regard to the proceedings at Mainz he was not interested, because, as the saying goes, they had reckoned without their host.[1] He had not the slightest idea how the decision could stand to obey neither the Council nor the pope, since obedience must be shown either to the former or the latter; there was no third court to which obedience could be shown in matters that concerned the faith or the salvation of souls. The Church would not tolerate its affairs and matters of faith being decided by the judgement of the princes. For the Holy Spirit was not subordinate to the princes, but they to it, and he himself for the sake of this resolution would not fear the loss of fortune or the punishment of martyrdom. As for Panormitanus showing himself so keen a defender of Eugenius, that baffled him, since no one had on other occasions shown up papal errors more than Panormitanus, through whose activity and persuasion the warning decree had been passed against Eugenius, and his suspension had been carried.[2] He was quite unaware of the reason for the change, seeing that Eugenius had not changed his life, nor could the Church remain in so great a schism.[3] He asked Panormitanus to consider carefully whether he was speaking in accordance with his conscience. The resolutions which should now be enacted were quite general ones, with no mention of the chief pontiff, and the truth of the faith was contained in them. If Eugenius took up an attitude opposed to them, it was preferable for the pope to be corrected rather than for the truth to be left out of account. When he had ended in this way, all were given notice to come to a session the next day. The Protector also asked the holy Council that none of their retainers should be allowed to come armed to the session, because he was ready to maintain the emperor's safe conduct, and together with the city council to restrain all who quarrelled from inflicting injuries.

When Saturday 16 May arrived, all who agreed with holding the session[4] came at the appointed hour. Louis, bishop of Lausanne, a Father of great counsel and great courage, began the mass. But the ambassadors of the princes, still anxious to make a gesture of some kind, had come into the choir of the church, and sending the

Concensem episcopos, uirumque non contemnendae peritiae, decanum Turonensem,[1] interfuturos se sessioni offerebant, si quatuor adhuc mensibus Eugenii depositio differretur.[2] Qui cum gratum responsum ab Arelatensi et quibusdam aliis primoribus habuissent, reuersi ad suos mutatum esse propositum inuenerunt. Iam enim solam primam conclusionem decretari uolebant; sicque iterum Arelatensem interpellarunt. Quibus responsum est uim maximam in duabus reliquis esse conclusionibus, easque praecipue uelle Concilium decernere. Si nollent oratores adesse, scirent concordiam a se fore interruptam, qui noluissent quod obtulerant obseruare. Quo responso et illi discesserunt et sessio celebrari occepit; nullus tamen Aragonensium praelatorum interfuit, nullusque omnino ex tota Hispania. Ex Italia soli Grossetanus episcopus[3] et abbas de Dona,[4] qui pro eorum constantia et firmissima ad bonum uniuersalis ecclesiae uoluntate mutari proposito non potuerunt. Doctores autem et caeteri inferiores magno in numero Aragonenses fuerunt, et omnes fere qui aderant ex Italia Hispaniaque, nec enim inferiores, sicuti praelati, principes timuerunt, maximaque tunc Aragonensium et Cathalanorum uirtus in inferioribus emicuit, qui sese minime necessitati ecclesiae denegarunt. Ex duabus aliis nationibus[5] mitrati fuerunt solum uiginti. Alii uero domi latebant, fidem in corde sed non in ore habentes. Cogitarat Arelatensis quod erat futurum, plurimasque sanctorum reliquias tota urbe perquiri iussit, ac per sacerdotum manus in sessione portatas absentium episcoporum locum tenere; quae res maxime deuotionem adauxit intantum ut uocato postmodum de more Spiritu Sancto nemo lachrymas continuerit. Erat nanque per totam ecclesiam tenerrimus ac suauis fletus bonorum uirorum, qui lachrymantes diuinum auxilium implorabant, quique matri ecclesiae ut opem ferret, magnum Deum deprecabantur. Inter alios quoque magnificus ille baro, imperialis protector, uberrimas ecclesiae lachrymas praestabat, et inter flendum haud modicam tali actu consolationem recipiebat.

Erat autem concio ipsa frequentissima, etsi enim episcopi haud multi erant, plena tamen omnia fuerunt subsellia procuratoribus

[1] Martin Berruyer.

[2] It will be recalled that the first three decrees laid down matters of principle (above, p. 20). The request now made was that the Council should not proceed to convict Eugenius of contravention of these three canons, and depose him, before four months.

[3] See above, p. 150, n. 1.

[4] Luchino; this Benedictine house was in the diocese of Como.

[5] France and Germany: for the 'nations' see Introduction, p. xvii.

bishops of Lübeck and Cuenca and the dean of Tours,[1] a person of no mean experience, they offered to attend the session if the deposing of Eugenius were held over for another four months.[2] On receiving a favourable reply from the cardinal of Arles and some other leaders, when they returned to their supporters they found that the plan had been changed. For now they were willing that only the first resolution should be made into a decree. So they appealed to the cardinal of Arles a second time. They were told that the greatest emphasis lay in the other two resolutions, and the Council particularly wanted to pass them. If the ambassadors did not want to come, they should realize that the responsibility for breaking the harmony would be theirs, as they had refused to keep to their offer. At this reply they left, and the holding of the session began. Yet none of the prelates of Aragon was present, and none at all from the whole of Spain. From Italy there were only the bishop of Grosseto[3] and the abbot of Dona,[4] who through their steadfastness and firm will for the good of the universal Church could not be turned away from their purpose. However doctors and other lower orders of the Aragonese were there in great number, and so were almost all who were there from Italy and Spain, for the lower orders did not, like the prelates, fear the princes, and among the Aragonese and Catalans the greatest courage shone forth in the lower orders, who never held themselves back from the need of the Church. From the two other nations[5] only twenty wearers of the mitre were present. The others were in hiding at home with their faith in their hearts and not in their mouths. The cardinal of Arles had considered what was going to happen, and had ordered search to be made for the very many relics of the saints throughout the whole city, so that borne by the hands of priests at the session they should fill the places of the absent bishops. This so greatly increased the devotion that when, as usual, the Holy Spirit had been invoked, nobody restrained his tears. For throughout the whole church there was soft and gentle weeping by the good men, who with tears implored divine aid, and prayed to almighty God that he would bring help to their mother the Church. Among others that distinguished baron, the Imperial Protector, made a copious show of tears for the Church and with his weeping thus gained great comfort.

Now the meeting was very full. Even if there were not many bishops, the benches were packed with bishops' proctors,

episcoporum, archidiaconis, praepositis, prioribus, presbyteris, ac diuini et humani iuris doctoribus, quos aut quadringentos aut certe plures esse diiudicaui; quos inter nullum unquam probrum, nulla rixa, nulla unquam contentio fuit, sed alter alterum in professione fidei hortabatur, unanimisque omnium esse consensus ad defendendam ecclesiam ostendebatur. Decretum uero Massyliensis episcopus[1] apprime nobilis legit, cui cum Albigaunensi episcopo tanta familiaritas ac fraternitas fuit ut gemini dicerentur. Nam et domi forisque semper simul cernebantur. Quae res eo mirabilior uidebatur, quo ipsi in factis ecclesiae discordantiores ostendebantur, cum et Albigaunensis aduersus decretum protestationem legisset et Massyliensis decretum, atque una ex domo lector utriusque exisset; sed erat (ut quidam putant) in uno ueritas, in altero simulatio. Breuis lectio decreti[2] fuit, nam et ipsum breue erat; fuit tamen eius lectura attente audita, nec ullum uerbum incassum cecidit. Factoque fine, 'Te Deum laudamus' ex una parte cantatum est, ex altera responsum, 'Te dominum confitemur'. Sicque alternatim summa cum laetitia et omni alacritate finitus est hymnus, et sessio dissoluta, quae fuit in numero aliarum tertia et trigesima; quae si (ut diximus) et quieta fuit et ultra omnes pacifica, nihil mirandum est. Ea nanque in die celebrata est quae ipsius pacis et quietis matri Mariae Virgini est dedicata.[3] Nec enim sua in die aut seditiosum aliquid aut turbulentum fieri beata Virgo in suo praesertim templo[4] admisisset. Vidimus nanque alias, cum decretum electionis loci[a] publicari deberet, quia futura erat praegrandis discordia, Virginem ipsam bis impediuisse, quo minus in suo die publicaretur, fuitque res illa Marti dimissa.[5] At nunc quia pacifica res fuit, non solum in sabbato sessionem fieri permisit, sed miraculose etiam uoluit ut generalis concio pro re ipsa concludenda in sabbato haberetur.[6]

Ea quae secuta est Veneris die secunda et uigesima Maii, oratores principum praeter omnium spem generali congregationi et actibus Conciliaribus se miscuerunt, eo uel saltem facto praeteritae sessioni praestantes assensum. In qua celebranda si patres errassent, nequaquam fas erat oratores principum cum eisdem

[a] loci β; locum α

[1] Louis de Glandèves, whose translation to Marseilles from Vence was confirmed by the Council in May 1438 (*Mon. Con.* III. 104); died 1440.

[2] In substance the first three articles so long under discussion; cf. above, p. 20. These were now declared to be articles of faith: cf. *Mon. Con.* III. 278; Mansi, XXIX. cols. 178–9.

[3] Cf. above, p. 154, n. 2.

[4] The cathedral was dedicated to the Virgin.

[5] Cf. Haller, VI. 665–6 (27 Oct. 1439).

[6] Above, p. 154.

archdeacons, provosts, priors, priests, and doctors of canon and civil law, whom I judged to be four hundred strong or indeed more. Between them there was no abuse, no quarrel, no dispute at any time, but each encouraged the other in his profession of the faith and agreement was shown to be unanimous for the defence of the Church. The decree was read by the very distinguished bishop of Marseilles,[1] whose friendship and brotherhood with the bishop of Albenga were so close that they were called 'the twins'. For both at home and abroad they were always seen together. This seemed all the more surprising as they were shown to be considerably at variance in the business of the Church, since the bishop of Albenga had read a protestation against the decree, and the bishop of Marseilles the actual decree, and the reader of each document had come from the same house; but there was, in the belief of some, truth in the one and pretence in the other. The reading of the decree[2] took a short time, because it was short itself, and its reading was heard with attention, and no word fell unheeded. When it had ended, 'We praise thee, O God', was chanted from one side of the church, and the response was made from the other, 'We acknowledge thee to be the Lord'. So with great gladness and fervour the canticle was sung right through antiphonally, and the session ended, being the thirty-third in number; and if, as we have said, it was quiet and peaceful beyond all others, this is not surprising. For it was held on the day dedicated to the Virgin Mary, the mother of peace and quiet.[3] On her day the blessed Virgin would not have permitted any discord or disturbance to happen, particularly in her own church.[4] For we have noticed at other times when there was due to be published the decree about the place for an election, because there was going to be very great strife, the Virgin herself twice prevented the publishing taking place on her day, and the matter was postponed to a Tuesday.[5] Now, however, because the matter was a peaceful one, she not only allowed the session to take place on a Saturday, but miraculously was willing that the general congregation[6] for the settlement of the matter should be held on a Saturday too.

On the following Friday, 22 May, the ambassadors of the princes contrary to everyone's expectation joined in the general congregation and the proceedings of the Council, by this act at least showing their assent to the past session. If in holding it the Fathers had erred, it would not have been at all right that the

patribus concilium celebrare; sed existimati sunt remorsu conscientiae tacti, iam abhorrere quod egerant, quod de oratoribus Caesareis ac Gallicis nequaquam fuit obscurum. Lubecensis nanque episcopus id sibi absentiae causam praestitisse dixit, quoniam iussu Caesareo ad pacem fuisset destinatus, ex qua re non decuisset eum alicui negotio interesse, unde ille perturbaretur, cum quo pax esset pertractanda; se tamen sessionem praehabitam plurimum commendare, decretumque in eadem promulgatum optimum se ac sanctissimum credere, ueritates quoque in eo contentas apud se semper indubitatas fuisse, eisque et nunc et usque ad mortem uelle adhaerere. Turonensis autem archiepiscopus, plurium literarum et ornatae prelatus eloquentiae, pro se ac suis collegis loquens, audisse se inquit inter aliquos sibi esse detractum, quod in sessione illa sanctissima regem suum non honorassent, quem maxime tueri fidem ac exaltare deceret, qui ideo esset prae caeteris regibus nomen sortitus 'Christianissimum'; habere se tamen non illegitimam excusationem, quando eos qui essent ad pacem missi nihil omnino agere conueniret, quo suam impedirent legationem. Duo quoque iniustitiae fore genera, quibus aut fienda non fierent, aut fierent non fienda. Primumque non semper obligare, quod oporteret temporis, loci, personarumque rationem habere, ultimum uero semper tenere. Neque in eo se incidisse, qui nihil turpitudinis admisissent. Circa primum tamen posse aliquibus uideri se errasse, quod in ueneranda sessione non affuissent, sed esse quoque hic quod responderent, quia si sessionem talem adissent, inutiles postmodum tractatui pacis cum Eugenio se reddidissent; ideoque, licet desyderassent tam sancto negotio interesse, secutos se tamen fuisse exinde exemplum Pauli, qui licet cupere 'dissolui et esse cum Christo,'[1] adhuc tamen ut magis prodesset ecclesiae differebat. Sicque se nunc fecisse, quoniam non idcirco abfuissent, quia de conclusionibus dubitarent, quas ueras sanctasque reputarent, et quibus usque ad martyrium adhaererent, sed ne tractatui pacis pro qua uenissent, redderentur inepti; se

[1] Phil. 1: 23.

ambassadors of the princes should go on holding a council along with the same Fathers; but they were thought to have had a touch of remorse, and by now to loathe their actions, as was quite evident in the case of the ambassadors of the emperor and of France. For the bishop of Lübeck explained that the reason for his absence had been that by the emperor's orders he had been appointed to make peace, so it would not have been fitting for him to take part in any business which would have upset the person with whom peace had to be negotiated. Yet he much approved of the session just held, and believed that the decree passed at it was excellent and holy. The truths contained in the decree had in his own mind never been in doubt, and both now and till his death he wished to adhere to them. Moreover the archbishop of Tours, a prelate well lettered and of polished eloquence, speaking for himself and his colleagues, said that he had heard from some that they had been criticized for not showing honour in that holy session to their king, who was bound especially to protect and uplift the faith, and for that reason when compared with other kings had gained the name of 'most Christian'. Yet he had a valid excuse, as it was improper for those sent to make peace to do anything at all which would be a hindrance to their mission. There were two kinds of unrighteousness, not doing what should be done, and doing what should not be done. The former did not always make one guilty, as it was necessary to take account of time, places and persons; the latter always made one answerable. In this they had not been involved, as they had done nothing that brought disgrace. Yet with regard to the former they might seem to some to have been in error, because they had not been present at this venerable session, but here too they had a possible reply, that if they had attended such a session they would have made themselves useless afterwards for negotiating peace with Eugenius. Therefore even if they had wished to take part in so holy a matter, they would nevertheless have followed the example of Paul, who though he desired 'to depart and to be with Christ',[1] yet put it off, so that he might be of greater benefit to the Church. Their actions now had been similar, since they had not been absent because they had any doubt about the resolutions, which they thought true and valid, and to which they would adhere even as far as martyrdom, but so that they should not be made unfitted for the negotiating of peace, for which they had come. However, what they had not done in person they had

tamen quod suis non fecissent, in personis domesticorum impleuisse, quod omnes honorare sessionem iussissent.

Voluissem tunc praelati alicuius magni esse loco; nec enim non castigati transissent, qui se post digitum latere[1] arbitrabantur. Etenim per Deum excelsum, quid est quod pacis tractatui officiat declaratio ueritatis? Aut si officit, cur pari loco non habeatur qui declarat et qui declaranti consentit? En quid amplius testibus indigemus? Ecce quod ipsi principum oratores inimicum ueritatis Eugenium esse dicunt. Sed transeo ista, sat enim postea Eugenius cognoscere se Turonensem inimicum sibi[2] ad ipsum regem Franciae scripsit; solum restat ut pariter Lubecensis expediat.[3]

Arelatensis uero, postquam finem Turonensis fecit, gratias egit Deo, qui sic suam tueretur ecclesiam, quique post nubilum serenitatem quoque praeberet. Laudatisque Imperatoris erga ecclesiam et ipsius regis Franciae beneficiis, ipsos etiam Lubecensem et Turonensem magnifice commendauit, qui et in Concilio saepe et proximis diebus in Maguntia autoritatem defendissent; praecipue tamen praesentem actum laudibus extulit, qui et publice ueritatem confessi fuissent, et ab ecclesiae fide se minime sequestrassent. Ingressusque rei gestae narrationem, fuisse se Pisis ac Constantiae inquit, nec unquam sessionem uidisse aut quietiorem aut deuotiorem, tum propter lachrymas omnium, qui in tantae rei prosecutione plorabant, tum propter sanctorum reliquias, quae in manibus sacerdotum aduectae et deuotionem et autoritatem rei maiorem addebant. Necessariumque illud fuisse decretum asseruit ad reprimendam Romanorum pontificum ambitionem, qui se supra uniuersalem ecclesiam extollentes, omnia pro libidine sua se posse arbitrabantur, ne posthac ecclesiam unus homo, nunc Bononiam, nunc Florentiam, rursus Bononiam, mox Ferrariam, et deinde iterum Florentiam, ut Eugenius attentauit,[4] traduceret; utque deinceps Romani pontifices paululum animum a temporalium solicitudine rerum retraherent, qui, ut ipse uidisset, nequaquam de spiritualibus cogitarent. Ideoque quo esset sanctior quoque necessarior illa sessio, eo laudabiliorem et omnibus patribus gratiorem ipsorum oratorum adhaesionem fuisse, propterea

[1] A proverbial expression?

[2] Cf. Valois, II. 218 and *Mon. Con.* III. 330, where the Council is informed of a letter from the pope to the king of France dated 31 May 1439 bitterly criticizing the French delegation at Basle and the archbishop in particular.

[3] This allusion is not explained.

[4] References to Eugenius IV's translation of the Council to an Italian town; ultimately the papal council had opened at Ferrara in Jan. 1438 and had been transferred to Florence in Jan. 1439, where it was currently sitting. Cf. Introduction, p. xix.

carried out through their followers, all of whom they had told to respect the session.

I wish I had been at that moment in the place of some great prelate, for they would not have gone unpunished who thought they were hidden behind a finger.[1] In the name of God on high what obstacle is the declaring of the truth to the negotiating of peace? Or if it is an obstacle, why make any difference in the position of him who does the declaring and of him who agrees with the declaration? What further need have we of witnesses? Why even the very ambassadors of the princes say that Eugenius is the enemy of the truth. Yet I pass over that. For Eugenius afterwards wrote to the king of France himself that he was aware that the archbishop of Tours was an enemy of his.[2] It remains only for the bishop of Lübeck to make a similar statement.[3]

The cardinal of Arles, when the archbishop of Tours had ended, gave thanks to God for guarding his Church in this way, and bringing a clear sky after the clouds. Praising the services rendered to the Church by the emperor and the king of France, he paid a splendid tribute also to the bishop of Lübeck and the archbishop of Tours who, both often in the Council and also recently in Mainz, had defended its authority; and he particularly praised their present action in admitting the truth publicly and in not withdrawing from the faith of the Church. Entering upon an account of what had been achieved, he said he had been at Pisa and Constance, and had never seen a session quieter or more full of devotion, both because of the tears of all who felt sorrow in the pursuance of such a matter and because of the relics of the saints, which, borne in the hands of priests, gave the proceedings added devotion and authority. He maintained that the decree had been necessary to check the Roman pontiffs' ambition, who, raising themselves above the universal Church, thought they might do all at their own will, [and necessary also] to prevent one man from transferring the Church now to Bologna, now to Florence, now back to Bologna, soon afterwards to Ferrara, and then a second time to Florence, as Eugenius attempted;[4] next that the Roman pontiffs should withdraw their thoughts somewhat from anxiety about temporal matters, seeing that, as he had noticed, they never thought about spiritual ones. So the more holy and the more necessary that session was, the more praiseworthy and pleasing to the Fathers had been the adherence of the ambassadors, since

quod actum esset nec minus propter absentiam, nec plus propter adhaesionem ualuisse. Atque iis dictis et ipse assurrexit, et congregatio dissoluta est. Nunc depositionem, quo pacto transierit, qui secuturus est liber exponet.[a1]

COMMENTARIORVM AENEAE SYLVII SENENSIS DE GESTIS CONCILII BASILIENSIS LIBRI PRIMI

FINIS

[a] V *adds*: Scriptum anno domini 1444° die xxv[a] mensis Aprilis

[1] On the hiatus at this point see Introduction, p. xxix. The narrative resumes (below, p. 188) with the preliminaries of the election and thus omits the formal deposition of Eugenius 25 June 1439 (below, p. 188, n. 7). Cf. H–L. VII. 1070–1, 1073 for other transactions at Basle in May and June.

what was done had validity no less because of their absence and no greater because of their adherence. With these words he rose, and the congregation broke up. Now how the deposition passed off will be related in the book that follows.[1]

END OF BOOK I OF THE COMMENTARIES OF
AENEAS SYLVIUS OF SIENA
ON THE PROCEEDINGS OF THE COUNCIL OF BASLE

COMMENTARIORVM AENEAE SYLVII PICCOLOMINEI SENENSIS DE GESTIS CONCILII BASILIENSIS

LIBER SECVNDVS

APPREHENDIT Dominus arma et scutum, et exurrexit in adiutorium ecclesiae.[1] Eaque sic adiuta, gaudens exultat in Deo suo, qui eam uestimentis salutis induit; et quasi sponsam decoratam corona et ornatam monilibus, iustitiae indumentis circundedit eam.[2] Traditum est superioribus Commentariis quo statu nostra demum aetate ecclesia fuerit, quam Eugenius pauloante Papa ut uentus arundinem exagitauit.[3] Verum est tamen, quod ore aureo Ioannes praedixit, quia 'non cessat ecclesia impugnari, non cessat insidias pati, sed in nomine Christi semper superat, semper uincit. Et quamuis alii insidientur, quamuis repercutiant eam fluctus, fundamentum tamen, quod supra petram est, non quassatur.'[4] Quocirca mentita est iniquitas Gabrieli,[5] et perdidit eum Dominus in malitia sua; quo Synodali sententia ex apostolica sede praecipitato, factus est Dominus in refugium ecclesiae, gregique suo pastorem largitus est, qui derelicta (ut spes optima est) uisitabit, dispersa quaeret, confractum sanabit, carnes pinguium non comedet, et id quod stat sapienter enutriet.[6] Quam rem ut omnes Christicolae plane intelligant, enarrandus est mihi in eo qui sequitur libro electionis ordo, quo nunc Amadeus, Sabaudiae dux sapientissimus, in Romanum pontificem sit assumptus.

Deposito igitur (sicut iam monstrauimus) ex Romano pontificio Gabriele Condulmario,[7] uocatisque ipso die prioribus patrum in capitulari loco maioris ecclesiae, an expediret illico nouum creari pontificem, an in tempus differri consultatum est. Quibus festinanda electio pontificis uidebatur, plenum periculis dicunt[a]

[a] dct' VW; dictae α

[1] Cf. Ps. 35 (34): 2.
[2] Cf. Isa. 61: 10.
[3] Cf. Matt. 11: 7.
[4] Cf. above, p. 44, n. 1.
[5] Eugenius IV.
[6] Cf. Zech. 11: 16.
[7] The pope was deposed at the thirty-fourth Session, 25 June 1439: Mansi, XXIX. cols. 179–81; H–L. VII. 1069. Cf. above, pp. xxix and 186 n.

BOOK II OF THE COMMENTARIES OF AENEAS SYLVIUS PICCOLOMINI OF SIENA ON THE PROCEEDINGS OF THE COUNCIL OF BASLE

THE Lord took hold of shield and buckler, and stood up for the help of the Church.[1] Thus assisted, it is joyful and rejoices in its God, who clothed it with the garments of salvation, and covered it with the robes of righteousness, like a bride decked with ornaments and adorned with jewels.[2] The previous Commentaries have described the position in our time of the Church, which Pope Eugenius just previously shook like the wind shaking a reed.[3] Yet what John said with his golden voice is true: 'The Church does not cease to be assailed, it does not cease to suffer treacherous attacks, but in the name of Christ it always prevails, always conquers. Though some lie in wait, though the waves buffet it, still its foundation, which is on rock, is not shaken.'[4] Therefore the wickedness of Gabriel[5] lied, and the Lord destroyed him in his malice. When he had been driven from the apostolic see by the judgement of the Synod, the Lord came to the rescue of the Church, and bestowed a shepherd on his flock, who, there is good reason to hope, will visit what is cut off, will seek what is scattered, will heal the broken, will not eat the flesh of the fat, and will feed wisely what stands still.[6] That all the worshippers of Christ may clearly understand this, in the book that follows I must relate the order of the election by which Amadeo the wise duke of Savoy was adopted as Roman pontiff.

So when Gabriel Condulmaro was deposed,[7] as we have shown, from the Roman pontificate, when the leaders of the Fathers had been summoned on the same day in the chapter-house of the cathedral, it was debated whether it was desirable that a new pontiff should immediately be elected, or whether this should be put off for a time. Those anxious to hurry on the choosing of a pontiff asserted that it was full of dangers for a community of this kind

congregationi huiusmodi sine capite gubernari. Morbum esse in tota urbe pestiferum, qui non solum pueritiam et iuuentutem, sed uiros etiam fortes aetate et aridos senes, quibus innoxia pestis esse solet, depopularetur. Eamque luem primo ex aduenis ad pauperes urbis, et inde ad diuites, denique etiam ad ipsos Concilii patres aduolasse. Praedicare augere timorem, et omnia, sicuti fit, plus uero extollere. Decretum[1] nequaquam obstare, quo cautum esset sexaginta diebus post uacationem supersederi. Id nanque intelligi, cum extra locum Concilii sedes uacaret; nec expectandum esse ut principes per Gabrielem suasi obsisterent, quibus scribenda unico nuncio foret et Gabrielis depositio et alterius assumptio.

Alii uero quibus supersedendum esse uidebatur, nec carere Concilium capite, quod Christus erat, asseuerabant, nec rectorem desyderare, quod per praesidentes et alios officiales gubernaretur. Pestis autem in tali re mentionem non esse habendam, quoniam nec timenda mors esset uiris fortibus, nec pro fide Christi pugnantibus iniici metus tormenti possit. Eum tamen qui modo in urbe grassaretur morbum iamiam facto iudicio[2] sperandum esse commitescere, qui propter neglectam iustitiam creditus fuerat inualescere. Principibus uero in re tam ardua inuitis potius quam neglectis utendum esse, nec uerendum fore, quin eo casu fortes fortuna sit adiutura.[3]

Re igitur inter omnes diligenter trutinata, licet 'quot homines, tot sententiae' forent, et 'suus cuique mos'[4] esset, constare tamen inter omnes uidebatur utilius esse statim eligere, differre honestius. Eam ob causam Ioannes Segouius, summa scientia uir: 'Diuersis hinc atque hinc patres', inquit, 'rationibus trahor; ut tamen maturius rem ex animo colligo, ea mihi demum sententia stat ut electionem festinam humani, dilationem uero bimestrem diuini consilii putem. Mihi enim non uidetur quod sic factum legibus rescindi posse, decretique nostri non solum uerba, sed mentem quoque seruandam censeo. Quapropter si mihi credetis, honestatem potius periculosam sequemini quam utilitatem securam, licet re uera secerni utilitas ab honestate non queat.' Vicit igitur

[1] The decree referred to here and in what follows was passed at session vii (6 Nov. 1432) and laid down an interval of sixty days if an election of a pope occurred while the Council was in session; this was to enable absent cardinals to attend. At session xxxv (10 July 1439) this interval was reaffirmed (cf. below, p. 192, n. 4; Mansi, XXIX. cols. 42–43, 181–2).

[2] That is the deposition of Eugenius, now referred to in the text as Gabriel, since he is no longer pope.

to be governed without a head, and that there was throughout the city a destructive plague, which not only was sweeping away children and youths, but men strong in years as well as withered old men whom the plague does not usually harm. This pestilence had sped first from strangers to the poor of the city, then to the rich, finally even to the Fathers of the Council. Proclaiming it increased the alarm, and, as usually happens, exaggerated everything. [They maintained] that the decree[1] stipulating that there should be an interval of sixty days after a vacancy was no obstacle, for that was taken to apply to a vacancy in a see away from the place of the Council. Nor should they wait for the princes to be persuaded by Gabriel and raise objections. By one and the same message they should learn of Gabriel's deposition and the adoption of a successor.

Others, who wanted an interval, maintained that the Council did not lack a head namely Christ, and that it did not need a ruler, as it was governed by the presidents and other officials. No mention should be made of the plague in such a matter as neither should brave men fear death nor fear of torture grip those fighting for the faith of Christ. The disease which was now raging in the city would, it was to be hoped, grow less severe now that the judgement[2] had been given, as it had been thought to gain strength because justice was being neglected. In so difficult a matter it was better to find the princes unwilling rather than overlooked and, there should be no fear of fortune in that case not aiding the brave.[3]

So when the matter had carefully been examined by all, though there were as many views as men, and each had his own usage,[4] yet there seemed to be general agreement that it was more advantageous to hold an election at once, more honourable to postpone it. For this reason John of Segovia, a man of great knowledge, said, 'I am torn, Fathers, this way and that by opposing considerations, yet the longer I ponder over the matter my view remains that human counsel advises a quick election, but divine counsel a two months' postponement. For I do not believe that legal enactments of this kind can be repealed, and I consider that there must be kept not only the letter but the spirit of our decree. So if you will be persuaded by me, you will take an honourable path involving risks, rather than a safe and advantageous one, though it is not really possible to separate

[3] Cf. Cicero, *Tusc. Disp.* ii. 4, 11; Terence, *Phormio*, 203. [4] Cf. *Phormio*, 454.

inter patres dilationis sententia, duobusque mensibus expectandum esse decreuerunt.[1] Interim missi ad principes nuncii depositionem Romani pontificis in Synodo factam ubique gentium publicarunt. Corruptus tamen interea coeli tractus et 'letifer annus' nequaquam purgabatur, sed crescente indies tabida lue, 'linquebant' plurimi 'dulces animas, aut aegra trahebant corpora'.[2] Quare orta est subita trepidatio patribus, nec quid agerent satis consultum habebant, neque tutum se transferre putabant neque manere. Qui tamen permanendum duxerunt alios quoque tenuerunt ut qui famem et hostiles insidias superauerant in terra pestis[3] persecutione non uiderentur deficere; quia tamen non omnes teneri poterant, caute prouisum est ne per cuiusquam recessum dissolui Concilium uideretur, utque solidius res firmarentur, lecti sunt ad huiusmodi curam nonnulli patres, quos 'de stabilimento' appellauere,[4] quorum postea in longum tempus potestas durauit.

Cunque iam steriles exureret Syrius agros, omnesque arerent herbae,[5] latius undique grassata est pestis, et feruescens dietim morbus incredibile est quantas animas Orco demiserit;[6] horribile uisu erat horatim funera per uicos exportari, semperque aut Dominicum corpus aut unctionis extremae sacramentum in uiarum compitis esse, et ubique planctum, ubique gemitum exaudiri. Nulla expers luctus in tota urbe domus patebat, nullibi aut risus cerni, aut iocus poterat; illic matronae uiros, illic uiri uxores deflebant. Ibat per urbem omnem uterque sexus; et illi natos, illi parentes, alii fratres, alii amicos desyderabant. Vt tamen pauidior quisque fuit, sic alter alterum sermone uitabat. Et alii quidem domi manebant, alii uero per urbem euntes narium et oris spiracula captatis aduersus pestem odoribus claudebant. Cadebat sine numero urbana plebecula; utque in primo autumni frigore syluarum folia concidunt, sic iuuentutis corpora expirabant.[7] Tantaque morbi uis fuit, ut aliquem nunc in platea laetum et

[1] Cf. above, p. 190, n. 1.

[2] Cf. Virgil, *Aen.* iii. 137–40.

[3] Preceded by famine conditions, as it so often was, the plague began at Basle in the spring of 1439 and was at its height in the summer. Aeneas Sylvius describes it again in his *Commentaries*, pp. 26–28.

[4] Notably to scrutinize applications to withdraw from Basle: *Mon. Con.* III. 338; Haller, VI. 539 (30 June 1439); those appointed were the patriarch of Aquileia, the bishop of Lausanne, the abbot of Dona, and Augustinus de Insula. The problem of the Fathers withdrawing from the Council is also dealt with in the decree of session xxxv (10 July 1439, Mansi, loc. cit.) which, in providing for the *stabilitas* of the Council, refers to a decision of 12 Dec. 1438 declaring that the Council could not be regarded as dissolved as a result of the departure of any of its individual members.

[5] Cf. Virgil, *Aen.* iii. 141–2. Virgil, like other writers, associates Sirius, the dog-star, with heat. Cf. *Georg.* ii. 353; *Aen.* x. 273.

advantage and honour.' Among the Fathers then the opinion in favour of postponement prevailed, and they decided to wait two months.[1] In the meantime messages were sent to the princes, and published everywhere the deposition of the Roman pontiff in the Synod. Meanwhile, however, the expanse of the heavens was tainted, and the 'death-bringing year' was in no way cleansed, but as the wasting pestilence grew daily, very many 'gave up their sweet lives, or dragged about sick bodies'.[2] For this reason a sudden fearfulness came upon the Fathers, who were not sure what they should do, and did not think it safe either to move away or to stay. Yet those who thought they should stay, kept back others as well, so that those who had beaten hunger and the wiles of the enemy on earth, might not appear to fail at the attack of the plague.[3] Yet because not all could be kept back, the careful precaution was taken that anyone's departure should not make it appear that the Council was breaking up. To put this matter on a firmer basis, several Fathers were appointed to see to this kind of thing, whom they called 'the Permanency Committee',[4] whose power lasted for a long time afterwards.

When Sirius was now scorching the fields with drought, and all the grass withered,[5] the plague raged everywhere more widely, and the disease, gaining in virulence every day, sent an incredible number of souls down to Orcus.[6] It was dreadful to see funeral processions every hour in the streets, and always at the street corners there was the Lord's body or the sacrament of extreme unction, and everywhere wailing and groaning was heard. No house in the whole city was free of mourning, nowhere could laughter or joking be observed. At one place matrons were weeping for their husbands, at another, husbands for their wives. Throughout the whole city both men and women were on the move, and some were mourning for children, some for parents, some for brothers, others for friends. Yet as everyone grew frightened, so everyone avoided contact with others. Some stayed at home, others, as they went through the city, guarded their noses and mouths against the plague by the use of perfumes. The lower orders of the city went down beyond all counting and, just as in the first autumn chill the leaves of the woods fall, even so the young expired.[7] So great was the virulence of the disease that after seeing someone in the street now

[6] Cf. Virgil, *Aen.* ii. 398; ix. 527. 'Orcus' is one of Virgil's names for the abode of the dead in the underworld.
[7] Cf. Virgil, *Aen.* vi. 309–10.

ualidum cernens, post horam decimam humatum fore audires. Iamque tot erant morientium funera, ut sepulturae loca deforent. Quapropter exaratis omnibus coemiteriis foueas in parochiis peramplas fecerunt ubi pluribus congestis cadaueribus terram superinduxerunt.[1] Quam ob causam ita exterriti patres erant, ut nullus iam in eorum facie sanguis rubesceret.

Permaxime tamen inopina et subita mors Ludouici protonotarii cunctos exterruit, quem (sicuti supra retulimus) uirum robustum, aetate florentem, et utriusque iuris scientia eminentissimum, paucissimis horis inuidiosus oppressit morbus.[2] Cecidit et paulo post Ludouicus, patriarcha Aquileiensis,[3] uir grandaeuus, et in aduersitatibus enutritus, nec quem optauerat diem electionis papae potuit cernere. In eo tamen partem consolationis recepit, quoniam prius depositum Gabrielem uidit, quam moreretur. Laetusque (ut ante praedixit) tale nuncium in orbem portauit alium. Hic septem diebus aegrotauit, et (ut quidam uolunt) incuria magis sua quam ui morbi defunctus est. Fuitque eius obitus omnibus patribus amarissimus. Iamque duas Concilii columnas prostratas esse dicebant, protonotarium et patriarcham; quoniam iure alter, facto alter ueritatem Synodi defendissent. Delatus est hic feretro super ceruices hominum patriarchali habitu uestitus, faciem ostentans similem dormienti, usque ad Carthusiam,[4] quem omnis patrum lachrymans secuta est turba; ibique ante altare sepultus iacet. Per idem temporis diem clausit in terra Suitzerorum uir summa doctrina, eleemosynarius regis Aragonum,[5] in Argentina paulopost Ebronensis episcopus,[6] in Spira abbas Vergiliacensis,[7] et inter Budam ac Viennam Austriae Ioannes,[8] Lubecensis episcopus. Sed ii ultimi etiam illud commemorandum in morte gesserunt. Nanque ubi adesse migrationis horam sensere, compluribus ad se uiris grauibus accersitis, coram ipso Christi corpore, quem statim sumpturi, et ante cuius tribunal infra paucas horas comparituri erant: 'Vos omnes qui adestis', dixerunt, 'orate Deum, ut illos conuertat qui Gabrielem pro summo pontifice recognoscunt; quia in eo statu saluari non possunt'; seque in fide Basiliensis Concilii morituros professi, absque ulla excusatione

[1] On the plague in Basle see R. Wackernagel, *Geschichte der Stadt Basel*, I. 522–5 and refs. p. 637.

[2] Cf. his eulogy above, pp. 100–2 and cf. p. 96.

[3] Between 7 and 19 Aug. 1439. Cf. above, p. 12.

[4] Cf. above, p. 102, n. 3.

[5] Cf. above, p. 20, n. 5, and p. 104.

[6] Cf. above, p. 16, n. 2.

[7] Cf. above, p. 142.

[8] Cf. above, p. 10, n. 5.

cheerful and well, you would hear ten hours later of him being buried. There were so many funerals that burying places were insufficient. So when all the cemeteries were filled by interments, they made large pits in the parishes, in which they collected many corpses and covered them with earth.[1] For this reason the Fathers were so alarmed that none had any trace of ruddy colour in his face.

Most of all the unexpected and sudden death of Lodovico, the protonotary, alarmed everyone for, as we have related above, he was a strong man in the flower of his youth, and pre-eminent in the knowledge of both branches of law, when within a very few hours this hateful disease struck him down.[2] There died also shortly afterwards Ludwig, patriarch of Aquileia,[3] a man of a great age and brought up amid adversity, who was not permitted, as he had wished, to witness the day of the election of the pope. In regard to this he did have some consolation since he saw Gabriel deposed before he died. With gladness, as he said beforehand, he bore such news into another world. He was ill for seven days and, as some will have it, died rather through his own lack of care than through the virulence of the disease. His death came as a bitter blow to all the Fathers. Now they were saying that two of the pillars of the Council were laid low, the protonotary and the patriarch, since the one had defended the truth of the Synod in law, the other in deed. The latter, wearing the robes of a patriarch, and with his face visible and like that of a sleeper, was carried on a bier on men's shoulders as far as the Charterhouse,[4] and the whole concourse of Fathers followed weeping. He was buried there, and lies before the altar. At the same time there ended his days in Switzerland a man of great learning, the almoner of the king of Aragon,[5] in Strasbourg shortly afterwards the bishop of Hebron,[6] in Speyer the abbot of Vézelay[7] and between Buda and Vienna in Austria, Johann, bishop of Lübeck.[8] These last even accomplished something noteworthy in their death. For when they felt that the time of departure was near, they summoned several grave Fathers, and in the presence of the very body of Christ, of whom they were about to be partakers and before whose judgement-seat they were destined within a few hours to appear, they cried, 'All you who are present, pray to God to convert those who acknowledge Gabriel as the chief pontiff, because in that state they cannot receive salvation', and professing that they would die in the faith of the Council of Basle, without any making of excuses and like men

dormientibus similes ad Dominum migrauerunt. In Bohemia quoque legatus sacri Concilii, Constantiensis episcopus,[1] uirtutis exemplar decessit. Eratque et intra Concilium et extra ubique timor et tremor. Fuerat in Concilio per plures annos abbas de Dona,[2] Cumanae diocesis, uir mundo pauper, Deo autem diues, quem nec preces ullae, neque minae ullae unquam a recto proposito flexerunt; mendicareque potius in ueritate patrum uoluit quam in mendacio aemulorum abundare. Quapropter dimissis dominis, qui sibi uictum praebebant, in peste permansit; qua etiam ipse tactus migrauit ad patres, unamque tantum uaccam testatus suo monasterio legauit. Ex camera Arelatensis percussus Henricus capellanus[3] triduo expirauit. Ex officio scriptorum bullarum octo defuncti sunt; inter quos etiam uir summa bonitate Arnoldus Kempenich,[4] tunc rescribendarius, decessit. Ex scriptoribus sacrae poenitentiariae aut totidem aut plures ceciderunt. Omnisque ordo patrum confossus fuit. Ex doctoribus magnus defecit numerus.

Qui uero aegritudinem incidebant, admodum pauci liberabantur; unus tamen inter alios Aeneas Sylvius Senensis, morbo percussus, diuina adiutus euasit gratia. Hic enim, sepulto amico suo, Iuliano Romano,[5] quem tenere adamauit, sequenti nocte ulcus persensit, triduoque morti uicinus iacuit, desperantibusque domesticis suis inunctus est, totaque urbe ab amicis pro mortuo deploratus; ut tamen diuinae pietati collibuit, spacium uitae longioris recepit.[6] Sed heu rerum humanarum instabilis ordo, heu fallax promissio mundi! Aeneas, qui suo in corpore mori non potuit, in alieno est mortuus. Paruo nanque post tempore ex Tridento rediens,[7] Ioannem Pinanum[8] ex Rothomagensi ciuitate oriundum, uenenosa febre et incuria medicorum extinctum repperit; quo nuncio ita turbatus fuit, et ita mente alienatus ut animae suae dimidium sibi subtractum esse ostenderit, neque deinceps ille sibi ad res Conciliares ardor, aut ad literarum studia uigor manserit, uixque animulam, qua nunc spirat, retinuisse se diceret. Fuit autem Ioannes honestis parentibus natus, literis ingenuis eruditus, experientia rerum perdoctus, ingenio uigil, et animo uastus; apud cardinalem Arelatensem literas primus obsignabat. In re Conciliari sic diligens et expertus erat ut eum

[1] Philibar de Montjeu, at Prague.

[2] Cf. above, p. 192, n. 4.

[3] De Bona: Haller, VI. 503.

[4] This name is not listed among the chancery clerks in 1439 (Haller, VI. 775) but an Arnolphus Champerich is mentioned as 'scriptor concilii' in Sept. 1435 (Haller, III. 518).

[5] Cf. *Commentaries*, p. 27.

[6] Aeneas also had treatment from a doctor whom he describes as 'lucky but ignorant'. It is described in the *Commentaries*, p. 27.

[7] 7 Oct. 1439: Haller, VI. 625.

[8] Jean Pivan: *Mon. Con.* II. 724; cf. Pérouse, p. 352.

asleep, they departed to the Lord. In Bohemia too a legate of the holy Council, the bishop of Coutances,[1] died, a pattern of virtue. There was everywhere both inside and outside the Council fear and trembling. There had been in the Council for several years the abbot of Dona[2] in the diocese of Como, a man poor in this world, but rich in God, whom no prayers or threats ever turned aside from the straightness of his purpose; he preferred to be a mendicant in the truth of the Fathers than to be well off in the mendacity of the envious. So sending away those monks who looked after his needs, he remained amid the plague; and stricken by it also, he departed to his fathers, bequeathing to his monastery his property, a single cow. From the household of the cardinal of Arles, Henry, the chaplain,[3] was attacked and died within three days. From the office of the writers of bulls eight perished, among whom passed away Arnold Kempenich,[4] a man of great kindness, at that time the clerk of rescripts. Of the clerks of the sacred penitentiary as many or more went down. Every rank of Fathers suffered losses. Of the doctors a great number was lost.

Very few of those who incurred the sickness gained deliverance. One of them was Aeneas Sylvius of Siena, who when stricken by the disease, escaped through divine aid. For after the burial of his friend, Giuliano Romano,[5] whom he dearly loved, on the following night an ulcer developed and for three days he lay on the verge of death. When his servants gave up hope he received unction, and throughout the city was mourned by his friends as dead. Yet by the will of divine compassion, he received a longer stretch of life.[6] But alas for the shifting nature of human affairs, alas for the world's treacherous promise! Aeneas who could not die in his own person died in that of another. For shortly afterwards returning from Trent,[7] he found dead through a venomous fever and the carelessness of the doctors Jean Pivan,[8] who came from the city of Rouen. This news so disturbed him and drove him so far out of his right mind that he appeared to have lost the half of his life, and from then on he did not retain the same interest in the affairs of the Council, or the same keenness in the study of letters, and he said that only with difficulty did he cling to the remnant of life that gives him breath. Now Jean was born of gentle parents, had received a liberal education, was thoroughly experienced in affairs; cautious by nature, he had a wide intellect. He was the chief secretary of the cardinal of Arles. In conciliar business he was so

inter primos locent quorum obitus sacro Concilio onerosi fuerunt. Cum Aenea uero non tantum socius, sed alter Aeneas erat. Ferenda tamen fuit omnibus illa fortuna; nec quisquam impune praeteriit, quin aut suum aut alterius indoluerit casum.

Illis autem diebus quibus feruidior erat pestis, quibusque dietim plus quam centum apparebant funera, magnae apud Arelatensem habitae preces sunt ut uicinum aliquod in rus secederet; eratque omnium domesticorum aut familiarium eius uox eadem: 'Quid agis, spectate pater? Fuge hunc saltem lunae defectum, salua tuum caput, quo saluo saluamur omnes, quo etiam pereunte omnes perimus; quod si te pestis opprimat, ad quem confugiemus? Quis nos reget, quis ductor huius fidelis exercitus erit? Iam tuam cameram irrepsit uirus, iam secretarius tuus, iamque cubicularius tuus mortem obiit. Consydera discrimen, et salua teipsum et nos.' Sed neque illum preces neque domesticorum funera flectere potuerunt, uolentem potius cum uitae periculo saluare Concilium quam cum periculo Concilii saluare uitam. Sciebat enim quoniam se recedente, pauci remansissent, facileque committi fraus in eius absentia potuisset; quocirca sicut in re bellica milites omnia discrimina subeunt, cum medios inter hostes imperatorem conspiciunt, sic patres Concilii pestem erubuerunt fugere, cum praesidentem in eodem periculo secum permanere uiderunt. Quae res opinionem illorum euertit, qui patres in Basilea commorantes non fidei ueritatem, sed propria quaerere commoda garriebant; nullum enim[a] est in terra commodum quod permutare cum uita mortales soleant. Illam nanque qui mundo seruiunt omnibus rebus anteponunt; et illi quidem (ut est in Cicerone)[1] nihil habentes in uita iucundius uita, ducere uitam cum uirtute non possunt. Hi autem nostri, murum inexpugnabilem pro domo Dei se exhibentes, superatis omnibus quas Gabriel struxit insidiis, superatis etiam difficultatibus quas sterilis annus produxit, ad extremum quoque uiuendi cupiditate posthabita, periculum superauere, ueritatemque sacri Concilii usque in hoc tempus incommutabilibus animis defendere non dubitarunt.

Transactis autem post depositionem Gabrielis diebus decreti, uisum est patribus ad electionem pontificis intendendum, habitisque inter primates de modo procedendi sermonibus, auisatum est,

[a] enim V; *om.* α

[1] Cf. *Rhetorica ad Herennium*, iv. 14, 20 (now no longer attributed to Cicero).

painstaking and well versed that he was held to be among the chief of those whose deaths embarrassed the holy Council. To Aeneas he was not so much an associate as another Aeneas. Yet all had to suffer that fate. No-one escaped scot-free without mourning his own mischance or that of another.

At that time when the plague grew more rife and when every day more than a hundred funerals were witnessed, the cardinal of Arles was much pressed by requests that he should move somewhere into the neighbouring countryside. All his servants and intimates used the same words: 'Honoured Father, what are you doing? Avoid at least this waning of the moon. Save your own head, as with you safe we are all safe, but if you perish, we all perish. If the plague should attack you, with whom shall we take refuge? Who will rule us, who will be the leader of this loyal army? The poison has already crept into your household, and your secretary and your chamberlain have both died. Consider the risk and save both yourself and us.' Neither the prayers nor the deaths of his servants could move him, as he wished rather at the risk of his life to save the Council, than save his life at the Council's risk. For he realized that, if he withdrew, few would have remained and trickery could easily have been carried out in his absence. Therefore, just as in warfare soldiers endure all hazards when, in the midst of the foe, they see their commander, in like fashion the Fathers of the Council were ashamed to flee the plague when they saw their president staying with them in the same peril. This confounded the belief of those who chattered about the Fathers spending time in Basle in search not of the truth of the faith but of their own profit, as there is no profit on earth that mortal men are in the habit of exchanging for life. For those who are slaves of the world put life before all things, and those who, as Cicero has it[1] hold nothing in life pleasanter than life cannot lead virtuous lives. These people of ours, displaying in themselves an unsurmountable bulwark before the house of God, overcoming all the plots devised by Gabriel, and all the hardships caused by the barren year, putting aside finally even the desire to live, overcame the danger and did not hesitate with unalterable hearts to defend the truth of the holy Council right up to this time.

Now when the statutory days had passed after the deposition of Gabriel, the Fathers resolved to attend to the election of a pontiff, and the leaders exchanged views and held discussions about the

et tandem in deputationibus et in plenaria congregatione conclusum duos et triginta patres ex corpore Concilii assumi debere, omnes in diaconatus ordine constitutos, qui suscepto[a] iureiurando per sanctam Synodum ordinato, una cum cardinali Arelatensi intrantes conclaue, Romanum Papam eligerent. Deputationi tamen cui 'de communibus' nomen est, soli quatuor et uiginti ad celebrandam electionem recipiendi cum cardinali uidebantur, eosque in sacerdotio requirebat. Obtinuit tamen, ut semper fit, quod tribus placuit; quapropter decretum super ea re factum est.[1] Interea domus[2] conclauis sine intermissione parabatur. Qua perfecta ad nominationem xxxii. qui cum cardinali papam eligerent circa ipsum Octobris principium uentum est; fuitque res primo ingressu apprime difficilis, et aliis quidem uno, aliis alio modo nominare electores placebat. Aperuit tamen denique Gulielmus, archidiaconus Metensis, uir et naturali sensu et acquisito memorabilis, cuiusque supra in relatione processus[3] papae meminimus, uiam unam, quae, primo per deputationem fidei approbata et per alios reiecta, ab omnibus tandem maturius pensantibus recepta est. Aiebat enim grauissimus ille doctor tres esse in Concilio patres quibus res ista committi posset, quorumque fidem totum Concilium crederet secuturum. Tres autem uiros hos fore dicebat Thomam, abbatem de Dunduno,[b] ordinis Cisterciensis, diocesis Candidae Casae, uulgo de Scotia[c][4] nuncupatum; Ioannem de Segouia,[5] archidiaconum de uilla Vissosa in ecclesia Ouetensi;[d] ac Thomam de Corcellis,[6] canonicum Ambrianensem, in sacra theologia magistros. Quibus sobrie laudatis quoniam notae[e] uirtutis essent, hos primum tres fore ex electoribus Romani pontificis statuebat; iis quoque committi electionem reliquorum nouem et uiginti, quos clam omnibus inter se nominarent, nec ante diem publicarent quae introitum conclauis immediate foret praecessura. Qua re in deputatione fidei approbata, missi ad alias deputationes sunt[f] Franciscus de Fuxe,[7] theologus, ac Aeneas Senensis, qui rem aliis suaderent, sed suspicantibus aliis fraudem esse, frustra omnis suasio fuit. Quoniam tamen nulla per alios expeditior aut securior uia demonstrabatur, stetit deputatio fidei

[a] suscepto W; suscepti αV [b] Dre'dra' (*following* Dund' *cancelled*) V
[c] Graecia αγ [d] Ouetensi (Ouethensi) W; Onetensi α *corr.*; Metensi α
[e] notae W; uerae V; uice α [f] fuit αγ

[1] At the thirty-seventh session, 24 Oct. 1439: Mansi, XXIX. cols. 185–8.
[2] Below, p. 230.
[3] Above, p. 12, n. 15. This is the passage which suggests that a book now missing dealt with the 'processus papae'. See Introduction, p. xxix, and n. 2.
[4] Cf. above, p. 16, n. 4.
[5] Cf. above, p. xxviii.
[6] Cf. above, p. 13, n. 3.
[7] Cf. above, p. 20, n. 6.

method of procedure, and at length in the deputations and in a general congregation it was decided that thirty-two Fathers should be drawn from the body of the Council, all [at least] ordained as deacons, who taking an oath prescribed by the holy Synod, should enter a conclave with the cardinal of Arles and elect the Roman pope. The deputation, however, which is called that 'for general business', considered that only twenty-four persons should be admitted with the cardinal as electors and it wanted these to be of the priesthood. The view of three deputations, as is always the case, prevailed, and a decree on this matter was carried.[1] In the meantime work was going on all the time to prepare a house[2] for the conclave. When it was finished, about the beginning of October they proceeded to nominate the thirty-two who were to be the electors of the pope along with the cardinal. At the start the business was particularly difficult. Some wanted to nominate the electors in one way, others in another. In the end Guillaume, archdeacon of Metz, a person noteworthy both for his innate and his acquired sense, whom we have mentioned previously in speaking about the process against the pope,[3] disclosed one method which, approved by the deputation on faith and rejected by the others at first, in the end was accepted by all when they gave it longer thought. This grave doctor said that there were three Fathers in the Council who could be entrusted with this matter, and whose good faith he believed the whole Council would accept. These three, he said, were Thomas, abbot of Dundrennan, of the Cistercian order, in the diocese of Whithorn, commonly called Thomas of Scotland;[4] John of Segovia,[5] archdeacon of Villa Vezzosa in the church of Oviedo; and Thomas de Courcelles,[6] canon of Amiens, all masters of theology. Praising them in measured terms because they were of well-known virtue, he was of the view that these should be the first three of the electors of the Roman pontiff, and to them should be entrusted the choosing of the remaining twenty-nine, whose nomination they should make in secret and not publish before the day immediately preceding the entry into the conclave. So when approval of this had been given in the deputation on faith, the theologian, François de Fuxe[7] and Aeneas of Siena were sent to the other deputations to recommend this course to them but, as all suspected a trick, their recommendation was ineffective. Yet since no simpler or surer method was devised by others, the deputation on faith stood by its

semper in sententia. Interiectisque nonnullis diebus, iterum Franciscum atque Aeneam praedictos ad deputationes alias destinauit; eo addito ut, si placeret deputationibus aliis, uirum alium sibi tres patres coassumerent. Hoc autem ideo factum est ne maxima omnium Germanica natio nullum se inter tresuiros habuisse conqueri posset. Abbatem nanque illum de Scotia uideri potius Gallicum quam Germanum[1] nonnulli submurmurabant, fuisseque in hoc tam grandi negotio non insularem sed mediterraneum hominem, qui alios nosset, assumendum; quae adiectio animos fere omnium placauit. Ac post multas rei discussiones in hac sententia consonatum est.

Nominati et electi sunt tres uiri supradicti pro tribus ex electoribus Romani episcopi, iisque plenaria facultas commissa est eligendi, si uellent, et assumendi secum unum, duos, aut tres alios, prout eis uideretur; qui assumpti et electi similem et eandem secum potestatem haberent facultate, mandato, uice et autoritate sacri Concilii nominandi et eligendi restantes electores ipsius futuri summi pontificis et etiam alios officiales pro conclaui necessarios, ita quod nullus per eos eligendus aut nominandus, electus et nominatus censeretur, nisi a maiori parte ipsorum eligentium nominatus electusque foret. Iniunctumque eis est ut reciperent et nominarent ipsos restantes electores ex toto corpore Concilii, habendo respectum ad nationes et deputationes in Concilio existentes, quantum fieri posset. Receptumque a praefatis tribus iuramentum est, quo stricti sunt uiros idoneos et timorem Dei habentes nominare, electosque per ipsos usque ad publicationem eorundem in generali congregatione aut iussione iussu Concilii faciendam nemini reuelare, sed ipsam electionem sic per eos celebrandam sub eorum sigillis in loco securo et sub fida custodia usque ad ipsam diem publicationis tenere. Quae res tertio idus Octobris[2] in generali congregatione peracta est, mirumque omnibus uisum est ac miraculo simile rem tantam, tam necessariam, tamque optatam tribus duntaxat uiris potuisse committi; fecit tamen omnia uirtus, omnemque fraudis suspicionem probata triumuirorum bonitas procul extrusit. Re autem hac conclusa, uidebatur cardinalis Arelatensis praeter opinionem omnium expeditionem differre. Et alii quidem, ut est multitudo ad detrahendum prona,

[1] A reference to the political association of Scotland and France.

[2] On 13 Oct. 1439: *Mon. Con.* III. 406; Haller, VI. 630–1.

view. After the lapse of some days it again sent the same François and Aeneas to the other deputations with this addition that, if other deputations preferred it, the three Fathers should co-opt another. This came about so that the German nation, the largest of all, could not complain that it had no representative among the three. For some people were murmuring that the abbot from Scotland seemed more like a Frenchman than a German,[1] and that in so important a business a man not from an island but from the continent, who knew others, should have been chosen. This addition quietened the minds of almost all. After many discussions agreement was obtained for this view.

The three men afore-mentioned were nominated and chosen as three of the electors of the Roman bishop, and they were given full power to choose, if they wished, and co-opt one, two or three others, as they saw fit. These, when co-opted and chosen, were to have similar power and the same as theirs, of nominating and choosing with the permission and by the order of the holy Council and in its name and by its authority the remaining electors of the future chief pontiff and other officials necessary for the conclave, provided that no-one to be chosen or nominated by them should be considered as chosen and nominated unless nominated and chosen by a majority of those making the choice. They were charged with accepting and nominating the remaining electors from the whole body of the Council having regard as far as they could to the nations and deputations of the Council. The three men already mentioned took an oath binding them to nominate suitable and God-fearing persons and not to reveal to anyone those chosen by themselves until the public announcement of the same in the general congregation or by an instruction to be made by the Council's order, but to keep the list of those to be chosen by them in this way under their seal in a safe place and under secure guard until the day of making it public. This was settled in the general congregation on 13 October,[2] and it seemed surprising and almost miraculous to all that business so important, necessary, and desirable could have been entrusted to only three persons. Yet their virtue brought this about, and the well-tried goodness of the triumvirs banished all suspicion of trickery. On the conclusion of this business it appeared that the cardinal of Arles was putting off the settlement of the matter contrary to the general expectation. Some—so ready is a crowd to criticize—were

eam mordebant, alii contra ipsius intentionem properari electionem studebant. Quam rem ut ille intellexit, praeter consuetudinem suam, quem nunquam hactenus maledicta curare perpendimus huiusmodi, rerum querimoniam deputationibus fecit; tantumque dicendo effecit ut se penitus expurgato, eos qui sibi detraxerant in odium ac contemptum adduxerit, fidemque erga Concilium suam probatiorem reddiderit.[1] Dumque ista geruntur, iam fama in orbem ierat cessasse apud Basilienses pestem, electionemque Papae accelerari. Quapropter ad spectaculum tantae rei ex diuersis regionibus complurimi aduolarunt, inter quos etiam plerique insignes praelati profecti sunt.

Cumque iam plenius solito Concilium esset, et omnes fere redissent quos pestis fugauerat, uolentes tresuiri commissionem per Concilium factam exequi, coassumpto sibi Christianno de Gregregino,[2] praeposito ecclesiae Sancti Petri in Brumia Olomucensis diocesis, ex umbilico nationis Germanicae oriundo, in theologia magistro, et recti iudicii et constantis animi uiro, quinto Calendas Nouembris in domo fratrum Minorum conuenientes nominationem sibi commissam peregerunt, eamque iuxta mandatum Concilii obsignatam custodiuerunt. Prius tamen quam id ageretur, uiros expertos ex singulis nationibus in colloquiis habuerunt, quorum relatu et mores hominum persenserunt, et qualis quisque in sua patria haberetur, subtili indagine didicerunt. Complures quoque ad eos suopte ingenio decurrebant, quibus uel laudare amicum uel reprobare inimicum studio fuit, quos illi ueritatis cupidi, et ne in tanta re fallerentur anxii, libenter audiebant; nullumque eos in sacro Concilio perpetratum latuit malum, et multa etiam foris acta senserunt. Quo fit ut nullum magis hodie de moribus hominum quam triumuirale iudicium expectetur. Hi ergo quarto Calendas Nouembris ex iussu Concilii relaturi quid egerant in congregationem uenerunt, quo loci iam omnis (ut aiunt) incorporatorum coetus confluxerat, nec illa die ex his qui poterant quisquam defuit. Et quoniam nulli unquam tresuiri se aperuerant, quanto secretior res erat, tanto desyderatior omnibus uidebatur.

[1] On Aleman's hesitation and subsequent self-defence see Pérouse, pp. 309–13.

[2] Canon of Olmütz and a theologian; president at this time of the German nation: *Mon. Con.* III. 416; Haller, VI. 352, 713–25, etc.

attacking it, others were eager that the election should be hurried on contrary to his intention. When he realized this, departing from his usual practice, for we have never considered up to now that he worried about abuse of this kind, he complained of these matters to the deputations. His words were so effective that he cleared himself completely, brought his critics into hatred and contempt, and created greater certainty about his good faith towards the Council.[1] While this was happening, a report had spread round the world that the plague had abated among the people of Basle, and that the election of a pope was being hastened. So to witness this important event very many rushed there from different countries, among whom many distinguished prelates set out.

Since the Council was now fuller than usual, and almost all had returned whom the plague had put to flight, the triumvirs, anxious to carry out the commission assigned by the Council, co-opted Christian von Königgräz,[2] provost of the church of St. Peter at Brünn in the diocese of Olmütz, coming from the heart of the German nation, a master of theology, and a person of sound judgement and a steadfast purpose; and meeting on 28 October in the house of the Franciscans they carried out the task of nomination entrusted to them. In accordance with the Council's instruction they kept their list guarded under seal. Yet before that was done, they held conversations with knowledgeable persons from each nation, from whose information they gained a knowledge of men's characters, and learned by careful investigation what reputation each enjoyed in his own country. Many persons too had access to them by their own wish, who were interested in supporting a friend or belittling an enemy, to whom the triumvirs willingly listened in their eagerness for the truth and anxiety not to be deceived in this important matter. No misdeed committed in the sacred Council was concealed from them and they had information too about many actions outside. The result is that no judgement is today more eagerly awaited about men's characters than that of one of these triumvirs. So on 29 October in accordance with the Council's instructions they came to the congregation to report their actions. There the whole body of the 'incorporated' (as they are called) had gathered and that day no-one who could come was absent. Since the triumvirs had revealed their secrets to no one, the matter, through being so concealed,

Confabulari autem omnes inuicem, multa de tribusuiris dicere, multa etiam de nominatione uaticinari, et alii istum, et alii illum electorem futurum contendere; et ut affectio et ueri similitudo trahebat, quemque sic ratiocinari. Quia tamen nihil certi habebant, mira omnibus erat audiendi cupiditas. Et alii quidem festiuas induerunt uestes, alii seruitores nouos conduxerant, alii etiam domum amicis commendauerant, qui se futuros in numero electorum arbitrabantur;[1] fit enim nescio quomodo ut se quisque supra uirtutem aestimet suam, quorum ambitio magis postea irridetur quam impleatur.

Cardinalis autem Arelatensis in tanta re anxius, et pluribus occupatus negociis, aliquanto tardius uenit quam tempus exegit, expectationemque sui non sine admiratione omnibus praebuit; qui tamen ut ad subsellia resedit, mora sua primitus excusata: 'Hodie', inquit, 'magna res agitur; in nominatione quae statim aperietur status ecclesiae pendet. Si tresuiri quibus rem commisistis bene egerint, fateor quippe tardiuscule me uenisse; si autem male, nimis cito assum.' Quae uerba et trementi uoce, et ore pallido, atque ex abundantia cordis pronunciauit, qui sic locutus, aspectu tristis, animo turbatus, et oculis minax cunctis terrori erat; tantumque mentis moerorem ostendit ut plurimi conlachrymati sint, qui eius in fronte statum suum condiscunt. Verebatur nanque optimus ille pater ne tresuiri, spretis maioribus praelatis, plures ex inferioribus accepissent; quae res eo erat suspectior, quoniam nunquam scire aliquid de mente triumuirorum potuerat. Qui ut corrugatam tunc cardinalis frontem inspexerunt, quasi post coruscantem aërem ad sustinendam procellam se parauerunt. Timor tamen omnibus fuit ne illo iterum die scinderetur ecclesia, periculosiorque illo tumultus formidabatur, quem loci alias electio peperit.[2] Iam enim ut quisque mente conceperat, sic aut laudationi aut uituperationi triumuirorum se accingebant. Quibus cognitis, uisum est tribusuiris ante aperturam tabularum parumper sermocinari, et animos audientium prius placare quam laederentur, nominationisque suae tunc causas aperire, cum audiri possent;

[1] And that consequently they would be housed for a time in the conclave.

[2] Cf. above, p. 144, n. 2.

caused the greater general curiosity. Discussion was rife among all, there were many remarks about the triumvirs, there was much forecasting about the nomination, and some maintained that one man, others that another would be an elector, each reasoning as he was led by his own inclinations and by probability. Yet because they had no definite information all had a tremendous eagerness to listen. Some even wore their best clothes, others had hired new servants, others too had entrusted their houses to their friends, in their belief that they would be included in the number of the electors.[1] Somehow or other it happens that a man whose ambition is in the upshot laughable rather than successful over-estimates his own worth.

Now the cardinal of Arles, anxious about so important a matter, and busy with many tasks, arrived rather later than the occasion demanded, and made all await him with some surprise. When he sat down facing the benches, he first apologized for his lateness. 'Our business today', he said, 'is important. On the nomination which will be revealed forthwith the whole state of the Church depends. If the triumvirs to whom you entrusted the matter have done their work well, I admit I have come a little late; but if they have done it badly, then I am here too soon.' These words he uttered with trembling voice and a pale face and from the fullness of his heart. This remark of his, his gloomy appearance, his disturbed mind and threatening look caused alarm in all, and he displayed such mental anguish that very many recognizing in his face their own state shed tears with him. For this excellent Father was afraid that the triumvirs had ignored the greater prelates, and had accepted more from the lower clergy. He had all the more reason for suspecting this because he had been unable to learn anything about the intention of the triumvirs. They, when they saw the cardinal's brow wrinkled, prepared as though after a bright sky to experience a storm. Yet all were afraid of the Church being on that day split again, and a more dangerous disturbance was feared than the one which at another time was caused by the choice of place.[2] For according as each had made up his mind, so they were making themselves ready either to praise or to criticize the triumvirs. On learning this the triumvirs thought it advisable, before opening the lists, to say a few words, and gain the good will of their hearers before they were offended, and explain, while they could gain a hearing, the reasons for their

scientes quia post uulnus inflictum nemo benignus est auditor. Locutus pauca prius est abbas Scotus,[1] triumuir, et post eum Ioannes Segouius.

Vt igitur nulli se spretos crederent, qui forent omissi, praefatiunculam istiusmodi praemiserunt: cogitatum se maximum habuisse, quos uiros intra conclaue reciperent, quosque extra dimitterent, opusque sibi uisum fuisse non minus extra quam intus uiros habere sensatos, qui et conclaue tuerentur, et fieri nouitates in Synodo prohiberent; idque ex Platonis summi philosophi praeceptis se didicisse, qui rectores ciuitatum sic curare totum rei publicae corpus iubet ne, dum partem aliquam tueantur, reliquas deserant.[2] Quae res eos etiam commonuerit electores quoque sic per prouincias nominare ne honoratae aliae, neglectae aliae uiderentur. In electis uero magnam curam habuisse ne uel episcopum sine plebe, uel abbatem sine monasterio sumerent.[3] In omnibus autem per se nominatis aut bonitatem singularem, aut nobilitatem cum bonitate, aut summam scientiam cum bonitate et nobilitate se inuenisse; et in episcopis quidem cum cardinali, qui episcopus esset, numerum esse Apostolis aequatum. Abbates septem, theologos quinque, inter luminatos ac doctores nouem, omnes autem in presbyteratus ordine constitutos. Alios quoque officiales a se nominatos, et dignitatibus esse et uirtutibus insignitos, uicecamerarium quidem unum, custodes conclauis octo, caeremoniarum clericos duos, promotores duos, procuratorem fiscalem unum, soldanum[4] unum; quam circa nominationem habuisse se et ad deputationes, ut iniunctum sibi fuerat, oculum. Quibus dictis aliquantisper multitudinem placauerunt; factoque miro inter omnes silentio, apertae sunt nominationis tabulae, quas Ioannes Segouius legit; fuitque omissus in illis nationum ordo, onerosum enim triumuiris putatum est nationem nationi praeferre. Ideoque ut quisque prior aut praelatura aut dignitate fuit, sic prius est nominatus. Ego autem nequaquam timebo nationum seruare ordinem qui Constantiae fuit seruatus, nec mihi inuidiam timeo, quia nec praepositis gratiam, nec postpositis iniuriam faciam. Ordinem nanque istum neque nobilitas neque maioritas sed tempus peperit, quia ut quaeque natio uerbum Dei prius suscepit, sic prior habetur; nec aut laudi est mihi aut uituperio,

[1] Thomas Livingstone; cf. above, p. 16, n. 4.

[2] *Republic*, iv. 419–20, but perhaps as referred to in Aristotle, *Politics*, 1264^{b}.

[3] i.e. titular bishops and abbots holding *in commendam*.

[4] With police jurisdiction.

nomination, realising that after the infliction of a wound no hearer is well-disposed. First the Scottish abbot[1] who was a triumvir said a few words, then John of Segovia. So that none who were left out should think themselves ignored, they delivered a short preamble like this.

They had held a long discussion about which persons they should include in the conclave and which they should keep outside, and it had seemed advisable to them to keep men of true intelligence outside as well as inside, to protect the conclave and prevent upheavals in the Synod. This they had learnt from the teaching of the great philosopher Plato, who tells the rulers of states to look after the whole body of the state in such a way that in maintaining part of it they do not abandon the rest.[2] This was a reminder to them to nominate electors among the provinces in such a way that it did not appear that some were being respected and others disregarded. Among the chosen they had taken the greatest care that they should not take either a bishop without a diocese, or an abbot without a monastery[3]. Furthermore in all those named by them they had found either outstanding goodness, or nobility together with goodness, or the greatest knowledge together with goodness and nobility, and among the bishops, including the cardinal who was a bishop, the number was equal to that of the Apostles. There were seven abbots, and five theologians, nine men of learning and doctors, all ordained priests. Other officials had also been nominated by them distinguished for their rank and qualities, one vice-chamberlain, eight guardians of the conclave, two clerks of ceremonies, two promoters, one procurator fiscal, one soldan.[4] In regard to the nomination they had kept an eye on the deputations, as they had been charged. By these words they somewhat calmed the throng, and in an unusual and general silence the nomination lists were opened, which John of Segovia read. The order of the nations was omitted in them, as the triumvirs thought it invidious to put one nation before another. So the order of mention corresponded with seniority in prelacy or rank. I, however, shall not be afraid of keeping the order of nations which was observed at Constance, and I am not afraid of any ill-feeling, as I shall show no favour to those I put first, and do no harm to those I put later. This order owes its origin not to nobility or greatness but to time, because as each nation received the word of God before the next, so it is given seniority. I have

dummodo Christianus sim, maiorum meorum uel matutina uel uespertina conuersio, nec plus habet in Euangelio qui mane ad uineam uenit quam qui uesperi.[1] Nationem tamen Italicam etiam sedes beati Petri et Romanum imperium facit priorem; seruabimus ergo ordinem nationum, faciliorem que legentibus praestabimus intellectum.

Illud tamen prius sciendum est cardinalem Arelatensem, non nominationis triumuiralis gratia, sed iure proprio ad electionem uenisse. Ideoque primum eum extra nationum ordinem pono, eundemque locum caeteri cardinales habuissent, si qui aut reintegrati ecclesiae, aut Eugeniana labe minime commaculati in tempore aduenissent. Primus itaque omnium electorum cardinalis fuit Arelatensis, uir et constantiae insuperabilis et prudentiae incomparabilis, cuius uirtuti haud asscribere titubauerim quaecunque in Concilio gesta sunt; quia nec sine illo praelati perseuerassent, nec alicuius principis umbra protexisset. Sed pergo ad nominationem.

Ex Italica natione recepti sunt:

episcopi:

Gulielmus Vercellensis,[2] uir et in Concilio notus et in patria dilectus, et origine quidem Gallicus, dignitate uero Italicus, et in quo praedecessoris odor sui Eusebii[3] adhuc spirat;

Georgius Augustensis,[4] ex clarissima Salutiarum familia genus ducens, ac non solum sanguine sed animi quoque generositate et uirtutibus nobilis;

Ioannes Eporgiensis,[5] et literis et probitate clarus, ac senilem prudentiam in aetate adhuc iuuenili ostendens:

Ludouicus Taurinensis,[6] claris ortus parentibus, et scientia iuris eminens, et moribus ubique honestis excultus;

abbates:

Aleranius Sancti Benigni Fructuariensis,[7] uir tam moribus quam aetate grauissimus, cui ex nobilissima domo de Carretto origo est, quae tantae olim sublimitatis fuit ut imperatores quoque habere meruerit. Et huic quidem germanus est Matthaeus, Albigaunensis episcopus, cuius in omni re prudentiam per

[1] Matt. 20: 1–16.

[2] Guillaume Didier, formerly bishop of Belley. He resigned Vercelli in 1452.

[3] See above, p. 122, and *Golden Legend*, 1 Aug.

[4] Bishop 1433–40.

[5] Giovanni de Parella, died 1479.

[6] Lodovico de Romagnano, died 1469.

[7] A Benedictine house in the diocese of Ivrea. The subsequent reference is to the tradition referred to above, p. 156, n. 2. Carretto is in Liguria.

no grounds, so long as I am a Christian, for praising or blaming those before me for being converted in the morning or in the evening; in the Gospel he who comes in the morning to the vineyard does not get more than he who comes in the evening.[1] The Italian nation does, however, gain prior place through the see of the blessed Peter and the Roman Empire. So we shall keep the order of the nations, and make things easier for our readers to grasp.

Yet it must first be known that the cardinal of Arles came into the election not through nomination by the triumvirs, but of his own right. So I set him first outside the list of the nations, and the other cardinals would have held the same place if they had either been reunited to the Church, or free from the stain of Eugenius's dishonour, and had arrived in time. Foremost then of all the electors was the cardinal of Arles, a person of unsurpassed steadfastness and incomparable wisdom, to whose high qualities I should not hesitate to ascribe the achievements of the Council, as the prelates would never have continued without him, nor would the shadow of any prince have protected them. However, I pass on to the nomination.

Of the Italian nation there were included:

the bishops:

Guillaume of Vercelli,[2] a man both well known in the Council and well loved in his own country, French in origin but Italian by his office, in whom there still breathes the odour of his predecessor Eusebius;[3]

Giorgio of Aosta,[4] descended from the distinguished house of Saluzzo, and noble not only in blood but in his greatness of mind and virtues;

Giovanni of Ivrea,[5] noted for learning and uprightness, displaying an old man's wisdom at a youthful time of life;

Lodovico of Turin,[6] of distinguished parentage, outstanding in legal knowledge, and adorned with all-round nobility of character;

the abbots:

Aleramo of St Benignus at Fruttuaria,[7] a man great in both character and years, who came from the noble house of Carretto, which once was of such prominence that it was worthy of providing emperors too. A kinsman of his is Matteo, bishop of Albenga, whose wisdom in every matter for many years the

plures annos sacrum Concilium demiratum est. Et horum sane qui alterum uidet, utrunque uidet, sic est uterque et habitu corporis et uiuendi consuetudine assimilis.

Iacobus de Secusia,[1] et annis et prudentia antiquus;

doctores:

Frater Ioannes de monte Canuto, praeceptor domus Sancti Antonii de Reuersio, cuius in toto ordine Sancti Antonii[2] magna existimatio est, quique post magnum abbatem secundus habetur, et hic in Italia beneficium habet, in Gallia parentes;[3]

Frater Bartholomaeus de Prouanis, praeceptor domus de Clauacio[4] eiusdem ordinis, uir bonitate non minus quam doctrina amabilis;

cumque iis uiris ad eligendum Romanum pontificem Italicorum natio est admissa.

Ex natione Gallica, quae et ipsa secunda est, cuiusque in ecclesiam Dei permaxima extant beneficia, nominati sunt:

ex archipontificali dignitate:

Ioannes Tarantasiensis,[5] uir uita praestans, et omnis inimicus ambitionis, quique inuitus ad tantam dignitatem uocatus fuit;

ex pontificali:

Franciscus Gebennensis,[6] antiquus Romanae curiae officialis, uir ut parui eloquii sic magnae intelligentiae, et cuius iudicium in omni re ardua sit praeponendum;

Bernardus Aquensis,[7] iurisconsultus admodum oculatus subtilisque; quia tamen ob notissima corporis impedimenta infestamque sibi podagram hic se excusauit, Ludouicus Massyliensis[8] in eius locum suffectus est, uir animo uastus, et ab omni simulatione alienus, quem talem puta, qualem audis, nusquam fallax, nusquam deceptor; et hic sententiam in Gabrielem latam publice legit, cum ille ex Romano deiectus pontificio fuit.[9]

[1] Abbot of Susa, diocese of Turin.

[2] The Hospital Brothers of St. Antony, founded in the Dauphiné in the late eleventh century, followed the rule of canons regular. The seat of the grand-master was at Saint-Antoine (Isère), dioc. Vienne. See Helyot, *Hist. des ordres religieux*, new ed., II (Paris, 1792), 110–16.

[3] This revealing remark shows that even at the time it was evident that the 'Italian nation' was represented among the electors exclusively by men from the Savoy–Piedmont region. Cf. Valois, II. 181–2.

sacred Council has admired. Whoever sees one of these sees the other too, so alike are they in bodily appearance and manner of living.

Giacomo of Susa,[1] an elder in years and wisdom;

the doctors:

Brother Jean of Monte Canuto, prior of the house of St. Antony of Reversio, whose reputation is great throughout the whole order of St. Antony,[2] and who is considered second after the great abbot. He has his office here in Italy and his relatives in France.[3]

Brother Bartolomeo Provana, prior of the house of Chivasso[4] of the same order, a man no less lovable for his goodness than for his learning.

In the person of these men the Italian nation was given a share in the election of the Roman pontiff.

Of the French nation which comes second, and whose services towards the Church of God are very important, there were named:

of the rank of archbishop:

Jean of Tarentaise,[5] a man of outstanding life, the foe of all ambition, who had been called unwillingly to such high rank;

of the rank of bishop:

François of Geneva,[6] a former official of the Roman curia, a person of small eloquence yet great understanding and whose judgement on every difficult matter is to be preferred;

Bernard of Dax,[7] a very discerning and clever doctor of law, but because of his well-known bodily ailments and the gout that plagued him, he excused himself, and Louis of Marseilles[8] was appointed in his place, a man of vast intellect and devoid of all insincerity, whom you must imagine to be as you hear, in nothing treacherous or a deceiver. He it was who read out in public the verdict delivered against Gabriel, when he was deposed from the Roman pontificate.[9]

[4] Dioc. Ivrea.

[5] Jean d'Arces, promoted cardinal by Felix V in 1444 and by Nicholas V in 1449; died 1454.

[6] François de Mez, a Benedictine who was promoted cardinal by Felix V in 1440; died 1444.

[7] Bernard de La Planche, a Benedictine canonist; deprived of Dax by Eugenius in 1439, promoted cardinal by Felix V in 1440.

[8] Louis de Glandèves; cf. above, p. 180, n. 1. [9] Above p. 188, n. 7.

ex abbatiali:

Raimundus Conchensis,[1] scientia iuris pontificii apprime callens, multaque in rebus conciliaribus experientia tritus, quique pro sancta Synodo compluribus legationibus functus est;

ex gradu theologico:

Nicolaus Tibout,[2] Normannus, uir quondam negociosae, nunc autem nimium senescens ociosae uirtutis;

Ioannes de Valle,[3] Brito, et patriam uirtutem et ingenium ostendens;

Thomas uero Corcellis[4] triumuir fuit.

ex iurisconsultis:

Gulielmus Hugonis,[5] archidiaconus Metensis, uir nec prudentia ulli praedictorum nec scientia inferior.

Hi omnes cum cardinali Arelatensi ex tota Gallia ad electionem Romani papae uocati sunt.

Ex natione Germanica, quae omnium est amplissima, recepti sunt:

ex episcopali praeeminentia:

Fredericus Basiliensis,[6] nobilitate generis et humanitate in omnes eximius;

ex abbatiali:

Conradus de Luzella,[7] Cisterciensis ordinis, uir, ut monachum decet, et a pompa seculi et ab omni superbia remotus; ac

Thomas de Scotia,[8] triumuir;

ex doctorali:

Detzelaus,[9] archidiaconus Cracouiensis, Polonus genere, conuersatione uero suauis et doctus;

Ioannes Vuyler,[10] decanus Basiliensis, uir mansuetus, et sciens plura quam praedictus;

Henricus de Iudaeis,[11] in splendida urbe Coloniensi natus, humanitate ac doctrina patriam redolens;

Iacobus de Saltzburga,[12] canonicus Ratisponensis, uir neque precibus neque minis commutabilis;

[1] A Benedictine house, diocese of Rodez.
[2] Canon of Coutances.
[3] Rector of Plounéor, diocese of Saint-Pol de Léon.
[4] Cf. above, p. 13, n. 13.
[5] Cf. above, p. 13, n. 15.
[6] Frederick zu Rhein, died 1451.
[7] Abbot of this Cistercian house in the diocese of Basle; cf. *Mon. Con.* III. 424.
[8] Cf. above, p. 16.
[9] Derzelaus Nicolai de Borzinow, a canonist.
[10] Johann Wyler, a canonist.

of the rank of abbot:

Raymond of Conques,[1] particularly skilled in the knowledge of canon law, and well-versed in the affairs of councils through his great experience, who had served on many missions for the holy Synod;

of the rank of theologian:

Nicolas Tibout[2] of Normandy, a man of merit once active, but now passive through his advanced age;

Jean Valle,[3] a Breton, an example of his country's virtue and genius;

Thomas de Courcelles[4] was a triumvir.

of the doctors of law:

Guillaume Hugues,[5] archdeacon of Metz, a man in wisdom and knowledge not inferior to any of those mentioned already.

All of these together with the cardinal of Arles were called from the whole of France for the election of the Roman pope.

From the German nation, which is the largest of all, there were included:

of episcopal pre-eminence:

Frederick of Basle,[6] in nobility of descent and in culture outstanding among all;

of that of abbot:

Conrad of Luzella[7] of the Cistercian order, a man, as befits a monk, removed from both wordly pomp and all pride; and

Thomas of Scotland,[8] a triumvir;

of that of doctor:

Derzelaus,[9] archdeacon of Cracow, a Pole by race, pleasant and learned in conversation;

Johann Wyler,[10] dean of Basle, a mild man with greater knowledge than the last named;

Heinrich von Jude,[11] born in the fine city of Cologne, in culture and learning typical of his country;

Jacob von Salzburg,[12] canon of Regensburg, a man who could not be moved by prayers or threats;

[11] A lawyer: for his name cf. Haller, VI, index.

[12] Jacob Friesheimer von Salzburg, a lawyer: cf. *Reichstagsakten*, XIV. 280, etc.

Christiannus[1] autem (ut supra diximus) iam in consortio triumuirorum erat assumptus.

Ex natione Hispanica, quae et ipsa uastissimos habet ac per-nobiles campos, quatuor Christianis regibus et uno infideli regnata,[2] hi sunt ad electionem magni pastoris accersiti:

pontifices:

Otho Dertusensis,[3] consilii utilis, et animi stabilis, totaque conuersatione perlepidus; hic ea in sessione qua lata est in Gabrielem depositionis sententia praesedit, nec post, quamuis plurimi pestem fugerent, de recessu habuit mentionem, fidus semper et Arelatensis comes et ecclesiae filius.

Georgius Vicensis[4] summa doctrina et grauitate, quo nemo pluribus nemoque grauioribus apud principes Concilii causa legationibus usus est, quas cum magnis uitae periculis magnisque peregit sumptibus. Qui etiam illud singulare fecit, is enim ut uidit principes Gabrielis causam tueri, et oratoribus suis praefinita loqui praecipere Eugenianis, legatione regis sui, quam tunc apud Synodum gerebat, se abdicauit, ne cum aliis principum nunciis dicere aduersus conscientiam cogeretur. Quod si alii fecissent episcopi, nequaquam autoritatem ecclesiae principes cum sua neutralitate paruipendissent; sed omnium malorum quae in ecclesiam irruerunt partem maximam ipsimet induxerunt sacerdotes.

Ludouicus Visensis,[5] uir et amicus amico et conuersatione perplacidus; hic orator Ioannis Portugaliae regis praestantissimi in Concilio fuit, quo uita functo[6] etiam in Concilio mansit. Tribusque ipsius Concilii honorificentissimis legationibus functus est. Iuit ad Graeciam[7] cum uiro prudentissimo Ludouico Lausanensi,[8] quem et uiarum, et periculi, et honoris habuit comitem. Iuit Coloniam et ad ducem Burgundiae potentissimum collega Ludouici protonotarii, et ambo quidem in reditu per quendam ex comitibus Palatinis Rheni capti sunt, et iussu Gabrielis in custodiam mancipati. Qua

[1] Cf. above, p. 204, n. 2. He ranks as one of the five theologians mentioned above, p. 208.

[2] The rulers of Aragon, Castile, Navarre, Portugal, and the Moorish kingdom of Granada.

[3] Cf. above, p. 104, n. 6.

[4] Cf. above, p. 12, n. 10.

[5] Luis de Amaral, deprived of Viseu in 1439, made cardinal by Felix V in 1444.

[6] João I had died in 1433.

[7] The bishop of Parma was another member of the delegation, led by the bishop of Lübeck, which left Basle in Feb. 1437. See Haller, v; and Gill, pp. 71–83 and references.

Christian[1] too, as we have said already, had been co-opted by the triumvirs.

Of the Spanish nation, which possesses vast and noble plains, governed by four Christian kings and one infidel,[2] there were summoned to the election of the great shepherd:

the bishops:

Otón of Tortosa,[3] a helpful counsellor, level-headed, and very charming in all his conversation; he presided at that session when the vote of deposition was passed against Gabriel, and afterwards, though many fled from the plague, he never mentioned withdrawing, always a faithful companion of the cardinal of Arles and son of the Church.

Jorge of Vich,[4] of the greatest learning and dignity; no-one served on more numerous and more important missions to the princes on behalf of the Council, which he accomplished with great danger to his life and much expense. He also took an unusual line of action, for when he saw that the princes were supporting Gabriel's cause and were telling their ambassadors to give a message previously decided to the followers of Eugenius, he resigned from the mission of his king on which at that time he was serving at the Synod, so that he should not be compelled with other envoys of the princes to speak against his conscience. If other bishops had done this, the princes would not have belittled the authority of the Church by their neutrality; but of all the ills that fell upon the Church the majority the priests brought upon themselves.

Luis of Viseu,[5] a good friend to his friends and of calm conversation. He was ambassador to the Council of João, the distinguished king of Portugal, and remained at the Council even after the king died.[6] He served on three most distinguished missions of the Council. He went to Greece[7] with that wisest of men, Louis of Lausanne,[8] whom he had as sharer of his travels, danger, and reputation. He went to Cologne and to the most powerful duke of Burgundy as colleague of Lodovico the protonotary, and on their way back both were captured by one of the Counts Palatine of the Rhine, and by Gabriel's orders were put under guard. In

[8] Cf. above, p. 148, n. 4.

in re uirum se priscae uirtutis Visensis ostendit. Namque cum libertas sibi abeundi dimisso collega fieret, nunquam se inquit carceres egressurum, nisi cum socio.[1] Iuit et in eas Galliae partes quibus Britannia hodie nomen est, ducisque illius excellentissimi animum ad Concilium flexit.[2]

Abbates recepti sunt:

Petrus Sancti Cucuphatis,[3] uir solers et monasteriorum gubernationi aptissimus; ac
Antonius Arularis,[4] et aspectu et alloquio gratus;

doctores:

Bernardus Buscho,[5] canonicus Ilardensis, iudicii non minus recti quam firmi; et
Raimundus Albioli,[6] canonicus Tirasonensis, sensum habens et mores aetati conuenientissimos;
Ioannes quoque Segouius,[7] triumuir, ex hac natione electioni interfuit.

Hi quoque ex quatuor nationibus nominati ad eligendum Papam fuerunt. Anglici uero idcirco recepti non sunt, quia non aderant, nec alii assumi poterant quam praesentes.[8]

Officiales autem circa conclaue necessarii uocati sunt:

Ludouicus, episcopus Lausanensis, *uicecamerarius*, uir summi exercitii summaeque uigilantiae, et ad officium sibi commissum non solum aptus sed necessarius, cuius in negociis singulis diligentia in sacro Concilio et in omnibus rebus bonitas in tota Christianitate perspecta est;

custodes conclauis: Perceuallus,[9] Bellicensis episcopus, non minus re bonus quam aspectu:
Nicolaus Grossetanus,[10] genere nobilis et fidelitate insignis, quem et pro seruitio ecclesiae et pro defensione fidei spoliari

[1] For this episode (early Feb. 1438) see *Mon. Con.* III. 55. Their captor was the duke of Bavaria; their captivity lasted only a few days. But cf. *Reichstagsakten*, XIII. 567–8 note.

[2] Jean V, in the summer of 1439: Haller, VI. 487, 489, 490, etc.

[3] A Benedictine house, diocese of Barcelona (*Mon. Con.* III. 424).

[4] A Benedictine house, Arles-sur-Tech, diocese of Elne (both places now in dep. of Pyrénées-Orientales).

[5] A canonist.

[6] Another canonist.

[7] Ranking as a theologian. Cf. p. 208.

this affair the bishop of Viseu displayed an antique courage, for when he had the chance of leaving his colleague and going away, he said that he would never come out of the prison unless his comrade came too.[1] He went also to those parts of France called today Brittany, and made the distinguished duke well disposed towards the Council.[2]

The abbots included were:

Pedro of St. Cucuphas,[3] a clever man, well suited to the governing of monasteries; and

Antonio of Arulara,[4] pleasant both in appearance and address;

the doctors:

Bernard Buscho,[5] canon of Lerida, whose judgement was as correct as steady;

Raimondo Albiol,[6] canon of Tarazona, the possessor of sense and character most suited to his years;

John of Segovia,[7] the triumvir, was also present from this nation at the election.

These were nominated from the four nations to elect the pope. The English were not admitted because they were not present, and none but those present could be included.[8]

Officials needed at the conclave were also named:

Louis, bishop of Lausanne, was the *vice-chamberlain*, a man of the greatest experience and vigilance, not merely fit for the duty assigned to him but indispensable, whose attention to details was evident in the sacred Council and his goodness in all matters was evident throughout the whole of Christendom.

The *guardians of the conclave* were the bishops, Percivale, bishop of Belley,[9] notable for good words as well as for good looks, and Niccolò of Grosseto,[10] of noble birth and remarkable fidelity, who did not shrink from being deprived of his

[8] On the English connexion with Basle, virtually ended after the rapprochement between Philip of Burgundy and Charles VII in 1435, see A. Zellfelder, *England und das Basler Konzil* (Berlin, 1913), and A. M. E. D. Schofield, 'The first English delegation to the council of Basel', *Journal of Ecclesiastical History*, XII (1961), 167–96.

[9] Percivale de Balme, died 1460.

[10] Cf. above, p. 148, n. 5.

beneficiis non piguit, ueritatem cum paupertate quam mendacium cum diuitiis eligentem;

Ioannes sancti Michaëlis de Clausa[1] Taurinensis diocesis, praestanti ingenio, et Franciscus Abundantiae,[2] tam scientia et uirtute quam temporalibus bonis abundans, monasteriorum abbates;

Franciscus de Fuxe,[3] theologus, professione minor, eloquentia magnus;

Gulielmus de Constantia, canonicus[4] Spirensis, antiquus pontificii iuris interpres;

Ioannes de Turicella, decanus Segobricensis,[5] iurisconsultus; ac Theodericus Nagel, canonicus Rigensis, probitate cognitus;

clerici gratia ceremoniarum: Aeneas de Piccolominibus, Senensis, canonicus Tridentinus;[6] ac Michaël Brunout, canonicus Beluacensis, in eo exercitio longo tempore tritus;[7]

promotores qui antea in Concilio per plures annos negocia promouerant: uiri docti et constantes, Hugo Berardi,[8] et Ioannes Slitzenrode;[9]

procurator fiscalis, qui antea fuerat uir exercitatus: Robertus Magnani;[10]

soldanus[11] uero: Petrus de Atro, qui etiam ab initio nascentis Concilii eo in officio laudabiliter se habuerat.

Hi fuerunt uiri conscripti ex nominatione triumuirali, qua per Ioannem Segouium lecta (ut antea diximus)[12] exhilaratus est cardinalis animus, qui usque ad illam horam trepidus stupidusque permanserat, nec persuaderi sibi poterat nominationem istiusmodi fieri. Vt autem uidit episcopos et abbates in magno numero assumptos, et nationes quae in Concilio erant, aequis portionibus honoratos, et animi simul uigorem, et frontis recepit colorem. Factusque laetus sereno uultu concionem quoque exhilarauit, quae, illo moestitiam ostendente, non tristis esse non poterat. Habuit ergo cardinalis de nominatione facta magnifica uerba, triumque patrum uirtutem magnopere commendauit, qui et in Concilio se semper bene habuissent, et nunc optime; posteaque

[1] Abbot of this Benedictine house.

[2] A canonist, abbot of Abbondance, diocese of Geneva: *Mon. Con.* III. 424.

[3] Above, p. 20, n. 6. [4] Above, p. 14. [5] And canon of Urgel.

[6] Elsewhere, *Commentaries*, p. 28, Aeneas says that he was named but that he was unwilling to accept ordination and hence an ecclesiastical career. He was thus only present as a clerk of ceremonies. He had been made canon of Trent by the time of the conclave (cf. Haller, VI. 678 and above, p. 196 and n. 7) and not as is suggested by the editors of *Commentaries*, p. 28 n., as a result of a bull of Felix V in 1442, which is also what Wolkan implies, I. i. 117 n.

benefices for the service of the Church and the defence of the faith, choosing truth with poverty rather than falsehood with riches; the abbots of monasteries, John of St. Michael of La Chiusa[1] in the diocese of Turin, outstandingly gifted, and François of Abbondance,[2] abounding in knowledge and virtue as well as temporal goods; François de Fuxe,[3] the theologian, a friar minor but major in eloquence; Wilhelm von Konstanz,[4] canon of Speyer, a long-established interpreter of canon law; John of Turicela, dean of Segorbe,[5] a doctor of law, and Dietrich Nagel, canon of Riga, well known for his uprightness.

As *clerks of ceremonies* there were Aeneas Piccolomini of Siena, canon of Trent,[6] and Michel Brunout, canon of Beauvais, long experienced in that duty.[7]

The promoters who previously for several years had promoted business in the Council were the learned and steadfast Hugo Berard[8] and Johann Slitzenrode.[9]

The procurator fiscal, who had much previous experience, was Robert Magnani.[10]

The soldan[11] was Peter de Atro, who from the very beginning of the Council had performed that duty in praiseworthy fashion.

These were the men enrolled in accordance with the nomination of the triumvirs, and when this had been read out by John of Segovia, as we have previously said,[12] the cardinal's mind was cheered, for up to that moment he had remained fearful and bemused, and he had been unable to persuade himself that a nomination of this kind was being made. When, however, he saw bishops and abbots included in great number, and the nations present at the Council being awarded fair shares, his mind regained its activity and his face its colour. Thus made happy he cheered the assembly too with his unclouded brow, an assembly which could not but be gloomy when he was a picture of sadness. So the cardinal uttered complimentary words about the accomplishment of the nomination, and greatly commended the quality of the three Fathers, whose conduct had always been good in the Council but

[7] He had earlier been made clerk of ceremonies to the Council: Haller, VI. 99, etc.
[8] M.A., from Toul: Haller, III.
[9] Hugolin spells 'Sleczinrode': Haller, VI *passim*.
[10] M.A.
[11] Cf. above, p. 208, n. 4.
[12] Above, p. 208.

concionem dimisit. Eaque die occupati omnes fuerunt ad praeparandos in conclaui necessarios conuictus. Sero autem singuli electores ad cardinalis domum uocati de cameris diuidendis intra conclaue sermonem intra se habuerunt. Et quoniam camerarum magna differentia erat, uidebatur praelatis diuisionem secundum dignitates fiendam; atque ut quisque dignior et antiquior esset, sic prior locum sibi assumeret. Nec ferendum esse dicebant ut cardinalis et archiepiscopus cum doctoribus ueniret ad sortem; quo casu ridiculum esset, si cardinalem infra et doctorem supra locari contingeret. Cumque praelati essent numero plures, omnesque uno ore loquerentur, desperata res uidebatur de sortibus cogitare; utcumque tamen res iret, uisum doctoribus est etiam pro se uerba facere. Dicebant igitur priscas consuetudines non debere rescindi, in omni conclaui obseruatum ut camerae per sortem diuiderentur, neque id inter cardinales tantum, sed etiam inter cardinales et alios fuisse; Constantiae[1] cardinales admodum multos, non tamen respuisse cum episcopis et doctoribus sortem subire. Praelatos autem nimium sibi ipsis fauere, qui cum essent numero plures, sententiam magis uocibus quam rationibus obtinerent; si sine sorte fiat electio camerarum, timendam esse collusionem, inter electores quoque timendum schisma, ne stantes infra et rigentes frigore locatis supra inuideant. Quibus rationibus cardinalis euictus in sententiam doctorum consensit; ac post eum uir bonus, episcopus Dertusensis, prophetatus est. 'Si quis enim est', ait, 'cui nocitura sors sit, ego ille sum, quem ultimum sors efficiet; ne tamen aut priscas consuetudines euertamus, aut inuidiosi doctoribus simus, utilius puto rem sortibus transigi.' Eiusque in sententiam conclusum est. Eademque ipsa hora missi sunt ad conclaue ex omni statu electorum cum cardinali Arelatensi, qui sortes super cameras ex consilio uicecamerarii iacerent. Scripta igitur sunt electorum nomina singulatim per scedulas, quae omnes clausae ac permixtae in quodam birreto reconditae sunt, atque exinde ad primam digrioremque cameram uentum est, ubi tunc cardinalis Arelatensis manum iaciens in birretum scedulam quae sibi sorte obuenit recipiens legit, eamque uicecamerarius in fronte ipsius camerae confixit; sicque successiue per ordinem factum est

[1] The election of Martin V at Constance was the only previous conclave where the cardinals had been joined by other orders (cf. Introduction, p. xiv); procedure for the election at Basle was modelled on Constance.

now was best of all, and then he dismissed the meeting. That day all were busy making the necessary arrangements for living together in the conclave. Late in the day individual electors, summoned to the cardinal's house, discussed the allocation of the rooms in the conclave. Since there was a great difference between the rooms, the prelates thought that the allocation should be made according to rank, and that priority in making the choice of place should go according to rank and age. They held it intolerable that a cardinal and an archbishop should share the chances of the lot with doctors. In such a case it would be absurd if it happened that the cardinal was placed low and a doctor high. Since the prelates were in the majority, and were unanimous, it seemed a forlorn hope to think about drawing lots. Still the doctors decided, however the matter should go, to put in a word for themselves. So they said that the former practices should not be abandoned, that in every conclave the rule had been to assign the rooms by lot, and this had been not only among the cardinals, but among the cardinals and the others. At Constance[1] the cardinals, who were quite numerous, had not refused to submit to the lot along with bishops and doctors. The prelates were favouring themselves too much, seeing that by reason of their majority they were getting their way by their votes rather than by reasoning. If the choice of rooms took place without lot, collusion was to be feared, and division too among the electors, with those standing below and stiff with cold envying those placed above. The cardinal was convinced by these arguments and gave his agreement to the view of the doctors, and after him that good man, the bishop of Tortosa, made a prophetic utterance. 'If there is anyone', he said, 'whom the lot is going to harm, it is myself, whom the lot will make last, but that we should not overthrow former practices or offend the doctors, I think it better that the matter should be dealt with by lot.' It was settled in accordance with his view. The very same hour persons were sent to the conclave from every rank of the electors together with the cardinal of Arles, to cast lots about the rooms under the direction of the vice-chamberlain. So the names of the electors were written singly on small slips, all of which were folded and shuffled and hidden in a cap, and then they came to the first and worthiest room, where the cardinal of Arles plunging his hand into the cap, picked out the slip that he happened to come across, and read it, and the vice-chamberlain fixed it on the outside of the room; and

ut intraturi sequenti die electores conclaue eam sibi cellam noscerent assignatam, ubi suo nomini obuiarent.[1] Fuitque primus omnium decanus Basiliensis, ultimus uero, ut uaticinatus extiterat, Dertusensis episcopus.

Miraque in re hac distributio sortis fuit, aut potius diuina dispensatio, quae consilia hominum reprobans, doctorem primum, episcopum autem postremum fecit, cum statuissent ante praelati cellulas sibi digniores asscribere. Id tamen in utroque bonitatis est uisum ut neque decanus ex primo loco superbierit, neque ex ultimo Dertusensis episcopus condoluerit; sed illum indigne se credere, istum digne locatum humilitas faciebat. Sequenti autem die, quae fuit Veneris iii. Kalend. Nouembris, habita est generalis congregatio, conclusaeque sunt proximarum deputationum deliberationes. Sessioque mox secuta est;[2] diuina autem officia cardinalis Arelatensis celebrauit, quo nemo ceremonias nouit melius. Sermonem autem ad electores post Euangelium decantatum Marcus, insignis memoriae theologus habuit;[3] qui, enumeratis depositi Gabrielis criminibus, suadere electoribus nitebatur, ut uirum assumerent, qui contraria imitaretur prioribus, quique omnia euitans Gabrielis uitia, ut ille calumniis odiosus fuit, sic se iste assumendus iustitia praestaret ıcceptum, et ut ille rapax, sic iste continens esse studeret.

Erat templum ubique populo plenum; stabant inter columnas superiores nobiles urbis matronae, respectumque in concionem habentes ordinem rerum non sine deuotione consyderabant. Aderat Ioannes de Tierstein comes,[4] qui loco imperialis protectoris cathedram adimplebat. Aderat consulatus urbanus et alii complures nobiles rem insolitam conspecturi, seruabaturque inter omnes silentium. Extra ecclesiam quoque ciues in armis erant, si quod scandalum pararetur, prohibituri. Tantusque ad spectaculum eius rei confluxerat populus ut neque in templo neque in plateis recipi posset, magnaque undique intra ecclesiam haberetur pressura. Vt igitur cardinalis Arelatensis intra missarum solemnia communicasset, uocati sunt ad altare communicaturi etiam secundum ordinem electores. Tumque archiepiscopus Tarantasiensis et decem alii episcopi communicarunt, post autem septem

[1] The allocation of rooms is given in detail by Hugolin: Haller, VI. 680–1.

[2] The thirty-eighth session, on the same day 30 Oct.

[3] This is not mentioned by either Hugolin or Segovia; perhaps Marco Bonfilii, on whom see Haller, VI, index.

[4] See above, p. 134, and n. 3.

like this it went on right through in succession, so that the electors on entering the conclave the following day might recognize the room assigned to them when they came across their own name.[1] The first of all was the dean of Basle and the last, just as he had prophesied, the bishop of Tortosa.

The assignment by lot, or rather by divine dispensation, was surprising in this matter in that it rejected the plans of men and put a doctor first and a bishop last, when the prelates had previously decided to assign the better cells to themselves. Virtue was displayed in both persons, seeing that the dean did not show pride in the foremost place nor the bishop of Tortosa feel indignation in the last, but humility made the former feel that he did not deserve his place, and the latter that he did deserve his. On the following day, Friday 30 October, a general congregation was held, and the deliberations of the last deputations were passed. A session soon followed.[2] The celebrant of the divine office was the cardinal of Arles, the person with the best knowledge of the ritual. After the singing of the Gospel, Marcus, a theologian of happy memory, preached a sermon to the electors.[3] Mentioning the crimes of the deposed Gabriel, he urged the electors to choose a man who would take as a pattern the opposite of his predecessor's actions, and avoid all Gabriel's faults. Just as Gabriel was disliked for his lying accusations, so the man to be adopted should shew himself acceptable because of his justice, and just as the former was rapacious, so the latter should strive to restrain himself.

Every part of the church was filled by the people. Between the upper pillars stood the noble matrons of the city, who paid attention to the assembly and watched the whole process of affairs with great devotion. There was present Count Johann of Thierstein,[4] who occupied a seat as deputy for the Imperial Protector. The city magistrates were there and many other nobles to watch the unusual ceremony, and silence was kept among all. Outside the church too there were citizens in arms to prevent any trouble arising. Such great crowds had gathered to watch the ceremony that room could not be found for them in the church or in the streets, and inside the church was contained a throng packed all round. When the cardinal of Arles had communicated in the celebration of the mass, the electors were called to the altar to communicate in due order. So then the archbishop of Tarentaise and the ten other bishops communicated, after that the seven

abbates, exinde quinque theologi, ac demum iurisconsulti nouem; qui accedentes altare genibus flexis et lachrymis ubertim fusis, sacratissimae susceperunt eucharistiae sacramentum. Eratque uenerandum spectaculum tot eximios antistites, totque praeclaros patres, nudam ante Dominicum sacramentum ostentantes caniciem cernere, et alios quidem orantes, alios uero illachrymantes conspicere. Deuotionem autem maxime cardinalis adaugebat, qui pontificalibus indutus uestibus, nudato et caluo capite, Dominicum corpus quibusque ministrabat, confessionemque in re tali solitam singulis repetebat; ac secutus piissima Saluatoris Domini nostri Iesu Christi uestigia, quemlibet deosculabatur, hortatus plurimum ut quam quisque posset, pura anima susciperet Dominum. Quam rem sic ordinate, sic solenniter, sic deuote peregit ut ex uidentibus nemo tenuerit lachrymas, nisi qui pectus habuit aut saxeum aut ferreum. Post haec finita missa, et congregatione generali peracta, praelati omnes infulas et uestimenta sessioni accommoda susceperunt. Inuocata altis uocibus per omnes patres Spiritus Sancti gratia, peractisque litaniis et orationibus, ac omni solennitate sessionis impleta, Ludouicus, episcopus Lausanensis, ambonem ascendit, triaque illic per ordinem legit. Primo responsionem Synodalem ad famosum Gabrielis libellum, cui principium est 'Moyses',[1] secundo limitationem quandam circa decretum de electionibus dudum in Synodo editum, tertio uero nominationem triumuiralem, quam ex certa scientia sacrum Concilium approbauit.[2] Quibus lectis, interrogati patres utrum placeret. Responsum est ab omnibus: 'Placet'.

Exhinc requisiuit Lausanensis iurisiurandi formam ab electoribus praestandam publice legi, electoresque iuxta Concilii ordinationem iurare. Primus igitur cardinalis Arelatensis, aperto decretorum libro, formam iuramenti[3] cunctis audientibus legit, moxque requisitus ut ita iuraret: 'Ego', inquit, 'reuerendissimi patres, coram Domino meo, Iesu Christo, cuius modo sacratissimum corpus indignus peccator manducaui, cuique in tremendo et magno finali iudicio de omnibus per me factis, rationem sum redditurus, promitto, iuro et uoueo quoniam in hoc electionis negotio, ad quod nunc uolente Concilio mittimur, nil aliud quaeram quam populi Christiani salutem et uniuersalis ecclesiae

[1] Eugenius IV's constitution 'Moyses', 4 Sept. 1439, challenged the validity of the decree of conciliar supremacy passed at Constance in 1415 (cf. Introduction, p. xiii), and declared the clergy at Basle schismatics and heretics. See Valois, II. 175–6.

[2] The three decrees are printed in Mansi, XXIX, cols. 191–8.

[3] The form of the oath to precede the election was enacted at session xxiii (25 Mar. 1436): Mansi, XXIX, col. 111. Aeneas's Latin is a paraphrase.

abbots, then the five theologians, and lastly the nine doctors of law, who, approaching the altar, on bended knee and copiously shedding tears received the sacrament of the most holy eucharist. It was an awe-inspiring sight to see so many distinguished bishops and so many famous Fathers displaying their grey hairs uncovered before the Lord's sacrament, and to behold some praying, some shedding tears. Their devotion was much increased by the cardinal, who in his pontifical vestments, with bared and bald head, administered to each the Lord's body, and repeated to each the words of faith usual in such a ceremony; and following the most holy footsteps of our Lord and Saviour, Jesus Christ, he kissed each after urging him seriously to receive the Lord with as pure a soul as he could. This he did with such orderliness, solemnity and devotion that no one who witnessed it kept back his tears unless he had a heart of stone or steel. Afterwards, when the mass was ended, and the general congregation completed, all the prelates put on the mitres and vestments suited to the session. When the grace of the Holy Spirit had been invoked in a loud voice by all the Fathers, and the litanies and prayers had been completed, and all the solemnities of the session accomplished, Louis, bishop of Lausanne, mounted the pulpit and there read three decrees in due order, first the reply of the Synod to the notorious pamphlet of Gabriel beginning, 'Moses',[1] secondly a certain resolution regarding a decree recently published in the Synod about elections, thirdly the nomination by the commission of three, which the holy Council approved from sure knowledge.[2] When these had been read, the Fathers were asked whether they agreed. All replied, 'Agreed'.

Next the bishop of Lausanne requested the public reading of the form of oath to be taken by the electors, and the taking of the oath by the electors according to the Council's directions. First then the cardinal of Arles, opening the book of decrees, read the form of oath[3] in the hearing of all, and shortly afterwards when requested to take the oath in this form, declared: 'I, most reverend Fathers, in the presence of my Lord, Jesus Christ, whose most sacred body I, an unworthy sinner, have just eaten, and to whom at the dread and mighty final judgement I am to give account of all my actions, promise, swear, and vow that in this matter of the election, to which by the will of the Council we are now being sent, I will seek nothing but the well-being of the Christian people

bonum. Idque mihi curae erit studere ne autoritas generalium Conciliorum uilipendatur, ne fides catholica expugnetur, neue patres in Concilio persistentes opprimi possint; hoc quaeram, hoc sollicitabo, ad hoc uiribus totis incunbam, nihil in hac re aut mei aut meorum amicorum causa faciam, sed solum Deum et ecclesiae suae utilitatem respiciam. Hoc animo, hac mente, hoc denique corde conciliare suscipio iuramentum.' Fuitque eius sermo et uiuax et terrificus, omniumque astantium commouit animos. Post eum autem electores alii suo ordine iurauerunt. Quae res electioni post factae maximam praebuit autoritatem. Quis enim non illum summo pontificio dignum putet, qui tot sacerdotum episcoporumque iudicio sit comprobatus, praesertim cum illi antea suscepto Dominico corpore iusiurandum praestiterint, nullum se electuros, nisi quem sciuerint tantae idoneum dignitati? In eadem etiam sessione et uicecamerarius et custodes conclauis et clerici ceremoniarum et promotores iureiurando promiserunt officium suum sine fraude exercere. Quibus peractis omnibus, hora iam post meridiem tertia, adhuc populo ieiunante, cantatum est undique, 'Te Deum laudamus', et organis respondentibus alternatim, usque ad finem completus est hymnus.

Quo facto, egressi sunt pueri in stolis albis admodum multi longum processionis ordinem facientes, quos secuta pars cleri urbani est. Et post ueneranda incorporatorum multitudo cum doctoribus et uniuersitatum oratoribus, qui longis honestisque uestibus orantes incedebant. Exinde sacerdotes urbani excolendas sanctorum reliquias in ulnis gestantes proficiscebantur. Mox uero Ludouicus Lausanensis crucem argenteam ante se habens, sequentibus quatuor clericis incedebat. Post uero cardinalis Arelatensis adhuc et mitra et auratis refulgens uestibus, deuoto et desyderanti populo benedicens. Exinde infulati episcopi et abbates ad processionem ornati, innumerabili populo subsequenti procedebant. Sicque aliis orantibus, aliis suspirantibus, usque ad ostium conclauis est processum, armatis hinc atque inde propter custodiam conclauis existentibus. Vt uero ad conclaue uentum est, receptis electoribus dimissi sunt caeteri. Intromissi sunt etiam dominorum seruitores concessi. Non tamen ostium conclauis

and the good of the whole Church. It shall be my concern to take active measures that the authority of the general Councils be not despised, that the catholic faith be not confuted, and that the Fathers who remain in the Council cannot be defeated. This will I seek, for this will I be anxious, to this will I apply all my efforts; in this matter I will do nothing for my own sake or that of my friends, but I will only regard God and the interests of his Church. With this mind, this intention and finally this heart I take the Council's oath.' His words were both lively and awe-inspiring, and impressed all those present. After him the other electors took the oath in their order. This ceremony conferred great authority upon the subsequent election. For who would not think him worthy of the supreme pontificate who was approved by the judgement of such a number of priests and bishops, especially when after partaking of the body of the Lord they took an oath that they would elect no-one but him whom they knew to be suitable for that great office? At the same session too the vice-chamberlain and the guardians of the conclave and the clerks of ceremonies and the promoters promised on oath to do their duty without fraud. On the completion of all of this, at three in the afternoon, with the people still fasting, all chanted, 'We praise thee, O God', and with the organs accompanying the antiphony the canticle was sung right through to the end.

After this a very large number of boys went out in white stoles, forming a long procession, followed by a number of the city clergy. After them came the reverend multitude of the incorporated [members of the Council] together with doctors and delegates of the universities, praying as they marched in their long ceremonial robes. Next the priests of the city set forth, carrying in their arms the venerable relics of the saints. Soon after went Louis, bishop of Lausanne, with a silver cross in front of him and four clerics following. After him came the cardinal of Arles, still gleaming with his mitre and gilded vestments, blessing the devoted and eager people. Next the bishops wearing mitres, and abbots decked for the procession marched with a countless throng following. Thus with some praying and some sighing they proceeded right to the door of the conclave, armed men being posted on this side and that to guard the conclave. When they reached the conclave, the electors were admitted and the rest sent away. There were also allowed inside the servitors permitted to their masters.

statim est clausum, sed usque ad nonam ante medium noctis horam familiaribus patuit res deferentibus opportunas, permissique usque id temporis sunt amici ad amicos accedere. Cardinalis autem sic processionaliter ingressus, sequentibus electoribus, in sacello quod celebrandis missis paratum erat, ante altare et ante ipsum Christi uexillum genibus flexis, et nudo capite, orationibus Deo porrectis, et domui et habitatoribus benedixit; sicque positis pluuialibus et mitris, illuc se quisque recepit ubi nomen suum recognouit. Cum uero iam noctis uenissent tenebrae, ingressus est protector cum quibusdam ciuibus, et ut quisque locatus esset uisurus, et uoluptatem magnam ex tanto ordine suscipiens. Post eum uero intrauit Lausanensis uicecamerarius, et ipsum secuti sunt custodes conclauis; aliqui ex iis singulas cameras diligenter rimati, et personarum et rerum examen habuerunt, excussuri extra conclaue, si quid contra leges reperissent, nihilque praeter ordinem inuenientes abierunt. Et hora, ut dictum, nona tam intra quam extra obserata est ianua, et undique admoti pessuli cum catenis tenacibus.

Sed quoniam de conclaui sermo est, necessarium existimo ipsius formam conscribere. Domus[1] erat in medio urbis apud plateam cathedralis ecclesiae loco edito et patenti, quam nobiles quondam in usum struxerant chorearum, et supra et infra perlatas habentem aulas; et superiorem sane, quoniam igne poterat calefieri hyemi, inferiorem aestati deputauerant. Hic igitur conclaue haberi posse est uisum ut esset domus orationis, ubi fuerat lasciuiae campus, et succederent mores, ubi uitia triumpharant. Constructae ergo illic sunt et supra et infra mansiunculae opportunae, quarum numerus aequatus est electoribus, una superadiuncta, quae ceremoniarum clericis deseruiret. Fuit autem structura earum admodum facilis, nec enim aut saxo aut robore ligneo parietes instruxerunt medios, sed positis in columnarum morem ex abiete sudibus cortinas simplices uisuque penetrabiles pro parietibus texuerunt. Camerarum forma plerumque quadrata fuit, perbreuis tamen, et angusti uix lecti uniusque mensae capax; luce autem omnes fere carebant, exceptis admodum paucis quae spiracula quaedam in angulis conclauis habuerunt. In mediis uero cellulis perpetua mansit obscuritas, nec sine candela aut legere aut esse

[1] *Das Haus zur Mücke* was the premises of a patrician social club: Wackernagel, *Geschichte der Stadt Basel*, I. 525–6 and refs. p. 637. The house had earlier been used for meetings of the deputations.

Yet the door of the conclave was not at once shut, but right up to nine in the evening it was open to servants who were bringing things that were of use, and up to that time the visits of friends were allowed. The cardinal on entering thus in procession with the electors following, in the chapel which was ready for celebrating masses, before the altar and before the very cross of Christ on bended knee and bareheaded, offered prayers to God and blessed the house and its occupants. Laying aside their copes and mitres each went to the place where he recognized his name. When the darkness of night had come, the Protector and certain citizens went in to see how each had been placed, and gained great pleasure from such systematic arrangements. After him the bishop of Lausanne, the vice-chamberlain, entered, and the guardians of the conclave followed. Some of them carefully examined the separate rooms, inspecting the persons and objects, with the intention of putting outside the conclave anything they found contrary to the rules, and on finding nothing unusual they went away. At the ninth hour, as has been said, the door was barred on both the inside and the outside, and on both sides the bolts were applied with strong chains.

Since I am mentioning the conclave, I consider it essential to describe its arrangement. The house[1] was in the middle of the city, in the cathedral square in a high and open place. Nobles had once built it to be used for dancing and it had very wide rooms above and below. The upper, since it could be heated by a fire, they had assigned to the winter and the lower to the summer. Here then it appeared that a conclave could be held, so that there might be a house of prayer where there had been a display of wantonness, and that morality should follow where vice had triumphed. So there were constructed in it both above and below suitable quarters equal in number to that of the electors, with one extra to serve for the clerks of ceremonies. Their construction was quite simple, as they did not build the partitions of stone or timber, but setting up fir poles like pillars, they interwove as walls mere bark through which one could see. The shape of the rooms was square for the most part, yet very small, and hardly big enough to hold a narrow bed and a single table. They almost all were without light except for very few, which had ventilation-holes in the corners of the building. In the middle cells there was permanent darkness, and no one could either read or eat without a candle. In these

potuit quisquam. Noxque una iis fuit dierum septem; ac camerae inferiores plus etiam incommodi habuerunt, quia in solo positae frigidissimo loca piscibus magis quam humanis apta corporibus praebuerunt. Quocirca omnes qui eas inhabitauerunt reumaticum morbum ex humore nimio contraxerunt et, tanquam alter alterum irrideret, tussientes inuicem respondebant, nec illi frigori ullum erat remedium; uestes enim et uillosae pelles magis grauabant quam calefacerent. Ignem uero habere loci angustia nec periculum nec fumus permittebat. Murus conclauis et grossus undique et altus fuit. Omnesque fenestrae clausae fuerunt, paruis admodum foraminibus ad commune lumen dimissis.

Exterius uero etiam cancelli circa conclaue fuerunt; nec appropinquare muro aliquis poterat, nisi armati custodes, qui die noctuque intra ipsos cancellos excubabant. In media uero parte ipsius conclauis in modum fenestrae ostiolum fuit, et hoc quidem duabus exterius clauibus, una interius claudebatur. Et illarum quidem alteram uicecamerarius, alteram protector custodiuit. Istam uero cardinalis Arelatensis habuit, nec ulli unquam tradidit, nisi ceremoniarum clerico, Aeneae, cum aut admittendi cibaria aut emittendi coenarum reliquias fuerat tempus; bis namque ante prandium, et totiens post prandium reserabatur ostiolum. Et bis quidem recipiebantur fercula, bis autem remittebantur fragmenta. Quibus in rebus hic modus obseruabatur. Erant (ut antea diximus) in conclaui familiares, qui dominis suis electoribus seruiebant, doctoribus singuli, praelatis bini; extra uero ut quisque potuit, sic habuit seruitores. Et illi quidem qui extra remanserunt cibaria comparabant, quae horis indictis in lignea capsa depicta, quam cornutam appellant, usque ad conclauis ostium deferebantur; et ne suspicio ueneni esset, degustare tam pocula quam cibaria cogebantur. Exinde per custodes conclauis examen fiebat ne uel litera uel aliud quiduis praeter eorum scitum intromitterentur. Quare omnia in manum[a] uicecamerarii praesentabantur. Et ille extendens ad ostiolum manus praesentabat Aeneae, ceremoniarum clerico, cui soli cum socio licebat adhaerere fenestrae. Itaque nec qui extra erant mandare aliquid in conclaue poterant, nisi per uicecamerarium, nec qui intra dictare aliquid foris, nisi per clericum. Et oportebat omnia alta uoce et latina dicere ut qui protectoris erat

[a] manum γ; manu α

there was one single night lasting seven days. The lower rooms had features that were even more inconvenient since, built on the cold ground, they afforded places better suited to fishes than to human bodies. So all who occupied them contracted bad colds from the excess of moisture and, as though mocking one another, they answered each other's coughs. There was no cure for that coldness, for clothes and furs added weight rather than heat. Because of the place's small dimensions both the danger and the smoke made having a fire impossible. The wall of the building was both thick and high all round. All the windows were shut, with a few quite small openings left to provide light for all.

On the outside there were also railings round the conclave, and no one could come near the wall but the armed guards, who kept watch day and night within the railings. In the middle part of the conclave itself there was a wicket gate like a window, shut by two keys on the outside and one on the inside. Of the former one was kept by the vice-chamberlain, the other by the Protector. The cardinal of Arles had the inside one and did not hand it over at any time to anyone except Aeneas, the clerk of ceremonies, when it was time either to let in food or send out the remnants of the meals. For twice before lunch and as often after lunch the wicket-gate used to be unfastened. Twice the trays were admitted, and twice the fragments were sent out. The procedure in this matter was this. There were, as we have said previously, servitors in the conclave, who served their masters the electors, one each for the doctors and two each for the prelates. Outside each had such servitors as he could afford. Those who remained outside used to prepare the dishes, which at set hours were carried to the door of the conclave in a painted box of wood called a horned-box, and so that there should be no suspicion of poison they were compelled to taste both food and drink. Next an examination by the guards of the conclave took place, that no letter or anything else be brought in without their knowledge. So everything was presented into the hand of the vice-chamberlain, and he, stretching out his hands to the wicket-gate presented it to Aeneas, the clerk of ceremonies, who alone with one companion was allowed to stay at the window. So neither could those outside hand anything into the conclave unless through the vice-chamberlain, nor those inside send any message out unless through the clerk. It was obligatory to say everything aloud and in Latin, so that the Protector's interpreter

interpres intelligeret quae mandarentur. Cum uero emittendi reliquias coenarum hora aduenerat, uocabantur per clericum ceremoniarum familiares cum cornutis, qui uenientes ad cancellos interiores ipsi clerico omnia assignabant, et ipse extra fenestram uicecamerario contradebat; mittebantur etiam extra paropsides et alia mensarum ornamenta quae lauacro indigebant. Et ea etiam perquirebantur nequid ab intra emitteretur literarum, fueruntque aliquae deprehensae, quae stultitiam magis familiarium quam rem proderent. Nonnulli etiam in ipsis uasorum fundis sculpentes literas commouere amicos tentauerunt; sed inuentis omnibus, nec graue aliquid nec quod ab electoribus proueniret compertum est. Vt uero perquisita singula erant quae extra mittebantur, quicquid coenarum supererat, pauperibus Christi dabatur. Qua ex re plus quam ducenti uitam trahebant. Quo circa cum omnibus longissima uideretur conclauis mora, solis huiusmodi pauperibus est uisa breuissima. Illud etiam custodes conclauis libenter obseruabant, ne ad electorum escam diuersae species cibariorum deferrentur. Et oportebat quidem aut carnibus tantum aut piscibus uesci, aut, si neque hoc neque illud placebat, ouis et caseo. Rursusque qui carnibus utebatur una specie contentari debebat, nec qui bouem habuit uti etiam oue potuit. Id quoque in piscibus fuit, nec enim cui murena est intromissa offerri quoque anguilla potuit. Si quis autem in legem commisit, partem alteram in ostio perdidit. Idque cum prima die familiares incaute commisissent, et dominis suis, quasi nuptias celebrantibus, dubiam afferrent coenam,[1] omnes in ostio spoliati sunt, nec plus una specie intromissum est. Quos inter Cracouiensis etiam archidiaconus diminutionem tulit. Cui cum oues et anatinae[a] carnes afferrentur, subtractae auiculae sunt, orante in porta famulo ut quod plus esset, id domino dimitteretur; sperabat nanque ex anate[b] partem, ex ouibus autem partem non sperabat; dominus tamen auiculas praeoptasset. Ideoque cum spolium sensit ubique conquestus est publiceque testatus, nunquam se diem postquam sacerdos fuit tulisse peiorem. Ac cum rogaretur ne admirationem haberet, quoniam id idem obtigisset cardinali: 'Proh!', inquit, 'cardinalem mihi aequiparas, hominem Gallicum, parcum, euentrem aut, ut uerius loquar, non hominem? Ego apud eum meo infortunio sum

[a] arietinae $\alpha\gamma$ [b] ariete $\alpha\gamma$

[1] Terence, *Phormio*, 342; Horace, *Sat.* ii. 2, 77.

might understand the message. When it was the time to send out the remnants of meals, the servants with the horned-boxes were summoned by the clerk of ceremonies; they came to the inner railings and handed everything to the clerk himself, and he delivered it through the window to the vice-chamberlain. The dishes were sent out and the other table furnishings that needed washing. These too were inspected, so that no kind of letter might be sent from inside, and some were detected, revealing rather the folly of the servants than anything of substance. Some too inscribed letters on the bottoms of the vessels and tried to alert their friends; but when all had been found nothing was discovered of any importance or coming from the actual electors. After the detailed examination of the things being sent out, the remnants of the meals were given to Christ's poor. From this more than two hundred obtained sustenance. Therefore whilst the duration of the conclave seemed very long to everyone else, to such poor persons alone it seemed very short. The guardians of the conclave also willingly saw to it that different kinds of food were not sent in for the electors' meals. It was obligatory to eat either meat only or fish, or, if neither the one nor the other was acceptable, eggs and cheese. Again he who took meat had to be satisfied with one kind only, and he who took beef could not have mutton too. The same was true of fish, and he who had lamprey sent in could not be offered eel as well. If anyone broke the rule, he lost one of the dishes at the door. When on the first day the servants had carelessly been guilty of this, bringing for their masters (as though celebrating a wedding) a dinner with several choices,[1] all were deprived at the door, and not more than one kind was let in. Among them the archdeacon of Cracow suffered loss. When mutton and duck were being brought in, the birds were taken away from him, as the servant begged at the gate that his master should be allowed the larger helping, for [the servant himself] was hoping for a portion of the duck, but did not want a portion of the mutton; yet his master would have preferred the birds. So when [the archdeacon] noticed the loss, he went round to complain, openly maintaining that he had never endured a worse day since he became a priest. When he was asked not to be surprised as the same thing had happened to the cardinal, he cried, 'What! Are you comparing me with the cardinal, a Frenchman, austere and without a stomach, or to speak more accurately not a human being at all? As ill luck

locatus, omnia quae facit perlustris mihi cortina indicat; nec adhuc aut bibere eum aut comedere uidi et, quod mihi molestius est, insomnes noctes insomnesque dies ducit. (Quanquam nulla est apud nos dies!) Aut legit semper, aut negociatur. Nulla ei minor quam uentris est cura; mihi nihil cum eo commune est. Ego Polonus sum, ille Gallicus; mihi ardet, illi friget stomachus; illi sanitas, mihi mors ieiunium est. Ego, ni multum comedam et multum dormiam, cito deficiam; illi econtrario omnia sunt. Ieiunent Gallici, et Poloni comedant.' Quo dicto cunctos in risum uertit. Et quoniam de hoc faceto et hilari homine fecimus mentionem, id quoque non praeteribo; ea nanque infelicitas eius fuit ut famulus eius, qui extra mansit, semper ad ostium ueniret ultimus cum cibariis. Ex qua re ortum in ostio prouerbium fuerat ultimum esse qui prior esuriret. Fuit autem haec lex de cibariis antiquitus aliter instituta. Primis enim tribus diebus nulla erat cibariorum apud ueteres limitatio. Quarta die ad unam speciem redigebantur. Nona uero sublatis aliis solum panis et aqua electoribus tradebatur. Clemens[1] autem uti clementia cupiens rigorem legis in modum qui nunc seruatur moderatus est. Id quoque inter electores seruatum extitit, patentibus nanque pransitatum et coenitatum, ut sic oculis omnium testibus factis luxuriae modus fieret. Et cibaria quippe inter se missitare non licebat, uinum licebat. Rigidusque huiusmodi legum non solum obseruator sed custos etiam fuit Ioannes Segouius, qui non aliter uiolare alienas leges exhorruit quam suas proprias apud Romanos Antius Restio, de quo illud memorabile[a] fertur eum foris, quoad uixit, postea non coenasse, ne testis fieret contemptae legis quam ipse bono publico pertulisset.[2]

Sed (ut eo redeam, quo sum digressus) electores postquam obseratum ostium fuit, ac postquam aliquantisper in suis conuenerant mansiunculis, egressi ad uisitandum se inuicem sunt, atque ut quisque in sua camera esset, prospiciebant. Quibus in locis non aliter se uicissim recipiebant ac si ex longa peregrinatione redissent. Eaque uisitatione ad magnam noctis partem producta, tandem ad quietem est itum; horaque post medium noctis tertia ad matutinas singuli experrecti sunt, orantesque usque ad quintam

[a] memorabile W *MSS. of Macrobius*; memoriale αV

[1] The severities laid down for conclaves by Gregory X at the Council of Lyons in 1274 (*Vbi periculum*) were softened by Clement VI in 1351 (*Licet in constitutione*).

[2] In this passage 'eum foris . . . pertulisset' is a quotation from Macrobius, *Satur.* iii. 17, 13. (Incidentally Macrobius uses 'memorabile' just previously.) Antius Restio was the proposer of a law against extravagant expenditure on food 'a few years after' the similar law of Aemilius Lepidus in 78 B.C.

would have it I have been put beside him, and the transparent screen reveals to me all that he does. Up to now I have never seen him drinking or eating, and, what is more irksome to me, he spends his nights and days without sleep, though in fact we have no day! He is always either reading or doing business. He bothers less about his stomach than anything. I have nothing in common with him. I am a Pole, he a Frenchman. My stomach is hot, his is cold. Hunger is health for him, death for me. If I do not eat a lot and sleep a lot, it will soon be the end of me. He, however, has all he wants. Let the French fast and the Poles eat.' With these words he amused all and, since we have mentioned this witty and cheerful person, I shall not pass over this too; for such was his bad luck that his servant, who remained outside, was always the last to come to the door with his food. From this there had grown up a saying at the door that he was last to eat who felt hunger the first. Now the rule about food had run differently in olden days. For in former times there was no restriction on food during the first three days. On the fourth day they used to be restricted to only one kind. On the ninth day everything else was taken away, and only bread and water were given to the electors. Clement,[1] however, wishing to show clemency, modified the harshness of the law to the form that is now observed. This too has persisted and has been observed among the electors, namely lunching and dining in public, so that with the eyes of all to witness there should be a limit to luxury. They were not permitted to exchange food, but only wine. Not merely a stern observer but also a guardian of the rules of this kind was John of Segovia, who dreaded as much the violation of other people's laws as Antius Restio among the Romans did that of his own. Of him it is recorded as remarkable, that to avoid seeing broken the law which he had passed for the general good, he did not dine out thereafter as long as he lived.[2]

But to return from my digression, the electors, after the door was shut and after they had gathered for a time in their own quarters, went to pay visits to one another, and looked to see how each fared in his own room. To their places they would come back in turn as though they had returned from a long journey. This visiting was prolonged until late at night, but eventually they retired to rest. At three a.m. each of them woke up for his matins, and praying until five, they then devoted themselves to the office

exinde missarum officio se tradiderunt, et alii quidem in suis cellulis, alii uero in communibus altaribus celebrabant. Episcopi nanque altaria plerunque portatilia apud se traduxerant. Clerici uero ceremoniarum diuersis in locis intra ipsum conclaue tria altaria erexerant, ut possent complurimi celebrare. Vt uero dies illuxit, uniuersi ad communem missam uenerunt; qua completa, et decantato hymno quo Spiritus Sanctus euocatur,[1] habitis in concilio patribus, de modis et conclaui obseruandis consultatum in medio est. Isque communi consilio receptus est ordo: statutum est singulis noctibus quatuor supra, et quatuor infra ex seruitoribus assumi uigiles, qui noctes inter se partientes curam haberent ne uel ignis uel alia quaeuis res nocumento esse posset. Cui rei nemo uigilantius incubuit quam Rubinus, antiquus cardinalis de Cypro[2] nobilissimi familiaris. Cuius excubatione nequaquam dubitauerim pleraque euitata fuisse discrimina. Exinde cautum erat ut post mediam noctis horam inter quartam et quintam euigilatio per omnes fieret; tumque usque ad septimam, ut cuique animo esset, aut oraret aut celebraret, postea uero ad communem missam omnes accederent. Qua peracta, et Spiritus almi efflagitato patrocinio, concilium iniretur, utque in eo scrutinium fieret; et eo finito, prandium haberetur. Ac deinde, ut quenque uoluptas traheret, sic uel legeret uel quiesceret usque ad horam post meridiem tertiam, quo tempore iterum intrantes concilium illorum merita in examen ducerent, qui praecedenti scrutinio nominati fuissent; mature inter sese consulerent, quo nunc ecclesiae modo ferri auxilium posset. Dimisso uero concilio, hora circiter post meridiem septima coenaretur, ac post horis tribus ad quietem se cuncti redigerent. Eoque modo tam diem quam noctem partiti sunt.

Omittam illam sanctissimam uitam beatam et omni stricta religione mundiorem; ubinam gentium talis patrum est chorus, ubi tantum scientiae lumen, ubi prudentia, ubi bonitas est, quae horum patrum aequari uirtutibus queat? O integerrimam fraternitatem! O uerum orbis terrae senatum! Quam pulchra, quam suauis, quam deuota res fuit, hic celebrantes episcopos, illic orantes abbates, alibi uero doctores diuinas legentes historias, audire, et unum ad lumen candelae scribentem cernere, alium uero grande aliquid meditantem intueri! Quid est quod aliqui in Hispaniis

[1] The 'Veni, Creator Spiritus'.

[2] Hugues de Lusignan, died 1442. Though still considered a friend of the Fathers at Basle and mentioned in the conclave as a possible pope (see the letter of Aeneas to Siena quoted by Valois, II. 182, n. 3), he was actually in Cyprus. Some of his *familiares* are mentioned in earlier conciliar proceedings but not named: Haller, III. 149, 406. Rubinus was presumably servant at this time to a member of the conclave.

of mass, and some would celebrate in their own cells, and some at the common altars. For the bishops in most cases had brought in with them portable altars. The clerks of ceremonies had set up three altars in different places within the actual conclave, that as many as possible might celebrate. When day dawned, they all came to a common mass. When this was over, and the hymn was sung invoking the Holy Spirit,[1] the Fathers were kept in council and they considered together the procedure for the conclave. By general agreement the following arrangement was adopted. It was decided to have each night four servitors above and four below assigned as watchmen, who should divide up the nights, and should take care that no fire or anything else should cause harm. To this duty no one gave more watchful attention than Rubinus, formerly servant of the most noble cardinal of Cyprus.[2] I feel no doubt that through his watchfulness many dangers were avoided. Next it was ordered that all should be awakened between four and five in the morning, then till seven as each pleased he should pray, or celebrate, and afterwards all should come to the common mass. When this was over, and the assistance of the comforting Spirit had been requested, they should hold a meeting and at it a ballot should take place. When this was over they should have lunch. Then as the inclination moved each he should read or rest until three in the afternoon; at this time entering into council again they should consider the merits of those named at the preceding ballot. They should take thought together at some length on how aid could be brought to the Church. When the meeting broke up at about seven in the evening, they should have dinner, and within the next three hours all should retire to rest. In this way they divided up day and night alike.

I will pass over that most holy blessed life, purer than all strict religion. Wherever is there such a band of Fathers, where such a splendour of knowledge, where the wisdom and the goodness that can be compared with the virtues of these Fathers? What a perfect brotherhood! What a true senate of the whole world! How fair, how pleasant, how holy an experience it was to hear bishops celebrating here, abbots praying there, elsewhere doctors reading the holy narratives, and to discern one writing by the light of a candle, to behold another in meditation on some lofty theme! What is the reason why some people in Spain give such

locum quendam tantopere laudant nomine Guadalupum,[1] Cartusiam Gallici in Delphinatu siue Sabaudia[2] commendant? Potuitne unquam religio hac excellentior inueniri? Ac ego existimo illis in locis irriguos magis fontes et splendidas cellas aliaque aedificia esse admirationi quam homines. In nostro uero conuentu caetera contemnenda, uiri duntaxat admirandi fuerunt. Quorum modestiam nemo potuit satis contemplari; nullae illic rixae, nullae contentiones, omnia in amicitia, omnia in dilectione fiebant. Illic cum exeuntem cellam aut Christiannum aut alium quempiam ex antiquioribus uidisses, non alium certe uidere putasses quam uel magnum Antonium, uel Paulum Simplicem, et illum sane Hilarioni, illum Paphnucio, illum uero Amoni[3] aequiparasses. Plus etiam hoc in loco quam in Antoniana solitudine reperisses, siquidem Hieronymo etiam et Augustino obuiasses, quorum literae in conclaui fuerunt, in eremo non fuerunt. Custodiebatur inter dominos magna charitas, inter famulos bona dilectio, inter utrosque optimum silentium. Et isti in dominos obedientes, illi in seruitores benigni erant; nulla superbia, nullus liuor, nulla simultas uigebat, suus cuique status placebat; nihil secretum, nihil occultum fuit, omnia scire uicinum oportuit quae fecit uicinus. Sed neque mihi tacendi familiares uidentur, quorum numerus fuit duo et quinquaginta. Itaque omnes animae quae ingressae sunt conclaue tres de nonaginta dinumeratae sunt, fueruntque inter seruitores conplures et docti et ornati uiri. Erant cum cardinali Arelatensi Stephanus Plonerii[4] et Petrus de Tridia,[5] doctores et archidiaconi; cum archiepiscopo Tarantasiensi, Antonius Pioceti, iurisconsultus, qui auditor etiam Rotae aliquando fuit.[6] Cum Basiliensi episcopo officialis[7] suus, uir non minus doctus quam facetus. Fuerunt et alii complures et docti et egregii uiri. Quapropter facile potest quis dominorum excellentiam recognoscere, ubi uirtutes familiarium non ignorat.

Sed iam tempus admonet ut scrutiniorum seriem referamus et modum. Eo ergo in loco ubi et cardinalis et Vicensis episcopi cella fuit atque aliae nouem, hinc atque hinc sedilia posuerunt. In summo loco ara erat sacra, et ante ipsum puluinar cardinali stratum. Ad cuius dextram sedebat archiepiscopus Tarantasiensis, et ad sinistram Dertusensis antistes, et successiue hinc et inde gradatim reliqui electores assidebant. Ante ipsum uero cardinalem

[1] The Order of Guadalupe was a congregation of reformed Franciscan houses and ultimately constituted a branch of the Observant Franciscans.

[2] Mother house of the Carthusian order.

[3] These five names are those of early saints in fourth-century Egypt and are meant to suggest the austerity and inspiration of members of the conclave.

[4] Archdeacon of Embrun.

[5] Archdeacon of Lodève.

[6] A canonist from Agde; the Rota was the principal court of the Curia and one existed also at Basle.

praise to a place called Guadalupe,[1] while the French commend the Chartreuse in Dauphiné or Savoy?[2] Could religion ever be found more excellent than here? My view is that in those places it was the flowing springs and noble cells and other buildings rather than the men that called for admiration. At our assembly, however, all else deserved contempt, and only the men admiration. At their restraint no one could gaze long enough. There were no quarrels and no disputes, everything took place in friendship and affection. There, when you saw leaving his cell either Christian or some other of the older fathers, you would have thought you were beholding either the great Anthony, or Paul the Simple, and you would have compared one to Hilarion, one to Paphnutius, and one to Ammon.[3] You would have found more even in this place than in the solitude of an Anthony from encountering Jerome too and Augustine, whose writings were in the conclave but not in the wilderness. Among the masters great love was maintained, among the servants good affection, among both excellent silence. The latter were obedient to their masters, the former kindly towards their servitors. No pride, spite, or anger prevailed, each being satisfied with his own position. There was nothing secret, nothing hidden. A neighbour was bound to know all a neighbour's actions. I must not leave unmentioned the servants also, numbering fifty-two. So there had entered the conclave eighty-seven souls. Among the servitors were several men of both learning and distinction. There were with the cardinal of Arles Etienne Plovier[4] and Pierre de Trilhia,[5] doctors and archdeacons; with the archbishop of Tarentaise the doctor of law, Antonio Piocheti, who for a time was also an auditor of the Rota.[6] With the bishop of Basle was his official,[7] a man no less learned than witty. There were several others as well both learned and eminent. So anyone aware of the qualities of the retainers can easily realize the distinction of the masters.

However, the time now prompts me to describe the order and arrangement of the ballots. In that part then where the cardinal's cell was and that of the bishop of Vich and nine others they placed benches on both sides. There was a holy altar at the top end, and before it a cushioned seat was placed for the cardinal. On his right sat the archbishop of Tarentaise, and on his left the bishop of Tortosa, and the rest of the electors sat one after the other in order of seniority on one or the other side. In front of the cardinal was

[7] Johannes Meminger, 'officialis' or judge of the episcopal court.

scabellum, et supra scabellum ex argento peluis stabat. Huc audita missa, et decantato Spiritus Sancti hymno,[1] singuli electores uenerunt, et eorum quilibet scedulam suam iecit in peluim. Easque postmodum singillatim cardinalis recepit, et legit, atque, ut ipse legerat, quatuor alii ex electoribus lectionem ipsius scribebant. Scriptio autem scedularum huiusmodi erat: 'Ego, Georgius, Vicensis episcopus, eligo in Romanum pontificem illum uel illum', poteratque unum uel duos uno in scrutinio nominare. Et inscribebat se quilibet electorum nomine proprio, ut sic in lectione[a] scedularum seipsum quisque recognosceret, possetque contradicere, si [quis] aliter quam ipse diceret scripsisset; quae res exclu debat omnem dolum. Vt autem omnes scedulae lectae erant, et nominationes eorum conscriptae, fiebat per scrutationes numeri ad numerum collatio. Et nisi in unum aliquem duas scedularum partes reperiebant concurrere, easdem igne cremabant.

Igitur primo scrutinio confecto, compertum est plurimos esse in papam nominatos, nullum tamen habere uoces sufficientes; septemque et decem eo ipso die ex diuersis nationibus ad pontificatum fuisse uocatos constat, unus tamen omnes superauit uir praestantissimus Amadeus,[2] dux Sabaudiae, decanus militum Sancti Mauricii[3] de Riparia Gebennensis dioecesis, quem iam coelibem ac religiose uiuentem sexdecim electores primo scrutinio dignum qui gubernaret ecclesiam censuerunt. Exinde hora post meridiem tertia habita est in concilio electorum de nominatis diligens inquisitio, atque ut quisque opinatus est, aut extulit nominatos, aut depressit. Ea tamen habita est Amadei relatio, ut in sequenti scrutinio, quod celebratum est quarto nonas Nouembris, ipse Amadeus unam de uiginti, ac deinde in tertio unam et uiginti, et rursus in quarto unam et uiginti uoces habuerit; quia tamen nullus adhuc duas habere partes compertus erat in omni scrutinio, exustae sunt scedulae. Cumque ad electionem summi pontificis una duntaxat uox desyderaretur, multiplicari orationes et augeri deuotiones placuit, ut dignaretur Deus in unum concorditer uota dirigere, qui pastoralem curam super Dominicum gregem susciperet digne. Et quia proximior aliis Amadeus Romano pontificio uidebatur, habiti sunt in communi sermones multi de uita et moribus eius. Et alii non esse homini laico cito imponendas manus dicebant, quod uideretur omnibus monstri simile principem

[a] lectione W; electione αV

[1] The 'Veni, Creator Spiritus'.
[2] See Introduction, p. xx.
[3] The order Amadeo had himself founded.

a stool, and on it stood a silver bowl. After hearing mass and singing the hymn of the Holy Spirit,[1] the electors came here one by one, and each of them cast his voting slip into the bowl. Afterwards the cardinal took them separately and read them out, and four others of the electors would write down what he had read out. Now the wording of the slips was like this: 'I, Jorge, bishop of Vich, choose this man or that to be Roman pontiff', and it was possible to name one man or two at a single ballot. Each of the electors wrote down his own name so that when they were read out he might recognize himself, and could object if anyone had written what was different from his opinion, which made fraud quite impossible. When all the slips had been read and their nominations written down, then the numbers were examined to see how they compared. Unless they found that two-thirds of the slips agreed on any one person, they burnt them in a fire.

So when the first ballot was completed, it was found that there were several nominations for the papacy, but none had enough votes. It is common knowledge that on that day from the various nations seventeen were proposed for the office of pontiff, but all were outstripped by one man of great distinction, Amadeo,[2] duke of Savoy, dean of the knights of St. Maurice,[3] of Ripaille in the diocese of Geneva. Now that he lived a celibate and religious life sixteen electors at the first ballot considered him worthy of governing the church. Then at three in the afternoon a careful inquiry was made in the council of electors about those who had been nominated, and each in accordance with his views either praised or disparaged those nominated. Yet such was the report given about Amadeo, that in the next ballot held on 2 November he gained nineteen votes, in the third twenty-one, and twenty-one again in the fourth, but because nobody yet was found to have gained two-thirds of the votes in any ballot, the slips were burnt. Since for the election of the chief pontiff there was only one vote short, they agreed that prayers should be multiplied and intercessions increased, that God might deign to direct their votes in harmony towards a single person, who should undertake worthily the pastoral care of the Lord's flock. Because Amadeo seemed nearer than others to the office of Roman pontiff, many general discussions took place about his life and character. Some said that they should be in no haste to lay their hands on a layman, because it would seem monstrous to all that a secular prince

seculi ad Romanum pontificium accersiri; quae res nimium ecclesiasticis derogaret uiris, quasi nullum haberent tantae dignitati idoneum. Alii hominem qui fuerit coniugatus, cuique proles esset, ineptum sacerdotio existimabant. Alii Romanum episcopum legisdoctorem esse oportere asseuerabant, multisque literis praepollentem.

Quae uerba ut audiuerunt, alii mox assurgentes longe aliter dixerunt. Et Amadeum quidem, etsi doctor non foret, peritum tamen et doctum esse, qui cum alias in iuuentute sua literarum studiis insudasset, non titulos sed scientiam quaesiuisset; eumque et diuinum officium optime nosse, et horas canonicas obseruare, septiesque dietim Domino dicere laudes. 'Quod si de uita', inquit alius, 'huius principis edoceri uultis, iam me, obsecro, audite, qui eum et "intus et in cute noui".'[1] Nempe hic homo ab ineunte aetate ac lacteis (ut aiunt) annis magis religiose uixit quam seculariter, parentibus quidem obediens et paedagogis obsequiosus; semper autem Dei timore imbutus, nec unquam aut uanitati aut lasciuiae operam dedit, nec unquam puer de domo Sabaudiae natus tantam prae se indolem aut spem tulit. Quibus ex rebus qui eum intuebantur, magnum sibi aliquod portendebant. Nec fefellit opinio, siquidem uir postquam adoleuit, animum semper ad alta leuans apud inclytae memoriae Sigismundum Caesarem forensi certamine Gebennensem euicit comitatum, moxque deinde familiam suam honoribus cumulans ducales suscepit infulas.[2] Ac si scire cupitis eius regimen, et quale et quantum fuerit, illud primum cognoscite, uirum hunc post obitum patris iam annis circiter quadraginta regnasse. Cuius tempore regina uirtutum semper iustitia floruit. Audiens enim per seipsum subditos, nunquam uel inopes opprimi uel circumueniri imbecilles permisit. Ipse pupillis tutor, ipse uiduis aduocatus, ipse pauperibus protector fiebat,[3] nusquam in territorio suo aut rapinis locus aut latrociniis patuit; diuites ac pauperes aequali iure apud se habebat, nec terracolis onerosum, nec aduenis importunum se exhibens, nullaque in patria grauis exactio pecuniarum fuit, satis se diuitem existimans, si patricolas abundare cognosceret, sciens quia boni pastoris esset non deglubere oues suas, sed tondere.[4] In eo tamen praecipue

[1] Persius, iii. 30.

[2] The purchase of the county of Geneva in 1401 was contested and settled in Amadeo's favour by Sigismund in 1422. He acquired the ducal title in 1416.

[3] Cf. St. Bernard, *De consid.* iv. 7 on what the pope should be.

[4] A saying of the Emperor Tiberius, quoted by Suetonius, *Tib.* 32.

should be summoned to the office of Roman pontiff, which would lower the credit of ecclesiastics as though they had nobody suited to so great an honour. Others thought that a man who had been married, and who had issue, was unsuited to priesthood. Others asserted that the bishop of Rome should be a doctor of law and pre-eminent in scholarship.

On hearing these remarks, others quickly rose and spoke very differently. Amadeo, even if he was no doctor, was experienced and learned, who when at times in his youth he had worked hard at scholarship, had sought knowledge rather than academic degrees; and he was entirely familiar with the divine office, observed the canonical hours, and seven times a day uttered praises to the Lord. Another said, 'If you wish to be informed about the life of this prince, listen to me now, I beseech you, as "I know him intimately and closely".[1] For this man from the beginning of his life and his babyhood, as the saying is, has lived more in a religious than a secular fashion, obedient to his parents and deferential to his tutors. Moreover, filled always with the fear of God, he never gave himself up to vanity or wantonness, and no boy born to the House of Savoy ever displayed such character and promise. The result was that those who observed him prophesied greatness for him. Their belief did not play them false, seeing that when he grew up, lifting his mind always to lofty things, before the Emperor Sigismund of famous memory he won in a legal action the rank of count of Geneva, and soon afterwards, loading his family with honours, gained the rank of duke.[2] If you want to know what his rule was like, and how great it was, first learn this, that he has reigned for about forty years since his father's death. In his time justice, the queen of virtues, has flourished always. For listening in person to his subjects, he has never allowed the poor to be oppressed or the weak to be deceived. Himself he became the guardian of orphans, the pleader for widows, and the protector of the poor.[3] Nowhere in his territory was there any place for theft or plunder. Rich and poor he treated with equal justice, neither showing himself burdensome to his native subjects nor exacting to strangers, and there was no harsh taxation in that land. He considered he was wealthy enough if he knew that his fellow countrymen had plenty, knowing that it is the sign of a good shepherd not to skin his sheep but to shear them.[4] In this, however, he showed particular care, that his

sollers exhibuit studium, ut et pace subditi eius fruerentur, et nulli sibi finitimi causam succensendi haberent. Quibus artibus non solum paternum dominium tranquille gubernauit, sed alia quoque sponte ad eum uenientia superadiecit. Nulli unquam intulit bellum, illato uero resistens, semper de pace magis quam de uindicta cogitauit, et hostes singulos beneficio potius uincere quam gladio studuit. Vxorem unicam duxit,[1] eamque uirginem nobilem, et formae et pudicitiae admirabilis. Familiam omnem suam non solum manus sed oculos etiam abstinentes habere uoluit; fuit in eius domo summa honestas, summa obseruantia morum, et in seculari palatio claustralis obseruabatur religio.

'Ac ubi thori consors uitam commigrauit in aliam, ubi ducatum eius firmatum et ad posteriores sine controuersia uenturum perspexit, animum qui semper religiosus et Deo dicatus fuerat patefecit, et qualem in corde gestaret uoluntatem demonstrauit. Contempto nanque seculi fastu, omnique pompa mundiali despecta, uocatis secum charissimis amicis in eremum concessit; ubi constructo mirae deuotionis et artis monasterio, in seruitium Dei se relegauit, et tollens crucem suam, secutus est Christum.[2] Quo loci per plures annos conuersatus singularis sanctimoniae dedit odorem, uestes quidem non alias induens, nisi quae possent frigus arcere, epulasque non alias sumens, nisi quibus pelli fames ualet; uigilansque ad plurimam noctem, nullam unquam diuini officii horam neglexit. Cumque ibi pulcherrimum Deo et beato Mauritio sacellum construxisset, et honorificum sacerdotum collegium ordinasset, diebus illic singulis tres missas, duas quidem legi, unam autem decantari audiuit; tantusque illo in monasterio seruatus est rigor disciplinae, tanta honestas, tanta religio ut nusquam sub coelo putem aut sanctiorem aut deuotiorem inueniri locum. Quocirca non nouiter, ut quidam ante sentire sunt uisi, hic princeps ad ecclesiam uenit, qui natus Christianus ex progenitoribus iam mille annis et ultra Christianis, nunc Deo in monasterio seruit. Id autem quod de uxore dicitur nihilipendo, cum non solum qui uxorem habuit sed uxorem adhuc habens queat assumi. Cur enim disputant doctores an uxoratus electus in papam uxori soluere debitum teneatur, nisi quoniam etiam coniugatus recipi possit? Fueruntque (ut scitis) etiam in matrimonio pontifices, nec Petrus Apostolorum princeps uxore caruit.[3]

[1] Marie de Bourgogne, whom he married in 1393 and who died in 1422.

[2] Cf. Matt. 16: 24; Mark, 8: 34; Luke 9: 23. The duke began to reside at Ripaille in Oct. 1434.

[3] For St. Peter's wife, see Mark 1: 30. Popes who had been married did occur —for instance in the eleventh century—but were not particularly respectable.

subjects should enjoy peace and that none of his neighbours should have cause for wrath. By these arts he not only governed peacefully the realm of his father, but added others that came to him of their own accord. He never declared war on anyone, resisting when it was declared on him. He was always more concerned with peace than with revenge, and tried to win over individual enemies by kindness rather than the sword. He had one wife,[1] a young woman of noble birth, and of outstanding beauty and chastity. He wished all his household to restrain not merely the hands but the eyes. In his house there was the greatest uprightness, the strictest observance of morals, and in a palace that was secular there was observed the religion of the cloister.

'When his spouse departed to another life, when he saw that his dukedom was assured and would pass to his descendants without dispute, he revealed a mind that had always been religious and devoted to God, and displayed the purpose he was cherishing in his heart. For despising secular pride and disregarding all worldly pomp, he summoned his dearest friends, and withdrew into a hermitage, where he built a monastery of wondrous devotion and art; banishing himself into the service of God, and taking up his cross, he followed Christ.[2] For many years he has dwelt in this place, and has given forth an odour of great sanctity, wearing no clothes except what could keep out the cold, and eating no food but what sufficed to banish hunger. Watching far into the night he has missed no hour of divine office. When he had built there a fair shrine for God and the Blessed Maurice, and had established an honourable college of priests, he has heard there three masses each day, two said and one sung, and such strictness of discipline has been maintained in that monastery, such uprightness, such religion that I think nowhere under heaven is found a holier or more devout place. So it is not just recently, as some seemed previously to suppose, that this prince has come to the Church, who, born a Christian of ancestors Christian for a thousand years and more, now serves God in a monastery. As for what is said about his wife, I hold that of no importance, since not only a widower, but a man with a living wife can be chosen. For why do the doctors discuss whether a man with a wife, when elected to the papacy, is bound to discharge his duty to his wife, unless this is because a man with a spouse can be admitted? As you know, there were several married pontiffs, and Peter,[3] the head of the

Quid ista modo obiicimus? Fortasse non esset peius sacerdotes quamplures uxorari, quoniam multi saluarentur in sacerdotio coniugato, qui sterili in presbyteratu damnantur. Sed de hoc alias. Illud autem mihi risu magis quam responso dignum uidetur, quod de filiis est obiectum. Etenim cur filii praesertim natu grandes, pontifici patri sint impedimento? Nunquid ait scriptura: "Vae soli, quoniam si ceciderit, non habet subleuantem se?"[1] Hoc imputari principi modo non poterit. Sunt enim illi filii duo,[2] et forma et ingenio admodum praestantes. Quorum alter princeps Pedemontensium, alter comes est Gebennensium. Hi patriam Sabaudiae absente patre gubernabunt, indigentique sibi auxilia subministrabunt. Iam enim regere ac praeesse populis didicerunt. En quid mali hoc est habere Romanum antistitem potentes filios, qui patrem contra tyrannos iuuare queant?

'Proh! reuerendissimi patres, sane quo magis huius peruersi temporis procellam intueor, quo magis angustias animo euoluo quibus ecclesia in hac nostra tempestate percutitur, eo magis non utile tantum, sed necessarium esse arbitror hunc ipsum eligi principem, existimaboque misericordiam Domini super nos factam, si eum uidero huius cymbae suscepisse gubernaculum. Consyderate, oro, paulisper: quibus in terminis sumus, quibus angustiis premimur, quibus periculis agitamur, quis principum est huic sacro Concilio obediens? Alii nec Concilium hic esse fatentur, nec mandata nostra suscipiunt; alii uerbo hic esse concilium dicunt, facto apud Florentiam fore ostendunt. Quamuis enim uerbis et literis ecclesiam hic esse non negent, promotiones tamen apud Gabrielem depositum procurant. Hic est status ecclesiae, his procellis nauis illiditur; surrexerunt filii impii aduersus matrem, qui nec suscepti lactis nec materni laboris memores eam spernunt, eam lacerant, eam colaphizant. Quid hic fiendum est? Nudumne hominem eligemus, qui nostris principibus magis derisui quam uenerationi habeatur? Non sunt hodie secula quae uirtutem respiciant. "Probitas", ut est apud satyricum,[3] "laudatur et alget." Pauper locutus est, et dicunt: "Quis et hic?"

[1] Cf. Eccl. 4: 10.

[2] Louis (d. 1465), who succeeded to the duchy, and Philip (d. 1444), count of Geneva.

[3] Juvenal, i. 74.

Apostles, was not without a wife. Why do we raise such objections now? Perhaps it would not be worse for as many priests as possible to take a wife, since many would be saved in a married priesthood who are damned in one that is celibate. Yet about this at another time. Moreover the objection made about his sons seems to me more worthy of ridicule than a reply. For why should sons, particularly when they are grown up, be a hindrance to a father who is pontiff? Surely the scripture says: "Woe to him that is alone, for if he falls, he has not anyone to help him up."[1] Such a charge cannot be brought against the prince, as he has two sons,[2] in looks and intellect quite outstanding. One of these is prince of Piedmont, the other count of Geneva. These will govern their country of Savoy during their father's absence, and when he needs help they will supply it. For already they have learnt to rule and be in charge of peoples. What evil is this that the bishop of Rome should have powerful sons, to be able to help their father against tyrants?

'Most reverend Fathers, the more I contemplate the tempest of this perverse time, and the more I turn over in my mind the difficulties by which the Church in this calamity of ours is stricken, the more I think it not merely useful, but essential that this prince be elected, and I shall consider that the Lord's mercy has been shed upon us, if I see that the duke has undertaken to steer this boat. Reflect for a moment, I beg you, upon the limits within which we are set, upon the straits by which we are close pressed, upon the dangers by which we are tossed. Which of the princes shows obedience to this holy Council? Some neither admit that there is a Council here, nor accept our orders. Some in word say that there is a Council here, but in deed show that there is one at Florence. For though in words and letters they do not deny that the Church is here, it is with the deposed Gabriel that they obtain preferment. Such is the state of the Church, such the tempests that beat upon the ship. Undutiful sons have risen against their mother, and forgetful of the milk afforded to them and of their mother's labour, they despise her, tear her in pieces, and knock her about. What is needed now? Shall we choose a defenceless man to be held by our princes in ridicule rather than in reverence? The present generation does not show respect for virtue. "Uprightness", to quote the satirist,[3] "is praised yet freezes." When a poor man has spoken they say, "Who is this?" Virtue is certainly

Bona est equidem uirtus, sed multum interest ad nostrum propositum an in potente sit, an in paupere. Vobis eligendus est gubernator qui non solum consiliis sed etiam uiribus nauim regat. Validus uentus est; nisi et consilium bonum sit et brachia fortia, frangetur malus, et periclitabuntur omnes. Exinde recens ante oculos est quia uirtutem impotentem nihilipendunt principes. Nunquid maxima uirtus hic ostensa est, qui nullum timentes aut uitae aut bonorum periculum pro ueritate Christi tamdiu pugnastis? Debuerant principes terram deosculari, ubi gressus uestri fuissent; quia tamen potentes praelati ac famosi cardinales a nobis defecerunt, uidetis quid principes fecerint. Aspicit tamen ex alto maximus atque optimus Deus talia, iisque (ut puto) resistet insolentiis. Saepius ego illorum opinioni assensus fueram, qui expedire dicebant temporale dominium ab ecclesia secerni. Opinabar namque et sacerdotes Domini ad diuina mysteria reddi expeditiores, et principes seculi erga clerum fieri obedientiores. Nunc autem didici quoniam ridiculosa est sine potentia uirtus, nec aliud est Romanus pontifex sine patrimonio ecclesiae quam regum et principum seruus. Quod praeuidens diuina pietas Romanam ecclesiam dotari per Constantinum[1] et locupletari uoluit, ut qui, spreto spirituali gladio, aduersus fidem et bonos mores tumultuarentur, potenti brachio possent compesci. At cum hodie terrae ecclesiae, partim per Gabrielem, partim per alios occupentur tyrannos, prouidendum nobis est ut uirum talem eligamus, qui et recuperare patrimonium queat ecclesiae, et in quo Christi uicariatus non contemnatur, cuiusque potentiae clypeo eorum contumacia conteratur qui rationem contemnunt et ueritatem. Ad quas res nemo (ut mihi uidetur) aptior est Amadeo, duce Sabaudiae, qui alterum in Italia, alterum uero in Gallia pedem habet, cui omnes fere Christianorum principes aut sanguine attinent, aut amicitia fauent, cuiusque quanta sit uirtus, iam supra retulimus. Quid igitur hunc haereamus eligere? Nemo est quem magis dari sibi aduersum Gabriel quam istum timeat. Pereat igitur eo gladio quo putauit. Nemo est qui magis pacare ecclesiam quam iste possit. Quaeritis in pontifice deuotionem? Nemo est eo deuotior. Quaeritis prudentiam? Iam intelligitis ex anteacta uita quis sit. Quaeritis

[1] Lorenzo Valla's celebrated essay denying the authenticity of the Donation of Constantine was being written at about this time (spring of 1440).

a good thing, but it makes a good deal of difference to our purpose whether it is found in a powerful or a poor man. You must elect a steersman to control the ship not merely by his counsels but by his strength. The wind is strong; unless there are both good counsel and strong arms, the mast will break and all be in danger. You have had too a recent object-lesson of virtue that is powerless being held of no account by the princes. Surely the greatest virtue has been shown here, where without any fear of risk to life or property you have fought so long for Christ's truth? The princes should have kissed the ground where your footsteps had been. Yet because powerful prelates and celebrated cardinals have deserted us, you see what the princes have done. God, however, in his greatness and goodness, beholds such things from on high, and will, I believe, oppose those acts of insolence. Very often I used to agree with the view of those who said it was desirable to remove temporal dominion from the Church. For I thought that the priests of the Lord would become more fitted for the divine mysteries, and the secular princes would become more deferential towards the clergy. Now, however, I have learnt that virtue is ridiculous without power, and that the Roman pontiff without the patrimony of the Church is nothing but the slave of kings and princes. The divine compassion foreseeing this willed that the Roman Church be endowed by Constantine[1] and made rich, so that those who in contempt of the spiritual sword caused disturbance against faith and good order could be controlled by a strong arm. Since, however, today the lands of the Church are possessed partly by Gabriel and partly by other tyrants, we must look to it that we choose a man capable of recovering the patrimony of the Church and in whom the office of the vicar of Christ is not despised, and by the shield of whose power the obstinacy is crushed of those who despise reason and truth. For those duties nobody, I think, is more suitable than Amadeo, duke of Savoy, who has one foot in Italy and one in France, to whom almost all the princes of Christendom are either close in blood or well-disposed in friendship, and the extent of whose virtue we have already related. Why then should we hesitate to choose this man? There is nobody whose opposition Gabriel fears more. May he die then by the very sword by which he thought [he might]. There is no one who can better make the Church peaceful. Do you look for devotion in a pontiff? No one is more devout than he. Do you look for wisdom? You know

iustitiam? Populus eius est testimonio. Siue potentiam, siue uirtutem efflagitatis, hic omnia sunt. Quid moramini? Agite, obsecro, bonis hominibus hunc eligite; hic fidem augebit, hic mores reformabit, hic autoritatem ecclesiae conseruabit, hic aduersarios reprimet, hic pacem Christiano populo condonabit. Non audistis eos qui de futuris praedicant has fluctuationes ecclesiae praenunciantes, annum qui iam instat quadragesimum iis terminum tribulationis assignare? Nunquid iamdudum audistis papam iis temporibus eligi debere, qui consolaturus Sion,[1] omnia ponat in pace? Et quis erit, obsecro, ille, qui talia queat implere, nisi istum assumamus? Credite mihi, scripturas impleri oportet, et trahet (ut spero) animos uestros, etiam si nolimus, Deus;[2] tamen uos quod rectum et sanctum est uolentes potius agite.'

Haec cum ille dixisset, maxima electorum pars sibi fauendo arrisit, eamque habuerunt uerba eius efficaciam, ut sequenti scrutinio perfecta res sit. Nonis enim Nouembris dum clerus ciuitatis circa conclaue cum reliquiis sanctorum staret, et processio praelatorum Spiritus Sancti gratiam inuocaret,[3] horam circiter ante meridiem decimam, aperto scrutinio, et facta collatione (ut moris est) numeri ad numerum, compertum est Amadeum, ducem Sabaudiae, religiosissimum principem, iuxta decretum Concilii in papam fore electum, sexque et uiginti uoces in eum concurrere. Quapropter subito inter omnes coorta laetitia est, omnesque rem gestam amplissimis uerbis collaudarunt. Quocirca uocatis notariis, et intromissis testibus, confectum est de ipsa electione chirographum. Qua re sic peracta, remissis testibus, horam circiter post meridiem primam ad eas fenestras quae in plateam uersae erant factus est impetus, omnesque ualuae securibus infractae, atque illinc miranti populo nouitatem crux argentea est ostensa. Erat iam tota ciuitas in platea, omnisque multitudo in fenestram tendebat oculos, electum sibi nominari desyderans. Tunc cardinalis Arelatensis facto signo crucis, in nomine Patris et Filii et Spiritus Sancti electi pontificis nomen publicauit, et oratione praemissa, populo benedixit. Postque hora iam tertia praelati cum pluuialibus et mitris, ac clerus urbis cum reliquiis ad cancellos conclauis uenientes, electores similiter exornatos ad

[1] Isa. 51: 3, Zech. 1: 17.
[2] Cf. Job 34: 14.
[3] The 'Veni, Creator Spiritus'.

already from his past life what he is. Do you look for justice? His people can give evidence for him. If it is power or virtue that you demand, all these are present in him. Why do you delay? Come now, I beg you elect him for the sake of the virtuous. He will increase faith, correct morals, maintain the authority of the Church, restrain its enemies, and give peace to the Christian people. Have you not heard that those who foretell the future, when prophesying these upheavals of the Church, fixed for them this fortieth year which is now upon us as the end of the tribulation? Surely for a long time you have been hearing that a pope should be chosen at this time who would comfort Sion[1] and set all things in peace? Who, I beseech you, will be he who can fulfill such things, unless we take this man? Believe me, the scriptures should be fulfilled, and God will gather [to himself], I hope, your minds,[2] even if we be unwilling. Yet willingly, rather, do what is right and holy.'

After these words the majority of the electors was favourably disposed to support him. His words were so effective that at the next ballot the matter was brought to a close. For on 5 November while the city clergy were standing outside the conclave with the relics of the saints, and the procession of prelates was invoking the grace of the Holy Spirit,[3] at about ten in the morning the ballot was opened, and when the numbers were compared in the usual fashion it was found that Amadeo, duke of Savoy, a most religious prince, according to the decree of the Council was chosen as pope, and twenty-six votes agreed in his favour. Suddenly therefore joy sprang up among all, and all praised this achievement in the warmest terms. Therefore calling in notaries, and admitting witnesses, they executed a document about the actual election. When this was over, the witnesses were sent back, and at about one in the afternoon a rush was made towards the windows that gave upon the square, and all the shutters were broken down with axes, and from them a silver cross was displayed to the populace wondering at the novel sight. The whole community was already in the square, and the whole crowd stared at one window, wanting to be told the name of the person elected. Then the cardinal of Arles making the sign of the cross proclaimed the name of the elected pontiff in the name of the Father, Son, and Holy Spirit, and after a prayer blessed the people. Afterwards at three the prelates with copes and mitres, and the clergy of the city with the relics coming to the railings round the conclave, led out the

maiorem ecclesiam reduxerunt; ubi gratiarum actionibus magnis Deo exhibitis, iterum populo, qui erat innumerabilis, publicata per cardinalem electio est. Ac deinde cum maxima omnium iocunditate hymnus laetitiae et organis et humanis uocibus est decantatus, et congregatio dissoluta.

Quocirca laudent omnes populi Deum, quia pastorem habemus, qualem ipse dedit amandum bonis et malis timendum.[1]

COMMENTARIORVM AENEAE SYLVII SENENSIS DE GESTIS CONCILII BASILIENSIS LIBRI SECVNDI

FINIS

[1] Extracts from the printed text of the *Commentaries on the Council of Basle* in the *Opera* (Basle, 1551) dealing with the conclave (from p. 230 above to the end) are printed with a German translation by Berthe Widmer in her biographical anthology of Aeneas's writings: *Enea Silvio Piccolomini, Papst Pius II* (Basel/Stuttgart, 1960), pp. 166–76.

electors similarly garbed to the cathedral, where great thanksgivings were offered to God, and a second time the election was proclaimed by the cardinal to the people, who were beyond counting. Then amid the great joy of all a hymn of gladness was raised by the organs and human voices, and the congregation dispersed.

Wherefore let all peoples praise God, because we have a shepherd and one such as he himself has given to be loved by the good and feared by the bad.[1]

END OF BOOK II OF THE COMMENTARIES OF

AENEAS SYLVIUS OF SIENA

ON THE PROCEEDINGS OF THE COUNCIL OF BASLE

INDEX OF QUOTATIONS AND ALLUSIONS

A. THE BIBLE

Vulgate references are stated in parentheses where these differ from those of the Authorized Version.

B. CLASSICAL, PATRISTIC, AND MEDIEVAL SOURCES

GENERAL INDEX

Normally references are to pages of Latin text but proper names are in vernacular forms. For scriptural authorities named in the text see Index of Quotations and Allusions.